D1216629

METAPHOR

METAPHOR: An Annotated Bibliography and History

by WARREN A. SHIBLES

THE LANGUAGE PRESS

Box 342 Whitewater, Wisconsin 53190

ISBN 0-912386-00-2

Library of Congress Catalog Card
Number 72-157087

By the same author:

Philosophical Pictures (Kendall-Hunt, Dubuque, Iowa) 1969

Wittgenstein, Language and Philosophy (Kendall-Hunt) 1969 (1970)

Models of Ancient Greek Philosophy (Vision Press, London) Feb. 1971

An Analysis of Metaphor (Mouton, The Hague, Netherlands) May 1971

Printed in the United States of America

"The greatest thing by far is to be a master of metaphor. It is the one thing that cannot be learned from others. It is the mark of genius."

Aristotle

"Indeed, as the documents of science pile up, are we not coming to see that whole works of scientific research, even entire schools, are hardly more than the patient repetition, in all its ramifications, of a fertile metaphor."

Kenneth Burke

"Certainly philosophy is no other than sophisticated poetry."

Montaigne

"A philosophical treatise has never been written which did not depend upon the use of metaphor."

D. Berggren

"Metaphor has always been one of the central problems of philosophy."

D. Berggren

"The subject of metaphor is inexhaustible."

Bréal

"Both philosophers and poets live by metaphor."

S. Pepper

"Someday the history of the metaphor will be written, and then we will know the truth and the error that these conjectures hold."

Borges

"The most fruitful modern criticism is a rediscovery and recovery of the importance of metaphor."

C. Brooks

"We are witnessing a radical change in the whole conception of the function and fittingness of metaphor, and with it, a revolution in the conception of poetry."

C. Brooks

"Any history of thought might begin and end with the statement that man is an analogical animal."

S. Buchanan

"We have come to give you metaphors for poetry."

Yeats' spirits

"What too are all poets and moral teachers, but a species of Metaphorical Tailors."

Carlyle

"You have taught generations of Amherst students that for gaining an insight into life, a metaphor is a sharper and brighter instrument than a syllogism."

Robert Frost Litt. D. citation

"Metaphor was the beginning of wisdom, the earliest scientific method."

C. Day-Lewis

"Men think in terms of models."

K. Deutsch

"The whole of nature is a metaphor of the human mind."

Emerson

"Metaphor ought to be entirely banished from the severer compositions of philosophy."

Fitzosborne

"To know is to use metaphor."

Friquegnon

"All thinking is metaphorical."

Robert Frost

"Metaphors are among man's highest achievements in being presentational and value-charged."

J. Hagopian

"The history of philosophy should be written as that of seven or eight metaphors."

T. Hulme

"The most profound social creativity consists in the invention and imposition of new, radical metaphors."

R. Kaufmann

"Something like a paradigm is prerequisite to perception itself.... Paradigms prove to be constitutive of the research activity."

T. Kuhn

"All our truth, or all but a few fragments, is won by metaphor."

C. S. Lewis

"Literalness we cannot have."

C. S. Lewis

"Metaphor is as ultimate as speech itself, and speech as ultimate as thought. If we try to penetrate them beyond a certain point, we find ourselves questioning the very faculty and instrument with which we are trying to penetrate them."

J. Murry

"And what therefore is truth? A mobile army of metaphors.... Truths are illusions of which one has forgotten that they are illusions."

Nietzsche

"To know is merely to work with one's favorite metaphors."

Nietzsche

"I recommend a microscopic venture, concerned with tracing fine distinctions according to the imagery appropriate to each art form."

M. Osborn

"Students...need to become more familiar with analogical forms of reasoning...and metaphoric association in particular.... An expanded training program would appear desirable."

M. Osborn

"Any supreme insight is a metaphor."

H. Parkhurst

"Poets, it is said, anticipate science.... Every writer and every speaker works ahead of science, expressing analogies and contrasts, likenesses and differences, that will not abide the apparatus of proof.... The finest instrument of these discoveries is metaphor, the spectroscope of letters."

Sir Walter Raleigh

"What is not verbally odd is devoid of disclosure power."

I. Ramsey

"A better understanding of metaphor is one of the aims which an improved curriculum of literary studies might well set before itself."

I. A. Richards

"As philosophy grows more abstract we think increasingly by means of metaphors that we profess <u>not</u> to be relying on."

I. A. Richards

"Most sentences in free and fluid discourse turn out to be metaphoric."

I. A. Richards

"What we have to do is to watch metaphors at work tricking us and our fellows into supposing matters to be alternatively much simpler and much more complex than they are."

I. A. Richards

"The conduct of even the plainest, most 'direct' untechnical prose is a ceaseless exercise in metaphor."

I. A. Richards

"Language is vitally metaphorical."

Shelley

PREFACE

This book took several years of intense research involving the great task of obtaining bibliographical materials from every major library and from as many sources as possible and checking these sources. Each major article, book, dissertation, etc. in each major language was then read and a summary made. The main ideas of these articles or the important or especially new and interesting ideas were then written up as the annotations which appear here.

The madness required to create this book arose from doing a previous book entitled An Analysis of Metaphor. It became clear that one of the most important features of philosophical systems, poetry, and theories of any sort was that they were highly metaphorical. It was also clear that no one had given an adequate analysis of metaphor. This situation led to an attempt to find out as much as possible about the subject of metaphor. It is hoped that this volume will serve to promote further research on the subject of metaphor.

In addition to An Analysis of Metaphor another work will soon be published giving a presentation and critical interpretation of the major views on metaphor from Aristotle to the present time. This work will treat accounts too extensive to be fully annotated in this bibliography.

I would like to express my appreciation for all those who have helped to make this book possible. This includes the cooperation of nearly every major library in the United States and Europe and especially the Harold Andersen Library at Whitewater, Wisconsin. Those who assisted, too numerous to mention, include translators, typists, students to whom some of this material was presented.

Warren Shibles
Wisconsin State University
Whitewater, Wisconsin 53190

Table of Contents

INTRODUCTION

The traditional ideas concerning metaphor are contained in the annotations and indexed. I have therefore chosen in the following account to add some new considerations and dimensions:

I. METAPHOR AS AN ART FORM.

Metaphor is an art form in its own right. We usually think of metaphor as a technique in poetry or prose for which certain rules apply, certain standards of acceptability are maintained. But once it is seen that plastic art, linguistics, music, philosophy, poetry, and everything including behavior and life itself can be seen as a metaphor, metaphor can be established as an art form on the same level as any other art. One may be involved in music or one may be involved in making metaphors. There is an art to making metaphors, seeing the world metaphorically, living metaphorically, and living metaphors. We perhaps do these things without fully realizing it. We are engaged in the art of metaphor when we whistle, or arrange flowers in a vase. This book is an investigation into the art of metaphor and an attempt to make clear the many aspects of that art. An attempt is made to show that metaphor has implicitly been regarded as an art and that now it has achieved its full justification as a form of knowledge, an art form, a subject which ought to be taught in itself isolated from those with which it was traditionally intertwined. Metaphor should be taught as a separate course in universities as well as in schools stressing the arts. Metaphor may be taught as one of the arts rather than as just a part of them.

Courses in aesthetics, literary criticism, creative writing, etc. should also place great stress on the topic of metaphor for an understanding which an analysis of metaphor can give to them. It seems clear that all poetry in one way or another is based on the metaphorical process and most critics claim that poetry is essentially metaphorical. If we know the boundaries, forms and possibilities of metaphor we are in a better position to understand poetry. A similar statement may be made about prose. What characterizes contemporary pop art and new art appears clearly to be a mere metaphorical juxtaposition for its own sake. Ice cream cones are juxtaposed with a woman's breasts, there are renderings of reverse mermaids (the top part is the fish), in one painting middle class men rain down from the sky and in another an apple is as large as an entire room. This sort of juxtaposition characterizes the contemporary movement in painting, new art, music, writing, film, theatre. This reminds us of the conceit and surrealism to some extent. These arts may be seen to involve metaphor, and so a knowledge of metaphor should help both the critic as well as the artist. The artist would be better able to see that he is creating a metaphor of tension, or that his metaphor is a deviation from forms of the past, or that it is a metaphor giving insight as opposed to the very popular mere juxtaposition of any two objects which do not usually go together.

In music, metaphor involves an implied story (tone-poem), marching or moving to music, relations of counterpoint, deviations from previously accepted standards of form, tonality, new sounds, etc. A knowledge of metaphor can help the artist to create delicate balances of tensive metaphor, deviations from the expected, insight metaphors, similes, etc.

II. THE "METAPHORICAL METHOD" AS A METHOD OF DOING PHILOSOPHY

In addition to regarding metaphor as an art in itself and as central to other arts I have in my own work attempted to establish it as a philosophical method (see index for relevant works). It may be called the "metaphorical method" of doing philosophy. It is based on the insight that each philosophy, school of science, etc. is based upon a number of basic metaphors which are then expanded into various universes of discourse. By seemingly incongruous juxtapositions new knowledge is attained and revealing hypotheses suggested. A knowledge of metaphor allows us to see what it is possible to say and how to say it. It also helps us to avoid being captivated by our metaphors which we unconsciously thought were literal truths. Perhaps the joke played most often on the thinkers of the past is that of their having taken their theories and ideas as literal truths. This is as true of scientists as of others.

Mathematics and geometry are metaphorical systems. We

apply numbers, lines, triangles, etc., metaphorically to objects we observe. We thought that Euclidean geometry yields the only description of reality. With the rise of non-Euclidean geometry we now know that there are various models or metaphors which may apply to the "real" world. Contemporary physicists now sometimes assert that we were seriously misled by taking the Cartesian coordinate system of three (or even four) dimensions as our model. The present view is often that models in science and philosophy do not merely illustrate otherwise obtainable knowledge but rather constitute it such that a diagram, formula, description, etc. is a part of the object. The considerations of the notion of seeing-as even suggest that metaphors and models partially determine how and what we actually see and observe. This has been more traditionally expressed by Kant's view that we see things in terms of a number of categories such as cause-effect, substance-quality, space and time and that these contribute to the constitution of an object in a dialectic and synthetic manner. These categories provide _a priori_ knowledge of reality because we impose them on reality. This may be expressed intuitively by the view that we see things in terms of what we know and that this limitation we impose on reality. It is like wearing blue glasses then noting that the world looks blue. The notion of seeing-as however is not bound to the narrow, now highly questionable Kantian categories.

The metaphorical method allows one to see the basic metaphors in each system of knowledge but also to create a number of types of metaphorical system. Nietzsche's system was oracular and highly poetic. His tensive language was suited to the rendering of a process theory or theory of the world as change, as a constant overcoming. Poetry and philosophy are united here because both are based on metaphor. Both poetry and philosophy reveal. Both may transcend traditional categories because of their unity of diverse or incongruous elements. A knowledge of metaphor allows a great diversity of style and style does not just illustrate but partly constitutes what is said. One's style and philosophy may be tensive, imagistic, a series of mere juxtapositions, mythic, archetypal, revealing, analogical, mystical, suggestive, pseudo-literal, persuasive, etc. It can no longer be held that language merely represents ideas. The philosophy resulting from each of these styles may yield significant irreducible differences. But mainly one is alerted to the different possibilities of style and to the resulting fact that many kinds of philosophy are possible. A philosophy may be presented as a mere "as-if," a mere fiction.

The content of the basic metaphor used may vary from that used in the past. The existentialists take psychological elements as basic metaphors, e.g. dread, anxiety, anguish. There are, of course, serious objections to these categories in contemporary philosophical psychology. But the point is that few had ever before made a few psychological states a basis for an entire philosophy. An example of extreme deviation from the sort of metaphor chosen as the basis of a philosophy is Sartre's view that life is like a wet piece of gum, life is sticky. He also spoke of life as nausea. His psychological metaphors were often negative in this way. It is not hard to see how religious writers could adopt these negative metaphors as creating a problem for which a diety could then be pointed to as the way out.

The metaphorical method involves noting that since definitions cannot be identities, they must be only models, metaphors, types of seeings-as, aspects, diagrams, maps, formulas, pictures, paradigm cases, etc. If no definition can be taken literally it must be taken metaphorically. This means that nothing has a unique single definition or essence but rather that it has an unlimited number of perspectives by which and through which one can view the "thing". Even the present account is only a viewing, a perspective, one way of considering the subject. This helps prevent us from being captivated by a single definition or metaphor.

A definition is considered as a metaphor because it helps us to organize a lot of facts about definitions. A definition like a metaphor may be expanded. Also like metaphor it may be compared to simile and analogy. A metaphor "the world is atomic," is open to an infinitely great number of interpretations. It is like an open rather than a closed simile. The form of an open simile is "X is like Y" without further specification. In a closed simile the specific sense in which X is like Y is given e.g. the world is like atoms in that both involve circular and elliptical motions. Thus both metaphor and simile are open or vague statements which await further clarification or expansion. A definition, then, as like a metaphor, needs to be developed or expanded in order for a perspective to arise and in order for it to become specific and intelligible.

There are some loose criteria one might follow in the expansion of a metaphor or definition. About a model or metaphor one should be able to answer a) What is it like within our experience? b) What does it mean? c) Is it relevant and useful? (The first two articles in my Philosophical Pictures treat this subject more fully.) It was the purpose of the preceding few paragraphs to characterize a method only implicitly used for centuries, one which has been in great need of clarification, but one which is inescapable. This method is what is meant here by the metaphorical method. It is recommended for all types of inquiry.

III. THEORIES OF METAPHOR AS OFTEN BASED ON A PSEUDO-PSYCHOLOGY.

In the annotations in this volume it is seen that many hold a Freudian view of metaphor. Many also hold that there are various faculties such as fancy and imagination and that there are a number of internal states such as emotion and inner ideas. These views are today no longer held by a great number of philosophers and psychologists. The behaviorists as well as philosophers often reject the notion that there is an id, ego, superego, unconscious mind, etc., in opposition to Freud. The work in contemporary philosophical psychology by Wittgenstein and Gilbert Ryle is especially clear on this rejection. The view that there is a mind, imagination, fancy, will, or other faculty within us causing us to do things is found to lack support. Descartes' dualism of mind and body has become an almost untenable position to maintain, although it appears in disguised form such as Chomsky's notion of "deep structure" which is a covert way of talking about the more traditional concept "mind."

Although this is not yet commonly accepted, I would like to suggest that, based on the above views of contemporary philosophical psychology, there is no such thing as the imagination. There is no evidence for imagination or that we have a mind. The traditional models or metaphors on which they were based (substance-quality doctrine, subject-attribute language pattern, naming fallacy, assuption of a cause) are now seen by many to be unintelligible. One test for a model, definition ,or metaphor, concerns whether it can be made intelligible to another person. Thus the view that one is an artist or creates because he has a good mind or good imagination lacks support. What we call imaginative usually is largely just a use of metaphor. A poet is said to use his "imagination" in situations in which he is constructing metaphors. When one metaphorically deviates from past custom or traditional method we often claim that he is "imaginative" or has a good "imagination" (or is a genius, or just plain mad). But that one constructs good metaphors is not evidence for or proof of the existence of an imagination or a mind as such. There are just the metaphors and the deep unknown.

To assume that art expresses emotion, mind, imagination, ideas, or an unconscious or even conscious mind is merely to engage in an unfounded pseudo-psychology. We do not have a clear knowledge of inner states, and the very terms "inner" and "state" are themselves metaphors. We speak about "mental states" as if they are there and are clear but upon examination we find that we assumed all these states without evidence. Can we, for example, isolate and have access to a single "idea"? We note that "idea" derives from "to see," and that words describing "mental states" are metaphors derived from words describing "external" objects. T. S. Eliot's "objective correlative" seems to suggest this view also but a close examination shows that Eliot was still held captive by the traditional mind-body, inner-outer dualism. We speak of ideas as "train" of ideas, "stream of thought," mental "process," etc. This is not to say that there is no "something or other" "going on" "in" us but to assume we know it and are clear about it as the terms idea, emotion, imagination suggest is to engage in pseudo-psychologizing. Instead of assuming we are familiar with internal states and then explaining art and metaphor in terms of them and psychological categories, we may examine language, metaphor, and what we do, first and from this attempt to find out what thinking is. For these reasons it also appears unacceptable to assert that metaphor and art are expressions of emotion, or of the unconscious or expressions of the age (via ideas). By asserting these statements we assume more than we have evidence for. Contemporary philosophers have attacked the view that emotion is just an "internal state". To say art or metaphor is an expression of the unconscious is like stopping the conversation. Few people would be prepared to continue to ask,"How do you know you have an unconscious mind?" However, this should be asked. The statement seems true because it cannot be refuted since by definition we never have access to an unconscious mind. But again, in contemporary philosophical psychology we find no evidence to support such an entity. One can give only an operational equivalence in terms of actual behavior patterns. The last few paragraphs also suggest reasons why it was said earlier that one can no longer maintain that language merely represents ideas or mental entities. (cf. A. MacIntyre, _The Unconscious_, and my articles on these subjects in _Philosophical Pictures_).

Thus it is suggested that many of the views presented in the annotations are based on a faulty psychology. I have, however, tried to refrain from criticism and interpretation within the annotations themselves and instead let this introduction serve as a caution.

IV. A NEW RHETORIC

The attempt to establish metaphor as an independent field of inquiry has special force in the area of rhetoric. Traditional rhetorical device may be thought of as a "language-game." Clarification may be given to such games or devices and a sound philosophical basis thereby provided for them. By concrete and extensive investigation of each rhetorical device one can establish a "new rhetoric," one philosophically acceptable, and one relating to everyday language, because it is from ordinary language that the philosophical support has its derivation. Thus this work on metaphor is meant in part as the establishment of a "new rhetoric." What characterizes philosophy, poetry, rhetoric and even science is that all are to a large extent attempts to "learn" our language.

V. SOME OBSERVATIONS ABOUT METAPHOR

The following is a list of some characteristics of metaphor which are not readily accessible in the annotations, or which none has spoken of, or which could stand to be given some emphasis. This is in no way a summary but rather some curious notes made while compiling this bibliography. A summary of the various statements made about metaphor may be obtained by reading the topic headings in the index. 1. Metaphor may be thought of as a deviation from: the expected, the normal, social custom, grammar, usual behavior, the familiar. 2. Metaphor may be used to dissolve traditional categories such as subject-object, fact-fiction, cause-effect, mind-body, reason-emotion, etc. It then may offer both insight and escape. 3. In "Metaphor is expressive," "expressive" is ambiguous because it may imply expression of ideas, or of emotions. In any case, the whole notion of expression seems to rest on the questionable view that words (marks) stand for ideas, meanings or internal states. "Express" means to "press out." But it is not clear what is "pressed out." 4. Metaphor is sometimes said to describe or reveal emotions. Novels are often thought to reveal or describe subtleties of emotion. It may rather be that the novelist <u>creates</u> emotions, that metaphor <u>creates</u> emotions. The reader then erroneously takes a creation for a description. This is especially harmful if the emotion created is complaining or undesirable, as is often the case in literature and art. 5. There seems to be no commonly accepted term for reverse personification. We "personify" objects but the reverse would be to "objectify" ourselves. But we think of "objectification" as being a favorable scientific term. Dehumanization might be the term I am looking for here. 6. Calderón used grammatical and rhetorical terms themselves as metaphors. He used metaphor as a metaphor. Poems have been and may also be written on metaphor. 7. Metaphor is usually spoken of metaphorically, for example, as a filter, vehicle, stereoscope, tension, etc. Metaphors give "light," are "mixed," or "pure," etc. 8. Poets and writers (e.g. Arnold, Imagists) often state that poetry will save the world, that it is the most important thing in the world. 9. The terms of a metaphor can both be literal or both terms can be metaphors. 10. "Pure poetry" often refers merely to poetry which is highly metaphorical. 11. One may approach a metaphor by trying to explain it or on the other hand by merely recognizing it. (cf. Richards: "To read the poem rightly would be to hear and come.") 12. How much of deity is merely metaphorical sexual euphemism and personification? 13. In ordinary-language philosophy the meaning of a word is its use in a language-game (a language context and a situational context) such that to determine what the word means one need only look at the use of the language in its situation e.g. "How do you do?" in the language-game of greeting someone. The expression has no separate meaning. Metaphor could be developed in terms of this meaning-is-its-use theory. 14. Metaphor has a temporal aspect. For example, "Man is a wolf" may be regarded as past, present, future, briefly, continually, etc. 15. An artist (a metaphorist) may be thought of as a person who makes flowers which never grow. He may however make metaphors which grow. 16. It is often said that metaphor is based on analogy but seldom stated acceptably what analogy is based on. 17. "Catachresis" Webster defines as "use of the wrong word for the context; use of a forced and esp. paradoxical figure of speech (as 'blind mouths')." 18. "Epithet" Webster defines as "a characterizing word or phrase accompanying or occurring in place of the name of a person or thing; the part of a taxonomic name identifying a subordinate unit within a genus; a term." This term contains the concept of synecdoche, substitution, metonymy, metaphor. 19. The notion of "poetic license" is really the notion of "metaphorical license," the idea that one needs special sanctions in order to use metaphor. Metaphor is often regarded as "the black art." 20. Allegory is sometimes defined as being solely metaphors. A novel may be written with the conscious intention of using only conceits. Similar things have been done but not with the awareness of these notions and of the nature of metaphor. 21. Metaphor seems to have much to do with future possibilities, hope, and expectation of something great. 22. One may and perhaps should take every term or every seemingly literal term and regard it as a metaphor, a fiction, e.g. in aesthetics take the term "form" as a metaphor, in mathematics, "point," "line," and "number." When we do this we often find they are in fact metaphors. 23. It is strange to ask, "What could he have been <u>thinking</u> when he constructed that metaphor? Does he just <u>use</u> it to 'express himself'?" It would seem that the metaphor comes first, and then we try to say something psychological or talk about the land of thought. 24. The imagists claim to use only images but in fact they were using metaphors, and only some of these contain terms for sensuous objects. 25. Metaphors are sometimes only elliptical for concrete things; they are summaries of experience. 26. The view that metaphor is based on resemblance is inadequate or irrelevant if we take into account the actual sensation these metaphors induce. While looking at a metaphor we do not and need not say "Now I am relating two terms." 27. One type of metaphor: pray as an experience rather than as a religious experience. Religion is lost but an experience gained. 28. Aristotle's stress on opposites in his philosophy could be responsible for the extravagance of the Italian and Spanish stress on the oxymoron and conceit. 29. Situations and behavior may be regarded as metaphorical e.g. attending a graduation with a very large fish in one's pocket. 30. We may also see situations in terms of the device of metaphor. We may see something as a metaphor. We may even see metaphor as a metaphor. We may see a hat on a bedpost as a metaphorical device: "Here is your man," but also "That is a metaphorical device." 31. One might ask, "Why do we want to regard such and such as a metaphor?" ; "How did we get led into it?" 32. <u>Ars</u> (art) derives from the Aryan root "<u>ar</u>" meaning "join, put together." This suggests the metaphorical process of juxtaposing. 33. Note the colloquial expression "I figure that..." in place of "I think that..." 34. It is important to read, understand, analyze metaphors but eventually to understand them one has to create them himself in all of their concreteness, givenness, mysteriousness. 35. Good metaphors just come--like the rain. Rain just comes--like good metaphors. 36. For a creative person a word is a thrilling experience, a philosophy, a wealth of imagery, a poem. 37. One can rejuvenate nearly every work in any paragraph. Ask one who thinks he is speaking literally why he is being so metaphorical. 38. Do we know how we think, then apply that theory to metaphor or rather learn how we "think" by observing how metaphor works? 39. "Poet" derives from the Greek word for "a maker." This suggests that one artificially constructs metaphors and does not merely copy nature. The conceit is often attacked because it deviates from a so-called "nature." 40. It is perhaps less acceptable to say that we proceed from intuition to metaphor, than that we proceed from metaphor to intuition. 41. The basic idea of metaphor accounts for the artists' requirement that art be always new. 42. Games, e.g. "You be the knight, I'll be the pawn," and acting out parts may be regarded as metaphors. 43. Metaphor may itself be regarded metaphorically in a great many ways. It may be regarded as a structure forcing us to see reality in a certain way--just as does the subject—predicate category. 44. Metaphor may sometimes be regarded as an emotional transfer, because we _want_ something to be something else. 45. Metaphor may be seen as giving old words new functions, adapting them anew. 46. One type of metaphor is repetition, identity and circularity, e.g. "The sky is sky," or the logician's "A is A," or "I am I". 47. The logic of the oxymoron is diverse, e.g. "Irrelevance is a tool of relevance." 48. In one aspect the problem of the nature of metaphor is the problem of what any word is. It is a word or expression which has complex uses and relations just as does any other word. Each word in our language may be regarded as a rhetorical device. This leads to a philosophical inquiry of language and a "new rhetoric." 49. One characteristic of metaphor is that it is an open-context statement, even more so than an open simile. It implies a great many things but _says_ little. 50. In creating a good metaphor it may sometimes help if one knows many details about the subject in question so as to allow or suggest many concrete, detailed relations. It may also help if one likes and is interested in the subject and such details. 51. We constantly hear dead metaphors such as "deep concern," "ride the fence," "advance to a higher plateau." The inquiry of metaphor initiates a rebirth of "dead" metaphors. 52. A look at the change in the definitions of metaphor in the various editions of the _Encyclopaedia Britannica_ shows its changing fortunes and its present high evaluation. 53. The main thing about learning a language seems to be to learn how words stand for things metaphorically, and how they are used metaphorically. 54. One may consciously regard "error" or any abstract term metaphorically as an object or natural process for purposes of constructing a hypothetical model. 55. "How does it feel?" involves the analogy of others' inner states to our own. (Problem of "other minds" as a metaphorical problem.) 56. Metaphors may differ in function from language to language and culture to culture. 57. Philosophical therapy often involves nothing more than making us see that what we thought was literal is metaphorical. 58. Man may be regarded as a "metaphorical animal." (If one wishes to put things in that Aristotelian manner.) 59. The "mind" may be thought to be constituted by metaphor. 60. _Macbeth_: "There's nothing serious in mortality.

All is but toys."

II, iii, 98-99

61. Metaphor often stresses simplicity, saying much in few words. 62. One may speak of chart or diagram metaphors as opposed to written word metaphors. Written word metaphors may also be con-

sidered as chart or diagram metaphors. 63. Metaphor may be posed as a question e.g. Is man a machine? Did you put jelly on your life? 64. One trouble with metaphor analysis is that we often want too simple an interpretation. An interpretation often gets to be nothing but a sterile, deductive, mathematical system or a visual model, thereby missing all of the subtlety of the metaphor itself as a "form of life." 65. Metaphor may be regarded as a type of knowing. 66. Even quotation marks are highly metaphorical. Also they often imply an outdated theory of language whereby words stand for "ideas." (cf. Phenomenological technique of "bracketing.") 67. Metaphor takes one to a country hitherto unseen. 68. One may see formulas in science as metaphors e.g. $E = mc^2$. These often relate hypothetical non-entities or "forces." 69. Descartes' "I think therefore I am" appears not to follow, to be based on unacceptable scholastic slogans, and on a confused notion of existence and thought. Nevertheless the statement may be regarded as a metaphor. 70. If one presents a theory of metaphor based on the views of Croce and Wittgenstein metaphor could have no analysis and we could only use and make metaphors. We need not assume that metaphor "has" an analysis, though we may play the game of analyzing. 71. Anger is partly the metaphors of anger. 72. Metaphor may be used to describe or stipulate. It may be used to create relations as well as render existing relations. 73. From time to time certain types of metaphor were rejected only to be revived later. If we could become clear about metaphor we would have a standard not to be reversed. 74. The view that metaphor simply reveals the abstract or the transcendental needs justification. This type of metaphor may rather be merely a trick of language. 75. Poetry is a clue to thought, when there is no thought as such. 76. If metaphors become literal, new metaphors may be deserving of more tolerance. We could consciously create effective ones rather than inherit those which chanced to come about. 77. Metaphor rather than standing for an idea may be regarded as the idea itself. Metaphor then does not stand for something else. It is itself. It is itself a use. 78. Metaphor has gradations of belief. It may be variously taken as serious, literal, hypothesis, fiction, false, play, a joke, etc. 79. Wittgenstein, Tractatus: His key metaphor is "The proposition is a picture of reality." 80. Commas and question marks among other grammatical marks may be regarded as metaphors. 81. Metaphor may be compared to the subjunctive. 82. We speak of the verb "symbolize." We should establish also the verb "metaphorize." We do constantly metaphorize situations. 83. We know about an author because of his metaphors, not vice versa. 84. Colette: "In love, no thing is small." (cf. hyperbole and metaphor) 85. "Mysterious" may be regarded as a performative utterance,i.e. to utter this word is to produce the mystery. 86. Every word, may be personified. 87. One might say that Dylan Thomas died of metaphors. 88. That we cannot easily generalize about metaphor may suggest that thought is equivalent to style. 89. Metaphor creates a new world, a world we would not have without it. 90. In metaphor, it is sometimes said, something big happens in a very small place. 91. Metaphor is often spoken of in terms of a formerly held, still carried over, principle of association of ideas. Jakobson's principles of 1) similarity and 2) contiguity amount to this. 92. Because metaphors relate all kinds of like and unlike things yielding unity in diversity and because the poet uses metaphors, the poet may come to think that all is one unity. 93. Metaphor may be thought of as an hypothesis, an exploration of new causes. Poetry presents new causal relations and hypotheses. 94. Metaphor serves as therapy. It offers escape from narrow causal laws, and psychological release. It also serves a basic need. Certain people must hear and create metaphors for their aesthetic fulfillment. Perhaps others could obtain increased satisfaction with a greater knowledge of the nature of metaphor. 95. Many speak of metaphor as serving to clarify. One may also purposely use metaphor to create obscurity and vagueness. This happens frequently in speeches. 96. One of the serious problems is not with what it is to be metaphorical but rather with what it is to be literal. 97. Metaphor is itself a structure forcing us to see reality in a certain way, just as the subject-predicate structure does. 98. In understanding a metaphor it is often the case that previous experience cannot be of help. An entirely new experience is needed and created. 99. In school and college one is usually given an inadequate and brief account of imagery and metaphor. Often one is merely told to look for the imagery and not told what that is. The present teaching of imagery, metaphor and simile in schools has been shown to be unenlightened. (cf. metaphor, in education) 100. Metaphor is often regarded as _constitutive_ of reality, thought and emotions. 101. Under the topic "metaphor, as basis of arts and sciences" it is pointed out that metaphor has a central role in uniting these seemingly diverse areas of knowledge. 102. Metaphor is frequently thought to be a source of knowledge. See "metaphor, as source of knowledge." 103. Metaphor is frequently thought to be an immediate irreducible experience. See "metaphor, as immediate experience"; "metaphor, origin of"; "metaphor, presentational","metaphor, as irreducible to literal." 104. Symbol, archetype, allegory, parable, and such terms seem to be various types of metaphors.

Aalders, Willem. De 'Analogia Entis' in het Geding Amsterdam: Noord-hollandsche uitgevers-maatschappy 1937

Abel, D. Herbert. "Paradox or Oxymoron" Classical Bulletin 34 (Dec. 1957) 23
In oxymoron both terms of a contradiction are expressed, e.g. bittersweet. In paradox the expected word is not expressed and the unexpected takes its place while the expected word is retained in the mind.

Abraham, Karl. Selected Papers of Karl Abraham London: Hogarth Press 1949 esp. p. 429
The most widely different languages tend to express only by indirect allusion, or metaphor, behavior which is based on sadistic impulses. These metaphors one can trace back to anal-erotic instincts.

Abrams, Meyer H. "Archetypal Analogies in the Language of Criticism" University of Toronto Quarterly 18 (July 1949) 313-327

_____. "Correspondent Breeze: A Romantic Metaphor" Kenyon Review 19 (1957) 113-130
Also in English Romantic Poets: Modern Essays in Criticism New York: Oxford University Press 1960 pp. 37-54
Breath is normally associated with life; thus one need not regard it as an archetype or product of deep racial memory, etc. One can always find (create) an archetype by getting general enough. But such a search negates the individuality and aesthetic quality of a poem.

_____. "Figurative Language" A Glossary of Literary Terms New York: Holt, Rinehart & Winston 1957 pp. 36-37. See also "conceit" pp. 15-16, "pathetic fallacy" p. 66
"In a metaphor a word which in ordinary usage signifies one kind of thing, quality, or action is applied to another, without express indication of a relation between them." It has a principal subject (tenor) and secondary subject (vehicle). A Petrarchan conceit is a hyperbolical comparison of a cruel but beautiful mistress. A Metaphysical conceit is an occult resemblance.

_____. The Mirror and the Lamp: Romantic Theory and the Critical Tradition New York: Oxford University Press 1953 "Metaphors of Expression" pp. 48-53, "Changing Metaphors of Mind" pp. 57-69, "Poetic Truth and Metaphor" pp. 285-289 Also pp. 3 -32
The Romantic critic of art based his views on metaphors, e.g. poetry is music, overflow of feelings, expression, imitation (mirror), etc. Metaphor is needed to discuss the activity of mind. In any period the theory of mind and of art are integrally related and turn on similar analogies. Various critics' views are presented.

Achinstein, Peter. "Models, Analogies, and Theories" Philosophy of Science 31 no. 4 (Oct. 1964) 328-350

Adami, Riccardo. *I tropi e le figure nelle orazioni di Demosthene* Programm d. Communalgymnas Triest 1885 51 pp.

Adams, E. W. "Metaphor, Simile and Analogy" *The London Quarterly and Holborn Review* 164 (July 1939) 378-380
Metaphor is an analogy, a multiple simultaneous mental perception or vision of two or more related things, not a "squint" but a real "stereoscopic" blending, an emotional and attributional transfer which illustrates and is "sartorial" (clothes the unfamiliar in the familiar) and "protective" (by making an object more familiar and so acceptable). "Analogy is an open window whence a man may look out to spy whether truth be in the neighborhood. Argument goes out for truth with net to capture and pin to impale, like a collector of specimens."

Adams, George P. *Man and Metaphysics* New York: Columbia University Press 1948 ch. 5 "The Mind's Excursive Power" pp. 125-153
Metaphor is an analogical transport of a meaning from one context to another more adequate context. Metaphors are used to describe the mind and only through metaphor can man know at all. "We are condemned to use metaphors."

Adams, John Quincy. *Lectures on Rhetoric and Oratory* New York: Russell and Russell 1962 vol. 2 "Figurative Language" pp. 249-306, "Figures, Metaphor, Allegory" pp. 307-327

Adams, Richard P. "Emerson and the Organic Metaphor" *Interpretations of American Literature* Charles Feidelson Jr. and Paul Brodkorb Jr., eds. New York: Oxford University Press 1959 pp. 137-152. Also in *PMLA* 69 (Mar. 1954) 117-130

Adank, Hans. "Essai sur les fondements psychologiques et linguistiques de la métaphore affective" Thèse de la Faculté des Lettres de l'Université de Genève 1939 191 pp. (cf. Cohen, Kent)
From his point of view of a synchronic, linguistic, psychology of association metaphor is an internal, value laden, emotive-intellectual transfer revealing subtle states and new ideas. He expands Bally's view of affectivity in linguistic psychology. Adank worked under M. Bally, Geneva School of Linguistics.

Addison, Joseph. *The Spectator* Cincinnati: Applegate and Company 1860
See especially the series on *Paradise Lost*: nos. 267, 273, 279, 285, 297, 303. Also nos. 411-421 "The Pleasures of the Imagination" and no. 62.
In no. 413 he agrees with Locke in regarding metaphor as ornamental delusion. The value of metaphor is in its pictorial significance. Metaphors should be pleasant, never ugly. In no. 595 he suggests that poems actually be painted or drawn with a pencil to see if they are consistent.

Adelung, Johann C. Über den deutschen Stil two vols. in one, third edition, Berlin 1789 esp. pp. 353-378 (Sum. in Phelps) He accepts and amends Gottsched's views on metaphor. Tropes are the work of nature, not artificial. Good metaphors are regarded as a work of genius.

Adler, Mortimer J. Dialectic New York: Harcourt, Brace & Co. 1927 p. 94ff
All language is thoroughly metaphorical. "Sugar is sweet" is no more literal than "The sun is Apollo." The meaning of a metaphor is true in its context. The metaphors in science are given a more fully developed context than in poetry.

Ağakay, Mehmet Ali. Türkçede mecazlar sözlüğü Ankara: Doğuş, Matbaasi 1948 (in Turkish)

Agarwala, D. C. "Yeats' Concept of Image" Triveni (India) 36 (July 1967) 23-25

Aguilar, José Raúl. Diccionario de Símiles Mexico, D. F.: Ediciones Lux 1941

Ahearn, E. "Rimbaud's Images Immondes" French Review 40 (Feb. 1967) 505-517

Aikin, John. Essays Literary and Miscellaneous 1811
Gives extensive and detailed method of personifying abstractions. He says personification gives the highest exercise of the imagination.

Aish, Deborah Amelia Kirk. La Métaphore dans l'oeuvre de Stéphane Mallarmé Thèse, Université de Paris. Paris: Librairie E. Droz 1938
Arts and sciences are concordant for Mallarmé. His metaphors aim to express universal analogy.

Alain [pseudonym of Émile Chartier]. Propos sur l'Esthétique Paris: Presses Universitaires de France 1949 esp. "De la métaphore" pp. 4-6
Metaphor is a condensed simile. Proverbs, titles of musical compositions, and fables are all metaphorical. In metaphor the idea is in the image. Ancient symbols are metaphorical.

Albani, Johannes. "Die Metaphern des Epheserbriefes Paulus" Zeitschrift für wissenschaftliche Theologie 45 (1902) 420-440 (cf. N. F. 10 (1902) 402ff)

al-Bāqillānī, Muḥammad ibn al-Ṭayyib. I' jāz al-Qur'ān (The Miraculousness of the Qur'ān) Series: Dhakhā'ir al-'Arab 12 (The Legacy of the Arabs) 1954 [1964] [In Arabic]

al-Jindt, 'Ali al-Sayyid Sulaymān. Fann al-jinās
On Arabic literature and metaphors.

al-Samarqandī, Abū al Qāsim ibn Abī Bakr al-Laythī. ...La Samarkandya, petit traité de rhétorique arabe ... Traduction et notes par Abderrezzak Lacheref ... Alger: P. Fontana 1905 [In Arabic]
On metaphors and figures of speech.

al-Sharīf, M. (See Ibn al-Sharīf)

al-Tha'ālibī 'Abd al-Malik ibn Muḥammab. Sihr al-balāghah wasirr al-barā'ah
On metaphor and figures of speech in the Arabic language.

Albert, W. "Metaphor of Origins in Horace" French Review 40 (Nov. 1966) 238-245

Alcuin. "Dialogus: Carolus Rex et Albinus Magister. Dialogus de Rhetorica et Virtutibus" Alcuini Opera Omnia, Patrologiae Cursus Completus J. Migne, ed. Paris 1863
cf. Wilbur Howell. The Rhetoric of Alcuin and Charlemagne A translation of Alcuin's Rhetoric. Princeton University Press 1941 esp. pp. 133-135
Alcuin says metaphor should add clarity. It may attain brevity. Figures should be drawn from appropriate materials. They should not debase a subject. A Christian commentator, he holds traditional views on metaphor.

Alden, Raymond M. "The Lyrical Conceits of the Elizabethans" Studies in Philology 14 (1917) 129-152

_____. "The Lyrical Conceits of the 'Metaphysical Poets'" Studies in Philology 17 (1920) 183-198
On Donne, Carew, Cowley. A sequel to his "The Lyrical Conceits of the Elizabethan." "A conceit involves the interruption or elaboration of the normal poetic process by a special intellectual process... [which] ...may be truly lyrical." Conceits are classified as 1) verbal (word-play), 2) imaginative (image-play) a) metaphor or simile b) personification c) poetic myth, or 3) logical (play of reasoning, paradox).

Aldington, Richard. "Modern Poetry and the Imagists" The Egoist 1 (1914) 201-203

Aldrich, Virgil C. "Image-Mongering and Image-Management" Philosophy and Phenomenological Research 23 (Sept. 1962) 51-61
"The point here is that one can make sense with images under appropriate controls and in collaboration with concepts."

_____. "Pictorial Meaning and Picture Thinking" The Kenyon Review 5 (Summer 1943) 403-412
Language may have a pictorial use rather than just a cognitive use. It may evoke pictures which are significant but neither true nor false. "This may be the only kind of sense that is being made even where the aim is to make statements about matters of fact."

_____. "Pictorial Meaning, Picture-Thinking, and Wittgenstein's Theory of Aspects" Mind 67 (Jan. 1958) 70-79
A discussion of Wittgenstein's notion of "seeing-as" or "aspect-seeing." Aldrich modifies this view to include in it an aesthetic image-exhibiting or picturing function of language rather than just meaning as use.

_____. "Picture Space" Philosophical Review 67 (1958) 342-352

_____. "Scientific Abuse of the Imagination" Journal of Philosophy 38 (May 8, 1941) 270-275

_____. "Visual Metaphor" Journal of Aesthetic Education 2 (Jan. 1968) 73-86
Wittgenstein's seeing-as notion is combined with Barfield's view of metaphor as a symbol whose form is simply B (from A is B). The meaning of A is liquidated into B. A visual metaphor may thus be produced which fuses or "expressively portrays" the thing to be seen and what it is seen as so that they lose their separate identities. B, the visual metaphor, is intuited or pretended. Picasso, who would, for example, put a wicker basket in place of goat's ribs stated, "My sculptures are plastic metaphors. It's the same principle as in painting."

_____. et al. "Symposium: The Sense of Dogmatic Religious Expression" Journal of Philosophy 51 no. 5 (Mar. 4, 1954) 145-172
About literal and metaphorical senses.

Aleksandrowicz, Don R. "The Meaning of Metaphor" Menninger Clinic Bulletin 26 (1962) 92-101
A Freudian account, but with practical clinical insight. Metaphor is a method of communicating with the patient, getting at the source of his problem and a method of correcting it. "Metaphors serve as a defense, allowing anxiety-laden conflicts to be expressed in a displaced form and yet experienced with a sufficient intensity. On the other hand, being an archaic form of language, they fit into the general regressive tendency to use archaic forms of thought and expression."

Allemann, Beda. "Metaphor and Antimetaphor" Interpretation: The Poetry of Meaning Stanley R. Hopper and David Miller, eds. New York: Harcourt, Brace, and World 1967 pp. 103-123
All language is metaphorical. Kafka is said to be antimetaphorical, i.e. no comparison is possible when he reduces a story step by step to an inexplicable core. Allemann calls "absolute metaphor" one that is not just comparison. It escapes logical analysis. He adds that language is inseparably bound up with objects.

_____, ed. Ars Poetica: Texte von Dichtern des 20. Jahrhunderts zur Poetik Darmstadt: Wissenschaftliche Buchgesellschaft 1966 esp. articles by Paul Celan and Lorca

Allen, Don Cameron. "Donne and the Ship Metaphor" Modern Language Notes 76 (April 1961) 308-312

_____. Image and Meaning: Metaphoric Traditions in Renaissance Poetry Baltimore: Johns Hopkins Press 1968
Literary themes and poetic figures are related in detail and traced back to early Greek poetry.

Allen, Gay W. "Figures of Speech" Encyclopaedia Britannica 9 (1961) 232A-234

_____. "Metaphor" Encyclopaedia Britannica 15 (1961) 328
"A figure of speech, which consists in the transference to one object of an attribute or name that strictly and literally is not applicable to it, but only figuratively and by analogy. It is thus in essence an emphatic comparison, which if expressed formally is a simile."

Allers, Rudolf, von. "Vom Nutzen und den Gefahren der Metapher in der Psychologie" Jahrbuch für Psychologie und Psychotherapie 3 (1955) 3-15
All languages use metaphor to grasp the mental, idealistic, extrasensory, and the external world. Metaphors familiar to one people or period may appear strange to another. Metaphor is almost always ambiguous. It is not based on simple analogy or the likeness of one single quality. The same verbal metaphor can relate in many ways. He discusses how the word "deep" is metaphorically used and misused in psychology. It is a mistake to take a metaphor literally, as psychologists often do, and to expand it uncritically. Freud's psychology is only a model and not a description of reality. Plotinus consciously used contradictory models showing that they are models or metaphors and not literal descriptions. Models must constantly be reevaluated critically. Mere metaphors should not be expanded into large systems. Modern psychology needs to take traditional philosophy into account.

Alonso, Dámaso. Estudios y ensayos gongorinos Madrid: Editorial Gredos 1955 pp. 42-46, 73-74

_____. La lengua poética de Góngora (Revista de filología española, 22) Madrid 1961 (Madrid: S. Aguirre 1935)

_____. Cuatro poetas españoles: Garcilaso, Góngora, Maragall, Antonio Machado Madrid: Editorial Gredos 1962

_____. Góngora y el "Polifemo" two vols. Madrid: Editorial Gredos 1961 vol. 1 ch. 3, 4, 7, 8 on style and metaphor
Ch. 7 "Metáfora e imagen" An image is a comparison of the real and unreal both of which are stated. In metaphor the unreal is stated, the real and the relation is only implied. Metonymy like metaphor is a substitution, but unlike it in being a real relation containing no unreal element. Synec-

doche is a real quantitative relation. All of Góngora's art is based on these.

Alston, William. Philosophy of Language New Jersey: Prentice Hall 1964

Alvarez de Miranda, Angel. La metáfora y el mito Madrid: Taurus 1963

Anderson, C. C. "The Latest Metaphor in Psychology" The Dalhousie Review 38 (Summer 1958) 176-187
"Man must describe 'the mind' or behavior in metaphor." Metaphors change rapidly in psychology but may be self-corrective. Freud's metaphors of mental pipes and fluids are unaccountable in terms of nerve tissue. James' "stream of consciousness" is rejected. Models must be functionally identical (not illustrative or lacking flexibility), heuristic, unambiguous, and must not confuse contexts. The latest metaphor "brain is a calculating machine" treats inner states as an unknown "black box" between stimulus and response. But behavioral ambiguity requires us to construct self-corrective, well-founded metaphors for such inner states. By means of metaphor the physical and psychological can be explored.

_____. "The Psychology of Metaphor" Journal of Genetic Psychology 105 (1964) 53-73
A search for the cognitive or mediational processes involved in metaphor. Metaphor involves categorizing and analogical reasoning which are also basic to all reasoning. It may involve an aroused state, puzzle-resolution, increased associations or internal cues, e.g. thermal cues for "go cool your engine." He opposes Pederson-Krag's view that metaphor reveals private subtleties because it lacks public verification.

Anderson, Charles. "Wit and Metaphor in Thoreau's Walden" USA in Focus: Recent Re-Interpretations publication of the Nordic Association for American Studies, vol. 2 Sigmund Skard, ed. Oslow: Universitetsforlaget 1966 pp. 70-93

Anderson, James B. "Analogy in Plato" Review of Metaphysics 4 (Sept. 1950) 111-128

_____. The Bond of Being New York: B. Herder Book Co. 1949
Thomistic view of analogy and metaphor. He denies there is a problem with Thomistic analogy. Metaphor is only a likeness, improper proportionality. The terms used in metaphorical analogies are not intrinsically analogical but are merely given an analogical reference by the mind. Metaphors are subjective and only yield possibilities. "Reality is as such analogical."

_____. Reflections on the Analogy of Being The Hague: Nijhoff 1967

_____. "Some Basic Propositions Concerning Metaphysical Analogy" Review of Metaphysics 5 no. 3 (March 1952) 465-472 Following the article are replies by George Burch, Richard Robinson, and Joseph Owens. Anderson makes an additional response to these replies.
A Thomistic view. Analogy is a four term relation with the common term present to each intrinsically but in its own way, not essentially or univocally but by a likeness of proper proportionality, and is rooted in the relation of essence to the act of existing, ultimately grounded on the imitability of the divine act of being. There is a cause-effect relation in analogy.

_____. "Bases of Metaphysical Analogy" Downside Review 66 (1948) 38-47

_____. "Mathematical and Metaphysical Analogy in St. Thomas" Thomist 3 (1941) 564-579

Anderson, W. D. "Notes on the Simile in Homer and His Successors" Classical Journal 53 (Nov.-Dec. 1957) 81-87, 127-133

Andrewes, M. "An Aspect of Horatian Imagery" Classical Review 62 (1948) 111-112

Andrews, E. "Slang and Metaphor" Chautauquan 23 (1892-1896) 462-466
Slang provides good metaphors and insights.

Antoine, Gérald. "Pour une méthode d'analyse stylistique des images" Langue et Littérature 161 (1961) 151-164 (cf. Pasini)

Apostel, Leo. "Towards the Formal Study of Models in Non-Formal Science" Synthese 12 (1960) 125-161

Applewhite, James. "Dante's Use of the Extended Simile in The Inferno" Italica 41 (1964) 294-309

Aptekar, Jane H. "Scons of Justice: Iconography and Thematic Imagery in Book V of The Faerie Queen" PhD diss. Columbia University 1967

Aquinas, St. Thomas. Summa Theologica and other works (see Cajetan and all entries on Thomistic analogy and metaphor)
Metaphor is both useful and necessary in representing divine truth. It allows us to represent the spiritual by means of the material likenesses and by means of our senses, thus allowing us some access to such things. It shows us we do not have literal description of divine truths. Knowledge of God is by means of four term analogy of proper proportionality (which serves as a basis of metaphor), e.g. God's being : God's essence :: created thing's being : created thing's essence, God : God's attributes :: man : man's attributes. We cannot predicate human characteristics of God literally or directly but only analogically. "To speak metaphorically is

not to speak falsely; for by such speech one does not intend to express the natures of the things which are signified by the [metaphorical] words one uses, but rather those characters which have a certain likeness to those things."
"All creatures are images of the first agent, namely God... therefore all things exist for the purpose of acquiring a likeness to God."

Arber, Agnes. "Analogy in the History of Science" Studies and Essays in the History and Science of Learning Offered in Homage to George Sarton M. F. Ashley-Montagu, ed. New York: Schuman 1947 pp. 219-233
"The genius of a researcher may indeed show itself more clearly in his choice of the analogies under which he views his problems than in his more rigidly scientific procedure."

Arbesmann, Rudolph. "The 'Malleus' Metaphor in Medieval Characterization" Traditio 3 (1945) 389-392

Arbusow, Leonid. Colores Rhetorici, eine Auswahl rhetorische Figuren und Gemeinplätze als Hilfsmittel für akademische Übungen an mittelalterlichen Texten Göttingen: Vandenhoeck & Ruprecht 1963 [1948] "Metaphora" ("Translatio") p. 83

Arendt, H. Die Metaphern in den dramatischen Werken Corneilles Marburg: 1889

Arestad, Sverre. "A Study of Keats's Use of Imagery" PhD diss. University of Washington 1938

Aristotle. Aristotle: On Poetry and Style G. M. A. Grube, trans. New York: Liberal Arts Press 1958

_____. Rhetoric and Poetics W. Rhys Roberts, trans. New York: Random House 1954
I Rhetoric On metaphor from the point of view of oratory. "We should give our language a 'foreign air'; for men admire what is remote, and that which excites admiration is pleasant." "It is metaphor above all that gives perspicuity..." "Use metaphors and epithets by way of illustration, taking care, however, to avoid what is too poetical." What one learns in metaphor is the genus by means of which two similar things may be related (cf. Poetics). "They [metaphors] set things 'before the eyes'; for we ought to see what is being done rather than what is going to be done." (This is especially true of words signifying actual objects.) Animation relates inanimate things to animate ones giving them a sense of motion or of actuality. Antithesis, riddles and humor are closely related and can help us to gain insight. In jokes "that which one would not have expected to be said is said and recognized as true." "Most smart sayings are derived from metaphor, and also from misleading the hearer beforehand. For it becomes more evident to him that he has learned something, when the conclusion turns out

contrary to his expectation, and the mind seems to say, 'How true it is! but I had missed it.'" "Antithesis is more instructive and conciseness gives knowledge more rapidly," e.g. "The stranger must not always be a stranger." "Generally speaking, clever enigmas furnish good metaphors; for metaphor is a kind of enigma, so that it is clear that the transference is clever." "The simile also is a metaphor; for there is very little difference." "The simile is a metaphor differing only by the addition of a word, wherefore it is less pleasant because it is longer; it does not say that this _is_ that, so that the mind does not even examine this."

II _Poetics_ (cf. Mackey, Goldthwait, Curran, McKeon) Metaphor is not a usual usage. "Metaphor consists in giving the thing a name that belongs to something else; the transference being either from genus to species, or from species to genus, or from species to species, or on grounds of analogy." This transference seems to reduce to substitution between terms already similar in being in a genus-species or species-species relationship. Since two terms are related to a third term they may be substituted for each other, e.g. since "sever" and "draw" both can mean "to take away" (genus) they can be substituted for one another. This seems to reduce metaphor to literal statement. Transference based on four term analogy is regarded as the more popular form of metaphor. Of the terms ABCD and the analogy B : A :: D : C we can metaphorically put D in place of B and B in place of D. Also we can metaphorically create a genitive link between B and C as seen in the following instance: If cup : Dionysus :: shield : Ares we can then say "cup of Ares." Also if old age : life :: evening : day, we may speak of evening as "old age of the day" and "old age" as the "evening of life." The four elements of the analogy are already known. Also one can say the shield is a "cup that _holds no wine_." He restricts proportional metaphor to ratio of B : A :: D : C and substitution between fourth and second terms thereby ignoring other relations. He says, "The greatest thing by far is to be a master of metaphor. It is the one thing that cannot be learnt from others; and it is also a sign of genius, since a good metaphor implies an intuitive perception of the similarity in dissimilars."

_____. "Topics" _Works_ W. D. Ross, trans. Oxford: Clarendon Press 1963 [1966]
He says here that metaphorical expression is always obscure.

_____. _The Basic Works of Aristotle_ Richard McKeon, ed. New York: Random House 1941
He discusses four term analogy in _Metaphysics_ 1048b, 5-7.

Arminius, Hermann. _Die Tropen und Figuren_ Innsbruck 1890
Metaphor is a transfer of one name of a concept to another based on similarity. It is a condensed parable. Extended metaphors are rarely used in everyday life. Four kinds of figures are: substantive, adjectival, verbal, extended.

Armstrong, Edward A. Shakespeare's Imagination: A Study of the Psychology of Association and Inspiration London: Peter Smith Press 1946; University of Nebraska Press 1963

Arnaiz, Marcelino. Las metáforas en las ciencias espíritu Madrid 1908

Arrom, José J. "Tres Metáforas sobre España e Hispano-América" Hispania 45 (March 1962) 40-42
Metaphors are suggestive, valuable, reveal new feelings and meanings. They are dangerous if used beyond their limits. Metaphor is not reality but a substitution of it for another reality. He discusses how metaphors such as "mother Spain" and Spanish America as a "branch of the Spanish trunk" are misleading.

Arroyo, Ciriaco M. "Algebra y Logaritmo: Dos Metáforas de Ortega y Gasset" Hispania 49 (May 1966) 232-237
In "Poetry new, poetry old" Ortega wrote that words are "logarithms" of things, images, ideas and sentiments, and can only be used as signs of values. He also said that poetry is the superior algebra of metaphors. Unlike his early views, he thinks the sign does not just signify but has a value of its own.

Arthos, John. "Figures of Speech" Encyclopedia of Poetry and Poetics Alex Preminger et al., eds. Princeton University Press 1965 pp. 273-274

Asch, Otto. "Bildsprache und Humor als Ausdruck geistiger Reife" PhD diss. Bonn; Würzburg: K. Triltsch 1936

Asch, Solomon. "On the Use of Metaphor in the Description of Persons" On Expressive Language Heinz Werner, ed. Worcester: Clark University Press 1955 pp. 29-45

_____. "The Metaphor: A Psychological Inquiry" Person, Perception and Behavior Renato Tagiuri and Luigi Petrullo, eds. Stanford University Press 1958 pp. 86-94
Even in historically independent languages persons and internal states are described in terms of outer objects, e.g. deep person, think straight, hard decision, or in terms of wind, fire, and sea. These words refer to the functional properties shared by the psychological and physical rather than to just sensory qualities.

Aschenbrenner, Karl. "The Semantics of Metaphor" 1969 27 pp. (unpublished essay. paper read in different form at Pacific Division of the American Philosophical Association, Sept. 1951)
Metaphor is a literal meaning, a new class inclusion on the basis of shared properties. "Metaphor is neither inherently pathetic nor semantically pathological." Metaphor cannot be de-

nied as true, since metaphors are too widespread. It is not just an emotional meaning for there are not two kinds of meaning, emotional and descriptive. He gives the following summary of his paper: "The metaphorical and literal meanings of given words or phrases must not be regarded as distinct types. A metaphor continues as such so long as it is necessary to resort to the literal meaning to decode it, and may be effective even when not decoded. Metaphors are dependent and indirect meanings, but do not represent a pathology of meaning."

Ashe, Geoffrey. "Meaning and Analogy" Hibbert Journal 49 (July 1951) 388-393
Meaning and universals presuppose analogies. The supposing of an orderly cosmos would give support to the analogical method.

Assfahl, Gerhard. Vergleich und Metapher bei Quintilian Stuttgart: W. Kohlhammer 1932

Atkins, J. W. H. Literary Criticism in Antiquity two vols. Cambridge 1934 [1961]
vol. II This is a summary of rhetorical figures from classical times to the eighteenth century.

Atkinson, William C. et al. "Culteranismo and Conceptismo" Encyclopaedia Britannica 20 (1968) 1127-1128
The seventeenth century movement, culteranismo, was represented especially by Góngora's Polifemo and Soledades. He attempted to re-latinize the language and used "every subtlety of which metaphor is susceptible." His poetry was not a cult of obscurity, but was sincere and timeless. Conceptismo plays on ideas; culteranismo on language. The conceptista "purveyed thought, and sought to shock the reader into attention by both the subtlety and the violence of his conceits, aiming always at the semblance of profundity."

Auden, W. H. "Squares and Oblongs" Poets at Work Charles Abbott, ed. New York: Harcourt, Brace & World 1948 pp. 171-181
Subject and idea are unimportant to the poet. Language is more important: "How can I know what I think till I see what I say?" On this view metaphor is not an expression of thought but constitutes it.

St. Augustine. Of Christian Doctrine, trans. J. Shaw in The Nicene and Post-Nicene Fathers vol. II Philip Schaff, ed. Grand Rapids, Michigan 1956. Also Contra Mendacium ad Consentium, III esp. 481 note 1.
Tropes give knowledge natural to man. They are important for understanding scripture. Tropes are valid only because based on ontological reality and instituted by God. Nature mirrors the divine.

Austin, H. D. "Multiple Meanings and Their Bearings on the Understanding of Dante's Metaphors" Modern Philology 30 (Nov. 1932) 129-140

_____. "Ten Debatable Dante Metaphors" PMLA 52 (March, 1937) 1-15

Austin, John. "Pretending" Essays in Philosophical Psychology Donald Gustafson, ed. New York: Doubleday 1964 pp. 99-116 (cf. Haworth.)
A discussion of the varieties of pretending brought out by examining ordinary language. The question is raised as to whether pretending involves an internal state or not. Pretending may not be a mere substitute for an internal state or another situation. It relates to metaphorical behavior, make-believe, party-forfeit, etc. and may be an as-if situation or genuine and not as-if.

E. B. "Notes on the Function of Metaphor" Metaphor Society for Pure English, tract number 11, p. 3 Oxford: The Clarendon Press
Metaphor expresses emotions by means of likenesses to them. Its effort should be proportional to the emotion presented. Unlike simile it does not express the point of resemblance. The terms of a metaphor should be unlike, except for material to immaterial analogies.

Babbitt, Irving. The New Laokoön Boston: Houghton Mifflin Co. 1910
The various synaesthetic experiments are found to be too subjective for the more humane purposes of art. The correspondences of the Romantics were too sensual and ignored the intellect. Images or the "pictures" of the poet word-painter should not be substituted for ideas.

Babcock, Sister Mary D. "Cummings' Typography: An Ideogrammic Style" Renascence: A Critical Journal of Letters 15 (1963) 115-123
Cummings' typographical and linguistic inventions function like Chinese ideograms.

Bachelard, Gaston. La psychanalyse de feu fifteenth edition Paris: Gallimard 1938 esp. pp. 213-219
Cf. M. Baym 1961
He speaks of "métaphores des métaphores."

Bacon, Wallace A. "Review of Wimsatt The Verbal Icon" The Quarterly Journal of Speech 40 (1954) 449-451

Baconsky, A. E. "Declinul metaforei" Gazeta Literară no. 24 (June 1961) ca. p. 25 (Source: Bălăet)

Baden, W. W. "The Principal Figures of Language and Figures of Thought in Isaeus and Guardianship Speeches of Demosthenes" PhD diss. Johns Hopkins University 1906

Baernstein, Jo-Ann. "Image, Identity, and Insight in The Good Soldier" Critique: Studies in Modern Fiction 9 (1967) 19-42

Bain, Alexander. English Composition and Rhetoric London 1893

Baker, A. J. "Category Mistakes" Australasian Journal of Philosophy 34 (1956) 13-26
Ryle's notion of category-mistakes as based on universes of discourse, or the breaking of rule-types, is inadequate. It should be based on fact, truth and falsity distinctions or on the fact that it leads to contradictions.

Bäker, Ferdinand. Die Metaphern in den Satiren des Horaz Programm Stralsund 1883 21 pp.

Baker, James. The Sacred River: Coleridge's Theory of the Imagination Baton Rouge: Louisiana State University Press 1956

Baker, Sheridan. The Complete Stylist New York: Thomas Crowell 1966 esp. pp. 155-158
Metaphor is a pretending, or shorthand for as-if, or a hyperbole. A metaphor should agree in its details and be consistent with the natural world. It illustrates and produces humor or visual pictures. Jane Austin reserved the most metaphors for her hollow character. Baker says scholars, unlike poets, should not use metaphors, though nearly all of our words are metaphorical.

Bălăet, Dumitru. "Aspecte ale metaforei întînăra poezie română" Viaţa Românească 21 (1968) no. 4, 95-104; no. 5, 91-99

Balakian, Anna. "Metaphor and Metamorphosis in André Breton's Poetics" French Studies 19 (1965) 34-41
For Breton interpreting reality metaphorically transforms it. He says, "Life is an ever restless aspiration toward transformation, which can make the earth more translucid than water and let the metal ooze out of its shell."

_____. "The Surrealist Image" Romanic Review 44 (1953) 273-281
She believes seriously in the metaphors of Breton, etc., such as "le désert vertical."

_____. The Symbolist Movement: A Critical Appraisal New York: Random House 1967

Balázs, Béla. Theory of Film Edith Bone, trans. New York: Roy 1953
About metaphorical montage in film.

Balkenhol, Anna. "Das poetische Bild bei Annette von Droste-Hülshoff, Münster in Westf." Forschungen und Funde 4 no. 3 (1916)

Ballard, Edward G. "Metaphysics and Metaphor" Journal of Philosophy 45 (April 8, 1948) 208-214
The difference between the literal and metaphorical is only based on convention, what we take at one time or period to be "clear." But every age sees and is captivated by its metaphors which are replaced by others later. Thought and language proceed by metaphor. Mathematics is only metaphorically related to things. For many the machine metaphor is taken literally. In metaphysics the transcendental terms, rest, motion, being, same, etc. as they apply to all things may serve as the basis for analogies.

Ballowe, James. "Mythic Vision in American Literature" Discourse 10 (1967) 324-332

Bally, Charles. La Langue et la vie Zürich: Niehans 1935; Paris:

Payot 1926
Concrete images are grasped by imagination, affective images by sentiment, and dead images by intellectual operations.

_____. "Le langage figuré" Traité de stylistique française third edition, two vols. Geneva: George & Cie; Paris: C. Klincksieck 1951 vol. 1 pp. 184ff. (Heidelberg 1909)
Metaphor is a comparison, or simile. Imagery renders subtlety of thought and feeling. Ideas cannot be detached from reality. Images are pictorial, emotive, intellectual (these overlap). Wild juxtapositions give insight or produce comic effect.

Balston, Giles. "Catchwords and Press Figures at Home and Abroad" Book Collector 9 (1960) 301-307

Bandyopadhyay, Pratap. Observations on Similes in the Naiṣadhacarita Calcutta: Sanskrit Pustak Bhandar 1966 142 pp.

Banks, Theodore. Milton's Imagery New York: Columbia University Press 1950

Barat, Emmanuel. "Le Style Poétique et la Révolution Romantique" PhD diss. Paris 1904

Barclay, E. Homeric Similes from the Iliad Designs London 1900

Barczat, W. De Figurarum Disciplina atque Auctoribus Pars. I Auctores Graeci. Göttingen 1904

Barfield, Owen. "The Meaning of the Word 'Literal'" Metaphor and Symbol L. Knights and B. Cottle, eds. Proceedings of the Twelfth Symposium of the Colston Research Society held in the University of Bristol, March 28-31, 1960 London: Butterworth 1960 pp. 48-63
"Literalness is a quality which some words have achieved in the course of their history; it is not a quality with which the first words were born."

_____. "Metaphor" New Statesman 26 (March 20, 1926) 708-710
Most words once referred to sensible objects or animal activity, e.g. "abstract" meant draw or drag, "thesis" meant to put, "analysis" meant to loose, "right" meant stretch or straight. He presents Müller's distinction between "poetic metaphor" (deliberate, consciously created) and "radical metaphor" (natural, unconscious use).

_____. Speaker's Meaning Middletown, Conn.: Wesleyan University Press 1967 esp. ch. 2 "Imagery in Language and Metaphor in Poetry"
Metaphor is a "look through" one meaning to another, a "translucence." All language is metaphorical. Whenever one meaning is apprehended through another it is a metaphorical process. Metaphorical terms precede literal ones, not vice versa.

_____. "Poetic Diction and Legal Fiction" The Importance of Language Max Black, ed. New Jersey: Prentice-Hall 1962 pp. 51-71
In symbolic metaphor we talk of B where A is just implied. We are not explicitly given "A is B." "Tarning" refers to hiding one meaning in another, saying one thing and meaning another without explicit comparison. "Any striking and original use of even a single word tends to be metaphorical and shows us the process of tarning." All language is metaphorical. In law there is continual metaphorical modification, e.g. limited companies are personified and regarded as individuals. We should be conscious of our metaphors. (cf. Nietzsche)

_____. Poetic Diction: A Study in Meaning New York: McGraw Hill 1964 [1928]
Metaphor is a synthesis based on a four term mathematical analogy. Metaphor was once immediate cognition of reality. It tries to recapture that experience. He thus rejects Müller's "root" or "radical" metaphor theory according to which words once represented physical objects and were metaphorically expanded to apply to mental and non-physical ones. Myth is the source of true metaphor. False metaphor is like allegory--a conscious hypostatization and synthesis.

Barnard, F. M. "Metaphors, Laments, and Organic Community" Canadian Journal of Economics and Political Science 32 (Aug. 1966) 281-301
Political discourse is largely based on metaphor, e.g. the state is like an organism or the state is an organism. Such metaphors can captivate us or help constitute their object. They thus may aid in conceptual and methodological analysis (cf. organism model) or provide a basis for a critique for the status quo. He discusses two organic models and their metaphorical imagery: 1) Herder's and 2) modern political romanticism.

Barone, Joseph M. "Sets, Switches and Metaphors" PhD diss. Princeton 1968
Metaphors are treated on the basis of Chomsky's work on generative-transformational grammar. Barone criticizes the Katz-Fodor interpretation of "deviant strings." Models of logical circuit design and set theory are employed. A detailed examination of D. Thomas' "Light breaks where no sun shines" is given.

Baroway, Israel. "Imagery of Spenser and the Song of Songs" Journal of English and German Philology 33 (Jan. 1934) 23-45
A comparison of the imagery of Spenser and the imagery of the "Song of Songs." The oriental imagery seems to contain "monstrous incongruity" of senses to the western reader, but such imagery is to be taken as an association of ideas rather than of sense images. It then becomes meaningful.

Barqueño, Pedro. Metáfora del barco, y otros poemas Granada 1962

Barton, Richard. Analogy of Divine Wisdom in the Material, Sensitive, Moral, Civil, and Spiritual System of Things second edition Dublin 1750 (Source: Wasserman TLS p. 181)
Real analogy of all things. "Every lump of matter, is a lesson of divine truths." True or controlled wit is given to man to discover these correspondences.

Barwick, Karl. Probleme der stoischen Sprachlehre und Rhetorik (Abhandlungen der Sächsichen Akademie der Wissenschaften zu Leipzig. Phil.-Hist. Klasse. vol. 49 no. 3) East Berlin 1957 pp. 88-111

Basaglia, Franco. "Kitsch ed espressione figurativa psicopatologica" Il Verri 15 (1964) 27-34
The art and figurative works of the mentally ill have been industrialized and turned into "kitsch" (i.e. trashy art). The art of the mentally ill is a language which only the psychiatrist can understand. This psychopathological testimony is the only significance of the art work. Ordinary art criticism cannot be applied to the art of the insane.

Bass, A. N. "Figuratively Speaking" Scholastic 27 (Jan. 25, 1936) pp. 7ff

Basset, J. E. "The Function of the Homeric Simile" Transactions of the American Philological Association 52 (1921) 132-147

Bate, Walter. "The Sympathetic Imagination in Eighteenth-Century English Criticism" ELH 12 (1945) 144-164

Battcock, Gregory. ed. The New Art New York: E. P. Dutton, Inc. 1966 254 pp.
The cover shows what may be called a visual metaphor: a face on a can. The accounts he gives of art are confused. Without intending to, they present the picture of art as a mere juxtaposition of objects (cf. visual metaphor), the metaphorical expression "art is art," and other unexpected repetitions in art itself. Also art is spoken of metaphorically as voyaging, destruction (metaphorical deviation from traditional categories), alive, pure, domestication of the outrageous, etc.

Baudelaire, Charles. Oeuvres Complètes 15 vols. Paris: L. Conard 1923-1952
See especially his essay on Victor Hugo and examples of synaesthesia in his poetry, e.g. in "The Artificial Paradises," "Correspondances." Everything corresponds to everything else.

Bauer, Jakob. Das Bild in der Sprache two vols. in one Ansbach 1878-1897
An important work on metaphor. He discusses the work of Grimm, Müller, Gerber, Hense, Cicero, Aristotle, Locke, Tryphon, Quintilian, Vischer, etc. with illustration from Homer, Tieck,

Goethe, etc.

Baum, P. F. "Chaucer's Nautical Metaphors" South Atlantic Quarterly 49 (Jan. 1950) 67-73

Baumgartner, Paul R. "Jonathan Edwards: The Theory Behind His Use of Figurative Language" PMLA 78 part 1 (Sept. 1963) 321-325
For Edwards the "adequation" of limited man to knowledge of God is by means of metaphors. They reveal the analogy of the sensual, finite world to God's. Metaphor is based on divine universal analogy.

Baur, Karl. Homerische Gleichnisse in Vergils Aeneid I. Progr. Freising 1891

Bausani, Alessandro. "Appunti sulle origini religiose della metafora parola-luce" Studi e materiali di storia delle religioni 24-25 (1953-1954) 26-35

Baym, Max I. "Brief Statement Concerning the Present State of the Study of Metaphor" Langue et Littérature 1961 pp. 375-376
A brief summary of his Books Abroad article on the present state of metaphor.

_____. "The Present State of the Study of Metaphor" Books Abroad 35 (Summer 1961) 215-219
A brief account of several theories of metaphor. He states that these accounts show that: 1) the nature of metaphor is embedded in the nature of language, 2) research into metaphor is important in many disciplines, 3) metaphor study can help unite the sciences and the humanities, 4) the subject is inexhaustible.

Baym, Nina. "From Metaphysics to Metaphor: The Image of Water in Emerson and Thoreau" Studies in Romanticism 5 (1966) 231-243

Beach, John. "Analogous Naming, Extrinsic Denomination, and the Real Order" Modern Schoolman 42 (Jan. 1965) 198-213

Beament, J. W. ed. Models and Analogues in Biology Symposium of the Society for Experimental Biology. Cambridge University Press 1960

Beardsley, Monroe C. Aesthetics New York: Harcourt, Brace and World, Inc. 1958 pp. 133-147, 159-162
One of the most adequate presentations of metaphor. He presents four theories of metaphor, accepting the last as best: 1) Emotive, 2) Supervenience (metaphors bear supernatural or transcendent meaning), 3) Literalist, 4) Controversion Theory (logical absurdity theory). On the last theory the metaphor is absurd if taken literally so a second level meaning is found to make sense of the metaphor. Beardsley accepts the

controversion view, but modifies it slightly in his later article, "The Metaphorical Twist."

_____. "Figurative Language" Practical Logic New York: Prentice-Hall 1964 (1950) pp. 94-125
Metaphor is a comparison between two unlike things. It must be literally false to be a figure. It needs interpretation for it contains implicitly a group of sentences some of which are true, others false.

_____. "Metaphor" Encyclopedia of Philosophy Paul Edwards, ed. New York: Macmillan vol. 5 1967 pp. 284-289

_____. "The Metaphorical Twist" Philosophy and Phenomenological Research 22 (March 1962) 293-307
He rejects the Object-Comparison View according to which a metaphor is an elliptical simile denoting the same object as before. This view overstresses object imagery and fails to account for properties only believed to be relevant. He favors his Revised Verbal-Opposition View (cf. his Aesthetics) according to which the two terms yield absurdity if taken literally. Thus there is a "twist" to connotative meaning in which the predicate gains a new intension. The revision involves including larger contextual considerations. In regard to verbal-opposition he notes that we know what the author is thinking because we see the word is used metaphorically not vice versa. A metaphor is as much a "saying" as a literal statement. We can only mean what we can say.

_____, P. Henle, and I. Hungerland. Symposium on Metaphor. The Seventeenth Annual Meeting of the American Society for Aesthetics, Cincinnati, Ohio, Oct. 29-31, 1959 (unpublished. Beardsley's paper was rewritten as "The Metaphorical Twist.")

Beaver, Joseph. "Lanier's Use of Science for Poetic Imagery" American Literature 24 (Jan. 1953) 520-533
Lanier uses concepts and images from various sciences in his poetry in an accurate and faithful manner.

Beck, Friedrich. Die Metapher bei Dante, ihr System ihre Quellen Neuburg a.d.D. 1896 (Wissenschaftliche Beilage des k.b. humanistischen Gymnasiums Neuburg a.d.D. für 1895-1896)

Becker, Otfrid. "Das Bild des Weges und verwandte Vorstellungen im frühgriechischen Denken" Hermes: Zeitschrift für Klassische Philologie Heft 4 Berlin: Weidmann 1937
This is a development of his PhD thesis, Leipzig 1935.

Bede, The Venerable. "De Schematibus et Tropis" Rhetores Latini Minores Carolus Halm, ed. Leipzig 1863 ch. 24, pp. 607-618
Metaphor is a transfer of both words and things. It is the transfer of a word from its proper signification to a non-proper similitude for adornment or necessity. Metaphor is a genus and other tropes are species. Metaphor and scripture are dis-

cussed. Bede is in the tradition of Donatus and Isidore and the classical and Roman tradition. His classifications are the same as Vendôme's. The four animate-inanimate transfers are presented.

Begelman, D. A. "Misnaming, Metaphors, the Medical Model and Some Muddles" Psychiatry 34 (1971) 38-58

Behrmann, Alfred. "Metapher im Kontext: Zu einigen Gedichten von Ingeborg Bachmann und Johannes Bobrowski" Der Deutschunterricht 20 no. 4 (Sept. 1968) 28-48

Beinhauer, Werner. "Beiträge zu einer spanischen Metaphorik" Romanische Forschungen, Zeitschrift für Romanische Sprachen und Literaturen 55 (1941) 1-56, 184-206, 280-336
He says that Brinkmann states that the Spanish language is the most figurative of all romantic languages, Stählin that Spanish metaphors reveal character and culture. The metaphors of a language give a more or less complete picture of the people who speak the language. Primitive man cannot use metaphors because he is not conscious of figurative usage; he does not think feeling rendered in terms of a part of the body is metaphoric. Faded metaphors may be rejuvenated. Brinkmann is cited as showing that a sense of humor plays a very important part in Spanish metaphor. This essay deals with metaphor of authors from the middle of the last century to contemporary authors. Beinhauer stresses examples of metaphor as models to be learnt. Every expression is to be shown in its organic context. Bold images are especially difficult for foreign readers, e.g. those of Gracián, Guevara, Quevedo, Calderón. Beinhauer quotes José Bergamin: "En España el lenguaje es superior a la literatura." That is, in Spain the common language is highly metaphorical, more so than literature.

_____. "La Metáfora religiosa en el español hablado" Verdad y Vida 4 (1946) 138-155
Shows harmony between earthly and divine things.

_____. Das Tier in der spanischen Bildsprache Hamburg: Hansischer Gildenverlag 1949 135 pp.

_____. Spanischer Sprachhumor Bonn 1932
He shows how irreverently the Spaniard plays with long respected expressions and how he revives them by means of novel variations. A sense of humorous play is important in Spanish metaphor.

Bel'skii, A. V. "Metaforich . . . " (Source: Korol'kov)

Benamou, Michel. "Wallace Stevens: Some Relations Between Poetry and Painting" Comparative Literature 11 (Winter 1959) 47-60
Stevens shows his pictorial method by juxtaposing pictures, e.g. in "Sunday Morning." These visual metaphors provide multiple perspectives and reveal mental reality as well.

Benn, Gottfried. Gesammelte Werke four vols. Dieter Wellershoff, ed. Wiesbaden 1958-1961
Stressing immediacy he distrusts and avoids simile and metaphor.

Bennet, J. "Review of M. Hesse 'On Defining Analogy'" Journal of Symbolic Logic 25 (March, 1960) 74-75

Bennett, Joan. "An Aspect of the Evolution of Seventeenth-Century Prose" Review of English Studies 17 (1941) 281-297

Bentham, Jeremy. Works eleven vols. John Bowring, ed. New York: Russell & Russell 1962 (cf. Ogden, Bentham's Theory of Fictions)
Poetry is no better than a game of pushpin. Non-sensible entities or fictions are metaphors and should not be confused with real sensed objects. Metaphors (or fictions) should be replaced with literal language.

Berefelt, Gunnar. "On Symbol and Allegory" Journal of Aesthetics and Art Criticism 28 (Winter 1969) 201-212

Berg, George. Metaphor and Comparison in the Dialogues of Plato PhD diss. Baltimore: Johns Hopkins University 1903; Berlin: Mayer & Müller 1904
He agrees with Sihler's dissertation on Plato's metaphors and takes Aristotle's treatment of metaphor as final. The best metaphors are in the Republic, the most are in Phaedrus.

Berggren, Douglas. "An Analysis of Metaphorical Meaning and Truth" PhD diss. Yale 1959
"A philosophical treatise has never been written which did not depend on the use of metaphor." He discusses the following theories of metaphor: 1) ornament, 2) analogy or structural metaphor, 3) expression, 4) symbolism, 5) utility notions, 6) tension (Berggren's view). The two minimal conditions for all poetic metaphors are 1) dual reference with a type-boundary, 2) textural principle of transference which transgresses without obliterating the type boundary thereby yielding type tension. There is both textual affinity and a denial of type identity, conjunction and deduction. Poetry discovers but also creates such affinities. Modes of metaphoric transference of type-boundaries are: pictorial, structural (analogy), emotional, linguistic analogy, or several of these. This is one of the most complete analyses of metaphor. It contains numerous historical and conceptual charts of metaphor theories and ideas.

_____. "From Myth to Metaphor" Monist 50 (Oct. 1966) 530-552
The meaning of religion and physics is either mythically ambiguous, literally nonsensical or absurd, or metaphorically tensional. Instead of trying to make myth less ambiguous by distinguishing it from ordinary objects of perception and so destroying it we should regard it as irreducibly tensional. Some sort of identity in difference is sought between the em-

pirical world and the world of religion or science. Metaphor helps constitute reality and is not mere illustration or ornament.

_____. "The Use and Abuse of Metaphor" Review of Metaphysics 16 (Dec. 1962) 237-258, (March 1963) 450-472
"Metaphor has always been one of the central problems of philosophy." The "abuse" of metaphor is to regard it as myth instead of as tensional. Scientific models are not just true or false, but rather explanatory and useful in a certain frame of reference. There is no comparison of theory with fact but rather a use of models in a tensive manner. Metaphor gives unity in diversity without loss of diversity. He accepts the notions of metaphor as a "lens," "filter," "stereoscope of ideas." Metaphor is anything standing for something else, even something non-verbal, e.g. map, diagram, mathematics, raised eyebrow. It must be literally false statement. It constitutes reality but is not paraphrasable. Three epistemic and overlapping principles of metaphor are: 1) pictorial comparison of the form A-B, e.g. "hawk-nose," 2) structurally repeated ratios, e.g. A : B :: C : D, 3) common emotional feeling or texture. He states that as a result of the insight of his tensive theory, "Most traditional and contemporary attitudes toward philosophical ontology will have to be revised." "Poetic textures" resulting from tensive metaphors are neither objects nor emotions but nevertheless are phenomenally objective, e.g. to see the "joy of the waves" is no more like seeing with our emotions than just seeing. To apprehend textures we must construe the world with feeling with an eye on both.

Bergmann, K. "Wie der Feldgraue spricht" Giessen 1916

Bergson, Henri. Laughter: An Essay on the Meaning of the Comic C. Brereton and F. Rothwell, trans. New York: Macmillan 1914

Bernard, Manfred. "Pindars Denken in Bildern; Vom Wesen der Metapher" PhD diss. Tübingen 1955 (Pfullingen 1963)

Berne, Eric. Games People Play New York: Grove Press 1964

Berry, Ralph. "The Frontier of Metaphor and Symbol" British Journal of Aesthetics 7 (Jan. 1967) 76-83
Metaphor and symbol are both generally perceptions of associations. A symbol is an intuitive perception which can as yet neither be apprehended better nor expressed differently. It is a specific with a general undefined, passive association, often recurring over a long period. It involves belief in the identity of the two images. It tends to the universal. A metaphor is a brief, non-recurring, conscious and active likeness relation linking specifics. It seeks a new and elusive fruition. Context determines the meaning of both symbol and metaphor. They cannot always be distinguished. A symbol is sometimes a cluster of metaphors.

Berthoff, A. E. "Allegorical Metaphor: Marvell's 'The Definition of Love'" *Review of English Studies* 17 (Feb. 1966) 16-29

Bertram, Heinrich. *Die Bildersprache Platons, ein Beitrag zur Würdigung der schriftstellerischen Kunst des Philosophen* Programm der Landesschule, Pforta I 1893, II 1895

Betar, George. Jr. "Imagination and Reality in Wallace Stevens' Prose and Early Poetry" PhD diss. University of Southern California 1962
He shows that imagination is tied to reality for Stevens.

Bethell, Samuel L. "Gracián, Tesauro and Nature of Metaphysical Wit" *The Northern Miscellany* 1 (Autumn 1953) 19-40

_____. "The Nature of Metaphysical Wit" *Discussions of John Donne* Frank Kermode, ed. Boston: D. C. Heath 1962

Bett, Henry. *Some Secrets of Style* London: Allen and Unwin 1932 277 pp. esp. pp. 238-247
Metaphor is a highly pictorial extension of an adjective. It is intrinsic to language and every style of writing is metaphorical. Etymologically words have metaphorical derivations, e.g. "companion" from "one who shares bread." The images of metaphors should be consistent. Far-fetched metaphors may be justified by successful use. Metaphors should accurately reflect emotions.

Betts, George H. "The Distribution and Functions of Mental Imagery" *Contributions to Education* 26 (publication of Teachers College, Columbia University) New York 1909

Beutmann, Margarete. "Die Bildwelt D. H. Lawrences" PhD diss. Freiburg im Breisgau 1940

Bevan, Ed. *Symbolism and Belief* New York: Kennikat Press 1938
Metaphor allows man to conceive the inconceivable and know the unknowable.

Bevis, William. "Metaphor in Wallace Stevens" *Shenandoah* 15 no. 2 (1964) 35-48
For Stevens metaphor is the basis of art and the "harmonium" (which is a tensive union of self and external world). There is also a tensive relation between metaphor and sensing directly (which is metaphorical also.) All reality is partly fictive. Stevens says, "The senses paint by metaphor" (i.e. we see metaphorically. cf. "seeing-as"); to be aware is to be fictively aware. Metaphor is a revealing aberration. Abstract-to-concrete metaphor is circular.

Beyer, C. *Deutsche Poetik* three vols. Berlin: B. Behrs Verlag 1900 vol. 1 "Die Metapher" pp. 156-169
Metaphor is a shortened, simplified, comparison. The idea is

not only compared with another but is named after another and represented by this other. The object of comparison takes the place of the subject of comparison. The following definitions of metaphor are given:
Zumpt--contracted comparison
Wackernagel--shortened comparison
Gottschall-concentrated comparison
Vischer--bringing in a vision from another sphere
M. Müller--transfer of the nature of one object to other objects.
Metaphor may be a single word or part of speech or a part of or a whole sentence. Metaphor may be classified as 1) spiritual 2) sensual 3) material 4) spirited.

Bickerton, Derek. "Prolegomena to a Linguistic Theory of Metaphor" _Foundations of Language_ 5 (1969) 34-52
A specifically linguistic approach to metaphor which claims to be the first. The Katz-Fodor-Postal formulation is irrelevant and deficient. A tentative linguistic system is developed to account for metaphor.

Biese, Alfred. "Die Metapher als psychologisches Problem" _Die Literatur_ 30 (1928) 696-698
A discussion of the views on metaphor of Aristotle, Quintilian, Cicero, G. Buck, Vico, Goethe, Jean Paul, Vischer, Nietzsche, Vaihinger, Tieck, etc. Metaphor is not a comparison but rather a necessary assumption stemming from the unconscious. It is not an illusion or fiction but a necessary means of giving things a personal significance. For Vico everything one does not understand is personified and so metaphor is a little myth. Metaphor precedes literal statement. Every idea is a picture. In the hypotheses of science better pictures are always being found. Metaphor draws out what is already in external objects. There is an external harmony of the world. The struggle between prose and poetry or metaphor will remain. "We see everywhere that the metaphorical imagination governs the life of the soul." The poet of the philosophy of "as-if" (Vaihinger) is Max Dauthendey.

______. "Das Metaphorische in der dichterischen Phantasie" _Zeitschrift für vergleichende Litteraturgeschichte und Renaissance-Litteratur_ 2 (1889) 317-339
The poet metaphorically transforms individual experience, unites the inner mental and outer world in reciprocal transference. All poetry is metaphor either projecting inner on the outer or outer on the inner world. Metaphor is the transformation of the seen through the medium of subjective sensitivity. The poet who loses himself in the figures of his imagination will come closest to recreating nature. Historically simile tends to become metaphor, a comparison or juxtaposition becomes fused. Metaphor is not decoration but is one of man's primary thought forms. Our most recent books on poetics and aesthetics still do not acknowledge this fact. Poetry, myth, and a child's imagination are alike in being attempts to give soul to nature.

Language creates metaphors through lightning-like combinations. Language is built by means of metaphor. Jean Paul has the richest metaphors of all German poets.

_____. "Die metaphorische Sprache in Goethes 'Iphigenie'" Lehrproben und Lehrgänge vol. 55

_____. Die Philosophie des Metaphorischen Hamburg und Leipzig: L. Voss 1893 229 pp.
A major work on metaphor. He discusses metaphor in language, myth, childhood fantasy, religion, ancient and modern philosophy, and in art (architecture, plastic art, painting, music and poetry). Laan (1942) gives the following account of this work: The metaphorical, not the same as metaphor, is not mere rhetoric or trope but the embodiment of the spiritual, a natural expression of the synthesis of inner and outer. Metaphor is the manifestation of the metaphorical in language and is rather shallow by comparison. Metaphor restricts itself to dualisms of body-soul, matter-spirit, self-world, etc. We spiritualize the material and materialize the spiritual. Although we think language insufficient to express our thoughts completely, still language and metaphor cannot be avoided. Metaphor is an evil but a necessary evil.

Bigsby, C. W. "The Violent Image: The Significance of Kenneth Brown's 'The Brig'" Wisconsin Studies in Comparative Literature 8 (1967) 421-430

Bilsky, Manuel. "I. A. Richards' Theory of Metaphor" Modern Philology 50 (Nov. 1952) 130-137
He opposes Richards' views that all language is metaphor, that comparison is between given and remembered data, a resemblance of like things, and he analyzes in detail the relations between tenor and vehicle.

Binswanger, Ludwig. Ausgewählte Vorträge und Aufsätze Bern 1955 (cf. Vonessen 1959)
Metaphor is worked out as the actual language of phenomenology. The precedence of the realm of the senses is called into question.

Birch, Austin H. "The Abuse of Metaphor" Hibbert Journal 45 (Apr. 1947) 234-240
Many of our simplest words are disguised metaphors, e.g. escape, incur, shield, etc. Metaphor is mere ornament which may "dazzle the eyes and distort the picture." They are only a means to an end, are usually obscure and unanalyzable, and so should be avoided. They do reflect national character or temperament.

Bjorkman, Gunnar. Metaforernas bleknande, en orientering (Akademisk arhandling-Göteborg) Uddevalla 1925

Black, Max. "Metaphor" *Proceedings of the Aristotelian Society* N.S. 55 (May 1955) 273-294. Reprinted in *Art and Philosophy* W. E. Kennick, ed. New York: St. Martin's Press 1964 pp. 449-465. Also in *Models and Metaphors* (see next entry) He presents three theories: substitution (catachresis or literal substitution), comparison (elliptical simile view), interaction (Black's view). In interaction, the new context [or "frame"] imposes extension of meaning upon the focal word; the old and new meaning must be attended together; two thoughts are connected and active together, interilluminate and cooperate. Metaphor is a two-way "filter" or "screen of associated commonplaces," e.g. we may "filter" or "battle" through the vocabulary of "chess." It is not a comparison and may involve an emotive shift. Metaphor depends on an author's views, intentions and the larger historical context. There are no strict rules for usage. It involves meaning, not just syntax. Any part of speech may be a metaphor.

_____. "Models and Archetypes" *Models and Metaphors* Ithaca: Cornell University Press 1962 pp. 219-243 (Review by Odegard) The application of his interaction theory of metaphor to an analysis of models and archetypes. A study of models and archetypes shows science and the humanities are not far apart. A "scale model" preserves relative proportions, an "analogue model" preserves structure isomorphically, e.g. hydraulic model of an economic system, a "theoretical model" is a mere description of a possible structure--a "talking in a certain way." An "archetype" is an unconscious or "submerged" model such that only later can a pattern of concepts be found and termed an archetype. Models do not merely illustrate but partly constitute their object and provide knowledge not otherwise obtainable.

_____. "Some Questions About Emotive Meaning" *Philosophical Review* 57 (March 1948) 111-126

Blackall, Eric. *The Emergence of German as a Literary Language, 1700-1775* Cambridge, Eng.: Cambridge University Press 1959 ch. 9 "The Revival of Metaphor" pp. 276-313 The views of Bodmer and Breitinger are presented as reviving the value of metaphor.

_____. "Irony and Imagery in Hamann" *Publications of the English Goethe Society* 26 (1957) 1-25

Blaga, Lucian. *Geneza metaforei şi sensul culturii* (Fundaţia pentru literatură şi artă) Bucarest 1937

Blair, Hugh. *Lectures on Rhetoric and Belles Lettres* Carbondale, Ill.: Southern Illinois University 1965 [8th edition London 1801] "Metaphor" pp. 295-314 Metaphor is based on the association of ideas. It ornaments. He revises Kames' "principle idea" and "accessory idea" to "visual sense" (tenor) and "figurative sense" (vehicle) respectively. One term pictures the other. Metaphor must give a good image and it must be possible for one to delineate it with a pencil.

Blake, William. Letter to Rev. Dr. Trusler [1799] from "A Vision of the Last Judgement" [1810] _Complete Writings_ Geoffrey Keynes, ed. London 1957. Also in Ellmann and Feidelson pp. 54-57 Mental things alone are real. "To me, this world is all One continued Vision of Fancy and Imagination." Matter changes and is an imposture but Visions are real and eternal. A very Platonic account.

Blanch, Robert J. "Poe's Imagery: An Undercurrent of Childhood Fears" _Furman Studies_ 14 no. 4 (1967) 19-25

Blanche, F. A. "L'Analogie" _Revue de Philosophie_ 30 (1923) 248-270

_____. "La Notion d'Analogie dans la Philosophie de St. Thomas" _Revue des sciences philosophiques et théologiques_ 10 (1921) 169-193

_____. "Une Théorie de l'Analogie: Éclaircissements et Développements" _Revue de Philosophie_ N.S. 3 (1932) 37-78

Bland, D. S. "The Pictorial Image in Poetry" _Twentieth Century_ 162 (Sept. 1957) 243-250
A criticism of Richards and Coleridge for opposition to and neglect of the function language has of evoking images. The purpose of much poetry is merely to evoke images, to call up pictures. "It is _because_ 'the acts of the mind itself' cannot be expressed directly that we have recourse to metaphor, to expression by means of pictures or analogies.

Blau, H. "Heaven's Sugar Cake: Theology and Imagery in the Poetry of Edward Taylor" _New England Quarterly_ 26 (Sept. 1953) 337-360

Bliesener, Irmgard. "Bild-Erlebnisse Coleridges und ihre Einwirkung auf sein künstlerisches Schaffen" PhD diss. Göttingen 1935

Blinderman, Charles S. "T. H. Huxley's Theory of Aesthetics: Unity in Diversity" _Journal of Art and Art Criticism_ 21 no. 1 (Fall 1962) 49-55
Attempts to show there is art in science and science in art.

Bloch, Alice. "Sight Imagery in _Invisible Man_" _English Journal_ 55 (Nov. 1966) 1019-1021, 1024

Bloom, E. A. "Vanity of Human Wishes: Reason's Images" _Essays in Criticism_ 15 (Apr. 1965) 181-192

Bloomfield, Leonard. Language New York: Holt, Rinehart & Winston 1964 [1933]

Bloomfield, Morton. "A Grammatical Approach to Personification Allegory" Modern Philology 60 (1963) 161-171
"Personification allegory" is the process of animating inanimate objects or abstract notions. Its main source is action and animate verbs, and predicates, and is not in a particular space and time. It points to a world of values and is not completely linguistic. "It yokes together rationality and metaphoric boldness." Has a useful bibliography.

Bluestone, Max. "The Suppressed Metaphor in Pope" Essays in Criticism 8 (1958) 347-354

Blume, B. "Sein und Scheitern: Zur Geschichte einer Metapher" Germanisch-romanische Monatsschrift 9 (1959) 277-288

Blumenberg, Hans. "Licht als Metapher der Wahrheit: Im Vorfeld der Philosophischen Begriffsbildung" Studium Generale 10 (1957) 432-447

_____. "Paradigmen zu einer Metaphorologie" Archiv für Begriffsgeschichte. Bausteine zu einem historischen Wörterbuch der Philosophie 6 (1960) 5-142, 301-305
Metaphors can be "remnants" on the way from myth to logos. They can also be fundamentals of philosophic language which cannot be rendered literally. These are "absolute metaphors." Determination of their function would be an essential part of the history of ideas. Kant calls absolute metaphor a symbol i.e. a reflection of an object that can be perceived of a completely different idea, to which a perception can never directly correspond. This article examines tests and limits of absolute metaphors, e.g. the metaphor of "powerful" truth. Absolute metaphors cannot be verified and have only a pragmatic truth [cf. Vaihinger]. They reveal the fundamental certainties, suppositions, expectations, activities, desires, etc. of an age. Metaphor does not just illustrate truth but helps to constitute it. Absolute metaphor defies complete logical analysis. He suggests we compile a typology of metaphors. Metaphors may not appear directly but may be suggested by a series of statements. They make revealed a possibility of understanding. He suggests a progression from concept to metaphor rather than the reverse.

Blümner, Hugo. "Der bildliche Ausdruck in den Reden des Fürsten Bismarck" (Source: Stutterheim 1941)

_____. "Die Metapher bei Herodotos" Neue Jahrbücher für klassische Philologie 143 (1891) 9-52

_____. Studien zur Geschichte der Metapher im Griechischen Leipzig: B. G. Teubner 1891 vol. 1 Über Gleichniss und Metapher

in der attischen Komödie
About comparison and metaphor in attic comedy. An extremely detailed extensive account of specific comparisons and metaphors classified according to general concepts, words relating to man and his activities, and nature (e.g. plants, animals, minerals, land, sea, astronomy, meteorology, etc.).

Boas, F. "Metaphorical Expressions in the Language of the Kwakiutl Indians" Race, Language, and Culture New York: Macmillan 1940 pp. 232-239

Bochénski, I. M. "On Analogy" The Thomist 11 (1948) 424-447
Bochénski suggests that logic cannot be separated from ontology and tries to formulate in terms of symbolic logic the Thomist's "analogy of proper proportionality." Logic, he thinks, deals with being. He treats analogy as an "isomorphic" relation, a similarity of relations.

______. Die zeitgenössischen Denkmethoden Bern: Francke Verlag 1954
Thomistic view. We do not know God's being yet we can predicate analogically of Him. There is an "isomorphic" relation between God's thought and our own. Creatures : God :: effect : cause.

Bode, Wilhelm. "Die Kenningar in der angelsächsischen Dichtung, mit Ausblicken auf andere Litteraturen" Inaugural diss. Strassburg. Darmstadt & Leipzig 1886

Bodkin, Maud. Archetypal Patterns in Poetry: Psychological Studies of Imagination London: Oxford University Press 1934 [1968]
She states, "An attempt is here made to bring psychological analysis and reflection to bear upon the imaginative experience communicated by great poetry, and to examine those forms or patterns in which the universal forces of our nature there find objectivation." Archetypal patterns or themes persist from age to age which reveal fixed emotional tendencies of a race or of all mankind. She modifies Jung's archetype theory.

______. Studies of Type-Images in Poetry, Religion and Philosophy New York: Oxford University Press 1951 184 pp.
A consideration of religious images and archetypes. Two main types of imagery of the Divine are Dionysian and Olympian. Writers shape beliefs by means of their presentations of images. Archetypes are difficult to define because of the "elusive, inter-penetrative, character of the psychic and spiritual life to which [they] apply."

Bodmer, Johann. Critische Abhandlung von dem Wunderbaren in der Poesie Faksimiledruck nach der Ausgabe von 1740 Stuttgart: J. B. Metzler 1966 (cf. Blackall)
Metaphor should picture. Their various types should be studied as an aid to style. Imagination recognizes real likenesses; fancy recognizes only a possible world.

_____. Die Discourse der Mahlern 1721-1722 Bibliothek älterer Schriftwerke der deutschen Schweiz. series 2, no. 2 Frauenfeld: J. Huber 1891
In "Poetry and Painting" he states, "A true poet will try to paint pictures on the imagination, which at a man's birth is devoid of impressions . . . . A writer's pen is his brush, and words are his colors . . . . The best poet will so paint his pictures that his readers will see the originals reflected as in a mirror."

_____. Vier kritische Gedichte Heilbron: Gebr. Henninger 1883

Boies, J. J. "Circular Imagery in Thoreau's Week" College English 26 (1965) 350-355

Boillot, Felix. "Images et métaphores" Le Français Moderne 22 (1954) 5-7
One may be complimented on one's metaphors only to find they are not really too original except for those few who have not heard them before. New metaphors soon become absorbed into the language as clichés. One may keep notebooks of metaphors for ready use but for the writer this would inhibit the imagination. He discusses whether one should use others' metaphors and concludes by quoting Chateaubriand: "The truly original author is not the one who does not copy others, but the one whom no one can copy."

_____. "Les métaphores fournies à la langue française par l'art littéraire et les activités qui s'y rattachent" French Quarterly 22 (Dec. 1929) 245-259 (unverified source)

_____. Répertoire des métaphores et mots français, tiré des noms des villes et des pays étrangers Paris: Les presses universitaires de France; Oxford University Press 1929

Boléo, Manuel de Paiva. A metáfora na língua portuguesa corrente Universidade de Coimbra 1935 41 pp.

Bomhoff, Jacobus G. "De metafoor in de literatuur" Handelingen van het Nederlands Filologencongres 27 (1962) 59-68

Bonnell, John K. "Touch Images in the Poetry of Robert Browning" PMLA 37 (1922) 574-598

Bonner, John. "Analogies in Biology" Synthese 15 (1963) 275-279

Bonnet, Rudolphus. "De tropis graecis capita selecta" PhD diss. Marburg 1921

Bonsiepe, Gui. "Visual/Verbal Rhetoric" Dot Zero (New York) 2 (1967) 37-42
"Classical rhetoric...is no longer adequate for describing and analyzing rhetorical phenomena in which verbal and visual

signs, i.e. word and picture, are allied." He presents a modern system based on syntactic and semantic distinctions, e.g. a picture of air with the caption "you never run out of air" to suggest an air-cooled car is better than a water-cooled one. This is called "visual/verbal parallelism." He applies rhetoric to advertising.

Borges, Jorge L. Historia de la Eternidad Buenos Aires: Emecé Editores 1953 pp. 43-67, 69-74
1) "La Metáfora" (trans. by N. Thomas di Giovanni in "Up from Ultraism" New York Review of Books Aug, 13, 1970 pp. 3-4.)
Kennings offer pleasing surprise but have no emotion to justify them. This is true of the metaphors of mannerism also. Both combine words alone without being based on perceived analogies. Poets' metaphors had at certain times related only certain things e.g. stars and eye, woman and flower, time and water, old age and lateness, sleep and death. This produces triviality. It is almost absurd to try to work out new metaphors. Every familiar and necessary affinity has been noted and recorded by someone. Still metaphors may restate these affinities anew and the virtue of metaphor lies in the words used. "Someday the history of the metaphor will be written, and then we will know the truth and the error that these conjectures hold."
2) "Las Kenningar"
Snorri Sturluson was the first to compile a glossary of kennings of Icelandic poetry. (He preferred kennings which were moderate and not too intricate.) Kennings were the first deliberate verbal pleasure of an instinctive literature. They relieve the difficulties of a rigorous metric. The kennings partly served to stimulate generosity with the aim of receiving gifts. Thus they referred to kings as "lord of rings" etc. For Borges, Culteranismo also is a frenzy of the academic mind. The kenning estranges us from the world. It produces the mystical puzzlement of metaphysics. It is difficult to translate these compound words into a language which does not use words in that manner.

_____. Idioma de los Argentinos Buenos Aires: M. Gleizer 1928 "Otra vez la metáfora" pp. 55-63 (cf. Gertel, Girardot)
Metaphorical extravagance is justifiable as a visible expression of intense emotion. It is a habitual and necessary part of language but is not the basic task of the poet and should not be put over the other rhetorical devices. It presupposes a poetic experience which when combined with metaphor makes for effective poetry. Metaphor is literary, not poetic.

_____. "Apuntaciones críticas: La metáfora" Cosmópolis (Madrid (Nov. 1921) 395-402

_____. Inquisiciones 1925 "Examen de metáforas" pp. 65-75

Metaphor is new, transcending noun-adj. categories. Abstract words are metaphors. Metaphor renders emotions. Metaphors unite concepts. He classifies metaphors, e.g., space-time transfer.

Boulanger, André. *Aelius Aristide et la sophistique dans la province d'Asie au IIe siècle de notre ère* Paris: de Boccard 1923 504 pp. esp. pp. 412-417

Boulton, Marjorie. "Figures of Speech" *Encyclopaedia Britannica* 9 (1968) 257-260
(*Britannica* had earlier regarded metaphor as a mere condensed simile.) Figures of speech are intentional deviations from literal statement. They are an integral part of language, consciousness, sensory perception, and earliest thought processes. They are not mere ornaments. Metaphors emphasize, clarify, stimulate thought, manifest exuberance, create connections, express what cannot be expressed otherwise. It shades into image and symbol and ranges from seriousness to joke. Psychiatrists treat dreams metaphorically.

Bourke, Myles. *A Study of the Metaphor of the Olive-Tree in Romans XI*. *Studies in Sacred Theology* 2 series 3 Washington: Catholic University Press 1947

Bouwsma, O. K. "The Expression Theory of Art" *Art and Philosophy* W. Kennick, ed. New York: St. Martin's Press 1964 pp. 261-282
He considers the expression "The music is sad." His main point is that difficulty arises with such a statement, which we normally make, only when we think of other "language games" or "forms of life." We should not think that the music is sad in the same way that Cassie is sad. We are not *seeing* the music *as* sad, not seeing the music in terms of or through Cassie's sort of sadness. The puzzlement about "The music is sad" vanishes when we realize that it arose from misleading analogies. The music *is* sad, it is not *seen-as* sad.

Bovie, S. P. "Imagery of Ascent-Descent in Vergil's Georgics" *American Journal of Philology* 77 (Oct. 1956) 337-358

Bowers, John. "Some Correlates of Language Intensity" *Quarterly Journal of Speech* 50 (Dec. 1964) 415-420 (See also Osborn)

Bowers, R. H. "Bacon's Spider Simile" *Journal of the History of Ideas* 17 (Jan. 1956) 133-135

Boyle, Robert R. "Metaphor" *The New Catholic Encyclopedia* 9 pp. 724-725
Three approaches to metaphor are 1) two beings, four terms related, 2) two terms identified, 3) three terms: one being, one act or quality, one bare nature the mind imagines to be in the object. Every metaphor has two nouns: 1) concrete, 2) abstract

and expressed only as a nature. It also contains a verb or adjective. Metaphor on the third view does not deal with the real in itself but only as it exists in the mind of the knower concentrating on the contingent act. "The aim of metaphor is to focus the human mind on the mystery of the dynamic real." A Thomistic view.

_____. Metaphor in Hopkins Chapel Hill: University of North Carolina Press 1961 231 pp. (review by Mary Hess)
Hopkins' and every profound artist's mind finds its fullest expression in metaphor. He gives the Catholic religion's interpretation of Hopkins' metaphors although he presents other views.

_____. "The Nature of Metaphor" The Modern Schoolman 31 (May 1954) 257-280
Unlike the traditional Thomist, Boyle holds that metaphor exists in the concrete order of real being. It is usually held that metaphor is improper proportionality not grounded on reality. Boyle states that metaphor deals with one being and several natures, and the mind ascribes another nature to a being which does not have that nature normally, e.g. "John is an ox." The strength of the ox (the ox's nature) is mentally ascribed to John because John is stronger than a man. "I consider metaphor as the mind's way of fixing its whole attention upon the peculiar quality of an individual being, so that the ultimate limits of metaphor coincide with the ultimate limits of the being involved; and who will measure these?"

_____. "The Nature of Metaphor: Further Considerations" The Modern Schoolman 34 (May 1957) 283-298. Reply by M. Slattery pp. 299-301
A Thomistic controversy. He discusses Slattery's views on metaphor. Boyle's view is that metaphor doesn't deal with or state any relation which exists in or between things in reality but rather it offers accidental being and a contingent name. It aims not at discursive meaning but at vision.

_____. "Review of Wheelwright, Metaphor and Reality" Christian Scholar 46 (1963) 174-178
Boyle attacks Wheelwright for concentrating on metaphorical terms rather than on judgment and being.

Boyle, Thomas E. "The Tenor in the Organic Metaphor: A View of American Romanticism" Discourse: A Review of Liberal Arts 11 (1968) 240-251

_____. "Thomas Wolfe: Theme Through Imagery" Modern Fiction Studies 11 (Autumn 1965) 259-268

Bozon, Brother Nicole. The Metaphors of Brother Bozon Trans. from Norman French by J. Constable, from the Library of the Honorable Society of Gray's Inns. Written in the fourteenth century

by a Franciscan Friar (London 1913). Also published in 1889 by the Société des Anciens Textes Français under the title "Les contes moralisés de Nicole Bozon Frère Mineur" (Reprinted by Franklin Publishers, 1968).
A collection of morals is drawn from animals. Universal analogy is assumed.

Bradford, M. E. "Meaning and Metaphor in Donald Davidson's 'A Touch of Snow'" _Southern Review_ 2 (1966) 516-523

Brand, Fritz. "Metaphern bei Alfred de Musset; ein Beitrag zum Verständnis seines Lebens, Leidens und Dichtens" PhD diss. Münster i. Westf. 1916 144 pp.
A series of specific metaphors is presented.

Brandeis, Irma. "Metaphor in the _Divine Comedy_" _Hudson Review_ 8 (Winter 1956) 557-575
The _Inferno_ has few metaphors but _Purgatorio_ and _Paradiso_ have many.

Brandenburg, Alice S. "Dynamic Image in Metaphysical Poetry" _PMLA_ 57 (Dec. 1942) 1039-1045
"Dynamic image" describes the way objects act and interact and underly metaphysical poetry, e.g. it explains mental by means of physical action. It is not static, sensuous, visual imagery. The reader is not supposed to notice the sensuous side of metaphorical images.

Braumüller, Richard. _Über Tropen und Figuren in Virgils Aeneis_ Programm d. Wilhelms-Gymn. Berlin. Part 1, 1877, 1-33; part 2, 1882, 1-20

Braun, A. _Versuch über die Tropen_ Munnerstadt 1847

Bréal, Michel. _Semantics: Studies in the Science of Meaning_ Mrs. Henry Cust, trans. New York: Dover 1964 [1900] ch. 12 "Metaphor" pp. 122-133
Language is transformed and develops by means of metaphor which is based on similarity and the need for new description. Etymology is a rich source of instances, e.g. "person" is from _persona_ meaning "mask." He says, "The subject of metaphor is inexhaustible."

Bréhier, Émile. "Images plotiniennes, et images bergsoniennes" _Les études bergsoniennes_ 2 (1949) 105-128

Breitinger, Johann J. _Critische Abhandlung von der Natur, den Absichten und dem Gebrauche der Gleichnisse_ Stuttgart: Metzler 1967 (summary in Phelps and Blackall)
Metaphor should be limited to oratory and poetry. It is a technique of clarification and aesthetic enjoyment.

_____. _Critische Dichtkunst_ two vols. Faksimiledruck. Stuttgart: J. B. Metzlersche Verlag 1966 [1740] esp. vol. 1 ch. 2 "Erklärung der poetischen Mahleren" (summary by Blackall) Four types of comparison are 1) illuminative, 2) decorative, 3) expressive, 4) instructive. Unlike Gottsched he defends the oxymoron, pathetic fallacy and metaphor. Metaphor produces an impression of <u>das Wunderbar</u> and gives a vivid picture. Imagination reveals likenesses in nature; fancy yields only a possible world.

Brennan, J. "Epitome Troporum ac Schematum: The Genesis of a Renaissance Rhetorical Text" <u>Quarterly Journal of Speech</u> 46 (Feb. 1960) 59-71

Brewer, D. S. "Metaphor and Symbol in the Sixteenth Century" <u>Essays in Criticism</u> 4 (1954) 108-111
Reply to Maurice Evans' "Metaphor and Symbol in the 16th Century." In the sixteenth century there was a trend away from allegorical treatment of the Bible and more allegorical treatments of classical literature.

Brinkmann, Friedrich. <u>Die Metaphern: Studien über den Geist der modernen Sprachen</u> (Die Thierbilder der Sprache) Bonn: A. Marcus 1878 600 pp.
He classifies metaphors: 1) living to inanimate, 2) sensuous to unsensed; and by grammatical form: metaphor 1) with a form of "to be," 2) with <u>fit</u> (make) or <u>heissen</u> (call), 3) by apposition or relative clause, 4) by apostrophe or address, 5) by genitive apposition, 6) genitive in other constructions, 7) of verb, 8) of adjective, 9) of adverb. He also speaks of metaphors which are common and exceptional, lingual and personal, current and literary, incarnate and non-incarnate. Brinkmann after a long theoretical account of metaphor presents an extensive and detailed account of animal metaphors of dog, horse, donkey, mule, cat, swan, bee, pig, chicken, sheep, pigeon and several others. Laan (1942) gives the following account of this work: Brinkmann regards metaphor as a "revelation of the human spitit," a "faithful mirror of visual and spiritual world of man." Metaphorical transfer is based on a partial resemblance between image and object. There need only be one essential quality in common between object and idea. There are as many metaphors possible as there are characteristics of an idea. "Chains of metaphors" are formed because for every metaphor a quality can be developed further by synecdoche, metonymy. A basic idea is the inexhaustible source for all transfers but it is in fact limited by the individual and collective spirit of the people.

_____. "Metapherstudien" <u>Archiv für d. Studium der neueren Sprachen und Literaturen</u> 54 (1875) 155-182, 337-366; 55 (1876) 327-362; 56 (1876) 343-376; 58 (1877) 193-220
A study of different objects used metaphorically.

Britton, Karl. "The Description of Logical Properties" <u>Analysis</u> 7

no. 2 (June 1940) 40-45 (cf. MacIver)
Mistaken theories on logic derive from the fact that common logical terms are metaphors originating in non-logical sources.

_____. "Review of Urban Language and Reality" Mind 50 (Apr. 1941) 165-176

Brodbeck, May. "Models, Meanings, and Theories" Symposium on Sociological Theory Llewellyn Gross, ed. Evanston, Ill.: Row, Peterson 1959
Positivistic theory of models relying heavily on the concepts of symbolic logic.

Brodeur, Arthur. The Meaning of Snorri's Categories Berkeley: University of California 1952
On Icelandic and Old Norse epithets and Scaldic poetry.

Bronson, Bertrand. "Personification Reconsidered" New Light on Dr. Johnson Fred Hilles, ed. New Haven: Yale University Press 1959 pp. 189-231. Also in ELH 14 (1947) 163-177

Brooke-Rose, Christine. A Grammar of Metaphor London: Secker and Warburg 1958. Reviews by R. Draper, A. Holder, E. Morgan, J. Nosek, J. Warburg. Review in TLS "Changing of Words by One Another" April 3, 1959 p. 196
A purely grammatical or syntactical analysis of metaphor to show how metaphor is expressed in each part of speech. Five types of noun metaphor given are: 1) simple replacement 2) the pointing formula (e.g. A...that B) 3) the copula (A is B) 4) the link with "to make" 5) genitive link (x of y). "In my study any identification of one thing with another, any replacement of the more usual word or phrase by another, is a metaphor." Metaphor is elsewhere regarded as a term which replaces a proper term resulting in a new fused entity.

Brooks, Cleanth, Jr. "The Heresy of Paraphrase" The Well Wrought Urn New York: Reynal and Hitchcock 1947. Contains "The Language of Paradox" and "The Naked Babe and the Cloak of Manliness." In "The Naked Babe..." Brooks examines several of Shakespeare's metaphors showing that though they are like conceits they are effective. In "Heresy..." he states, "The poem...is a simulacrum of reality...an 'imitation'--by being an experience rather than any mere statement about experience or any mere abstraction from experience [or paraphrase]."

_____. "The Language of Paradox" Criticism, the Foundation of Modern Literary Judgement Mark Schorer et al., eds. New York: Harcourt Brace 1948. Also in The Language of Poetry Allen Tate, ed. Princeton University Press 1942 pp. 37-61
All metaphor involves paradox, the awed surprise involving contradiction and qualification by analogies. All of our subtler states can only be expressed by analogy, metaphor and so by paradox. For this purpose the poet constantly disrupts language.

_____. "Metaphor and the Function of Criticism" Spiritual Problems in Contemporary Literature Stanley R. Hopper, ed. New York: Harper and Brothers 1952 pp. 127-137
"The most fruitful modern criticism is a rediscovery and recovery of the importance of metaphor." Poetry is metaphor. The poet speaks inevitably and necessarily in and through metaphor, not external to it. Metaphor is a mode of knowing as well as a method of discovery. Myths are great radical metaphors. They apprehend reality, give insight, are inexhaustible and cannot be reduced to literal language or paraphrased.

_____. "Metaphor, Paradox and Stereotype" The British Journal of Aesthetics 5 no. 4 (Oct. 1965) 315-328
A mean is needed between just setting images side by side, and extreme juxtaposition. Incongruity of the terms of a metaphor is needed to build up its tension and power. There is paradox in all poetry. Truth arises through absurdity and paradox. "Metaphor provides the best and sometimes the only way in which certain things can be said." One should master clichés to enliven them, releasing their energy, and to provide a controlling context for metaphors. Metaphor sometimes serves to produce humor.

_____. "Metaphor and Tradition" Modern Poetry and the Tradition Chapel Hill: University of North Carolina Press 1939 pp. 1-17
The introduction of supposedly bizarre and undignified figures of speech is causing a revolution in poetry. But there rather is no a priori formula for metaphor. It is instead functional in its context and must be judged individually and separately. To alter or remove the conceits of metaphysical poetry or metaphors of poetry is to destroy the poetry. Poets can only say certain things by using metaphor; they remake language. To appreciate such poetry may demand a revolution in our thinking about metaphor. Conceits are not necessarily too intellectual and demanding.

_____. "A Note on Symbol and Conceit" American Review 3 (1934) 201-211
Symbolist poetry is several metaphors or conceits which "communicate feelings with such subtley and detail as to preserve all their shades and nuances." It stresses sincerity and precision just as does science. Symbolist poetry is similar to metaphysical poetry in this respect. For both wit involves the adequacy of being aware of all the alternatives of a situation.

_____. "Three Revolutions in Poetry" Southern Review 1 no. 1 (1935) 151-163
"We are witnessing a radical change in the whole conception of the function and fittingness of metaphor, and with it, a revolution in the conception of poetry." Figures cannot be justified a priori, e.g. in terms of simplicity, ornamentation, or illustration. Rather each figure must be considered separately

and individually in terms of its function in its context.

______, and R. P. Warren. "Metaphor" *Fundamentals of Good Writing* New York: Harcourt Brace 1950 pp. 361-389. Also in *Modern Rhetoric* New York: Harcourt Brace and Co. 1949 pp. 403-441
Metaphor is a transfer of meaning, renders the general by the concrete, renders the unknown by the known, extends old names to new, is often untranslatable essential statement, defines emotions and attitudes, enlivens, illustrates, depends on contrast and provides a resemblance in difference, is the basis of the origin of language and the method by which it is extended, is essential to thinking, is not vague or mere ornament, depends greatly on context, may be mixed, may become jargon.

Brooks, Keith, E. Bahn, and L. Okey. *The Communicative Act of Oral Interpretation* Boston: Allyn and Bacon 1967 "Imagery in Literature" pp. 103-127
The role of imagery in literature is to clarify, illustrate, unify and amplify ideas. It intensifies emotion, creates and sustains a mood. Image is recalled sensory experience.

Brower, Reuben. *The Fields of Light: An Experiment in Critical Reading* New York: Oxford University Press 1951 esp. ch. 3, 5
Metaphor is an iconic expression standing for the subject expression, an icon instead of an image. It is saying one thing and meaning another. They may be implicit. Metaphor may take an infinite number of forms. Metaphors build on and interanimate with other metaphors to make up the key design of a work of art.

Brown, Bishop. *Things Divine and Supernatural Conceived by Analogy with Things Natural and Human* London 1733
Thomistic system of analogy presented extensively. The divine analogy is, unlike metaphor, a real correspondence in the nature of things.

Brown, Goold. *Grammar of English Grammars* London 1751 1102 pp.
Metaphor is "a figure that expresses or suggests the resemblance of two objects by applying either the name or some attribute, adjunct, or action, of the one, directly to the other." "A figure, in grammar, is an intentional deviation from the ordinary spelling, formation, construction, or application, of words." There are figures of orthography, etymology, syntax, and rhetoric.

Brown, James. "Metaphor and Meaning" PhD diss. State University of Iowa 1951
Three factors of word meaning: (W) known word meaning, (S) sentence meaning, (T) total meaning of sentence, are literal (⌊_↑) or metaphoric (⌣→) with respect to each other. Six combinations are given, e.g. W⌊_↑S, etc. Eight combinations of the three are given, e.g. W⌊_↑S⌊_↑T (straight narration),

W⌣→S⌣→T (e.g. "lend me your ears" where "ears" is literal

to the total meaning but metaphoric in a metaphoric sentence), etc.

Brown, Robert. "Metaphorical Assertions" Philosophical Studies 16 (1965) 6-8
It is a false "assumption that it is always possible to decide in the full context of any given utterance whether it is to be understood literally or metaphorically." Many statements are "boundary cases," not clearly literal or metaphorical.

Brown, Roger, R. Leiter, and D. Hildum. "Metaphors from Music Criticism" Journal of Abnormal and Social Psychology 54 (1957) 347-352
Subjects agree on choices on scale of the application of sensory non-auditory words to voice qualities, e.g., light-heavy, warm-cold, etc. Baritones' voices because of our past associations with such words are characterized as dull, coarse, closed, dark, heavy, rough, hard, thick; tenors' voices as bright, light, thin.

_____. Words and Things Glencoe, Ill.: Free Press 1958 esp. ch. 4 pp. 140-154

Brown, Stephen J. "Imagery of the Bible" Catholic World 122 (March 1926) 721-730, 123 (April 1926) 68-75 vol. 123 is on St. Paul's imagery.

_____. "Imagery in Literature: Metaphor in the Old Testament" Catholic World 126 (Jan. 1928) 433-439
In the Bible the object is not delighted in or contemplated for its own sake, but always for a moral or religious message. Its imagery is limited to religious illustration. Spiritual states are represented by words for physical acts, e.g., "to stretch out the hands" means to pray. God is spoken of in terms of metaphors.

_____. Image and Truth: Studies in the Imagery of the Bible Rome: Officium Libri Catholici, Catholic Book Agency 1955 161 pp.
Metaphor is based on four term analogy of proportion or relations, a relation of relations (a Thomistic view). It gives truth just as does literal language. He discusses hermeneutics which deals with how scriptural figures are to be taken. It is suggested that they mean no more than intended [if that can be determined]. Christ spoke metaphorically. Metaphors may be emblematic, express what is beyond experience, render the abstract by the concrete, picture the unfamiliar, and express thought in sensuous terms.

_____. The World of Imagery: Metaphor and Kindred Imagery New York: Russell and Russell 1966
An often quoted extensive analysis of imagery by a Thomist. He discusses the genesis, nature, function and sources of metaphor as well as related imagery such as simile, personi-

fication, metonymy, synecdoche, and gives numerous illustrations. He discusses imagery in Hebrew, Greek, rhetoric, homiletics, logic, theology, common speech, arts and crafts, the sciences, nature, occupations, the plant world, body and dress etc.

Browne, Richard J. "Review of L. Mittner 'Wurd: Das Sakrale in der Altgermanischen Epik'" Speculum 32 (July 1957) 588-589 "Wurd" often personifies fate. Kenningar are discussed. There was taboo-ritual in kenningar, magical power of fate or death inherent in sword or spear. A "varying-kenning" explains by varying a notion; a "concealing kenning" conceals the ugly or the taboo.

Bruchmann, Kurt. Psychologische Studien zur Sprachgeschichte Leipzig 1883

Bruckner, Ferdinand. [pseudonym of Theodor Tagger]

Brumleve, Sister Barbara A. "Whitman and Stevens: From an Organic to a Process Metaphor" PhD diss. St. Louis University 1969 They reveal a change from a closed universe to an open-ended universe of process.

Bruneau, Charles. "Review of Konrad Étude sur la Métaphore" Le Français Moderne 8 (1940) 74-77

_____. "L'image dans notre langue littéraire" Mélanges de linguistique offerts à Albert Dauzat par ses amis Paris: Éditions d'Artrey 1951 pp. 55-67

Bruner, Jerome. "What Social Scientists Say About Having an Idea" Printers Ink 260 (July 12, 1957) 48-52

Brunetière, Marie Ferdinand. "Les métaphores de Victor Hugo" Nouvelles questions de critique Paris 254-278; Paris: C. Lévy 1890

Brunner, T. F. "Function of the Simile in Ovid's Metamorphoses" Classical Journal 61 (May 1966) 354-363

Brunot, Ferdinand. Histoire de la langue française des origines à 1900 ch. 9 "Métaphorisme et Charabia"

_____. Précis de grammaire historique de la langue française third revised edition, Paris 1889 (Paris: Masson 1961) vol. 6 part 1 "Les images," "La métaphore" (cf. Adank p. 168, M. Baym 1961)

Buchanan, Scott. Poetry and Mathematics Philadelphia: J. V. Lippincott Co. 1962 [1929]
"It is by expansion of metaphor that fact becomes intelligible, the world measured, and the complexities of experience described in language. Any history of thought might begin and

end with the statement that man is an analogical animal." Metaphors are regarded as suppressed or elliptical similes. "Is like" ought to be substituted for the "is" in a metaphor.

_____. Symbolic Distance in Relation to Analogy and Fiction London: Kegan Paul, Trench, Trubner 1932

Buchmann, Hansmartin. "Die Bildlichkeit in Jean Pauls 'Schulmeisterlein Wuz'" PhD diss. Köln 1953

Büchner, H. "Das Oxymoron in der griechischen Dichtung von Homer bis in die Zeit des Hellenismus mit einem Überblick über seine Entwicklung" PhD diss. Tübingen 1951

Buck, Gertrude. Figures of Rhetoric Ann Arbor, Mich.: The Inland Press 1896

_____. The Metaphor: A Study in the Psychology of Rhetoric Ann Arbor, Mich.: The Inland Press 1899. Also PhD diss. University of Michigan
Originally the two terms of a metaphor, the spiritual and material, were one term and referred to the same thing. The primitive consciousness was first homogeneous and only later became heterogeneous and formed two terms. Metaphor is mental, not linguistic. It arises unconsciously and is tensive. Scientific and literal language derive from metaphorical language. The artificial conceit and mixed metaphor are "pathological" forms of metpahor.

Bueckendorf, Helmut. "Metaphorik in modernen technischen Bezeichnungen des Englischen" PhD diss. Köln 1959

Bühler, Karl. Sprachtheorie; die Darstellungsfunktion der Sprache Jena: Verlag von Gustav Fischer 1934 "Die sprachliche Metapher" pp. 342-356
A two-field theory of metaphor. Metaphor relates a demonstrative field with a symbolic field by an interactive leap.

Bulatkin, Eleanor. Structural Arithmetic Metaphor in the Oxford 'Roland' Columbus, Ohio: Ohio State University Press 1971

Bullinger, E. W. Figures of Speech Used in the Bible London: Eyre & Spottiswoode 1898 (Criticized by S. Brown I.T. pp. 158 ff.)
He says the "is" of a metaphor always and only means "represented." The two terms are to be taken literally and the figure lies wholly within the copula.

Bullitt, John, and Walter Bate. "The Distinctions between Fancy and Imagination in Eighteenth Century English Criticism" Modern Language Notes 60 (1945) 8-15

Bullough, Edward. "'Psychical Distance' as a Factor in Art and

Esthetic Principle" *A Modern Book of Esthetics* third edition Melvin Rader, ed. New York: Holt, Rinehart and Winston 1960 pp. 394-411
"Psychical distance puts the phenomenon out of gear with our practical self"; "this distanced view of things is not, and cannot be, our normal outlook"; "this sudden view of things from their reverse...comes upon us as a revelation"; "Its peculiarity lies in that the personal character of the relation has been, so to speak, filtered." [All of these statements may apply to metaphor. Max Black even spoke of metaphor as a "filter." And metaphor may be thought of as psychical distance.]

Bundy, Murray W. "'Invention' and 'Imagination' in the Renaissance" *Journal of English and Germanic Philology* 29 (1930) 535-545

_____. *The Theory of Imagination in Classical and Medieval Thought* Urbana: University of Illinois 1927

Bunge, Mario. "Analogy in Quantum Theory, From Insight to Nonsense" *British Journal for the Philosophy of Science* 18 (Feb. 19, 1968) 265-286

Burckhardt, Sigurd. "Metaphorical Structure of Goethes *Auf dem See*" *Germanic Review* 31 (Feb. 1956) 35-48

_____. "The Poet as Fool and Priest" *ELH* 23 (Dec. 1956) 279-298
On metaphor.

Burke, Edmund. *A Philosophical Inquiry into the Origin of Our Ideas of the Sublime and the Beautiful* J. T. Boulton, ed. New York: Columbia University Press 1958 [1757]
He opposes the view that art is visualization. He discusses imagery and imagination, e.g. one cannot visualize "next summer." Words usually are not accompanied by imagery. Poetry is best thought of as nearly imageless.

Burke, Kenneth. *Attitudes Toward History* Los Altos, Calif.: Hermes Publishing Co. 1959

_____. "Four Master Tropes" *Kenyon Review* 3 (1941) 421-438
Metaphor is seeing something in terms of something else, a "perspective by incongruity." It establishes reality which is a number of perspectives, e.g. human motivation may be considered from the perspective of conditioned reflex, chemicals, class struggles, neurosis, power, movements of planets, geography, etc. He gives and develops the following substitute name for each trope: 1) perspective, for metaphor, 2) reduction, for metonymy, 3) representation, for synecdoche, 4) dialectic, for irony. Each trope shades into or involves the other, e.g. dialectic may give representation by means of interacting perspectives yielding a reduction.

_____. A Grammar of Motives New Jersey: Prentice Hall 1945 530 pp. "Pathetic Fallacy" pp. 232-235, "Four Master Tropes" pp. 503-517 (cf. Osborn 1963)

_____. "The Imagery of Killing" Hudson Review 1 (1948) 151-161

_____. "Key Words for Critics" Kenyon Review 4 (1942) 126-132

_____. "On Motivation in Yeats" Southern Review 7 no. 3 (1942) 547-561
A discussion of Yeats' images, visions, metaphors and motivation (inner and outer) in relation to his work. "We have come to give you metaphors for poetry," Yeats' spirits said. Yeats complains that he is "all metaphor."

_____. "Myth, Poetry and Philosophy" Journal of American Folklore 73 (1960) 283-306

_____. Permanence and Change: An Anatomy of Purpose Indianapolis: Bobbs-Merrill Co. 1954; Los Altos, Calif.: Hermes Publishing Co. 1954 esp. ch. 3 "Perspective as Metaphor," ch. 4 "Argument by Analogy"
A "perspective by incongruity" involves taking a term out of its usual context and applying it to another to reveal new and unique connectives. Thus we should observe the subtlety of language to note incongruities. Abstraction is a metaphorical process. Works and even whole schools of science are just expansions of a metaphor (cf. T. Kuhn). Burke's theory of metaphor is often sociological, one's experience projected into society. Regarding "planned incongruity" he says, "Imagine, then, setting out to study mankind, with whose system of speech you are largely familiar. Imagine beginning your course of study precisely by depriving yourself of this familiarity, attempting to understand motives and purposes by avoiding as much as possible the clues handed you ready-made in the texture of the language itself."

_____. The Philosophy of Literary Form: Studies in Symbolic Action Baton Rouge: Louisiana State University Press 1941

_____. A Rhetoric of Motives New York: Prentice-Hall 1950 340 pp.

Burkland, Carl E. "Presentation of Figurative Language" Quarterly Journal of Speech 41 (Dec. 1955) 383-390
All language is figurative, but poetic language, being more original, seems difficult. "All art, in varying ways and degrees, is a distortion of the real for the purpose of expressive statement." Metaphor creates rather than copies. It fuses one image with another of a different class on the basis of something imagined or felt. Science and philosophy are based on metaphor. Plastic art is metaphorical.

Burleson, Richard A. "Color Imagery in GG" Fitzgerald Newsletter

(Charlottesville, Va.) 39 (1967) 13-14

Burlingame, Charles. "On the Logic of the 'Seeing As' Locution" PhD diss. University of Virginia 1965
An intensive discussion of the notion of "seeing-as" as represented by Wittgenstein, Hanson, Aldrich, Farre and others. [Metaphor may be thought of as a type of "seeing-as," a seeing of one concept or object in terms of another.]

Burmester, A. Über den Einfluss der Metapher auf die Entwicklung der Sprache Programm der Realschule Barmen 1863

Burnet, Lord James. (See Monboddo)

Burrell, David B. "Analogy and Philosophical Language" PhD diss. Yale University 1965 228 pp.
A discussion of analogy in Plato (dialectic), Aristotle (proportion), Duns Scotus (univocity and similarity), Aquinas (proportion without univocal sameness), etc. Burrell's view is that "we would locate the lever of analogous discourse in our decision to use an expression in an unusual way, coupled with the recognition that one is using it so." "There are different procedures for appraising, criticizing, and correcting analogies in different sorts of inquiry."

_____. "Religious Language and Logic of Analogy" International Philosophical Quarterly 2 (1962) 643-658

Burton, J. M. Honoré de Balzac and His Figures of Speech Princeton: Elliot Monographs, 8, 1921

Butler, Charles. Rhetorici Libri Duo London 1684 [1597]
On tropes and figures.

Butler, Joseph. The Analogy of Religion New York: F. Ungar 1961 [1867]
He offers a guarded claim for analogical reasoning.

Butter, Peter. Shelley's Idols of the Cave New York: Haskell 1954

Cabeen, C. W. *L'Influence de Giambattista Marino sur la littérature française de la première moitié du XVII siècle* Grenoble 1904

Cain, Albert C., and Barbara M. Maupin. "Interpretation within the Metaphor" *Menninger Clinic Bulletin* 25 (1961) 307-311
Therapists often overestimate or give a subjective interpretation of patients' metaphors. They overvalue every word. Caution is needed as the patient may suffer serious mental harm. Interpretation of metaphor should begin sympathetically with the patient's intentions in mind.

Cajetan, Cardinal. *The Analogy of Names* Pittsburgh: Duquesne University Press 1953 (See Vio)
He organizes Aquinas' theories about analogy into a theory. Analogy is divided into analogy of: 1) inequality, 2) attribution, 3) proportionality a) metaphor b) proper proportionality. Proportional metaphor only produces a world of as-if rather than of being so is of no use in metaphysics. It is "improper proportionality." In analogy by proper proportionality (four term analogy) each participant has a common characteristic only in proportion to its being. It is this type (3b) which Thomists usually accept as true.

Calin, W. "Patterns of Imagery in Anouilh's *Antigone*" *French Review* 41 (Oct. 1967) 76-83

Calvi, Lorenzo. "La metafora meccanicistica in medicina" *Il Verri* 15 (1964) 143-149

Calvör, Wilhelm. "Der metaphorische Ausdruck des jungen Wieland" PhD diss. Göttingen 1906

Cameron, V. "Two Parasites: The Metaphor and the Simile" *Canadian Bookman* 15 (Oct. 1933) 139 (Reply by Leaver)

Campbell, George. *The Philosophy of Rhetoric* Lloyd Bitzer, ed. Carbondale: Southern Illinois University Press 1963 [1851]

Canguilhem, Georges. "The Role of Analogies and Models in Biological Discovery" *Scientific Change* A. C. Crombie, ed. New York: Basic Books 1963 pp. 507-520

Capella, Martianus. *De Nuptüs Philologiae et Mercurii* Adolfus Dick, ed. Lipsiae 1925 [written about 410-440 A.D.]
He follows Cicero and Quintilian on metaphor.

Caracostea, D. "Dela metaforă la simbol" *Revista fundatiilor regale* (Bukarest) 9 no. 4 (1941-1942) 411-419

Cargill, Lt.-Col. S. *The Philosophy of Analogy and Symbolism* London and New York: Rider 1947

A mystical and cosmic attempt to formulate a comprehensive theory of analogy and metaphor.

Carman, Sid. "Dylan Thomas: Rhetorician in Mid-Career" Accent 8 no. 1 (Winter 1953) 56-59

Carney, James, and Richard Scheer. Fundamentals of Logic New York: Macmillan 1964 esp pp. 2-179
Metaphor is a comparison without the use of like, as, similar, or same e.g. "He is a tiger." Literal meaning is the dictionary meaning. A metaphor taken literally is false. Context mixing e.g. "The fog has feet" is a mistake, but metaphor is not. A metaphor can be partly reexpressed in non-metaphorical language, though the imagery becomes lost. "I see the middle of next week" is not paraphrasable and is mistaken context-mixing. He also discusses analogy in argumentation.

Carnochan, W. B. "Johnsonian Metaphor and the 'Adamant of Shakespeare.'" Studies in English Literature 1500-1900 10 (1970) 541-550

Carnoy, Albert. La Science du mot: Traité de sémantique Louvain 1927 esp. ch. 20 pp. 275-313
He gives four types of metaphor: perceptual, synaesthetic, affective, pragmatic. The chapter on metaphor consists of examples of each type of metaphor. The term "métecsémie" is used to designate a change of sense from its proper order.

Carpenter, Frederic I. Metaphor and Simile in Minor Elizabethan Drama PhD diss. University of Chicago 1895 New York: Phaeton Press 1967
He follows Brinkmann on metaphor. Metaphor is contextual, dramatic, literally inexpressible, emotive sympathetic, or picturative. Not all imagery is trope. He distinguishes between figure of thought and figure of language. Elizabethans were noted for conceits. He discusses mainly Lyly (cf. euphuism), Peele, Marlowe, Kyd, Greene, Tourneur, Webster, Chapman, Jonson.

Carruth, Hayden. "Ideality and Metaphor" Poetry 72 (Aug. 1948) 270-273
A review of W. Stevens' "Three Academic Pieces." For Stevens the imaginative function is metaphorical, and through metaphor reality extends to, and is equated to, ideality. For him reality is perceived through metaphors and every metaphor is an experience of life.

Carter, Geoffrey. "Carlyle's Use of Metaphor in His Essays" PhD diss. University of Pennsylvania 1969
Carlyle's style is highly metaphorical. In his work he has: 1) quasi-mechanical metaphors (to expose the machine as a metaphor), 2) organicist metaphors, 3) cognition metaphors (inducing skepticism). Carlyle felt threatened by the machine. He found the part metaphors play in human affairs, i.e. root metaphors. Carlyle wrote, "What too are all poets and moral teach-

ers, but a species of Metaphorical Tailors." For Carlyle language for sensual objects is and was figurative.

Carter, Jane. Quintilian's Didactic Metaphors PhD diss. New York University 1910 New York: G. P. Putnam's Sons 1910

Caruth, Elaine, and Rudolf Ekstein. "Interpretation Within the Metaphor: Further Considerations" American Academy of Child Psychiatry Journal 5 no. 1 (1966) 35-45
Based on Sharpe's work it is asserted that metaphor may be used to establish communication with schizophrenic patients since it retains the needed distance from facing the real problem. A metaphor may even be acted out by the patient, e.g., setting fire to something may be a metaphorical expression of sexual feelings.

Carvalho, J. G. Herculano de. "Inovação e criação na linguagem. A metáfora" Revista da Universidade de Coimbra no. 20 (1962) 245-258
Discussion of the function, origin and value of metaphor. It is an imaginative force expressing a state of mind or being.

Caspers, W. Über die Tropen und Figuren Programm des Gymnasiums zu Recklinghausen 44, 1872

Cassiodorus (480-575 A.D.). Institutiones Divinarum et Humanarum Lectionum Leslie W. Jones, trans. and ed. New York: 1946 esp. II, 1-3; pp. 147-148
Figures of speech are transfers of words or thoughts. Ninety-eight transfers are given. Like Augustine he finds them suitable to literature and oratory. He follows Sacerdos' views.

Cassirer, Ernst. An Essay on Man Yale University Press 1944
Language is central to the investigation of thought and knowledge. It transfers or develops into various "symbolic forms" or areas of knowledge. "It is precisely this 'metaphorical transference' which contains our whole problem in a nutshell." Language helps constitute reality. This book is a condensed popular version of his Philosophy of Symbolic Forms.

_____. Language and Myth New York: Dover 1946
Metaphorical thinking underlies the analogous laws of myth and language. In a narrow sense metaphor is "the conscious denotation of one thought content by the name of another." In the broad sense it is "radical metaphor" i.e. a condition of myth and verbal concepts, a transformation or transmutation of experience into language and the creation of a new category. Myth and language determine each other reciprocally.

_____. Philosophy of Symbolic Forms 3 vols. Ralph Manheim, trans. New Haven: Yale University Press 1953-1957
The function of language is not to picture reality but to symbolize it. Human works are symbolic not physical. These symbols and symbolic forms help constitute reality or our

knowledge of reality. There is a mythically originated metaphoric transformation and increasing refinement of signs into autonomous symbolic forms such as science, art, etc. Consciousness involves the representation of one content through another.

Cavell, Stanley. "Aesthetic Problems of Modern Philosophy" Philosophy in America Max Black, ed. Cornell University Press 1965 pp. 74-97
We can and must be able to paraphrase metaphors, but that is not to say a paraphrase is an exact or literal rendering.

Cawdry, Robert. A treasurie or storehouse of similies... London: T. Creede 1600

Celan, Paul. Der Meridian: Rede anlässlich der Verleihung des Georg-Büchner-Preises Frankfurt: Fischer 1961. Also extract in Alleman Ars Poetica
"All tropes and metaphors tend to be reduced to absurdity," i.e. a metaphor is not just a logical comparison.

Chaitanya, Krishna. [pseudonym for K. K. Nair]

Chalmers, G. K. "Effluvia, the History of a Metaphor" PMLA 52 (Dec. 1937) 1031-1050

Chaneles, Sol. "The Metaphor of Dylan Thomas" M.A. thesis New York University 1950
Three phases of Thomas' imagery are: 1) 1934-1940 Freudian, 2) 1940-1945 Freudian and Biblical influence, 3) since 1945 Anglo-Catholicism influence. He was influenced by Hopkins' compound words, Hegelian dialectic (synthesis yielding insight as well as escape), James Joyce's metaphorical rendering of language, and Donne's metaphors. Thomas attempts by means of metaphors to free himself from the cycles of nature.

Chapin, Chester F. Personification in 18th Century English Poetry PhD diss. Columbia University New York: King's Crown Press 1955 (Has useful bibliography)
A discussion of the main writers on the subject. "When personification is placed in proper perspective, it is clear that it is also a device which gives truly imaginative expression to elements of thought and feeling which reflect that firm sense of actuality which is to be accounted one of the 'central virtues of the civilized mind.'" "No other type of metaphor which 18th century poets employ is more effective in conveying a sense of the real worth and dignity of those moral values which determine the patterns of civilized behavior."

Chapman, Loren J. "Confusion of Figurative and Literal Usages of Words by Schizophrenics and Brain-Damaged Patients" Journal of Abnormal and Social Psychology 60 (1960) 412-416 (cf. Vetter)
The schizophrenic made more literal and figurative errors than

brain-damaged patients. Those brain-damaged showed no more literal errors than a normal subject. Some subjects were quite atypical.

Charisius, Flavius Sosepater (fourth century). *Artis Grammaticae in Grammatici Latini* seven vols. Heinrich Keil, ed. Leipzig 1855-1880
Follows Donatus' views on metaphor.

Charney, Maurice. *Shakespeare's Roman Plays: The Function of Imagery in the Drama* Cambridge: Harvard University Press 1961

Charpentier, John. "Figures: Jean Giraudoux" *Mercure de France* 225 (1931) 96-99

Chase, Stuart. "Watch the False Analogy!" *Guides to Straight Thinking* New York: Harper 1956
Chase says watch false analogies and keep to "straight" thinking.

Cherkasova, E. T. "O metaforich..." (Source: Korol'kov)

Chesterton, G. K. "About Mad Metaphors" *As I was saying; a book of essays* London: Methuen and Co. 1936 pp. 1-6
Metaphors are dangerous especially since one "may have no head for figures." Metaphors can create a "mad" metaphysics.

Cheyne, George. *Philosophical Principles of Religion* two vols. London 1915
All things are based on divine analogy and so also on levels of analogy. The visible is thus analogous to the invisible, sensible to insensible, ectypal to archetypal, creature to creator. Simile is God's master plan.

Ch'i, Li. *The Use of Figurative Language in Communist China* Berkeley: University of California Press 1958
Etymology of words reveals a figurative basis of language which is a guide to the life and mind of each past age as well as present culture. War and revolution stimulate the creation of many new metaphors to meet new conditions. Communist Chinese metaphors are influenced by journalism which is less literary than it was.

Child, H. H. "Metaphorically Speaking" *Essays and Reflections 1948-1954* S. Roberts, ed. Cambridge: University Press 1948 pp. 167-168
We cannot express ourselves without metaphor and each sentence contains at least one.

Chisholm, A. R. "Le démon de l'analogie" (Mallarmé) *Essays in French Literature* 1 (1965) 1-6

Chomsky, Noam. *Syntactic Structures* Mouton & Co. 1957

Christiansen, Reidar. "Myth, Metaphor, and Simile" Journal of Myth: A Symposium Thomas Sebeok, ed. Bloomington: Indiana University Press 1955 pp. 64-80. Also in Journal of American Folklore 68 (Oct. 1955) 417-427

Chun, Ki-Taek. "A Psychological Study of Myth-Making: A Three Factor Theory of 'Metaphor-to-Myth Transformation" PhD diss. University of California, Berkeley 1969. See also T. Sarbin.

Church, Joseph. Language and the Discovery of Reality; a developmental psychology of cognition New York: Random House 1961
Relationships in psychological analogy test may be part-whole, cause-effect, higher-lower, sound or shape of words themselves, etc. Analogies express partial, metaphors total, equivalence. Werner Kaplan's test in which subject draws a line representing a statement, e.g. a proverb, resulted in the view that meanings involve imagery. Bühler's test results show that the child must be an adolescent or older to understand proverbs.

Cicero (pseudo author). Ad C. Herennium de Ratione Dicendi Harry Caplan, trans. Cambridge: Harvard University Press 1954 esp. p. 343
Written about 86-82 B.C., this is regarded as the oldest systematic Latin treatise on style. Author is unknown. He says, "Metaphor occurs when a word applying to one thing is transferred to another, because the similarity seems to justify the transference." Metaphor is used for vividness, brevity, to avoid obscenity, to magnify or minify and to embellish.

Cicero, Marcus. De inventione. De optimo genere oratorum topica H. Hubbell, trans. Cambridge: Harvard University Press 1960

______. De Oratore two vols. H. Rackham, trans. Cambridge: Harvard University Press 1942 [written 55 B.C.] See esp. Book 3
Everything can be related to everything else. Metaphor is a contracted simile, a borrowing, a transference based on resemblance. It may achieve brevity, embellish, clarify, give a picture, give pleasure. It should not be far-fetched or ugly or relate terms of high and low value.

Ciesielski, Elisabet. Vergleich und Metapher bei W. Wordsworth: Eine stilistische Studie nach Wordsworths: "Poems of the Imagination" PhD diss. Philipps Universität Marburg: Franz Fischer 1931 93 pp.

Clark, David. "'Metaphors for Poetry': W. B. Yeats and the Occult" The World of W. B. Yeats: Essays in Perspective R. Skelton and A. Saddlemyer, eds. Victoria, B. C.: Adelphi Bookshop 1965 pp. 54-66
In A Vision the spirit brought Yeats not scattered sentences of supernatural truth but "metaphors for poetry." Yeats was influenced by magic and mysticism of all sorts, e.g. theosophy, Buddhism, Irish myth, a St. Patrick centered religion, etc.

For Yeats there are elaborate correspondences between antinomies, e.g. visible and invisible.

Clark, Michael. "Humor and Incongruity" Philosophy 45 (Jan. 1970) 20-32
Ryle supposedly said to Isaiah Berlin after seeing the latter come from a symphony hall, "Been listening to some tunes, then?" Here subsuming tunes under the concept of symphony music is incongruous and so humorous. So also is, "G. E. Moore doing philosophy is like a man dancing in treacle."

Cleasby, Harold L. "The Metaphorical Use of Pronuba" Proceedings and Transactions of the American Philological Association 39 (1908) 21

Clemen, Wolfgang. Shakespeare's Bilder Bonn 1936. English trans., The Development of Shakespeare's Imagery Cambridge: Harvard University Press 1951 (Review by M. Crane)
Images foretell of events to come and unify the plays. Shakespeare's imagery gradually improved and became more significant.

Clutton-Brock, Arthur. "Dead Metaphors" Metaphor (Society for Pure English XI) Oxford: Clarendon Press 1922 pp. 11-14
"Metaphor becomes a habit with writers who wish to express more emotion than they feel, and who employ it as an ornament to statements that should be made plainly or not at all." Metaphors should be used freshly on each occasion. Context may help enliven an otherwise "dead" metaphor.

Coenen, G. F. "De comparationibus et metaphoris apud atticos praesertim poetas" PhD diss. Utrecht 1875 151 pp.

Coffey, M. "Function of the Homeric Simile" American Journal of Philology 78 (Apr. 1957) 113-132

Coffman, Stanley K. "Imagism" Encyclopedia of Poetry and Poetics Alex Preminger, ed. Princeton University Press 1965 pp. 377-378
An account of the theories of imagism and its relation to metaphor.

_____. Imagism: a chapter for the history of modern poetry Norman, Okla.: University of Oklahoma Press 1951

Cohen, L. Jonathan, and Avishai Margalit. "The Role of Inductive Reasoning in the Interpretation of Metaphor" Synthese 21 (1970)

Cohen, Marcel. "Review of Adank Essai..." Bulletin de la Société de Linguistique de Paris 41 (1941) 11-12

_____. "Review of Konrad Études sur la métaphore" Bulletin de la Société de Linguistique de Paris 40 (1939) 28-29

Cohen, Marshall. "Review of Philip Wheelwright Metaphor and Reality" Philosophical Review 74 (Oct. 1965) 548-550
Wheelwright's account of metaphor and tensive mythopoetics is unclear and unsupported. Cohen argues for a more positivistic "steno-language."

Cohen, Morris R. "The Logic of Metaphors--Figurative Truth" A Preface to Logic Cleveland: World Publishing Co. 1965 pp. 95-99
Metaphor is an emotional and primal perception of identity which later processes discriminate. It allows us to visualize the unknown by means of the known and is necessary for communication. The new is always metaphorical. Metaphor if taken literally is myth, and if not conscious leads to fallacy.

_____, and Ernest Nagel. An Introduction to Logic and Scientific Method New York: Harcourt, Brace and Co. 1934
Metaphor is not just derived from analogy. "Metaphors may thus be viewed as expressing the vague and confused but primal perception of identity, which subsequent processes of discrimination transform into a conscious and expressed analogy between different things."

Cole, Charles. "Metaphor and Syllogism" Massachusetts Review 4 (1963) 239-242
The Litt. D. citation from Amherst in 1948 to Robert Frost read, "You have taught generations of Amherst students that for gaining an insight into life, a metaphor is a sharper and brighter instrument than a syllogism."

Coleman, Elliott. "The Meaning of Metaphor" The Gordon Review 8 (1965) 151-163
Man is mixed metaphors of himself which control him. Metaphors depend on knowledge; are necessary; reveal reality, total unity, the Holy Ghost. "'In the beginning was the the word.'" It is metaphor to be ignorant in order to gain new knowledge.

Coleridge, Samuel T. Aids to Reflection in the Complete Works of Samuel Taylor Coleridge W. Shedd, ed. New York 1884 I, 117-373
Metaphor is inadequate because it is just a mechanical technique of comparison. He prefers the intrinsic relation in things. Analogy allows higher to be compared to lower.

_____. Biographia Literaria two vols. J. Shawcross, ed. London: Oxford University Press 1817 esp. I, 295-296
Now famous for his theory of the Imagination, he wrote (BL, XIV, 268): "The Imagination then, I consider either as primary or secondary. The primary Imagination I hold to be the living power and prime Agent of all human Perception, and as a repetition in the finite mind of the eternal act of creation in the infinite I am. The secondary Imagination I consider as an echo of the former, coexisting with its agency, and differing only in degree, and in the mode of its operation. It dissolves,

diffuses, dissipates, in order to recreate; or where this process is rendered impossible, yet still at all events it struggles to idealize and unify. It is essentially vital, even as all objects (as objects) are essentially fixed and dead." "The poet should paint to the imagination not to the Fancy." Genius consists in the presentation of such pictures.

_____. "A Lay Sermon" The Stateman's Manual Burlington: C. Goodrich 1932
He opposes private and abstract metaphors. They should be translated to picture language. Metaphor is a form of the "Fancy," not like a symbol which is an essential part of the whole which it represents.

_____. Shakespearean Criticism T. Raysor, ed. London: J. M. Dent; New York: E. P. Dutton 1960

_____. Unpublished Letters of S. T. Coleridge E. L. Griggs, ed. London 1932 esp. I, 155-156
Here he states that words are things: "Are not words, etc., parts and generations of the plant? And what is the law of their growth? In something of this sort I would endeavor to destroy the old antithesis between Words and Things; elevating as it were, Words into Things and living things too."

Collingwood, Robin. The Principles of Art Oxford: Clarendon Press 1964

Collins, Anthony. A Vindication of the Divine Attributes London 1710
A refutation of Bishop King's views. Analogy yields only an anthropomorphic deity or merely deceptive figures of speech.

Collins, Ben. "Joyce's 'Araby' and the 'Extended Simile'" James Joyce Quarterly 4 (1967) 84-90

Collins, Douglas C. "Kenning in Anglo-Saxon Poetry" English Association Essays and Studies 12 (1959) 1-17
A kenning is a metaphorical expression not of likeness but of identity. It "grew up and developed in pre-Christian verse and existed to express pagan ways of life and thought, [so] the poet in Christian times had considerable difficulty in adapting pagan language to Christian ideas..."

Colvin, Stephen S. "Methods of Determining Ideational Types" The Psychological Bulletin 6 (1909) 223-237

"Comparisons Beyond Compare" Golden Book 1 (March 1925) 394
A few examples of similes are given.

Compton, Gail Howard. "The Metaphor of Conquest in Dryden's The Conquest of Granada" PhD diss. University of Florida 1968

Comstock, Claire. "The Relevance of Images to the Processes of Thought" American Journal of Psychology 32 (1921) 196-230
He concludes that there is no irrelevant imagery. If imagery is present it is relevant.

Conger, George. Theories of Macrocosms and Microcosms New York: 1922
Examples of analogy in a cosmic scale.

Conroy, Marietta C. Imagery in the Sermons of Maximus, Bishop of Turin Catholic University of America Press 1966

Conzelmann, Otto. Metaphorik und Bildersprache im romanischen Volkslied PhD diss. Tübingen 1946 (Giessener Beiträge zur romanischen Philologie. Vienna 1947)

Cook, William, Jr. "Lord Jim as Metaphor" Conradiana 1 no. 2 (1968) 45-53

Cooley, T. L. "Heart of the Vergilian Simile" Educational Forum 3 (March 1939) 294-299

Coombes, H. "Imagery" Literature and Criticism Baltimore: Penguin 1953 pp. 43-63
Metaphor and imagery juxtapose images not ordinarily associated. If not too remote from our experience they can give precision, vividness, force, economy and impact.

Coon, Raymond. "The Reversal of Nature as a Rhetorical Figure" Indiana University Studies 15 (Sept. 1928) study no. 80
An analysis of "the impossible" as a figure, i.e., things which are impossible are regarded as figures of rhetoric, e.g., the statement, "We will be brothers until it snows in summer."

Cooper, D. "Concepts from Semantics as Avenues to Reading Improvement" English Journal 53 (Feb. 1964) 85-90
Metaphor is not mere ornament but a comparison some of whose elements are left out.

Cope, E. M. An Introduction to Aristotle's Rhetoric London: Macmillan & Co. 1867 (reprinted by W. C. Brown 1966) esp. Appendix B to book III, ch. 2, pp. 374-379
On metaphor and its use in the Greek and Roman tradition.

Cope, Jackson. The Metaphoric Structure of Paradise Lost Baltimore: Johns Hopkins Press 1962
He says he accepts Wheelwright's view that metaphor is paradox which inextricably reveals reality. Milton's metaphors reconcile the paradoxical modes of personal and interpersonal Christian expression.

Cope, J. I. "The 1654 Edition of Emmanuel Tesauro's 'Il Cannocchiale Aristotelico'" Italica 39 (1962) 273-275

Copleston, Frederick. "On Seeing and Noticing" Philosophy 29 (1954) 152-159
We can see things about us without noticing them because of familiarity. The reflective experience of noticing existence may be like this, a special seeing-as.

Correia, João Da Silva. "Duas palavras sôbre metaforismo sinestesico" Portucale 1 (1928) 279-287

Corrigan, Matthew. "Metaphor in William Blake: A Negative View" Journal of Aesthetics and Art Criticism 28 (1969) 187-199
Blake was preoccupied with mystical visions which he failed to communicate partly because he failed in his use of metaphors. He does not seem to understand the use of metaphor, and this not just because he rejects linguistic formulae. His general confusions may even stem from this lack.

Coseriu, Eugenio. La creación metafórica en el lenguaje Departamento de Lingüística pub. no. 9. Montevideo: Universidad 1956 31 pp.

Cosmo, U. "Intorno alla metafora" Scritti varii di erudizione e di critica in onore di Rodolfo Renier Torino: Fratelli Bocca Editori 1912 pp. 773-793
The two terms which unite in the synthetic "act of the spirit" to form the image are represented simultaneously. To materialize the metaphor is to destroy it--it is rather a synthesis, a given. "Not the meaning but the image in itself produces the esthetic emotion." Logic and concepts are no substitutes for images. Images have their own intimate nature and will not be analyzed by a theory or system.

Costello, Edward B. "Metaphors and Metaphysics" Journal of Thought 3 (July 1968) 141-151

Coster, Adolphe. "Baltasar Gracián 1601-1658" Revue Hispanique 29 (1913) 347-752
He attacks the agudeza.

_____. Baltasar Gracián Richard del Arco y Garay, trans., prologue and notes; Institucion Fernando el Católico 1947 esp. ch. 14-17 on ingenio, acutezza, conceptismo, cultismo.

Couch, A. and K. Keniston. "Yeasayers and Naysayers: Agreeing Response Set as a Personality Variable" Journal of Abnormal and Social Psychology (Now called Journal of Abnormal Psychology) 60 (1960) 151-174
On metaphor.

Coupland, R. "Simile and Metaphor in Brantôme [Pierre de Bourdeille]" Archivum Linguisticum. A Review of Comparative Philology and General Lingusitics 13 (1961) 50-77, 145-170
Brantôme's metaphors are not intrusive. His stature as a

writer is inferior to that of Rabelais or Montaigne but he is not inferior as a maker of images.

Courcelle, Pierre. "'Trames veritatis' La fortune patristique d'une métaphore platonicienne" Mélanges offerts à Étienne Gilson Toronto: Pontifical Institute of Mediaeval Studies. Paris: Vrin 1959

Cox, Leonard. The Arte or Crafte of Rhetoryke F. I. Carpenter, ed. Chicago 1899

Craddock, C. E. Style Theories as Found in Stylistic Studies of Romance Scholars (1900-1950) PhD diss. Washington D. C.: Catholic University Press 1952 (Studies in Romance Languages and Literatures 43, pp. 103-109)

Crain, Kenneth. Analogy of All Being New York: Philosophical Library 1970
All life's forms reflect a universal form based on basic principles of physics. Man works out his fate in an unconscious (in the Freudian sense) but nevertheless specified end, being unaware of the analogy of all being.

Crane, Hart. "The Dynamics of Metaphor" The Modern Tradition Richard Ellmann and Charles Feidelson, Jr., eds. New York: Oxford University Press 1965 pp. 158-162. A discussion with Harriet Monroe reprinted from Poetry 29 (Oct. 1926) 34-41
Metaphor has an emotional dynamics, is marked by connotation and is entrenched in pure sensibility. It is not governed by rules or science (which is itself metaphorical).

Crane, M. "One Key to the Bard's Meaning" Review of W. Clemen Development of Shakespeare's Imagery Saturday Review of Literature 34 (Oct. 20, 1951) 12ff

Crane, William. Wit and Rhetoric in the Renaissance, the Formal Basis of Elizabethan Prose Style New York: Columbia University Press 1937

Cranfield, C. "The Cup Metaphor in Mark 14:36 and Parallels" The Expository Times 59 (1947-1948) 137-138

Cranfield, L. "Review of C. Day-Lewis The Poetic Image" New Statesman and Nation 33 (June 7, 1947) 417-418

Creore, Ronsard. "Du Bartas and the Homeric Comparison" Comparative Literature 3 (1951) 152-159

Crétin, Roger. Les images dans l'oeuvre de Corneille Paris: Champion 1927

_____. "Lexique comparé des métaphores dans le Théâtre de Corneille et de Racine" PhD diss. Caen 1927

Croce, Benedetto. Aesthetic: As science of expression and general linguistic Douglas Ainslie, trans. New York: Noonday Press 1960 [1909] esp. "Rhetoric: or the Theory of Ornate Forms" We do not just have thoughts, then express them in words. To think is to express, to write, to take a pencil and draw. (On this view metaphor does not express thought but constitutes it.) To intuit, he says, is nothing else than to express. "In the aesthetic fact there are none but proper words." Metaphor is not improper usage. Aesthetic expression is regarded as a synthesis, even as "unity in variety" (cf. metaphor).

_____. "I trattatisti italiani del concettismo e Baltasar Gracián" Problema di estetica e contributi alla storia dell' estetica italiana second edition Bari 1923 pp. 313-348 He rejects the conceit. Although the scientifically oriented critics of the 1600's criticized the older views of the conceit their doctrines still remained grounded on the old Aristotelian views. The metaphor is still thought of as a clever ornament attached to the literal expression of thought. The writers of the 1600's thought of metaphor as an admirable thing in itself which teaches and entertains. Thus they advised accumulating and complicating metaphors to intensify them. But they stressed their richness and abundance in itself rather than regarding them as a simple means of expression. Gracián's views were basically Aristotelian and not especially valuable. Tesauro was Aristotelian also but had more rigor than Gracián. Matteo Pellegrini was the first to seriously attack the 17th century Aristotelians. He, though still Aristotelian, broke away from it. He regarded metaphor no longer as mere ornament but as the vehicle of thought. Croce believes that in general the 17th century criticisms were ineffectual because they started from the same Aristotelian and scientific assumptions. He states that the distinction between form (rhetoric) and content (logic) is inadequate. Rather the two are inseparable.

_____. La critica e la storia delle arti figurative Bari: G. Laterza & Figli 1946

_____. Logic as the Science of the Pure Concept D. Ainslee, trans. London: Macmillan and Co. 1917

_____. "Noterella sulla metafora" La Critica 38 (1940) 180-183 Also in Problema di estetica...pp. 160-164 As with Vico, metaphor is not artificial and witty, but spontaneous, natural, primitive, and popular or common, and a necessity of mind. To analyze the metaphor and simile is to falsify them because they are themselves perfect expressive unities. Poetry deals with the universal and unity of all things and ignores the distinctions of mind-body, animate-inanimate etc. Metaphor is not the transference of particular to particular, but restoration and resolution of the particular in the whole and the whole in the particular. The primitive, unanalyzed, undestroyed metaphor is sensuous and passionate. In science, philosophy, prose, and oratory, metaphor is a mere instrument, a means of directing attention to produce a practical result. Thus there metaphor is rejected in favor of literal language.

Cross, R. C. "Category Differences" Proceedings of the Aristotelian Society 59 (1959) 255-270
Ryle's notion of category-mistakes is illuminating as is also his noting of its connection with jokes. Category-mistakes deal with language rather than reality, however, and they do not always yield mistakes, e.g. "loud color."

Cummings, E. E. A highly metaphorical poet. Stresses metaphorical use of parts of speech not normally so used, especially prepositions (cf. Friedman).
An example of his poetry is as follows:
"who is this/dai/nty/mademoiselle/the o/f her/luminous/se/lf/
a shy (an/if a/whis/per a where/a hidi/ng) est/meta/ph/or/?
la lune"

Curran, Thomas. "The Theory of Metaphor: Tradition, Revolt, and Return" PhD diss. Fordham 1960
Metaphor is based on analogy. One thing is said, another meant. "The 'necessarily brief and deceptively modest' definition of Aristotle, with all its implications, commands my total acceptance." Curran is also Thomistic. A hierarchical, single and total theory of the universe must be obtained before a theory of metaphor can be meaningful. He proposes that we return to the mediaeval view of universal analogy of all things based on divine creation. He quotes Aristotle as an authority rather than presenting arguments for such views.

Curtius, Ernst R. European Literature and the Latin Middle Ages W. Trask, trans. Princeton Univeristy Press 1967 "Metaphorics," "Ape as Metaphor," "Grammatical and Rhetorical Technical Terms as Metaphors"

_____. "Schrift- und Buch-Metaphorik in der Weltliteratur" Deutsche Vierteljahrsschrift für Literaturwissenschaft und Geistesgeschichte 20 no. 4 (1942) 359-411

T. D. "On the Use of Metaphors" Blackwood's Magazine 18 (1825) 719-723
Plain unmetaphorical literal style is a myth. All written and spoken language is metaphorical. Even "metaphor" is metaphorical. Metaphor can render the abstract concrete and illustrate ideas. It is "not unclean" to mix metaphors. One need only look at their actual use in the specific case to see if they are acceptable.

Dahl, Cp. De natura similitudinum ex Homero Upsaliae 1797 [1791]

Dahlgren, Sven. "De Aeschyli metaphoris et similitudinibus a re navali deductis commentatio" PhD diss. Stockholm 1875

Daiches, David. "Imagery and Meaning in 'Antony and Cleopatra'" English Studies 43 (1962) 343-359

_____. "Images of America" Southern Review 1 (1965) 684-701

_____. "Myth, Metaphor, and Poetry" More Literary Essays London: Oliver & Boyd 1968 pp. 1-18. Also Royal Society of Literature of the United Kingdom N. S. 33 (1965) 39-55
Metaphor is seeing one thing as another, saying that they are the same and different. "To compare an egg to a house is to increase awareness of the place in human experience of both eggs and houses. In metaphor we both believe and don't believe." The metaphor is tensive and "achieves a new dimension for the literal truth."

Daitz, Edna. "The Picture Theory of Meaning" Mind 62 (Apr. 1953) 184-201

Dallas, Eneas. The Gay Science London: Chapman and Hall 1866 esp. I, p. 265 (cf. A. Ward)
He regards metaphor as a universal impulse toward harmony. Imagination and Fancy are not separate. Three types of similitude generated by the mind are: 1) Dramatic Form which asserts "I am that or like that," 2) Lyrical Form - "That is I or like me," 3) Epic or historical Form (metaphor) - "That is that or like that."

_____. Poetics: An Essay on Poetry London 1852 esp. pp. 189-216 on imagery

D'Alton, John F. Roman Literary Theory and Criticism New York: Russell and Russell 1962; (New York 1931) esp. pp. 94-96
Accepts Aristotle's theory of metaphor.

Damon, Phillip. Modes of Analogy in Ancient and Medieval Verse University of California Publications in Classical Philology vol. 15 no. 6, University of California Press 1961 pp. 261-334
He deals with Homer's similes, Sappho's similes, the "Imago Vocis" in Vergilian pastoral, etc.

Danielou, Jean. "The Problem of Symbolism" _Thought_ 25 (1950) 423-440
There are, as Augustine said, secret affinities in the nature of reality.

Dankmeyer, Johannes Willem. _Vergelijkingen in maleische literatuur_ Amstelveen-Amsterdam: Teerhuis and Klinkenberg 1945

Dannehl, Gustavus. "De tropis. Particula I. Translationum, metonymiae, synecdoches apud poetas aevi Augusti" PhD diss. Halle 1868 66 pp.

Darmesteter, Arsène. _La vie des mots étudiés dans leurs significations_ Paris 1887 [1950]

D'Avanzo, Mario L. _Keats' Metaphors for the Poetic Imagination_ Durham, North Carolina: Duke University Press 1967

_____. "Recurrent Metaphors for Poetry in John Keats' Works" PhD diss. Brown University 1963

Davidson, Edward H. "Review of Wimsatt _The Verbal Icon_" _The Journal of English and Germanic Philology_ 54 (Apr. 1955) 269-274

Davie, Donald. _Articulate Energy: An Inquiry into the Syntax of English Poetry_ London: Routledge & Paul 1955
He says that Aristotle's four term analogy is really six term. A discussion of the imagists, but mainly about types of syntax.

_____. "Berkeley's Style in _Siris_" _Cambridge Journal_ 4 (1951) 427-433

Davies, Cicely. "Ut Pictura Poesis" _Modern Language Review_ 30 (1935) 159-169
It was held that the harmony of nature provides a basis for the harmony of art such that poetry may be regarded as a painting. The value of metaphor is seen to be in its pictorial significance. A number of critics holding this view are presented.

Davies, Gardner. "The Demon of Analogy" _French Studies_ 9 (1955) 195-211, 326-347
On Mallarmé's analogies. Some are synaesthetic, humorous, conceits, physical resemblances, relations between abstract and concrete, etc.

Davies, H. "Lazamon's Similes" _Review of English Studies_ 11 (1960) 129-142

Davis, J. W. "Review of Turbayne _The Myth of Metaphor_" _Dialogue_ 2 (1963) 236-238

Davoine, Jean-Pierre. "Métaphores animales dans _Germinal_" _Études Françaises_ 4 (1968) 383-392

Day, Albert. "Metaphors and War" Christian Century 59 (March 18, 1942) 352-354 (See p. 340 for editorial "Mr. Day's Metaphors")
Thinking is metaphoric, but we should not be captivated by poor metaphors, e.g. war metaphors such as, "War is the judgment of God," or "War is surgery, unwelcome but often necessary."

Day, Angel. "A Declaration of All Such Tropes, Figures or Schemes, as...are speciallie used..." The English Secretary London 1595 part 2
Metaphor: "When a word from the proper or right signification is transferred to another near unto the meaning." It gives things properties they do not have.

Day, Robert A. "Image and Idea in 'Voyages II'" Criticism 7 (1965) 224-234
On Hart Crane.

Day-Lewis, Cecil. The Poetic Image London: Jonathan Cape 1947 [1961] (Review by Cranfield)
Metaphor involves the perception of a unity underlying and relating all phenomena. He once wrote, "Metaphor was the beginning of wisdom, the earliest scientific method."

De, Sushil K. History of Sanskrit Poetics two vols. second revised edition Calcutta 1960 (cf. Nair)

_____. Sanskrit Poetics as a Study of Aesthetics Berkeley: University of California Press 1963
Sanskrit poetics began with extensive, mechanical and grammatical analyses of figures of speech. Gunas are "excellences" or properties of figures. Rasa or "delectation" is a state of rising to the occasion of the reader's mind. When mind is contemplative and with wonder, free from doubt and obstacles it enjoys a state of generalized emotion susceptible to enjoyment of metaphor. De says metaphors are unique and cannot be governed by rules.

Debaisieux, Maurice. Analogie et Symbolisme: Étude critique de l'analogie comparée au symbolisme dans la connaissance metaphysique et religieuse Paris 1921

De Bruyne, Edgar. Études d'esthétique médiévale Brussels 1946
Discusses background of metaphor generally.

Degen, Heinrich. "Die Tropen der Vergleichung bei Johannes Chrysostomus" (Beiträge zur Geschichte der Metapher, Allegorie, und Gleichnis in der griechischen Prosaliteratur) PhD diss. Freiburg 1921

Degenhardt, Ernst. Die Metapher in den Dramen Victor Hugos Wiesbaden: Schwab 1900

_____. Die Metapher bei den Vorläufern Molières, 1612-54 PhD diss. 1886 Marburg: Elwert 1888 (A list of metaphors.)

De Laguna, Grace. "Professor Urban on Language" Philosophical Review 50 (July 1941) 422-431

Delaney, Howard. "The Doctrine of Four Term Analogy in Aristotle" PhD diss. St. Louis University 1958-1959 222 pp.

Delmond, J. "L'image dans le langage schizophrénique" Evolution Psychiatrique (Paris) 4 (1937) 1ff.

DeLozier, A. L. "List of French Similes" Modern Language Journal 21 (Jan. 1937) 264-271

De Melo, Francisco. A feira dos anexins: metaphoras Lisbon: Parceria A. M. Pereira, Livraria Editôra 1916 [1875]

Demetrius (c. 100 B.C.). On Style W. R. Roberts, trans. Cambridge: Harvard University Press 1965 pp. 257-487
Metaphor ornaments, clarifies, animates the inanimate to make it active, yields and renders mystery in the form of allegory. Metaphor is in all our language. It should be based on true analogy, and should not be far-fetched, used in excess, or relate things of greatly different value or esteem.

Demidoff, Alex. Laugh With Us: A Closer Look at What Novelists Really Say New York: Exposition Press 1957

DeMille, J. Elements of Rhetoric New York: Harper 1878 pp. 87-203

Demorest, D. L. "L'expression figurée et symbolique dans l'oeuvre de Gustave Flaubert" PhD diss. Paris 1931

Dempe, Helmuth. "Die Metapher als ambivalentes Symbol" Provinz: Pädagogische Monatsschrift für Erziehung und Unterricht (Frankfurt) 12 nos. 7-8 (1958) 359-367

Denbigh, K. G. "Use of Imagery in Science" Fortnightly 172 (Dec. 1952) 411-418
Metaphor serves as a model or hypothesis. This technique brings science and art closer, but science basically concerns thought and the general; art the feelings and the particular. There is no one model of anything, but many possible and overlapping models. The mathematical model is a loss of sense imagery.

Deneau, Daniel P. "Imagery in the Scenes of Clerical Life" Victorian Newsletter no. 28 (1965) 18-22

Derbolav, Josef. "Das Metaphorische in der Sprache Beitrag zu einer dialektisch-grenzbegrifflichen Sprachphilosophie der Wirklichkeitsnähe" in Festschrift für Robert Reininger Wien: Sexl 1949 pp. 80-113

"De vocabulis partium corporis in lingua Graeca metaphorice dictis" PhD diss. Leipzig (Genf) 1875

Deutsch, Karl. "Mechanism, Organism and Society: Some Models in Natural and Social Sciences" Philosophy of Science 18 (1951) 230-252
"Men think in terms of models." A model is a set of symbols or a physical matching object. Knowledge depends on physical and pictorial models such as the wheel, balance, thread, web. Mechanism and organism are models and were found to unsuccessfully account for social cohesion in society or for learning. Models from history, cybernetics and other areas are examined.

Deutschbein, Max. Neuenglische Stilistik Leipzig: Quelle & Meyer 1932 esp. pp. 86-104 "Vergleich, Metapher und Zitate"
Metaphor and simile transpose from one plane of speech to another. Simile transposes from the concrete thing realm (Sachsphäre) into a realm of internal images (Bildsphäre). These two spheres are connected by a "third comparison." It involves subjective and objective elements. The objective connection between the compared things and the subjective choosing of words clarify a certain feeling. (He follows Pongs' views here.) Romantics often use simile because they hold that being may be manifested in its different levels with different forms, moods, colors. Some types of simile are: 1) connection of two spheres e.g. by means of "as"; it may be used in the negative also--e.g. "We are no better than..." 2) use of "like." Here also the image sphere is more important than the thing sphere e.g. "He behaves like a child." 3) extended simile 4) as if, as though, simile. This is a "playing" in which subjective similarities predominate over objective. The sphere of images gains independence when an exaggeration is present. 5) use of "with" e.g. "She turned with the air of a landlady." This is like a metaphor. Simile and metaphor are ways of "viewing" in terms of concrete images. He gives diagrams to illustrate several types of metaphor and simile.

Dhorme, P. "L'emploi métaphorique des noms des partes du corps en hébreu et en akkadien" Revue Biblique 29 (1920) 465-506; 30 (1921) 374-399, 517-540; 31 (1922) 215-233, 489-517; 32 (1923) 185-212. Also in book form (Summary in S. Brown WI pp. 181-184)

Dick, Bernard. "Ancient Pastoral and the Pathetic Fallacy" Comparative Literature 20 (1968) 27-44

Dickey, James. "Metaphor as Pure Adventure" Lecture delivered at the Library of Congress, Washington D. C. Dec. 4, 1967
Metaphor is a given, a mystery which we can never understand,

a thing of the moment, putting together by rules we never understand but only feel, an action, a spontaneous happening, a making of truth rather than a telling of truth, a primitive magic and personal science, a contextual interchange. One or both of its terms are concrete, its correspondence has emotional charge, it gives liberation of mind and yields novelty, it begins with a picture in the head. Metaphor is not sheer juxtaposition and there is no adequate formula for making one. Metaphor is a recreation of the world rather than an understanding of it. It reveals aspects of the mind. For the poet the one great delight is to make metaphors--and it is great that this world allows them to be made in it. He views the world as always changing. One should make and collect good metaphors.

Diderot, D. Encyclopédie, ou dictionnaire raisonné des sciences, des arts et des métiers Genf-Neufchatel 1779 vol 21 pp. 703-710 "Métaphore" [Article initialed B. E. R. M.]
The article is mainly a quotation of the entire chapter, "La métaphore" in Cesar Du Marsais, Des Tropes.

_____, and Oscar Bloch. "Métaphore" Dictionnaire étymologique de la langue française Paris: Les Presses Universitaires de France 1932 (1765 vol. 10 pp. 436-440)

Dieckmann, Liselotte. "Metaphor of Hieroglyphics in German Romanticism" Comparative Literature 7 (Fall 1955) 306-312
The metaphor of "hieroglyph" underlies the many trends of thought which meet in German romanticism. It is the source of emblem books. Bible stories were regarded as hieroglyphic, for Platonists visible world is a hieroglyph of the invisible, nature is a hieroglyph of God, and linguists explored the relation of sign to object as hieroglyphic.

Dietel, Käthe. Das Gleichnis in der frühen griechischen Lyrik PhD diss. München 1940 Würzburg: Aumühle 1939

Dieter, O. A. "Arbor Picta: The Medieval Tree of Preaching" Quarterly Journal of Speech 51 (April 1965) 123-144

Diez, M. "Metapher und Märchengestalt" PMLA 48 (March-Dec. 1933) 74-99, 488-507, 877-894, 1203-1222

_____. "Principle of the Dominant Metaphor in Goethe's Werther" PMLA 51 (Sept.-Dec. 1936) 821-841, 985-1006
Goethe's Werther contains many metaphors.

Dillistone, Frederick W. Christianity and Symbolism London: Collins 1955

Diomedis. Grammatici Latini seven vols. Heinrich Keil, ed. Leipzig 1855-1880 esp. I p. 456
A minor grammarian of the Middle Ages. He follows the views

of Charisius who in turn follows Donatus on metaphor.

Disep, Herbert. "Formen bildlichen Ausdrucks bei den älteren griechischen Dichtern" PhD diss. Göttingen 1951

Djwa, Sandra A. "Metaphor, World View and the Continuity of Canadian Poetry: A Study of the Major English Canadian Poets with a Computer Concordance to Metaphor" PhD diss. University of British Columbia 1968
The dominant metaphors of Canadian poetry are discussed.

Döblin, Alfred. "Futuristische Worttechnik, Offener Brief an F. T. Marinetti" Der Sturm 3 (1913) 280-282
He criticizes Marinetti for attacking metaphor while still using metaphors in his poetry.

Dodge, Roger P. "The Image and the Actor" English Miscellany 17 (1966) 175-209

Donato, E. "Tesauro's Poetics: Through the Looking Glass" Modern Language Notes 78 (1963) 15-30

Donatus. Ars Grammatica Heinrich Keil, ed. Leipzig 1864 [c. 333 A.D.] vol. 4 (cf. Curran pp. 90-98)
Metaphor is a transference of words from animate to animate, inanimate to animate and vice versa, and inanimate to inanimate. He gives thirteen tropes, all other tropes being based on the genus-species relation. Tropes are verbal and are thought transfers for the sake of ornament or necessity.

Dondua, L. D. "Metafora v shirokom smysle i metafora poeticheskaya. K probleme znacheniya slova" Yazyk i Myshlenye 9 (1940) 57-64
On metaphor as an expansion of the word and poetic metaphor.

Donelly, Dorothy. The Golden Well: An Anatomy of Symbols New York: Sheed and Ward 1950

Dony, Yvonne P. de. Lexicon of Figurative Language New York 1957
Similar to Wilstach's collection of similes.

Dooyeweerd, Herman. De analogische grondbegrippen der vakwetenschappern en hun betrekking tot de structuur van den menselijken ervaringshorizon Amsterdam: Noord-Hollandsche Uitg. Mij. 1954

Dorfles, Gillo. "Myth and Metaphor" L'estetica del mito da Vico a Wittgenstein Milano: Mursia 1967. Also in Giambattista Vico: An International Symposium Giorgio Tagliacozzo, ed. Elio Tagliacozzo, trans. Baltimore: Johns Hopkins Press 1969 pp. 577-590
Vico's theory of metaphor is supported and elaborated. Metaphor is a partly cognitive and empathetic grasp of reality de-

riving from pre-conscious historical and cultural intuition. It arises like myth. Metaphor helps constitute our world and life. Man metaphorically transforms himself into the world.

_____. "Simbolo e metafora come strumenti di comunicazione in estetica" Il pensiero americano contemporaneo filosofia Rossi-Landi, ed. Milano: Edizioni di Comunità 1958 pp. 57-91
Art is metaphorical, not concealment as Boas thinks. It does not discuss values but presents them metaphorically. It delineates the possible. Dorfles discusses the views of C. Morris, Richards, Wimsatt, Langer, Empson, Arnheim, G. Stern, Weitz, Fenollosa, Dewey, D. Walsh.

Downer, James. Metaphors and Word-Plays in Petronius PhD diss. University of Pennsylvania 1905 Waco, Texas: Baylor University Press 1913

Downey, June. "The Imaginal Reaction to Poetry" University of Wyoming Bulletin 2 (1911)

_____. "Literary Synaesthesia" Journal of Philosophy, Psychology and Scientific Method 9 (1912) 490-498
Cases of actual experienced synaesthesia are distinguished from cases where it is only of literary value in the works of Poe, Swinburne, Shelley, Keats, Blake. While there is very slight evidence that the chosen poets experienced true synaesthesia, there is some justification in concluding that they enjoy, more than the ordinary reader, analogies between the senses.

_____. "The Metaphorical Consciousness" Creative Imagination: Studies in the Psychology of Literature New York: Harcourt Brace 1929

_____. "The Psychology of Figures of Speech" The American Journal of Psychology 30 (Jan. 1919) 103-115
A Freudian approach according to which metaphor reveals latent unconscious thoughts (by condensation, etc.), subtle states of mind and emotions. Metaphor is also involved in perceptual shifts (cf. seeing-as and visual metaphor). Images need not accompany metaphor and may be side by side, oscillating, or blending depending upon context and individual differences.

Downing, C. "How Can We Hope and Not Dream? Exodus as Metaphor: A Study of the Biblical Imagination" Journal of Religion 48 (Jan. 1968) 35-53

Drange, Theodore. Type Crossings PhD diss. Cornell University 1963 The Hague: Mouton 1966 (Review by R. Martin)
Type-crossings (cf. Ryle's "category-mistakes") are a priori falsehoods and can be known to be false independent of empirical evidence, e.g. Virtue is a fire-shovel, color the picture Socrates, smells are loud, moral perfection is a prime number,

the number five is heavy.

Draper, R. P. "Review of Brooke-Rose A Grammar of Metaphor" English Studies 47 (1966) 459-462
Brooke-Rose is too subjective in her presentation.

Dronkers, Abrahamus. De comparationibus et metaphoris apud Plutarchum PhD diss. Traiecti ad Rhenum, Utrecht: Boekhoven 1892

Dryden, John. "The Author's Apology for Heroic Poetry and Poetic License" Essays of John Dryden W. P. Ker, ed. Oxford: Clarendon Press 1900 vol. 1 pp. 178-190 [1677]
Cf. other essays of his: "A Parallel of Poetry to Painting" and "Preface to the Fables." Dryden says we read descriptions in poetry visually with an actual picture in the mind's eye. Metaphor is like bold colors in painting. He speaks also of "poetic license" needed by poets (which seems similar to license to use metaphor).

Dudding, Griffith. "The Function of Whitman's Imagery in 'Song of Myself' 1855" Walt Whitman Review 13 (1967) 3-11

Du Marsais, Cesar. Des tropes ou des différents sens dans lesquels on peut prendre un même mot dans une même langue Paris: Chez Mme Dabo-Butschert 1825 [1730] esp. pp. 103-117 "La Metaphore"
By the use of metaphor "we convert a noun's proper meaning to another meaning, which it can only bear by virtue of a comparison that resides in the mind." Also on misuse of metaphor.

Dumas, G. "Le symbolisme dans la langue" Revue Philosophique 117 (Jan. 1934) 5-38

Dumitrescu, I. "Review of Tudor Vianu Problemele metaphorei..." Limba Romîna (Bucharest) 7 no. 2 (1958) 86-87

Dumortier, Jean. "Les images dans la poésie d'Eschyle" PhD diss. Paris 1935

Dunbar, H. F. Symbolism in Medieval Thought and Its Consumation in the 'Divine Comedy' New Haven: Yale University Press 1929

Düntzer, Heinrich. Zu den homerischen Gleichnissen. Homerische Abhandlungen Leipzig: Hahn 1872

Durand, Gilbert. Les Structures Anthropologiques de l'Imagination; introduction à l'archétypologie générale Paris: Presses Universitaires de France 1960

Duval, Georges. Dictionnaire des métaphores de Victor Hugo Paris: Paiget 1888

Eastman, Max. The Enjoyment of Poetry New York: Scribner's 1913 esp. "Choice and Comparison"
A figure is direct, not indirect speech. Metaphor is a grammatical term for a rich adjective. There are two kinds of comparison: 1) illuminating and intensifying, 2) comparisons of reverie, e.g. allegory, fable, parables. "Direct metaphor" is allegory with no explanation of its symbols.

_____. The Literary Mind: Its Place in an Age of Science New York: Scribner's 1932 esp. part 4 ch. 1 sects. 5-6
Metaphor is a state of heightened consciousness. One can be "in a state of metaphor." Metaphor must depart from the ordinary, e.g. by use of comparison or synecdoche. It suggests impractical identifications. Any impractical identification is poetic in involving attentive consciousness. Some metaphors are thought poetic merely because they are obscure.

Eaton, Mary. "Imagery and Its Recall" Consider the Child London: Longmans, Green and Co. 1925 ch. 3

Ebersole, Frank B. "Metaphors and Particularly a Metaphysical Use of Metaphor" The Graduate Review of Philosophy 2 (Spring 1960) 16-32
Metaphysical metaphors, e.g. "substratum," have no literal interpretation and can be learned only from basic metaphors, not from the facts. The metaphysical metaphor is everlastingly puzzling. The meaning it has is that the author says it has.

Edel, Abraham. "Metaphors, Analogies, Models, and All That in Ethical Theory" Philosophy, Science and Method S. Morgenbesser, P. Suppes, and M. White, eds. New York: St. Martin's Press 1969

Edelman, Nathan. "The Mixed Metaphor in Descartes" Romanic Review 41 (1950) 167-178
The traveler, a metaphor of change, is contrasted with the architect, a metaphor of the static.

Edie, James M. "Expression and Metaphor" Philosophy and Phenomenological Research 23 (June 1963) 538-561
This is a phenomenological and existentialistic theory of metaphor proposing "to examine metaphorical expression from the point of view of an intentional theory of consciousness and to suggest that the necessity of speaking (and thinking) in metaphors is not an accidental weakness of human thought but an existential necessity . . ." Metaphor allows us to progress from the known to the unknown and point to new "life-world" experiences. A word is used to refer with a new purpose, a new intention to previous experience, in order to reveal new experience. Because thinking and language are metaphoric and metaphors limit the way we think we always need new and fresh ones. Metaphors build on metaphors at every step. He agrees

with Vico that words are etymologically and metaphorically carried over from bodies to apply to mind and spirit. Every word originally designated a concrete thing but came by metaphorical extension to refer to abstract things.

_____. "Vico and Existential Philosophy" Giambattista Vico: An International Symposium Giorgio Tagliacozzo, ed. Baltimore: Johns Hopkins Press 1969 483-495
Vico showed that thinking is impossible without using the method of metaphorical transposition. Like Merleau-Ponty, Vico is concerned with the ambiguous and chaotic. Metaphor helps name and clarify the chaos of preverbal experience. Because we think in metaphors and only later justify them we should not try to purify them but rather understand them.

Edwards, Jonathan. Images or Shadows of Divine Things Perry Miller, ed. New Haven: Yale University Press 1948
Analogical view of natural and divine worlds. He also wrote Book of Nature, A Grammar of Things.

Edwards, Thomas R., Jr. "Colors of Fancy: An Image Cluster in Pope" Modern Language Notes 73 (Nov. 1958) 483-489
The cluster image functions not philosophically but imaginatively.

Egan, Eileen. "Approaches to Metaphor as a Theoretical Concept" PhD diss. Catholic University of America 1966
Metaphor is a vital mode of language or of human perception or of all reality. It transcends the verbal but is not distinct from the knowing subject. She holds the Thomistic view of metaphor as analogy. Wheelwright, K. Burke and W. Stevens are discussed at length.

Egen, J. Über die homerischen Gleichnisse nebst einer Beispielsammlung Magdeburg 1790

Eichholz, Georg. "Das Gleichnis als Spiel" Evangelische Theologie 21 (1961) 309-326

Eicke, Otto. "Die kulturelle Bedeutung der Metapher in den Leitartikeln der Times von 1914-1920" PhD diss. Greifswald, Germany 1929
Newspapers are here regarded as "Metaphern-freundlich" and he shows how the spirit and culture of England is mirrored in the metaphors of the Times articles from 1914-1920.

Eigeldinger, Marc. "L'évolution dynamique de l'image dans la poésie française du romantisme à nos jours" PhD diss. Neuchâtel 1943

Einarsson, Stefán. "Skaldic Poetry" A History of Icelandic Literature New York: Johns Hopkins Press 1957 esp. pp. 44-68
Has useful bibliography.

The Skalds used heiti and kenningar (kennings). Heiti refers to poetical names, e.g. "salt" meaning "sea." Kenning consists of a proper name and a definer, and seems to be a substituted phrase, e.g. "sword liquid" for blood, "heather-fish" for snake. If there are many replacement substitutions they are called reknar, e.g. "ship" is "the hart of the ride of the ruler of the swan-path" as expanded from the kenning "horse of the sea."

Eisenstein, Sergei. The Film Sense Jay Leyda, trans. New York: Harcourt, Brace and World 1942 (cf. New York: Meridian Books, World Publishing Co. 1957: Film Form and The Film Sense)
The montage is a juxtaposition of two different film shots to yield a new creation, but one which reproduces the process by which new images are created in life. The "montage principle" includes the emotions and mind of the spectator.

_____. "The Image in Process" The Modern Tradition Richard Ellmann and Charles Feidelson, Jr., eds. New York: Oxford University Press 1965 pp. 163-169

Eisler, R. Wörterbuch der philosophischen Begriffe Berlin: E. Mittler 1929 vol. 2 p. 126

Ekstein, Rudolf. "Cross-sectional Views of the Psychotherapeutic Process with an Adolescent Recovering from a Schizophrenic Episode" American Journal of Orthopsychiatry 31 (1961) 757-775

_____, and Judith Wallerstein. "Choice of Interpretation in the Treatment of Borderline and Psychotic Children" Menninger Clinic Bulletin 21 (1957) 199-207

Eliot, T. S. "Dichterische Metaphorik" T. S. Eliot: Ausgewählte Essays 1917-1947 Ursula Clemen et al., trans. Berlin/Frankfurt 1950 (Hans Hennecke, ed. Berlin: Suhrkamp 1950) esp. pp. 69-70

_____. Selected Essays New York: Harcourt Brace 1960 [1950] (cf. Steadman)
Eliot's "objective correlative" is presented here. Metaphor is the poet's "perpetual slight alteration of language, words perpetually juxtaposed in new and sudden combinations, meanings perpetually eingeschachelt into meanings." "The only way of expressing emotion in the form of art is by finding an 'objective correlative'; in other words, a set of objects, a situation, a chain of events which shall be the formula of that particular emotion; such that when the external facts, which must terminate in sensory experience, are given, the emotion is immediately evoked.... You will find that the state of mind of Lady Macbeth walking in her sleep has been communicated to you by a skillful accumulation of imagined sensory impressions...."

Elledge, Paul. Byron and the Dynamics of Metaphor Nashville: Vanderbilt University Press 1968
In Byron there is juxtaposition of disparate concepts.

Elliot, John R. "Shakespeare and the Double Image of King John" Shakespeare Studies 1 (1965) 64-84

Ellis, Ronald. "A Grammatical Analysis of Metaphor" PhD diss. in progress, Cornell University (1971)
An analysis of metaphor in view of the theories of Levin, Riffaterre, Chomsky, Whalley and others. Transformational grammar is stressed. W. Stevens' poetry is examined.

Ellis-Fermor, Una. "The Functions of Imagery in Drama" The Frontiers of Drama London 1945 esp. pp. 77-95

_____. Some Recent Research in Shakespeare's Imagery Shakespeare Association London: Oxford University Press 1937

Ellmann, Richard, and Charles Feidelson, Jr. The Modern Tradition: Backgrounds of Modern Literature New York: Oxford University Press 1965
Includes: William Blake "The Eternal World of Vision," Flint and Pound "Imagism," H. Crane "The Dynamics of Metaphor," Max Ernst "Multiple Vision," Sergei Eisenstein "The Image in Process," Gide "The Reflexive Image," Yeats "The Completed Image," D. Thomas "A Battle of Images."

Elster, Ernst. Prinzipien der Literaturwissenschaft Halle: Max Niemeyer 1911 esp. vol. 2 Stilistik "Die metaphorische Apperzeption" pp. 111-139
Metaphor is conscious substitution into a different sphere involving analogy and a shared aspect. Its stages are 1) both images parallel 2) original image is only unconsciously thought 3) original image is remotely suggested 4) image is expressible intuitively but not in words. Metaphor needs importance, newness, contrasts, harmony of emotions, concreteness, trueness to life. The main measure of aesthetic value is the distance between the actual and the metaphoric image.

Embler, Weller. "Design as Metaphor" ETC 11 (Winter 1954) 101-112

_____. "Five Metaphors from the Modern Repertory" ETC 19 (1962-1963) 403-426
The five are prison, wasteland, monster, machine and hospital.

_____. "Metaphor in Everyday Speech" ETC 16 (Spring 1959) 323-342

_____. Metaphor and Meaning Deland, Fla.: Everett/Edwards 1966
Words, and so metaphors, determine thought and behavior; they make the world. A whole philosophy is contained in a metaphor and an age is known by its metaphors, e.g. the machine, the circle, etc. Art is a metaphorical expression of the inner

by means of the outer (cf. Eliot's "objective correlative"). This book contains most or all of Embler's various articles on metaphor.

_____. "Metaphor and Social Belief" Language Meaning and Maturity S. I. Hayakawa, ed. New York: Harper 1954 pp. 125-138
Also ETC 8 (1951) 83-93
Language arises out of social situations and often determines the thoughts we have. As beliefs are implicit in metaphors an age may be known by its metaphors.

_____. "The Metaphor of the Underground" ETC 25 no. 4 (1968) 392-406

_____. "The Novel as Metaphor" ETC 10 (Autumn 1952) 3-11

Emerson, Ralph W. "The Poetic Endeavor" The American Transcendentalist Perry Miller, ed. New York: Doubleday 1957 (cf. Keller)
Influenced by Kant and Coleridge. Genius implies imagination and use of figures and symbols. Trope is analogy. All thinking is a process of analogy. Nature is a trope. The whole of nature is a metaphor of the human mind. As a bird lands on the bough then flies in the air again so thoughts of God pause but for a moment in any form.

_____. Works five vols. Boston: Houghton, Mifflin and Co. 1881 esp. vol. 5 "Language" pp. 28-36 (cf. R. Adams)
"Parts of speech are metaphors, because the whole of nature is a metaphor of the human mind.... Every object rightly seen unlocks a new faculty of the soul."

Emmet, Dorothy. The Nature of Metaphysical Thinking London: Macmillan and Co. 1961
An examination of the role played by analogy in the various areas of knowledge. "Our concern will therefore be to study concepts drawn from particular relations within experience in so far as they claim to throw light on metaphysical questions about 'reality.'" The Thomistic doctrine of the "analogy of being" is examined and rejected.

_____. "Use of Analogy in Metaphysics" Proceedings of the Aristotelian Society 41 (1940) 27-46
She concludes that one cannot give a comprehensive theory of analogy.

Empson, William. "Donne and the Rhetorical Tradition" Kenyon Review 11 (1949) 571-587

_____. Seven Types of Ambiguity New York: Meridian Books, World Publishing Co. 1955
These seven types of ambiguity are relevant to metaphor, e.g. 1) a detail is effective in several ways at once such as in

subdued metaphor, 2) two or more alternative meanings are fully resolved into one, 3) puns, 4) contradictory meanings forcing one to invent interpretations, etc.

_____. The Structure of Complex Words New York: New Directions 1951 esp. "Metaphor" pp. 331-349
Metaphor is "a recognition that 'false identity' is being used, a feeling of resistance to it, and then a feeling of richness about the possible interpretations of the word, which has now become a source of advice on how to think about the matter, so that we regard it." All words for mental "processes" are derived from words for physical processes.

Ench, John. Wallace Stevens: Images and Judgments Carbondale: University of Southern Illinois 1964

Engelhard, R. De personificationibus in poesi atque arte Romanorum Göttingen 1881

Engstrom, Alfred G. "In Defense of Synaesthesia in Literature" Philological Quarterly 25 (1946) 1-19
Synaesthesia appeared even before Homer. It is intersensal, normal and healthy. It is a universal factor in human experience as well as in words.

Erdman, E. G., Jr. "Lope de Vega's 'De Absalon,' a laberinto of conceptos esparcidos" Studies in Philology 65 (Oct. 1968) 753-767 (In English)

Erhardt-Siebold, Erika von. "Harmony of the Senses in English, German and French Romanticism" PMLA 47 (1932) 577-592

_____. "Synaesthesien in der englischen Dichtung des 19 Jahrhunderts" Englische Studien 53 (1919) 1-157, 196-334

Ericksen, Donald H. "Imagery as Structure in Jane Eyre" Victorian Newsletter 30 (1966) 18-22

Ericson, Eston. "Metaphors for Heaven and Death" Anglia (Beiblatt) 48 (1937) 247-248

Erixon, Sigurd. "Metaphorical Language and Custom" Laos. Études comparées de folklore ou d'ethnologie régionale 1 (1951) 79-82
The phenomenon of metaphorically applying names of things to other things is common in every language and culture yet it has not been sufficiently studied by ethnologists and folklorists. A study of associations, comparisons or emotionally conditioned expressions requires in addition a cultural analysis.

Erlich, Victor. Russian Formalism: History--Doctrine The Hague Mouton 1954 (cf. Shklovskii)
Metaphor is regarded as "strange-making" insight. Sound repe-

tition is referred to as rhythmical metaphor or auditory simile. Jakobson distinguishes between figures of similarity and figures of congruity.

Ernst, Max. "Multiple Vision" The Modern Tradition Richard Ellmann and Charles Feidelson Jr., eds. New York: Oxford University Press 1965 pp. 163 ff.

Erwin, Edward. The Concept of Meaninglessness Baltimore: Johns Hopkins Press 1970 esp. chapt. 3 "The Category Mistake Argument" and chapt. 5 "Metaphor and Meaninglessness." Especially on Ryle, Drange and Max Black.

Esnault, Gaston. L'imagination populaire: métaphores occidentales. Essai sur les valeurs imaginatives concrètes du français parlé en Basse Bretagne comparé avec les patois, parlers techniques et argots français. Paris: Les presses universitaires de France 1925
He attempts to offer a semantic and linguistic study of the metaphors used in the local French of lower Brittany and give a general discussion of metaphor. Some statements about metaphor are: Metaphors are not chaotic or illogical but subjective and involve verbal fantasy. Metaphor is not a transfer of word from one meaning to another but is an intuition which transfers itself. The creation of a metaphor is a new mental impression pertaining to an object. The unknown is expressed in terms of the known. Metaphor is a condensed comparison by which the mind affirms an intuitive and concrete identity between two things. This identity is not a rational or scientific identity whose aim is to be true forever; it is a partial identity for the imagination, which expresses the present sensitive reaction of the subject. It must be pleasing to one of the five senses, through an instinctive (intuitive) meaning. An intuition is a kind of knowledge which is obtained immediately without need of previous knowledge. Psychologically a metaphor is a mental intuition of memory which covers over or masks either an intuition which is present and sensible, or another represented intuition. Linguistically metaphor is the name of an object which is given to another object, by reason of the intuitive resemblance between them, despite their intuitive differences, and without any explanatory discourse.

Eucken, Rudolf. Über Bilder und Gleichnisse in der Philosophie Leipzig: Veit and Co. 1880

_____. "Über Bilder und Gleichnisse bei Kant: Beiträge zur Einführung in die Geschichte der Philosophie" Leipzig 1906

_____. "Über Bilder und Vergleichungen bei Aristoteles" Neues Jahrbuch für Philologie und Pädagogik 99 (1969) part 1 pp. 248 ff.

Eusébio, Adelaide Ma. de Almeida. A Metáfora e a Comparação na

Prosa Literária do Século XV--Tese Lisbon 1949 (cf. Mendes)

Evans, David Owen. "Pierre Leroux and His Philosophy in Relation to Literature" PMLA 44 (March 1929) 274-287 (cf. Leroux)

Evans, Maurice. "Metaphor and Symbol in the Sixteenth Century" Essays in Criticism 3 (July 1953) 267-284 (Reply by D. Brewer) Metaphor had a basis in the religious notion of universal analogy which it now no longer has (cf. Wasserman). To extend a metaphor was almost like finding a religious allegory.

Evans, P. "Meaning of the Match Image in James' The Ambassadors" Modern Language Notes 70 (Jan. 1955) 36

Evans, R. O. "Conrad: A Nautical Image" Modern Language Notes 72 (Feb. 1957) 98-99

Fang, Achilles. "From Imagism to Whitmanism in Recent Chinese Poetry: A Search for Poetics that Failed" Indiana University Conference on Oriental-Western Literary Relations 1955 pp. 176-189
He discusses the imagist credo and movement and its influence on Chinese poetics and the Chinese literary revolution of 1917.

Farber, Eduard. "Chemical Discoveries by Means of Analogies" Isis 41 (1956) 20-26
Chemistry originated and grows by means of analogies, e.g. the periodic table of elements, comparison of atoms to cells, inorganic to organic, electrical conductivity to heat, etc. The use of analogy is essential but dangerous as it is a tentative prediction for which the facts are not all available. It may assume a universal analogy of all things.

Farre, George L. "Remarks on Swanson's Theory of Models" British Journal for the Philosophy of Science 18 no. 2 (Aug. 1967) 140-144
Swanson states that scientific models are used as metaphors, "lenses" or "filters" and carry over to theory. Farre argues that the metaphor or model does not help constitute theory but rather merely illustrates theory. "It is the structure of the theory that is imputed to the model and governs it."

Feidelson, Charles, Jr. Symbolism and American Literature Chicago: University of Chicago Press 1953 esp. pp. 58-65 (Summarized in L. Mackey 1965)
Metaphor is an "organic" interaction and conceiving of a collocation of words which cuts across and reshapes logical categories. It is not atomistic comparison, additive, a resemblance, an analogy, ornament, or verbal trick. It is a means of discovery by means of language. It is multi-significative and so literally unparaphrasable. Metaphor is the language of literature.

Feigl, Herbert. "Logical Empiricism" Readings in Philosophical Analysis Herbert Feigl and Wilfrid Sellars, eds. New York: Appleton-Century-Crofts 1949 pp. 9-11
Metaphor is not cognitive and its function is emotive and pictorial.

Feldkeller, Paul. "Die Einstellungsmetapher" Zeitschrift für Ästhetik und allgemeine Kunstwissenschaft 22 (1928) 147-165
Subjective metaphors cannot be explained by purely objective, conceptual thought. They are characteristic of poets, children, primitives, and women. They speak to the subconscious. Sometimes we relate human faces and landscapes or animal faces in subjective metaphorical ways. One sees his beloved subjectively rather than objectively. He discusses Hebbel's drama which the audience is made to view through its own subjective responses. Allegory is a type of subjective metaphor; symbolism is objective. "Action metaphor" is another form of

subjective metaphor, e.g. religious ritual with no objective significance. "Faucets run" is regarded as incorrect syntax rather than as a subjective metaphor.

Feldman, Asher. The Parables and Similes of the Rabbis Cambridge 1924

Felipe, Leon. "La intrépida metáfora demiúrgica" Revista Hispánica Moderna 34 (1968) 206-211

Feltenstein, Harry D. [T. Lira, pseudonym] "The Metaphor Roots of the Symbol" Unpublished Bowdoin Prize essay 1941
A discussion of metaphor through a lengthy and detailed analysis of Aristotle's theory of metaphor. Symbol is seen to be based on metaphor. "The nature of metaphor is not obvious." Every metaphor is a transposed mode of speech whereby in order to assert something about an object a, something corresponding is asserted about an object b which stands in a certain relation to the object a. Aristotle's theory of metaphor does not adequately stress the subjective and emotive aspect of metaphor. By use of metaphor we attempt to reach universals, discover similarity in dissimilarity, heighten emotional effect. There is an interaction between genus-species metaphor relations not just substitution of one for the other. The terms of the metaphor are not uniquely clear and determined and should not be so obscure as to lead to a puzzle or unintelligibility. The two terms of the metaphor he refers to as the "independent variable" (the subject), and the "dependent variable" (the transposed term). We immediately and intuitively grasp the relations between the two terms. The ineffable, (e.g. time, God) emotions, inner-life can be rendered only metaphorically. Poets often let words guide rather than try to force words into cognitive molds. "Poetry is written with words not ideas." He discusses Eliot's "objective correlative." Our metaphors tend to hypostatize entities but "this is as it should be."

Feltes, N. N. "George Eliot's Pier-Glass: The Development of a Metaphor" Modern Philology 67 (Aug. 1969) 69-71

Fennema, Elizabeth. "Mental Imagery and the Reading Process" Elementary School Journal 59 (Feb. 1959) 286-289 (Summary in Groesbeck 1961)
"A mental image is what an individual sees, hears, feels, or tastes in his own mind." Third and fourth grade children form mental images while they read. The intelligence tests stress the literal, while lower intelligence students formed more mental images than brighter ones who are faster readers. In creative reading children should be taught to read slower and form images.

Fenner, Dudley. The Artes of Logike and Rhetorike London 1584
"A metaphor is when like is signified by like."

Fenollosa, Ernest. "An Essay on the Chinese Written Character" Instigations of Ezra Pound New York: Books for Libraries Press 1920 [1967]
The Chinese character or ideogram uses material images or pictures to suggest immaterial relations. All speech is built on the basis of metaphor. The Chinese character allows us to watch objects move, relate and develop much as a scientist does. It shows its use rather than "juggles" thoughts. The relation between pictures is based on natural suggestion, overtone, universal analogy and is indeterminate. It forms a pictorial or visual metaphor--visual juxtaposition in succession--untranslatable by means of words or completed thoughts. (cf. Ezra Pound.)

Ferdière, Gaston. "Notes préliminaires sur les 'Portmanteau words' de Lewis Carroll (ou mots-valises) au cours de la schizophrénie" Acta neurologica et psychiatrica belgica 57 (1957) 993-1003
He says that the pormanteau words of Carroll's work (e.g. "frumius" for fuming and furious) and neologisms reveal a deep Freudian process of condensation in a moving and sensible manner. This insight may help locate psychiatric disorder.

Féré, Ch. "La physiologie dans les métaphores" Revue philosophique 40 (1895) 352-359
Metaphor is a transposition of a proper to an ordinarily improper meaning or use and is based on quality similarities or feeling. It unites material objects, unites ethical or intellectual fact with material fact, and it renders the abstract by means of the concrete. Our metaphors are often based on visual sensations, physiological states and physical gestures, e.g. "swollen with pride," "heat of passion," "burning with love," "He sees red," "bitter tears." Verbal expressions of the emotions seem to be only the expressions of involuntary physiological phenomena or reflexes. The physiological metaphor is also found in animal gestures and reflexes, primitives and psychotics. The horse may stamp its feet metaphorically to "communicate" something.

_____. "Les gestes métaphoriques chez les animaux" Comptes Rendus de la Société de biologie 1895 ca. p. 270

Ferguson, Charles W. "Words as Pictures" National Parent-Teacher 52 (June 1958) 14-16
We should cultivate the habit of thinking in metaphors. Metaphor is seeing one thing in terms of another. It adorns, clarifies abstraction, pictorializes, personifies objects and abstractions, compares bodies of knowledge, and expands language.

Ferguson, Donald N. Music as Metaphor: The Elements of Expression Minneapolis: University of Minnesota Press 1960
His task is "to explore...emotional consciousness and to find its metaphoric equivalent in the substance of music." All of the arts "strive for and often reach the vividness of metaphor,

the most vivid of linguistic devices for communication." Inflection metaphor may be obtained by inflection or pitch relations.

Fergusson, Francis. "The Metaphor of the Journey" Dante's Drama of the Mind: A Modern Reading of the 'Purgatorio' Princeton University Press 1953 pp. 3-13

Ferrater Mora, José. (see Mora)

Ferré, Frederick. "Mapping the Logic of Models in Science and Theology" Christian Scholar 46 (1963) 9-39
The notion of "model" is shown to be of central importance to theologians and philosophers as well as to scientists. He discusses whether or not models correspond to reality. They seem to function like metaphors (as-if thinking) and have the attributes of metaphors, e.g. the filtering of facts, giving freedom from a single universe of discourse, etc.

_____. "Metaphors, Models and Religion" Soundings 51 no. 3 (Fall 1968) 327-345
There is no non-metaphorical definition of literal. Metaphor is described metaphorically. Metaphor is literally false yet illuminates, organizes images and thought, shifts feeling from one object to another, suggests a new way of seeing the world, is a model, moves us to action, can permanently affect our perception of values, guides experiment, and represents the unrepresentable. Religious metaphors are open to debate and must be examined.

Figures of Speech Chicago: Coronet Films 1971
A student workbook for grades 10-12 dealing only with simile, metaphor, hyperbole, and personification. Metaphor is "the figure of speech that describes without using as or like." It helps avoid repetition, attracts attention, simplifies scientific description, and describes unfamiliar objects.

Filzeck, Karl. Metaphorische Bildungen im älteren deutschen Fastnachtsspiel PhD diss. Cologne Würzburg: Triltsch 1933

Fink, G. "Review of Pongs Das Bild in der Dichtung" Germanistik 2 no. 2 (April 1961) 198-199
Pongs fought the trend of separating the conscious from the unconscious; literature is rather seen as based on the unity of intellect and feeling. For him metaphor is "the primary creation of images through feeling." The supra-individual spirit is especially revealed in feeling. Thus he investigates the individuality of lyric poetry and attempts to outline the creative personality of the poet. On animation Pongs distinguishes between active-dynamic and passive attitude. The power of animation arises from the depth of feeling. These two forms with the parable lead to the mythical or mystical metaphor.

Finzi-Contini, Bruno. "Similitudini ed analogie; l'evoluzione del concetto di modello nella scienza e nella tecnica trieste" Università degli Studi di Trieste. Facoltà di Ingegneria 1958
Engineering models.

Fischer, Friedrich. _Über technische Metaphern im Griechischen mit besonderer Berücksichtigung des Seewesens und der Baukunst_... Inaugural diss. Erlangen: Friedrich Alexander Universität 1899. Pr. Straubing, Attenkofer 1900
Naval, art, science, and carpentry metaphors treated.

Fiser, Emeric. _Le symbole littéraire. Essai sur la signification du symbole chez Wagner, Baudelaire, Mallarmé, Bergson, M. Proust_ Paris: J. Corti 1941 esp. pp. 155-169 (cf. M. Baym 1961)
For Proust metaphor is a relation between sensation and memory occurring simultaneously. This is the dynamic or literary symbol.

Fishman, Burton J. "The Fatal Mosque: A Study of Visual Metaphor and Dramatic Convention in Renaissance Tragedy" PhD diss. Princeton University 1969

_____. _La théorie du symbole littéraire et Marcel Proust_ PhD diss. Paris 1941

Fiske, C. F. _Epic Suggestion in the Imagery of the Waverly Novels_ New Haven 1940

Fitzosborne, Sir Thomas. [pseudonym for William Melmoth] Letter 51 "On Metaphors" _Letters on Several Subjects_ London: Printed for R. Dodsley 1748
Metaphor is a comparison of one to many ideas. Metaphor may clarify, please, or embellish. It may be used in poetry and oratory, but "ought to be entirely banished from the severer compositions of philosophy."

Flanagan, John. "Review of J. Gold _William Faulkner: A Study in Humanism from Metaphor to Discourse_" _Journal of English and Germanic Philology_ 66 (July 1967) 479-480

Flanigan, Sister Thomas. "The Hound and Metaphysics" _America: National Catholic Weekly Review_ 101 (May 16, 1959) 331-333

_____. "The Use of Analogy in the _Summa Contra Gentiles_" _Modern Schoolman_ 35 (Nov. 1957) 21-37
A Thomistic view. The similitude between God and creatures is one of participation since God causes being.

Flasche, Hans. "Similitudo Templi; (on the history of a metaphor)" _Deutsche Vierteljahrsschrift für Literaturwissenschaft und Geistesgeschichte_ 23 (1949) 81-125

Flaum, Lawrence S. "A study of the understanding which 4th, 5th and 6th grade pupils in the Elementary School of Crawford, Nebraska have for figures of speech which appear in the basic history textbooks used in each of those grades" Greeley: Colorado State College of Education Field Study no. 1, 1945
History text figures showed 59.5 percent accuracy in understanding similes, 66.2 percent in personification, 75 percent in metaphors. He concluded that groups as a whole did not appear to have a high degree of understanding of the figures of speech on which they were tested.

Flavin, Robert J. "Animal Imagery in the Works of Nathanael West" Thoth (Syracuse University Department of English) 6 no. 2 (1965) 25-30

Fleischer, Walter. Synästhesie und Metapher in Verlaines Dichtungen Versuch einer vergleichenden Darstellung PhD diss. Greifswald: Ernst-Moritz Arndt Universität 1911

Fleissner, O. S. "Bilder und Gleichnisse in Gottfried Kellers Prosawerken" PMLA 55 (1940) 484-510

Fleming, Noel. "Recognizing and Seeing-As" The Philosophical Review 66 (Apr. 1957) 161-179 (cf. reply by Stadler)
A necessary but not a sufficient condition of recognizing X as Y by sight is seeing X as Y.

Flesch, Josef. Metaphysik des Symbols und der Metapher PhD diss. Bonn 1934
A Thomistic account of symbol and metaphor.

Fletcher, Angus. Allegory: The Theory of a Symbolic Mode Ithaca, New York: Cornell University Press 1964 (Review by W. Matthews)

Flint, F. Cudworth. "Metaphor in Contemporary Poetry" The Symposium 1 (July 1930) 310-335
Poetry is a form of vision. The poet sees the object he contemplates. All descriptions in science and of reality are metaphorical. "Logical sequences and traditional imagery are neither flexible nor subtle enough to render accurately the nuances of contemporary perception."

Flint, F. S. "The History of Imagism" The Egoist 2 (1915) 70-71

_____. "Imagisme" Poetry 1 (1913) 198-200

_____, and E. Pound. "Imagism" The Modern Tradition Richard Ellmann and Charles Feidelson Jr., eds. New York: Oxford University Press 1965 pp. 142-145

Foakes, R. A. "Suggestions for a New Approach to Shakespeare's Imagery" Shakespeare Survey 5 (1952) 81-92

Fodor, Jerry, and Jerrold Katz, eds. The Structure of Language New Jersey: Prentice-Hall 1964

Fogarty, Daniel. "An Approach to Metaphor" Roots for a New Rhetoric New York: Columbia University Teachers College, Bureau of Publications 1959 pp. 36-38
I. A. Richards' theory of metaphor is said to rest on his theory of abstraction. One abstracts an attribute from one reference and applies it to another reference. Fogarty agrees with this view.

Fogle, Richard H. The Imagery of Keats and Shelley: A Comparative Study Hamden, Conn.: Archon Books 1962 [1949]
Imagery includes metaphor and may be cognitive. Metaphor is an analogy or comparison of different "planes of consciousness." It depends heavily on context. It creates unity in diversity, and places feeling beside natural objects to objectify it. Keats and Shelley are compared for imagery of the types: sense, synaesthetic, empathetic, concrete and abstract, e.g. Keats is empathetic, Shelley not. In general, Keats is more rich, concrete and intense; Shelley more abstract and evanescent.

_____. "Metaphors of Organic Unity in Pope's 'Essay on Criticism'" Tulane Studies in English 13 (1963) 51-58

Folsom, J. K. "Mutation as Metaphor in The Education of Henry Adams" ELH 30 (June 1963) 162-174

Fónagy, Ivan. Die Metaphern in der Phonetik; ein Beitrag zur Entwicklungsgeschichte des wissenschaftlichen Denkens The Hague Mouton 1963
Books on phonetics and linguistics and for singers are rich in metaphors. Every sound has its own color, pitch is high or low, the voice is neutral, white, hard, brown, red, majestic, thoughtful, tart, cutting, trailing, broken, wet. Vowels are light, dark, sharp, thin, wide, feminine, masculine, hard, strong, fine, high, deep. Furthermore in tests with various age groups of normal subjects and those born deaf and blind we find that the sound i is in comparison with u, smaller, less thick, more lively, less sad, more friendly, less dark, less strong, harder, more beautiful, less bitter, less hollow. The front row vowels are light, the back row are dark. Consonants are designated metaphorically with the same or similar terms. Tests show that the sound r is more wild, rough, swirling, less smooth, more masculine than l. C is more wet than t. M and l are more sweet than t or k. R is more red than k. Metaphorical designations of sound characteristics are discussed e.g. frequency is high, sharp, thick, strong, heavy. Phonetic metaphors outside of phonetics are discussed e.g. in rhetoric, poetry, children's play, etc. He gives the acoustical and physiological basis of phonetic metaphors. Fónagy presents the unconscious basis of phonetic metaphor e.g. the consonants constrict air passages and show the imposition of the will on an obstructed free flow of air suggesting a

Freudian analysis based on the unconscious mind and its dynamics. Because r was found harder than l there is the suggestion that r may be found where wild, bitter struggles are considered. Also r was seen to emphasize masculine hardness e.g. in Baudelaire's poem "Don Juan aux Enfers." Fónagy thus refers to the r (after Hollós) as a masculine "erectional" sound. We also use sexual metaphors in speaking about speech e.g. "flow of speech." Fónagy suggests that such phrases as "to be in everybody's mouth" point to fantasies of verbal-oral incorporation. The last chapter is entitled, "Why Metaphor." The poet as well as the scientific grammarian describe metaphorically as if they were unable to describe correctly, as a child might say when his foot has gone numb, "I have soda water in my foot." This renders the unknown by means of the known. The scientist rather than the writer uses (necessary) metaphor in this way. Correct knowledge of how vowels (back and front) were obtained was slow. The grammarian uses metaphor because the object to be named, voice formation and accent, is unknown and scientifically unanalyzed. Grammarians, mystics, writers, young children, all of whom know nothing of front or back position of the tongue nevertheless understand which vowels are light and which dark. Such a first imperfect systematization can lead to a more scientific system. Fónagy bases the metaphorical character of sound on unconscious concepts (pre-conscious fantasy, free-association, etc.) He states, "In the metaphorical designation of a speech-sound is reflected one or the other unconscious impression connected with the quality of the sound, and that in a spontaneous manner." Metaphorical thinking is a "goal-oriented fantasying." The difference between the sound i and u is not based on conscious comparison of acoustic and articulatory qualities but rather on a pre-conscious (partly unconscious) fantasizing which is evoked by certain qualities of these sounds. The speech sounds are connected with the same metaphors in various languages and cultures and as well as for children born deaf. Thus such metaphors seem not to be arbitrary. They are probably based on kinaesthetic and tactile stimuli as well as preconscious and unconscious concepts connected with the movements of the speech organs.

Foote, E. "Anatomy of Analogy" Modern Schoolman 18 (Nov. 1940) 12-16

Force, Roland and Maryanne. "Keys to Cultural Understanding" Science 133 (Apr. 21, 1961) 1202-1206

Metaphors are culture-determined and give insight into culture and social organization. Examples from the Palau Islands are: elder females are called "mature coconuts," "my hand" is "my five," the structure of the turmeric plant serves as a model of their social relationships. All thought and perception are metaphoric. Metaphors are models of interpretation of our environment and the universe.

Fordyce, David. Dialogues Concerning Education fourth edition Cork 1775
There is a) capricious imagination based on false analogies, and b) true imagination reporting the natural analogies established by God (cf. Coleridge on imagination). Correspondence exists in nature, e.g. between beauty (images) and the moral realm. "Upon this foundation of Analogy, then, is the whole Superstructure of Metaphor, Allegory, and no small Part of Fable raised."

Forehand, Walter E. Jr. "The Literary Use of Metaphor in Plautus and Terence" PhD diss. University of Texas 1968

Foss, Martin. Symbol and Metaphor Lincoln: University of Nebraska Press 1966 [1949] (Review by Wimsatt)
Metaphor is a process of tension and energy which transcends all finite symbols. It transcends the many to realize a unity in tension and links the known with the unknown. He notes that every sentence, since it goes beyond dictionary definitions, is metaphorical.

Foster, Genevieve. "The Archetypal Imagery of T. S. Eliot" PMLA 60 (1945) 567-585

Foster, Steven. "Eidetic Imagery and Imagiste Perception" Journal of Aesthetics and Art Criticism 27 (Winter 1969) 133-145
Some of Jaensch's work on eidetic imagery parallels the imaginative intuition of the imagists. The images of the imagist have meanings and juxtaposed meanings allowing one a unique method of beholding, of perceiving reality.

Foultz, Frederick. (Made a collection of figures in everyday speech) M.A. thesis Berkeley: University of California c. 1957 (Source: I. Hungerland Poetic Discourse)

Fowler, B. H. "Imagery of the Prometheus Bound" American Journal of Philology 78 (Apr. 1957) 173-184

Fowler, Henry W. "Metaphor" A Dictionary of Modern English Usage second edition Oxford: Clarendon Press 1965 pp. 359-363
Churchill said that politicians often use metaphors to speak strongly because they are not sure what they want to say. Metaphors illuminate and vivify. Our language is built on metaphors. There is not a clear boundary between "live" and "dead" metaphors. He mentions metaphors which are unsustained, overdone, spoilt, mixed. One may change metaphors rapidly.

_____. "Some Notes on Metaphor in Journalism" Metaphor (Society for Pure English, tract no. 11) Oxford: The Clarendon Press 1922 pp. 4-10

France, Anatole. The Garden of Epicurus Alfred Allinson, trans. London: John Lane, The Bodley Head 1920 pp. 207-228

"The spirit possesses God in proportion as it participates in the absolute" literally translated becomes "The breath is seated by the shining one in the bushel of the part it takes in what is altogether loosed." Language is a metaphorical extension of words once denoting physical objects.

Francioni, Giacomo. "Review of Lauretano Ambiguità e metafora" Rivista di Estetica fasc. 2° (May-Aug. 1966) 283-286

Frankel, Hans. "Poetry and Painting: Chinese and Western Views of Their Convertibility" Comparative Literature 9 (1957) 289-307

Fränkel, Hermann. Die Homerischen Gleichnisse Göttingen 1921

Fraser, Donald. Metaphors in the Gospel London: Nisbet 1885; New York 1885

Fraser, William. "Metaphors in Aeschines The Orator" PhD diss. Johns Hopkins University 1897
A classification of metaphors based on subject matter or content. He distinguishes three kinds of metaphors: 1) naive or common, e.g. to "fall short," 2) intentional or purposeful, 3) technical, e.g. "horn" used as "wing of an army."

Fraunce, Abraham. The Arcadian Rhetorike London 1588

Frazer, Sir James. The Golden Bough New York: Macmillan 1923

Frazer, Ray. "Origin of the Term 'Image'" ELH 27 (June 1960) 149-161
"Image" is an ambiguous term. Its meaning was extended in the eighteenth century from that of a picture copy to that of a figure or metaphor. Dryden was the first to use image as referring to metaphor.

Freimarck, V. "Joseph Trapp's Advanced Conception of Metaphor" Philological Quarterly 29 (Oct. 1950) 413-416

Freire, Francisco José. [Candido Lusitano, pseudonym] Diccionario Poetico, para o uso dos que principião a exercitar-se na poesia portugueza Lisbon: Na Of. de S. T. Ferreira 1794
Similes in the Portuguese language.

Frentz, Thomas. "Some Psychological Aspects of Metaphor" M.A. thesis, University of Wisconsin 1967
An investigation of how the connotative meanings of metaphorical constituents are combined psychologically, e.g. whether the connotative meaning of the tenor is a function of the combined connotations of tenor and vehicle. He uses Richards' notions of tenor and vehicle and Osgood's connotative measurement scale.

Freud, Sigmund. The Complete Psychological Works of Sigmund Freud James Strachey, trans. London: Hogarth Press 1964 Freud uses metaphors to analyze dreams and deep mental ("primary") processes, e.g. "point" may refer to breast withdrawal in infancy and inner conflict. Although Freud does not say so metaphor may be thought of as a defense mechanism and vice versa, e.g. "condensation" is a metaphorical process. Only those elements are condensed into one picture which in emotional content are identical. Other defense mechanisms are repression, projection, introjection, sublimation, etc. We may perhaps think of Freud's "mechanisms" as tropes, metaphors or rhetorical devices. Freud also uses many bold metaphors by means of which he presents his own theory, e.g. mental events are described as the flow of fluid (flooding, pressure, dams, etc.), battles (e.g. "regression" is likened to troops giving ground in the face of the enemy), helmsman, horse and rider (ego and id), personification of mental events, play within a play (unconscious eludes a shrewd censor, etc.), "depth" processes and other spatial metaphors, etc.

_____. Jokes and Their Relation to the Unconscious James Strachey, trans. New York: W. Norton 1960; London: Hogarth 1960 Jokes combine opposites, reveal the hidden, are condensations as is dream-work, couple the dissimilar, are double meanings, are displacements, are formed in the unconscious, serve to give pleasure, lift repressions, begin with play and may be formed by analogy, e.g. alcoholidays.

_____. An Outline of Psycho-Analysis James Strachey, trans. New York: W. W. Norton 1949 esp. ch. 5 on condensation

Freudenthal, H., ed. The Concept and the Role of the Model in Mathematics and Natural and Social Science New York: Gordon and Breach 1961; Dordrecht, Holland: D. Reidel 1961

Freydorf, Roswith von. "Die bildhafte Sprache in Shelleys Lyrik" PhD diss. Freiburg: Quakenbrück 1935

Fricke, Gerhard. Die Bildlichkeit in der Dichtung des Andreas Gryphius. Materialien und Studien zum Formproblem des deutschen Literaturbarock. (Neue Forschung 17) Berlin: Junker und Dünnhaupt Verlag 1933

Friedland, Nathan. "Vergleich und Metapher in Voltaires Dramen" PhD diss. Marburg 1895

Friedman, Norman. E. E. Cummings: The Art of His Poetry Baltimore: Johns Hopkins University Press 1960

_____. "Imagery" Encyclopedia of Poetry and Poetics Alex Preminger, ed. Princeton University Press 1965 pp. 363-370 An extensive discussion of imagery and metaphor. "Imagery" is an ambiguous term sometimes referring to 1) literal sensuous images, 2) metaphors or figures of speech, or 3) non-discursive symbolic visions.

_____. "Imagery: From Sensation to Symbol" Journal of Aesthetics and Art Criticism 21 (Sept. 1953) 25-37
Imagery may be 1) mental, 2) rhetorical (metaphor), or 3)symbolic. Many images are ideas and are not visual at all. Poets may use the same images as literal and as metaphorical. Different people may have different images when reading a poem. Archetypes (often-repeated images) are stressed and examples given. Spurgeon's view that imagery reflects the author's tastes is rejected. Image often means merely a meaning.

Friedrich, Hugo. "Einblendungstechnik und Metaphern" Die Struktur der modernen Lyrik Hamburg: Rowohlt 1968 [1956] pp. 206-211
When Lorca transfers a forest into a clock this is a complete and equal interchange, not just metaphor as comparison. For modern and baroque poetry, metaphor is artificial and fantastic. Metaphor often forms a world opposite the real world. It is no longer an image to be looked at next to reality. Some types of metaphor are: attributive, verbal, appositive (leave off the article and shorten syntax), e.g. "church, stone woman" (Jouve); juxtaposition, e.g. "gold-coined afternoon" (Krolow); genitive-metaphor of identification, e.g. "The water's straw" (Eluard); genitive-metaphor involving realm exchange or semantic dissonance, e.g. "Deaf screams of the mirror" (Ungaretti). Modern poetry may be compared to "dissonance" in modern music and architecture. Freedom is sought in dissonant metaphor. The poet is alone with language but only language can save him.

Friend-Pereira, F. J. "Rosa Mystica: A Floral Metaphor in Middle-English Poetry" New Review 19 (1944) 9-22

Friquegnon, Marie-Louise. "Metaphor and Make-Believe" American Philosophical Association Bulletin 68th annual meeting of the Western Division, May 1970 Abstract of paper p. 10
Metaphor, make-believe and perspectives are discussed in relation to religion.

Frost, Henry W. "Figures of Speech" Galaxy 24 (1877) 204-210
Non-material concepts derive metaphorically from material ones. To know is to compare and thus to use metaphor. They permeate our thinking and constitute language. Metaphor must, however, be used with caution at times. He follows Max Müller's views.

Frost, Robert. Selected Prose of Robert Frost Hyde Cox and Edward Lathem, eds. New York: Holt, Rinehart and Winston 1949 esp. "Education by Metaphor"
People go to school to be educated because "they don't know when they are being fooled by a metaphor, an analogy, a parable...." "Poetry provides the one permissible way of saying one thing and meaning another." "All thinking...is metaphori-

cal." "The richest accumulation of the ages is the noble metaphors we have rolled up."

Fruit, John P. "The Evolution of Figures of Speech" _Modern Language Notes_ 3 (1888) 251-253
"Idea" comes from Greek "to see." An idea is a picture of what we have seen. The order of mental process is sensation, intuition, inference, ideation (picturing how the thing sensed and inferred must look). Cognition, feeling and conation need realization so that, e.g. we feel what is cognized. Metaphor provides realization by characterizing. It is an implied resemblance.

Fry, William F. _Sweet Madness: A Study of Humor_ Palo Alto, Calif.: Pacific Books 1963
Humor is metaphorical play and paradox. Paradoxes are shiftings of opposites, such as real-unreal, finite-infinite, process-void.

Frye, Northrop. _Anatomy of Criticism_ Princeton: Princeton University Press 1957
He combines Aristotle's and Aquinas' views on metaphor. "Metaphor: A relation between two symbols, which may be simple juxtaposition [literal metaphor], a rhetorical statement of likeness or similarity [descriptive metaphor], an analogy of proportion among four terms [formal metaphor], an identity of an individual with its class [concrete universal or archetypal metaphor], or statement of hypothetical identity [anagogic metaphor]." Literal metaphor is like the Chinese ideogram or "A;B," a simple juxtaposition. It may be merely a visual juxtaposition (visual metaphor). If the two terms are identified it is myth. Metaphor combines different universes of discourse. It may serve as a scientific hypothesis. Much of what we say may be reduced to the metaphor of a diagram.

_____. "The Archetypes of Literature" _Myth and Method: Modern Theories of Fiction_ James E. Metler Jr., ed. Lincoln: University of Nebraska Press 1960. Also _Kenyon Review_ 13 (1951) 92-110

_____. "Blake's Treatment of the Archetype" _English Institute Essays_ Alan Downer, ed. New York: Columbia University Press 1951 pp. 170-196

_____. "Elementary Teaching and Elemental Scholarship" _PMLA_ 79 (May 1964) 11-18

_____. _Fables of Identity: Studies in Poetic Myth_ New York: Harcourt 1963

_____. "Levels of Meaning in Literature" _Kenyon Review_ 12 (1950) 246-252

_____. "The Motive for Metaphor" The Educated Imagination Toronto: Canadian Broadcasting Corporation 1963 pp. 1-11
In metaphor one says "X is Y" which is logically impossible yet still significant and meaningful for man. "The motive for metaphor, according to Wallace Stevens, is a desire to associate, and finally to identify, the human mind with what goes on outside it, because...although we may know in part, as Paul says, we are also a part of what we know."

_____. "Yeats and the Language of Symbolism" University of Toronto Quarterly 17 (1947) 1-17

Fucke, Erhard. "Metaphern" Erziehungskunst: Zeitschrift zur Pädagogik (Stuttgart: Rudolf Steiners) 24 (Jan. 1960) 260-265

Fuller, M. E. "Subtle Metaphor: Crane's The Open Boat" English Journal 57 (May 1968) 708-709

Funk, Robert W. Language, Hermeneutic, and Word of God New York: Harper and Row 1966 esp. "The Parable as Metaphor" (Review by Perrin)
Metaphor is a transference of judgement, a context shift, having mystery, requiring participation in it, and creative of new untranslatable meaning. It is a unique method of knowing. In apprehending metaphor we make our own interpretations. There are no final ones, not even in religion. Parables are themselves metaphors.

Furbank, P. N. "Do We Need the Terms 'Image' and 'Imagery'?" Critical Quarterly 9 (1968) 335-345

Gáldi, L. "Review of Tudor Vianu Problemele metaphorei și alte studii..." Acta Linguistica. Academiae Scientiarum Hungaricae 8 (1958) 373-379

Gale, Herbert. The Use of Analogy in the Letters of Paul Philadelphia: Westminster Press 1964

Gale, Robert. "Art Imagery in Henry James' Fiction" American Literature 29 (March 1957) 47-63

_____. The Caught Image: Figurative Language in the Fiction of Henry James Chapel Hill: University of North Carolina Press 1964

Galinsky, Hans. "'Naturae Cursus': Der Weg einer antiken kosmologischen Metapher von der Alten in die Neue Welt" Ein Beitrag zu einer historischen Metaphorik der Weltliteratur Arcadia 1 (1966) 277-311; 2 (1966) 11-78, 139-172 Heidelberg: C. Winter 1968

_____. Die spätantiken Quellen einer kosmologischen Metapher Shakespeares und der anglo-amerikanischen Tradition. Ein Beitrag zur abendländischen Kontinuität dichterischer Bilder. Festschrift für Bischof Dr. Albert Stohr Ludwig Lehnert, ed. Mainz: Grünewald 1960 esp. vol. 2

Galton, Francis. "Statistics of Mental Imagery" Mind 5 (1880) 301-318
An attempt to use statistics "to define the different degrees of vividness with which different persons have the faculty of recalling familiar scenes under the form of mental pictures." Great individual differences were found. Some see no images at all.

Gang, T. M. "Hobbes and the Metaphysical Conceit--A Reply" Journal of the History of Ideas 17 (June 1956) 418-421
On G. Watson's "Hobbes and the Metaphysical Conceit." The conceit is not a daring metaphor but a play on words, or quibble. The conceit is "metaphysical" not because it is a wild comparison, but rather because it is a comparison between abstract and concrete where the concrete (vehicle) is taken seriously.

García-Girón, E. "La adjetivación modernista en Rubén Darío" Nueva Revista de Filología Hispánica 13 (1959) 345-351
On metaphor and synaesthesia.

García Lorca, Federico. Obras Completas Madrid: Aguilar 1967
"The metaphor unites two antagonistic worlds by means of an 'equine jump' of the imagination."

Gardiner, A. The Theory of Speech and Language Oxford: The Clarendon Press 1932 [1960] esp. pp. 165-170
Metaphor is a transfer or blending of object and language, "speech obsessed by language," which enriches feeling, renders

the abstract in terms of the concrete and visible (or pictorial). Metaphors are sometimes a natural unconscious principle or use of language, and sometimes are deliberate. New metaphors are difficult to obtain.

Gardner, William. "The Influence of the Metaphor upon Semasiology" The Classical Weekly 28 (1935) 201-205
Shows the ways in which metaphor by means of likeness and a sudden act of mind changes the meaning of words in the development of language.

Garlande, Jean de. Poetria ca. 1250
Traditional view of metaphor.

Gärtner, Helga. Bibliographie zur antiken Bildersprache Heidelberg 1964

Gates, Eunice. The Metaphors of Luis de Góngora PhD thesis Philadelphia: University of Pennsylvania Press 1933

Genther, Ludwig. Über den Gebrauch der Metaphern bei Iuvenal Programm des Gymnasiums Wittenberg 1878

George, François. Harmony of the World Guy le Fevre, trans. Borderie 1529
There is a correspondence of all things in the world, e.g. metals of the same principle as Mars, plants of the same principle as Jupiter.

George, Scott. "The Eighteenth Century Philosophy of Metaphor" PhD diss. Vanderbilt University 1943
Metaphor is "whenever we speak of one thing in terms of another, or when thoughts of two different things are supported by a single unit of meaning (word, phrase, sentence) whose meaning is a resultant of their interaction." The tenor and vehicle form an organic unity, each implying the other. New meanings cannot be said in any other way. The eighteenth century was characterized by atomistic views of thought and language (a one to one correlation between word, idea and object), a mechanical "association of ideas" and faculty psychology. This led to a view of metaphor as abnormal discourse or mere ornament, a set of *a priori* rules for the use of metaphor which paralyzed its function, and an unawareness that their theories of atomism, literalism, etc. were metaphorical and that they were using metaphors. The eighteenth century offered an unsatisfactory view of the nature of metaphor.

Gerber, Adolf. "Naturpersonifikation in Poesie und Kunst der Alten" Jahrbücher für klassische Philologie supplement to vol. 8 pp. 214-317

Gerber, Gustav. Die Sprache als Kunst three vols, in one Hildesheim: Goerg Ohms 1961 [1871-1874]

A major work on metaphor. An extensive account of language as an aesthetic object is given. Metonymy, synecdoche, sound figures, metaphor, etc. are discussed including historical accounts (e.g. Müller's radical and poetic metaphor), and compared with other tropes.

Gerber, H. E. "Reynolds Pendulum Figure and the Watchmaker" Philological Quarterly 38 (Jan. 1959) 66-83

Gerhard, E. S. "Origin of Figurative Speech and Faded Metaphors from the Classics" Education 49 (Jan.-Feb. 1929) 278-284, 355-371

Gerlach, F. D. Homers Einfluss auf die bildende Kunst d. Griechen Programm 1867

_____. Theorie der Rhetorik und Stilistik (Source: Stutterheim 1941)

Gertel, Zunilda. "La Metáfora en la estética de Borges" Hispania 52 (March 1969) 33-38
A summary of Borges' work on metaphor: For Borges metaphor is a spontaneous, emotive, identification of two or more concepts or images and must be based on experience. Any metaphor is a possible experience. It arises out of necessity due to the poverty of language. Borges once classified metaphors as 1) parallelism 2) synaesthetic 3) abstract-concrete 4) static-dynamic 5) antithesis. Metaphor requires a well-formed state of poetry. At the beginning and end of literature is myth. Borges believes that by the time of the Iliad all the necessary affinities and metaphors had been recognized and written.

Gibbons, Thomas. A Course of Lectures on Oratory and Criticism London: Printed for J. Johnson 1777 esp. lecture 22

_____. Rhetoric: Or a View of Its Principle Tropes and Figures Menston, England: The Scholar Press Limited 1969 [London 1767] esp. ch. 2 "The Metaphor Considered"
Metaphor is a contracted simile, a word removed from its proper signification to another on the basis of comparison. It means only what is intended, depends on context, and should be consistent, unmixed and used with discretion. A chain of metaphors results in allegory. He notes that metaphor is found in all subjects.

Gibson, Priscilla. "The Uses of James' Imagery: Drama Through Metaphor" PMLA 69 (1954) 1076-1084

Gibson, William M. "Metaphor in the Plot of The Ambassadors" New England Quarterly 24 (Sept. 1951) 291-305

Gide, André. "The Reflexive Image" The Modern Tradition Richard Ellmann and Charles Feidelson Jr., eds. New York: Oxford

University Press 1965 pp. 188-189

Gill, Jerry H. "Professor Edwards' Confusions" Mind 76 (Oct. 1967) 587-591

_____. "Review of Ian Ramsey Models and Mystery" Philosophical Review 74 (Oct. 1965) 550-553
Gill asks of Ramsey, "How does one distinguish between mystery and nonsense?" How do we know something is disclosed? He thinks Ramsey's approach is, nevertheless, better than the theologian's which retreats into "existential encounter."

Gilman, L. "Review of F. J. Wilstach Dictionary of Similes" North American Review 205 (Jan. 1917) 137-142

Gimeno, Amalio Gimeno y Cabãnas, Conde de. La metáfora y el símil en la literatura científica Madrid: Establecimiento tipográfico Huelves y compañía 1927

Ginsberg, Leon. "A Case of Synaesthesia" American Journal of Psychology 34 (1923) 582-589

Girardot, Rafael G. "El lenguaje de la metáfora y los géneros literarios" Jorge L. Borges: Ensayo de interpretación Madrid: Insula 1959 pp. 54-82
Universal history and philosophy are, for Borges, the history of a few metaphors. He stresses the ability of metaphor to correctly reveal secret and unlimited or multiple appearances of reality. Metaphors are not invented but are found. To metaphorize is only to reunite and recreate. Metaphor is the momentary intuitive contact of two images.

Glazier, Lyle. "The Nature of Spenser's Imagery" Modern Language Quarterly 16 (1955) 300-310

Gluskina, A. "K voprosu o stanovleniyi poeticheskovo obraza" Izvestiya Akademiya nauk SSSR, otdeleniye literatury i yazyka 7 (1948) 59-76
On the question of the definition of the poetic image.

Goblot, E. Le vocabulaire philosophique Paris 1920

Goheen, R. F. The Imagery of Sophocles' 'Antigone': A Study of Poetic Language and Structure Princeton University Press 1951

Gold, G. William Faulkner: A Study in Humanism from Metaphor to Discourse Norman: University of Oklahoma Press 1966 (Review by Flanagan)

Goldammer, Kurt. "Das Schiff der Kirche. Ein antiker Symbolbegriff aus der politischen Metaphorik in eschatologischer und ekklesiologischer Untersuchung" Theologische Zeitschrift 6 (1950) 232-237

Golden, Leon. "Aeschylus and Ares: A Study in the Use of Military Imagery by Aeschylus" PhD diss. University of Chicago 1958

Golden, Martha H. "Stage Imagery in Shakespearean Studies" Shakespearean Research Opportunities: The Report of the MLA Conference Riverside: University of California no. 1 1965 pp. 1-20

Goldsmith, Oliver. "On Metaphors" Works J. W. M. Gibbs, ed. London: George Bell and Sons 1908 vol. 1 pp. 361-377
"The metaphor is a shorter simile, or rather a kind of magical coat, by which the same idea assumes a thousand different appearances." It should be used sparingly, naturally and should arise from emotions. Any term can be used metaphorically. A metaphor cannot be pictured. He attacks metaphors in Hamlet's soliloquy on suicide because its metaphors cannot be represented by a painting on canvas.

Goldstein, Kurt. Aftereffects of Brain Injuries in War: Their Evaluation and Treatment New York: Grune and Stratton 1942 [1948] esp. pp. 152-207
Brain damaged patients could not use metaphor, compare implicit properties or understand metaphors.

_____. Language and Language Disturbances New York: Grune and Stratton 1948 [1960]
He treats imagery, imagery deviations and language deviations.

Goldthwait, John T. "Aristotle on Metaphor" (unpublished essay 1970)
A detailed discussion of Aristotle's theory of metaphor suggesting that his four kinds of metaphor (genus-species, etc.) are really based on four term analogies. Analogy involves class inclusion here. Metaphor for Aristotle is not to evoke images but to give names to things.

Gombrich, E. H. "On Physiognomic Perception" Daedalus (Winter 1960) 228-241

_____. "Visual Metaphors of Value in Art" Symbols and Values: An Initial Study L. Bryson, L. Finkelstein, H. M. Maciver, and R. McKeon, eds. New York: Harper and Brothers 1954 pp. 255-281
An art object embodies the metaphor of an equilibrium (negation, attraction, etc.) of values (e.g. nobility, security, simplicity, etc.). The metaphor involves a two-sided untranslatable experience dependent on the context and cannot have fixed symbolic meaning. We think in metaphors which captivate us. "Seeing cannot be separated from knowing (cf. seeing-as)."

Gonda, Jan. Remarks on Similes in Sanskrit Literature Leiden: E. J. Brill 1949

Góngora, don Luis de. The Solitudes of don Luis de Góngora Cambridge University Press 1965 (See Gates, Kane, B. Müller, Alonso, et al. on Góngora's metaphors and other of Góngora's works.)

González, Alberto Navarro. "Las dos redacciones de la *Agudeza*" *Cuadernos de Literatura* 4 (1948) 201-213 (on Gracián) He regards this as the most interesting book on baroque aesthetics. The first (1642) and second edition are compared showing that there is an increase of rules, examples, observations and thirteen new orations. The doctrine of *agudeza* (wit) remains the same. Brevity and elegance are diminished for the sake of clarity and intensity in the second edition.

González, Rafael. "Symbol and Metaphor in Náhuatl Poetry" *ETC* 25 (1968) 437-444

Goodman, Nelson. *Languages of Art* Indianapolis: Bobbs-Merrill 1968
Metaphor is a striking reclassification or change of several different "realms" (or universes of discourse). It is a deviation from past custom or habit. Non-verbal metaphors are also possible, e.g. a cartoon. Metaphors can be true or false. Tests apply to them such as comparison, checking of circumstance, looking again, etc.

Goodsell, Jane. "As Silly as a Simile" *Reader's Digest* 92 (June 1968) 69-70 (condensed from *Christian Herald*)
Similes are confused, e.g. brown as a berry, cute as a bug, etc.

Goodwin, Charles. "Apollonius Rhodius: His Figures, Syntax and Vocabulary" PhD diss. Johns Hopkins University 1890 (See *The Similes of Apollonius Rhodius* Johns Hopkins University Circulars 9 no. 81 1890)

Gordon, William J. *Synectics* New York: Harper and Row 1961
"Synectics" means from the Greek "joining together of different and apparently irrelevant elements." Metaphor construction by means of free-association is used as a method of discovery and problem solving in industry, the sciences, education, etc. Groups have been formed to create new ideas and inventions with this method. Part of the aim of synectics is to uncover the psychological mechanism basic to creative activity.

Gorrigan, Matthew. "Metaphor in William Blake: A Negative View" *Journal of Aesthetics and Art Criticism* (Winter 1969) 187-199

Gorter, Hermannus. *De interpretatione Aeschyli metaphorarum* PhD diss. University of Amsterdam Leiden: E. J. Brill 1889

Gottfried, Rudolf. "The Pictorial Element in Spenser's Poetry" *ELH* 19 (1952) 203-213

The pictorial element is only a minor ingredient of Spencer's art. Most of his imagery is auditory, not visual.

Gottlieb, Stephen A. "The Metaphors of Wanderer" Neuphilologische Mitteilungen 66 (1965) 145-148

Gottschall, R. Poetik Breslau 1858

Gottsched, Johann C. Ausgewählte Werke fourteen vols. Joachim Birke, ed. Berlin: Walter De Gruyter and Company 1968 esp. "Versuch einer Critischen Dichtkunst," "Ausführliche Redekunst," "Grundlegung einer Deutschen Sprachkunst" (Summary in Phelps)
Metaphor is decorative and misrepresents. Four attributes of a good metaphor are: 1) there is real similarity between figure and thing, 2) the figure is not contemptible or ridiculous, 3) the trope is not sought too far afield, 4) it makes everything more tangible than the actual experience.

Gourmont, Rémy de. "La métaphore" Esthétique de la langue française Paris: Mercure de France 1955 [1938] pp. 113-140

_____. Le Problème du Style Paris: Soc. du Mercure 1902 esp. ch. 7 pp. 83-107 (cf. Rémy de Gourmont: Selections from His Works Richard Aldington, trans. Chicago: P. Covici 1928 vol. 2 pp. 425-435)
Visual figures are needed. Style transforms words to vision. In speech everything is images. Imagination is just association of images from the senses. The smoothest discourse is a tissue of rugged metaphors.

_____. "Psychologie de la Métaphore" La Revue Blanche (Paris) 17 no. 129 (1898) 279-292

Gracián, Baltasar y Morales. Agudeza y arte de ingenio Madrid: Huesca 1642; Madrid 1648, 1649, 1720, 1729; Madrid: Biblioteca de Filósofos Españoles 1929; Madrid 1944; Buenos Aires 1942, 1944, 1945, 1957. Also The Complete Works of Gracián 1663-1960; Lisbon 1659; Antwerp 1669. (Editions vary slightly in content. The Ovejero edition Sarmiento says is poor. He favors the 1649 enlarged Huesca edition (see E. Sarmiento entry for summary.)) (Review by T. May, see M. Woods, Coster, et al.) Translated into English as "The Mind's Wit and Art" by Leland Chambers PhD diss. University of Michigan 1962
Wit or conceit (agudeza) is the agreement between two or more extremes or knowable contrasts, contexts, or antitheses, expressed by an act of the understanding. The conceit as the result of an act of the intellect may be classified by means of a rational system of categories. Gracián says, "Mere understanding without wit or conceit is a sun without light, without rays," and "What beauty is for the eyes and harmony for the ears, the conceit is for the understanding." The mental is regarded as superior to the senses, although he does

speak of sensuous metaphor and emblem conceit. Poetry is not just accidental or an appeal to the senses. Art perfects nature by an effort of the mind and is more diverse than nature. The conceit reveals reality rather than mere appearance. Reality is conceited, a mass of contrasts and oppositions. The conceit is a profundity or subtlety which is a quality of and gives life to every form of expression. Each sense has or can have some artifice in it. It delights and is best enhanced if it has a moral.

The conceit allows man to transcend himself and to gain public renown for all eternity. Gracián holds an aristocratic conception of literary taste. The conceit is more than rhetoric. It is about the whole of man in his world. The conceit is appropriate for both prose and poetry.

The mind is at its best when creating conceits which are not immediately comprehensible. Gracián, nevertheless, does at times advocate moderation in the use of conceits (e.g. Discourse no. 60).

Gracián is said to be especially influenced by Aristotle. In accordance with Aristotle's view that poets imitate nature it is thought that poets should imitate other poets as well. Gracián accordingly gives about nine hundred examples from poets to serve as good models. His points are often revealed only by contemplating the examples.

Four kinds of simple wit are:

1) correlation - similitudes, rivalry of opposites, disproportions, proportions, comparisons, contrasts, etc.

2) ponderation - paradox, exaggeration, maxims, satire, moral criticism, all witty observations. Ponderation is an attentive consideration of reasons in order to arrive at a judgment. Synonyms of ponderation are remark, mediate, weigh, consider. A ponderation is a solution to a metaphor or paradox.

3) ratiocination - riddles, retorts, illusions, proofs, a way of linking extremes by a rational process.

4) invention - plots, tricks, inventions in action and speech, a linking of extremes in a single concept. [There seems to be much overlap between categories.]

The term semejanza (comparison) refers to metaphor or simile. Metáfora refers usually only to an extended metaphor or allegory. Mistro, mystery, is used at times in the more religious contexts. He speaks of mysterious ponderations.

All wit is a harmony of extremes, concord and dissonance. The greater the disparity between extremes the greater the conceit of improportion. By becoming harmonized they give pleasure. He states, "Contrast is a magnificent foundation for all wit." The conceit is a subtlety of thought rather than of words. "Verbal wit" may be exemplified by puns, and "wit of action" is shown by pulling the carpet out from under someone or by the story of Columbus' egg. (Someone stated that anyone could have discovered America. In a type of rebuttal another asked "Can you or anyone present make an egg stand on end?" Noone could. The challenger then placed the egg on end by slightly flattening and cracking one end of the egg.)

Ingenio refers to talent, the mind, imagination, the power of creating wit. It is an intellectual process and one can therefore have rules for constructing conceits.

The first treatise concerns itself with simple wit, the second with compound wit. In compound wit many acts and parts are unified in a moral, artful, framework of discourse to achieve sublimity.

Some examples of the conceit follow:
"O snow, my flame."
"The dawn goes well with the sun." [circularity]
"Watching the light, but blinded by the light."
"Past joy and present grief." [time contrasts]
"Make haste slowly."

Góngora "was a swan with his harmony, an eagle with his conceits, in every kind of wit eminent." An example given from Góngora: "Body with little blood,
Eyes with much night,
The life and death of men
Found him on that field."

Wit is also produced by mystery (mistro) between extremes involving cause-effect, addition, circumstances, contingencies, etc. Such mystery can be powerful and contains the truth, e.g. "Impossible that something sad
Could happen to me while I'm gone
Since I have seen you glad."
One may also respond or act mysteriously. [Perhaps Gracián could have used certain Zen responses as an example, e.g. the Zen master may hit his pupil on the head with a stick as a reply.]

Names may in many ways be the source of wit, e.g. comedias reduced to come (gobble) & dia (day), or Dios (God) reduced to Di & os (I gave you).

Wit may involve turning another's words against him. It may also involve overstatement, e.g. "No need for day--you are the sun."

About paradox he states, "A paradox is a miracle of truth," e.g. that sadness gives pleasure (cf. masochism); and dying can give one life.

A conceit may be a striking remark plus an explanation, e.g. Someone praised a dish of blancmange and kept saying 'Amazing.' When asked what he found so amazing he replied, "Amazing how much chicken is missing!"

As an example of caustic and critical wit he gives: "Lost time married Ignorance, and they had a son whom they called Thoughtlessness, he married Youth, from whom he had many children: I-didn't think, I-didn't know,..."

He states, "By means of an exaggeration, stupidity can be commented on splendidly."

Of one who wastes much time on small things one may say, "He lit a bonfire to fry a radish."

Wit is best if related to a particular, concrete context and occasion. In one example given to illustrate this, a hair in milk causes death of a great man. Besides regarding the hair as merely an example of the concrete, Gracián speaks of it as an "emblem." The particular represents something like a universal. Emblem literature was popular at the time of Gracián.

Equivocal words yield profundity. They have tension which may become released thus producing a conceit.

Graham, A. J. Metaphors and Similes from Henry Ward Beecher Pilgrim Press (before 1899)

Graham, Angus C. ed., trans., and introduction. Poems of the Late T'ang Baltimore: Penguin 1965
He stresses imagism in Chinese poetry and shows the development of metaphor and imagery in the poetry.

Graham, Gladys M. "Analogy: A Study in Proof and Persuasion Values" Quarterly Journal of Speech 14 (Nov. 1928) 534-542
Arguments absolutely true or false are too simple to be meaningful. Analogy, however, realistically combines proof value and persuasive value. It rests on a cause-effect basis. Persuasive value is like "physiological analogy"--a similarity between two objects or circumstances. A superficial example, however, is the juxtaposition of a cigarette and a pretty girl.

Graham, V. E. "The Imagery of Proust" PhD diss. Columbia University 1953

_____. "Water Imagery and Symbolism in Proust" Romanic Review 50 (1959) 118-128

Grant, C. K. "Review of Turbayne The Myth of Metaphor" Mind 74 (1965) 140-141

Grapow, Hermann. Vergleiche und andere bildliche Ausdrücke im Ägyptischen Leipzig: J. C. Hinrichs 1920
On Egyptian metaphor.

Graupner, B. "De metaphoris Plautinis et Terentianis" PhD diss. Breslau 1874

Graver, Lawrence. "'Typhoon': A Profusion of Similes" College English 24 (Oct. 1962) 62-64

Gray, James. "Abstract and Concrete Imagery" Essays in Criticism 4 (1954) 198-206, 211-212 (Reply by F. Bateson pp. 206-211)
Gray distinguishes between abstract imagery (involving intellectual inquiry) and concrete imagery (self-evident and immediate). Bateson says there is no hard and fast line between them. All of language and metaphor is abstract. There is no

exclusively concrete poetic image, only an illusion of immediacy. Metaphor cannot be visualized.

Green, Z. E. "Observations on the Epic Similes in The Faerie Queen" Philological Quarterly 14 (July 1935) 217-228

Greenberg, R. A. "Patterns of Imagery: Arnold's Shakespeare" Studies in English Literature 5 (Autumn 1965) 723-733

Greene, Herbert E. "A Grouping of Figures of Speech Based on the Principle of Their Effectiveness" PMLA N.S. 1 (1893) 432-450 From least to most figurative are: literal, synecdoche, metonymy, stated simile (which becomes a metaphor if one term is suppressed), implied simile (omission of copula), metaphor, personification, imperfect allegory, pure allegory (pure figure). Like Coleridge, he distinguishes between fancy and imagination. Trope concerns meaning change; figure, the order of words. Metaphor is literally false but to the imagination it is true.

Greene, Theodore M. The Arts and the Art of Criticism Princeton University Press 1965 [1946] esp. pp. 109-113
Metaphor is the "application of name or descriptive term to an object to which it is not literally applicable." The two terms illumine and vitalize one another, fuse yet keep their own character thus providing tension. Metaphor is a revealing analogical comparison. It creates new images. In literature it is mainly a juxtaposition of the general and particular.

_____. "The Arts as Revelation and Communication: A Perspective on Metaphor and Reality" The Hidden Harmony: Essays in Honor of Philip Wheelwright New York: Odyssey 1966 pp. 23-40
An elaboration of Wheelwright's views.

Greene, W. "Aristotle on Metaphor" The Classical Weekly 39 (Jan. 1946) 94-95
An attack of A. E. Housman "The Name and Nature of Poetry." Housman says simile and metaphor are inessential. Greene says this is wrong as seen by Housman's own poetry.

Greenfield, Stanley. "Grammar and Meaning in Poetry" PMLA 82 (Oct. 1967) 377-387

Greenough, James, and George Kittredge. Words and Their Ways in English Speech Boston: Beacon 1900

Gregory, Joshua. "Metaphor and Analogy" Fortnightly 171 (N.S. 165) (April 1949) 260-267
Metaphor is a contracted simile, a comparison or analogy of two instances of a general notion. Analogies are necessary to thought, often serving as hypotheses. Analogies belong to logic; metaphors belong to aesthetics.

Greiff, Louis K. "Image and Theme in Dylan Thomas' 'A Winter's Tale'" Thoth (Syracuse University) 7 (1965) 35-41

Greilich, August. "Dionysius Halicarnassensis quibus potissimum vocabullis ex artibus metaphorice ductis in scriptis rhetoricis usus sit" PhD diss. Breslau 1886

Greimas, A. J. "Les relations entre la linguistique structurale et la poétique" Revue Internationale des Sciences Sociales 19 (1967) 9-17

Grenet, Paul. Les origines de l'analogie philosophique dans les dialogues de platon Paris: Boivin 1948

Greverus, J. Über die Gleichnisse und Bilder Homers Programm 1839

Grierson, Sir Herbert. Rhetoric and English Composition second revised edition London: Oliver and Boyd 1945
"In their origin figures were just as natural as crying or a dog's wagging tail." Metaphor may clarify, add concreteness and express emotions. Its two terms are linked by means of emotion. "Always ask, 'Do the words reflect the speaker's feelings?'"

Griffin, Leland. "The Edifice Metaphor in Rhetorical Theory" Speech Monographs 27 (Nov. 1960) 279-292

Griffith, Albert J. "Heart Images in Hawthorne's Names Emerson Society Quarterly 43 (1966) 78-79

Griffith, C. "Edward Taylor and the Momentum of Metaphor" ELH 33 (Dec. 1966) 448-460
Metaphors are effective.

Grindon, Leopold. Figurative Language: Its Origin and Constitution London: J. Speirs 1879

Groesbeck, Hulda. "The Comprehension of Figurative Language by Elementary Children: A Study in Transfer" EdD diss. University of Oklahoma 1961
An examination of figurative language to determine its relation to vocabulary, reading ability, intelligence, etc. The texts used were seen to contain figures which impair reading. She concludes, "Children in upper elementary grades should be given specific instruction designed to enable them to interpret more skillfully the figurative expressions which they encounter in their reading." She quotes Dewey, "To be playful and serious at the same time is possible, and it defines the ideal mental condition."

Groff, P. J. "Figures of Speech on Poems by Children" Elementary School Journal 63 (Dec. 1962) 136-140
Children in the intermediate grades do use figures of speech

and should be given greater instruction in the nature and use of figures.

Groom, Bernard. "The Formation and Use of Compound Epithets in English Poetry from 1579" S.P.E. tract no. 49 Oxford 1937

Groos, Karl. "Das anschauliche Vorstellen beim poetischen Gleichnis" Zeitschrift für Ästhetik und allgemeine Kunstwissenschaft 9 (1914) 186-207

_____. "Das Gleichnis im Erzählen der Dichtung" Verein deutscher Philologen und Schulmänner in Basel 1907 (See Downey (1919) p. 108)
He found that imaginal understanding is not always present in apprehension of figures, nor is it always visual. Other senses may be involved. Some react to the figure intellectually, others emotively or sensuously. An image may be of either term or both, but it was found more often (81 of 82 cases) for the figurative part.

_____. "Der paradoxe Stil in Nietzsches 'Zarathustra'" Zeitschrift für angewandte Psychologie 7 no. 6 (1913) 467-529

Grose, Christopher W. "The Rhetoric of Miltonic Simile" PhD diss. Washington University 1966

Gross, Harvey. Sound and Form in Modern Poetry Ann Arbor: University of Michigan Press 1964
"All expressive rhythms are variations upon a pattern of expectation. The 'prosody of prose' functions first as those departures from the normal grammatical structures of the language which set up lesser or greater impulses of meaning." He speaks of deviations from expectations, e.g. expressive delays and surprising repetitions, and departures from usual word order.

Gross, Nathan. "Conceit and Metaphor in Racine's Les Plaideurs" Symposium 20 (Fall 1966) 226-236

Gross, P. Die Tropen und Figuren Ein Hilfsbuch für den deutschen, lateinischen und griechischen Unterricht an höheren Lehranstalten Köln: Roemke 1880

Gryglewicz, F. "Métaphores sportives chez Saint Paul" Roczniki teologiczno-Kanoniczne 7 (1960) 89-107

Guetti, James. The Limits of Metaphor Ithaca: Cornell University Press 1967 (Review by Peter Brooks Partisan Review 25 (Fall 1968) 636-638)

Guichard, Léon. "La métaphore" Sept études sur Marcel Proust Cairo: Éditions Horus 1942 pp. 306-320

Guillén, Jorge. Language and Poetry: Some Poets of Spain Harvard University Press 1961. "Poetic Language: Góngora" pp. 25-76
Góngora is highly metaphorical, using a number of types of this method, e.g. tensive, remote, multi-level, symmetrical, etc. For him reality can only be approached by means of metaphor or indirect discourse.

Guiraud, Pierre. Langage et versification d'après l'oeuvre de Paul Valéry PhD diss. Paris 1953 Société de Linguistique de Paris Collection Linguistique 56 Paris: G. Klincksieck 1953

Gummere, Francis B. The Anglo-Saxon Metaphor PhD diss. Halle: University of Freiburg 1881
Metaphor is the basis of poetry. It arose in unconscious spontaneous confusion by primitive people, and only later became conscious and led to simile. Language progresses by metaphorical extension. He discusses the metaphor in Anglo-Saxon writing.

_____. "Metaphor and Poetry" Modern Language Notes 1 (1888) 83-84
Originally metaphor was due to the picturesque confusion of names. It then became more conscious simile and literal statement. The poet creates pictures.

Gunter, Garland. "Archetypal Patterns in the Poetry of Tennyson 1823-1850" PhD diss. University of Maryland 1967

Guss, Donald L. "Donne's Petrarchism" Journal of English and Germanic Philology 64 (Jan. 1965) 17-28
On conceits.

Haacke, Wilmont. Handbuch des Feuilletons three vols. Emsdetten: Verlag Lechte 1951 vol. 1 ch. 5 "Poetische Metaphorik und Symbolik um das Feuilleton" (von 1686 bis zur Gegenwart) pp. 269-402

Habbel, Joseph. "Die Analogie zwischen Gott und Welt nach Thomas von Aquin" PhD diss. Regensburg 1921

Hablützel, M. E. Die Bildwelt Thomas Deloneys. Ein Beitrag zur Erkenntnis von Zeitgeist und Gattungsgeschichte der englischen Renaissance. Diss. Zürich Siebnen. Schweizer anglistische Arbeiten, 16 1946

Hachtmann, Otto Wilhelm. Die Vorherrschaft substantivischer Konstruktionen im modernen französischen Prosastil Berlin: E. Ebering 1912
On simile.

Hafter, Monroe. Gracián and Perfection Harvard University Press 1966
"Gracián appeals to the indefinable quality of soul and vivacity to be achieved through pointed language, words laden with conceits."

Hagner, P. C. "Analogy" Journal of Philosophy 55 (Sept. 25, 1958) 855-862

Hagopian, John V. "Symbol and Metaphor in the Transformation of Reality into Art" Comparative Literature 20 (Winter 1968) 45-54
Alain Robbe-Grillet and Georg Lukács falsely deny or ignore metaphors. Rather novels are just expanded metaphors. Metaphors are deliberate, created, controlled and examined. They arise out of primitive synaesthesia to become models of reality, of value-charged experiences for contemplation. "Metaphors are among man's highest achievements in being presentational and value-charged."

Hagstrum, Jean. Samuel Johnson's Literary Criticism Minneapolis: University of Minnesota Press 1952 esp. pp. 116-117, 119-120
Metaphors are real and unreal at the same time.

_____. The Sister Arts: The Tradition of Literary Pictorialism and English Poetry from Dryden to Gray University of Chicago Press 1958 esp. pp. 129-170
The "poetry resembles painting" controversy.

Haight, Elizabeth. "Horace on Art: Ut pictura poesis" Classical Journal 47 (1952) 157-162, 201-213
Horace's Ut pictura poesis is often referred to, but he thinks of art as connotative rather than pictorial, and thinks that poetry is superior to painting (ut pictura poesis). For him art instructs; it does not merely delight by creating pictures.

Halbert, Cecelia L. "Tree of Life Imagery in the Poetry of Edward Taylor" American Literature 38 (1966) 22-34

Hale, David G. "The Body Politic: A Political Metaphor in Renaissance English Literature" PhD diss. Duke University 1965
Discusses the analogy between society and the human body.

Halio, Jay. "The Metaphor of Conception and Elizabethan Theories of the Imagination" Neophilologus 50 (1966) 454-461

Hamann, Johann Georg. Sämtliche Werke Wien: Thomas-Morus-Presse im Verlag Herder 1949-1950 (See his Aesthetica in Nuce; Schriften I, II)
Metaphor reveals the real essence of things giving a mystical revelation. All language is metaphorical.

Hampshire, Stuart. "Analogy of Feeling" Mind 61 (Jan. 1952) 1-12

Händel, Oskar. Tiermetaphern im französischen Gewerbe Leipzig 1908

Hangard, Johan. Monetaire en daarmee verwante metaforen; studiën over het metaforisch gebruik van de terminologie van muntwezen, onderzoek en bewerking van edele metalen en zegelwezen in de Griekse literatuur tot Aristoteles Groningen: Wolters 1963

Hankins, J. E. Shakespeare's Derived Imagery Lawrence: University of Kansas Press 1953

Hansen, Jens-Godber. "Bildhafte Sprache des Aeschylos: See und Schiffahrt in metaphorischer Verwendung" PhD diss. Kiel 1955

Hanson, Norwood. Patterns of Discovery Cambridge University Press 1961 (1958)
An application of Wittgenstein's notion of "seeing-as." Our theories and knowledge become a part of our seeing. "The knowledge is there in the seeing and not an adjunct of it." The task of the scientist is to see in new ways.

Hardie, W. R. "Metaphors and Allusive Language in Greek Lyric Poetry" Classical Review 5 (May 1891) 193-195
On Pindar.

Hardt, Manfred. Das Bild in der Dichtung. Studien zu Funktionsweisen von Bildern und Bildreihen in der Literatur München: W. Fink 1966

Hardy, Barbara. "Imagery in George Eliot's Last Novels" Modern Language Review 50 (Jan. 1955) 6-14
On imagery in Middlemarch and Daniel Deronda. "We find single images and clusters of images which recur throughout the long narratives, the recurrence acting as a mnemonic which helps the reader to see the book as a whole, binding together past and present in anticipation and echo . . . "

Harré, R. "Metaphor, Model and Mechanism" Proceedings of the Aristotelian Society N. S. 60 (Jan. 1960) 101-122
A theory must invent a mechanism, suggest the existence and sketch the character of mechanisms in regions previously inaccessible. Models or metaphors here do have empirical "cash value."

Harrell, Joe. "Some Notes on Conversion of Words in Poetry" Southern Review 7 (1941) 117-131
Metaphor is a conversion from one context to another, thus having a first and second intention. Metaphor cannot exist in isolation from material things or the literal. A somewhat Thomistic account.

Harrier, Richard. "Another Note on 'Why the Sweets Melted'" Shakespeare Quarterly 18 (1967) 67 (cf. Hobday)
On image-cluster linking, fawning dogs and melting sweets.

Harriman, Charles. "The Role of Metaphor in Cognition; Simple Natures in the Early Works of Descartes and Wittgenstein" PhD diss. in progress University of New Mexico (1971)

Harrington, David. "The Personifications in Death and Life a Middle-English Poem" Neuphilologische Mitterlingen 68 (1967) 35-47

Harris, D. F. "Metaphor in Science" Science N. S. 36 (Aug. 30, 1912) 263-269
Gives a number of examples.

Harris, Henry. "The Symbols of Imagery of Hawk and Kestrel in the Poetry of Auden and Day-Lewis in the Thirties" Zeitschrift für Anglistik und Amerikanistik 13 (1965) 276-285

Harris, James. Philological Inquiries London: C. Nourse 1781

Harrison, E. L. "Neglected Hyperbole in Juvenal" Classical Review 10 (1960) 99-101

Harrison, Frank III. "Concerning the Possibility of a General Theory of Analogy" PhD diss. University of Virginia 1961
Neither Cajetan, Plato, Aristotle nor Aquinas has a general theory of analogy, nor is it possible to have one. These are examples of "craving for generality, of overlooking the particular case." We can only talk about particular analogies used in particular cases. A Wittgensteinian approach to Thomistic theories of analogy and metaphor.

Harrison, Robert. "Erotic Imagery in Crashaw's 'Musicks Duell'" Seventeenth-Century News 25 (1967) 47-49

Hassan, Ihab. "Frontiers of Criticism: Metaphors of Silence" Virginia Quarterly Review 46 (Winter 1970) 81-95

Hatzfeld, H. "Three National Deformations of Aristotle: Tesauro, Gracián, Boileau" Biblioteca dell' Archivum Romanicum 64 (1962) 3-21

Haubrich, Werner. "Die Metaphorik des Sports in der deutschen Gegenwartssprache" Der Deutschunterricht 20 (Oct. 1968) 112-133

Haugsted, M. "Die Metapher als ästhetische Stilkomponente" Orbis Litterarum 1 (1943) 277-312

Havighurst, Walter. "Metaphor and the Short Story" (Phonotape) Cincinnati: Sound Seminars Co. (1970)
Short story technique and the role of metaphor is discussed.

Haworth, Helen. "Keats and the Metaphor of Vision" Journal of English and Germanic Philology 67 (July 1968) 371-394
Metaphor is a sort-crossing and pretense, and sometimes a kind of imaginary vision which is beautiful, dreamlike or erotic. Keats' visions are inspired by the concrete and natural, and are not visions of a spiritual, bloodless, unreal, abstract second world. Keats is no mystic. There is no second world, only pretense. Supernatural vision ruins beauty and cuts us off from the real world. Visions do not have special access to a second (or Platonic) world; they have no independent existence.

Hayner, Paul. "Analogical Predication" Journal of Philosophy 55 (Sept. 25, 1958) 855-862
A Thomistic account. We need to redefine analogy. The two terms related in analogy must have at least one property in common.

Headlam, W. "Metaphor with a Note on Transference of Epithets" Classical Review 16 (Nov. 1902) 434-442
Aeschylus and few others carry their metaphors through.

Hecht, Max. "Der metaphorische Bedeutungswandel, mit besonderer Rucksicht auf seine Entstehung" Festschrift zur Feier des 600 jährigen Jubiläums des Kneiphöfischen Gymnasiums zu Köngisberg i. Pr. am 23. Juni 1904. Königsberg: Hartungsche Buchdruckerei 1904
In metaphor is a spiritual act of union of two similar concepts. All men use metaphors. Metaphors 1) demonstrate, make the abstract tangible, clarify 2) animate the inanimate to make something more lifelike, truer and emotional 3) emphasize, arouse strong passion. Metaphor brings about change of meaning to yield a needed new name. There exists a thought similarity. Metaphor is a "lightning thought" (Stöcklein) grasped immediately and combined with the present circumstance, with due regard to the object being recalled. To be a success the comparison must be valid. Often bold leaps of thought into hidden areas bring out surprising metaphors. Metaphors of

various authors should be compiled since they reveal mental peculiarities as well as an entire age or culture.

Hegel, G. W. F. "Metapher, Bild, Gleichnis" Ästhetik F. Bassenge, ed. East Berlin 1955 [1820, 1835] esp. pp. 369-401. Also "The Metaphor, the Image, and the Comparison" The Philosophy of Art William M. Bryant, trans. New York: Appleton 1879 pp. 40-45
Metaphor is an abridged comparison. "Even in its highest degree it can appear only as a simple ornament for a work of art, and its application is found only in spoken language." Still he speaks of the oriental practice of juxtaposing unlike images.

Heidegger, Martin. Der Satz vom Grund Pfullingen: G. Neske 1957 esp. p. 89
Metaphor is located in the realm of metaphysics, not in the sphere of "wesentliches Denken."

Heilman, R. B. This Great Stage: Image and Structure in 'King Lear' University of Washington Press 1963

Heise, Wilhelm. Die Gleichnisse in Edmund Spensers 'Faerie Queene' und ihre Vorbilder PhD diss. Strassburg: Königsee 1902

Hemingway, Clara Edmunds. "The Use of Imagery" Poet Lore 50 (1944) 34-36

Hempel, H. "Origine et essence de la métaphore" Revue des langues vivantes (Bruxelles) 18 (1952) 166-179. Also "Essence et origine de la métaphore" Essais de philologie moderne Paris: Les Belles Lettres 1953 pp. 33-45 (cf. Pasini)
Metaphor is an unconscious resemblance or fusion of one sphere with a different one. It cannot be reduced to the literal. Four types of metaphor are the practical (to provide a needed name, to avoid taboo), rhetorical, affective, poetic. Only late did man learn to dissociate the physical and psychic.

Hemstead, Sylvia. "The Metaphor in James' The American: A Study in Textual Revisions" MA thesis New York University 1955

Henderson, G. P. "Metaphorical Thinking" Philosophical Quarterly 3 (1953) 1-13
Metaphysical systems are untranslatably metaphorical. They say something involving value, are apprasive and prescriptive rather than descriptive. They represent suggestively or metaphorically. The metaphysician is trying to persuade and uses a system based on a central metaphor to do so.

Henel, Heinrich. "Metaphor and Meaning" The Disciplines of Criticism Peter Demetz, Thomas Greene and Larry Nelson, Jr., eds. New Haven: Yale University Press 1968 pp. 95-123
A detailed criticism of Weinrich's "Semantik der kühnen Meta-

pher." He finds Weinrich's definitions inconsistent and untenable, and thinks metaphor should not be based merely on logical considerations.

Henkel, Heinrich. Das Goethesche Gleichnis Halle: Buchhandlung des Waisenhauses 1886

Henle, Paul. "Metaphor" Language, Thought, and Culture Paul Henle, ed. Ann Arbor: University of Michigan Press 1958
Metaphor is a transference involving antecedent similarity--one situation represents another "iconically" (C. S. Peirce's term), or induced similarity--a transference of similar feelings. Metaphor deviates from normal expectations and custom, and requires a clash of terms. It cannot be paraphrased without loss of meaning.

_____. "The Problem of Meaning" Proceedings of the American Philosophical Association Yellow Springs, Ohio: Antioch Press 1954 pp. 24-39

Henning, Hans. "Das Erlebnis beim dichterischen Gleichnis und dessen Ursprung" Zeitschrift für Ästhetik und allgemeine Kunstwissenschaft 13 (1919) 371-396

Hense, C. C. Beseelende Personifikation in griechischen Dichtungen mit Berücksichtigung lateinischer Dichtungen Shakespeares I Halle: Waisenhaus 1868, II 1877

_____. Über personifizierende Epitheta bei griechischen Dichtern, namentlich bei Pindar, Aeschylus, Sophocles Halberstadt Gymn. Programm 1855

Herder, Johann G. Sämmtliche Werke thirty-three vols. Bernard Suphan, ed. Berlin: Weidmannsche 1877-1913 esp. vol. 5 pp. 71ff
Every language has its own peculiar Metapherngeist. Metaphor has the value of reducing abstractions to the concrete. No rules can be given for the construction of good metaphors. Metaphor is poetic when it is in its primitive stages.

Hermann, Alfred. "Das steinharte Herz. Zur Geschichte einer Metapher" Jahrbuch für Antike und Christentum 4 (1961) 77-101

Hermogenes of Tarsus (ca. 170 A.D.) [also written Hermogenis]. Opera H. Rabe, ed. Bibliotheca scriptorum Graecorum et Romanorum Teubneriana Rhetores Graeci, vol. 6 Leipzig 1913 (in Greek). Also Stuttgart: B. G. Teubneri 1969

Hersch, Jeanne. Publié dans les Archives de Psychologie T. 23 Extrait paru à Genève 1931 (cf. Adank pp. 103-104)
On Bergson's imagery.

Herschberger, Ruth. "The Structure of Metaphor" *Kenyon Review* 5 (1943) 433-443
Metaphor makes statements about the world, and is accessible to prose paraphrase, but it also yields an aesthetic experience--one which serves as *therapy* for man's psychic needs. It is a likeness of unlike things able to reconcile opposites and contains tension.

Herzer, Jakob. "Metaphorische Studien zu griechischen Dichtern. I. Die auf 'Unglück und Verwandtes' bezüglichen Metaphern und Bilder bei den Tragikern" Programm der königlichen Studienanstalt, Zweibrücken 1884

Hesehaus, Clemens. *Deutsche Lyrik der Moderne von Nietzsche bis Yvan Goll. Die Rückkehr zur Bildlichkeit der Sprache*. Dusseldorf: A. Bagel 1961 "Das metaphorische Gedicht von Georg Trakl" pp. 228-257 "Günter Eichs Naturmetaphorik" pp. 449-454

Hess, M. Whitcomb. "Hopkins and the Metaphor in Poetry" *Spirit* 30 (March 1963) 21-24
Review of Boyle's *Metaphor in Hopkins*. Boyle in stressing metaphor theory in regard to Hopkins' work fails to do justice to the art of poetry. Poetry does not, as Boyle thinks, depend mainly on metaphor and metaphorical sound. It is the poetic subject matter of Hopkins' metaphors that gives them value.

Hesse, E. W. "Some Observations on Imagery in *La Vida es Sueño*" *Hispania* 49 (Sept. 1966) 421-429

Hesse, Mary. "On Defining Analogy" *Proceedings of the Aristotelian Society* N.S. 60 (1959-1960) 79-100 (Review by J. Bennet)
A logical analysis of analogy, such as Aristotle's four term analogy, in terms of the structure of an algebraic lattice. The lattice-algorithm allows the fourth term of a four term analogy to be calculated. A definition of analogies between words requires a thesaurus-like classification. This thesaurus is inadequate as a model of language structure and requires a modification of the lattice.

_____. "The Explanatory Function of Metaphor" *Logic, Methodology and Philosophy of Science* Proceedings of the 1964 International Congress Yehoshua Bar-Hillel, ed. Amsterdam: North-Holland Publishing Company 1965 pp. 249-259
Metaphor has cognitive implications, and the deductive model needs metaphoric modification to correct and replace literal description. She takes an interaction view of metaphor.

_____. *Models and Analogies in Science* University of Notre Dame Press 1966
Contains a discussion of material analogy, the logic of analogy, Aristotle's logic of analogy and the explanatory function of metaphor (discussed above). She deals with the question of

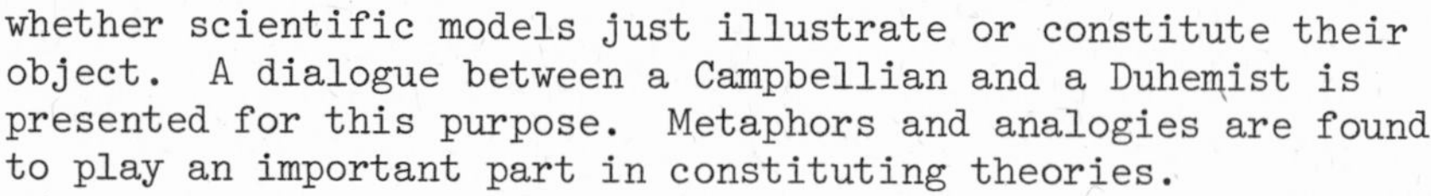

whether scientific models just illustrate or constitute their object. A dialogue between a Campbellian and a Duhemist is presented for this purpose. Metaphors and analogies are found to play an important part in constituting theories.

_____. "Models and Matter" *Quanta and Reality: A Symposium* New York: World Publishing Company 1964 pp. 49-57

_____. "Models in Physics" *British Journal for the Philosophy of Science* 4 (1953) 198-214

_____. Review of Turbayne *Myth of Metaphor*. *Foundations of Language* 2 (1966) 282-284
Turbayne has a confused thesis involving three not always consistent views. He seems to end with the view that, as Hesse emphasizes, we must abandon the search for the literal since all we can do is compare one metaphor with another.

_____. *Science and the Human Imagination* London: SMC Press 1954 esp. "Scientific Models" pp. 134-146
Analogies or metaphoric models in science may not just illustrate but rather determine the phenomena. They often cannot be reduced to similes or rendered in more precise terms without destroying their heuristic value. Analogies ("analogues") need not picture. The use of mathematics in describing nature is always merely analogical.

Hester, Marcus B. "An Analysis of the Meaning of Poetic Metaphor" (Abstract) *Linguistics: An International Review* 12 (1965) 107-109
Metaphor involves a type of imagery that is not observable. No conventions define the relevant relations between subject and predicate of the metaphor. The only appeal is to the metaphor as read.

_____. *The Meaning of the Poetic Metaphor; an analysis in the light of Wittgenstein's claim that meaning is use* The Hague: Mouton 1967. Also "An Analysis of the Meaning of Poetic Metaphor" PhD diss. Vanderbilt University 1964
Metaphor involves imagery and is known and excited by reading. He accepts much of Wittgenstein's theory of meaning but goes beyond this view by asserting that metaphors involve imagery. Reading is an act of seeing-as by which the relevant sense of a metaphor is found. "In an actual case of trying to discover a metaphor's meaning, we do not first recognize the metaphor, then read it, then analyze its meaning." The three are interwoven as an active seeing-as. The read metaphor has "presentational" immediacy.

_____. "Metaphor and Aspect Seeing" *Journal of Aesthetics and Art Criticism* 25 (Winter 1966) 205-212 (Reply R. Wajid 26

(1968) 389-90)
"The metaphor means...the metaphor realized in its imagistic fullness while being read." Poetic metaphor is a seeing-as or noticing of an aspect between the parts of a metaphor.

Heylen, V. "Les métaphores et les métonymies dans les épîtres pauliniennes" Ephemerides Theologicae Lovanienses 12 (1935) 253-290

Hick, John. Philosophy of Religion New Jersey: Prentice-Hall 1963 esp. pp. 71-72
Similar to the visual experience of "seeing-as" is that of "experiencing-as" which is a special insight into a situation e.g. to see an event in terms of human history.

Hill, Elizabeth. "What is an Emblem?" Journal of Aesthetics and Art Criticism 29 (1970) 261-265

Hill, Viola J. "Wordsworth's Imagery and What It Tells Us" PhD diss. Indiana University 1947

Hillenbrand, R. "Appreciation of Picturesque Language in the Intermediate Grades" Elementary English 36 (May 1959) 302-304

Hillman, Donald J. "On Grammars and Category-Mistakes" Mind N. S. 72 (1963) 224-234
A discussion of Ryle's notion of category-mistake, e.g. "Saturday is in bed" and Chomsky's tests for grammaticalness. Hillman suggests that we should talk of deviant-utterance rather than category-mistake.

Hillmann, Heinz. Franz Kafka: Dichtungstheorie und Dichtungsgestalt Bonn: H. Bouvier Co. 1964 pp. 136-47
Some comparisons used by Kafka have symbolic meaning. In his early works hypothetical (as-if) and comparative expressions (as) are realistically oriented but in later works they have a symbolic function. There is a sudden change from realistic to symbolic style. Kafka rarely used images and wrote in his diary that metaphors are one of the many things that make him despair of writing. By trying to avoid metaphor he hopes for precision. When he does use metaphors they are not spontaneous, but carefully thought out.

Hillyer, Robert. "Modern Poetry vs. the Common Reader" The Saturday Review of Literature 28 (March 24, 1945) 5-6
A simile is really an expanded adjective. It is a suggestion. But a metaphor identifies. "A metaphor matches the object quality by quality, and usually provides a picture appropriate in all its parts to the object."

Himelblau, J. "La Metáfora en la prosa de Alfonso Reyes" Hispanic Review 36 (Jan. 1968) 44-53 (cf. James Robb)

Hindermann, Federico. *Bilder der Liebes-Dichtung; Beiträge zu einer historischen Topik* Horgen-Zürich, Buchdr. F. Frei 1963

Hines, Leo. "Pindaric Imagery in G. M. Hopkins" *The Month* 29 (1963) 294-307

Hinz, Evelyn. "D. H. Lawrence's Clothes Metaphor" *The D. H. Lawrence Review* 1 (1968) 87-113

Hirzel, Arnold. Gleichnisse und Metaphern im *Rig-Veda*, in kulturhistorischer Hinsicht zusammengestellt und verglichen mit den Bildern bei Homer, Hesiod, Aeschylos, Sophokles und Euripides. Leipzig: Verlag von Wilhelm Friedrich 1890. PhD diss. Leipzig 1890 Also *Zeitschrift für Völkerpsychologie und Sprachwissenschaft* 17 (1889) 276-313; 347-415

Hispalensis, Isidore. (Bishop of Seville 602-636 A.D.) *Etymologiarum Libri* Patrologiae Cursus Completus J. Migne, ed. Paris. vol. 82 Book I of *Etymologiae*. (Isidori Hispalensis etymologiarum sive originum libri XX, W. M. Linsay, ed. Vol. I, Books 1-10, Oxford 1911)
Follows Donatus and Greek and Roman tradition on metaphor.

_____. *Opera Omnia* 7 vols. Rome 1798. Vol. 3, Books I, II

Hobbes, Thomas. *The Art of Rhetoric* London 1681 esp. 103-145
Metaphor is a transference of names from one like thing to another. It is inconstant, equivocal and deceitful. It may best be expressed literally.

_____. *The English Works of Thomas Hobbes* 11 vols. Sir William Molesworth, editor. London: John Bohn. Reprint Aalen, Germany: Scientia Verlag 1966 (See index of these volumes.)
He says the use of metaphor is one cause of absurd conclusions. It is misleading and metaphorical to say "The way goes, or leads hither," or "The proverb says..." Ways cannot go, and proverbs do not speak.

Hobday, C. H. "Why the Sweets Melted: A Study in Shakespeare's Imagery" *Shakespeare Quarterly* 16 (1965) 3-17 (cf. Harrier)

Hocke, Gustav René. *Manierismus in der Literatur: Sprach-Alchimie und esoterische Kombinationskunst* Hamburg: Rowohlt 1959 esp. pp. 68-111
A summary of various writers' views on mannerism and conceits. Metaphor involves the transfer of one thing to another and conveys incomprehensible things in pictures. It helps render the structure of reality. In antiquity it had a demonic power but today it is more like a riddle. The author discusses the views on conceit and metaphor of Tesauro, Marino, Gracián, Góngora, M. Peregrini, Wolfgang Kaiser, Goethe. Wars and social unrest cause bold, manneristic metaphors. Metaphor allows us to es-

cape fear and oppression. It is a type of linguistic magic.

Hodler, Gerhart. "Bemerkungen zur Verwendung von Vergleichen und Metaphern bei Euripides" in Festgabe Otto Regenbogen Heidelberg 1956 pp. 77-99

Hoernlé, R. F. Alfred. "Image, Idea and Meaning" N.S. Mind 16 (1907) 76-100

Hof, Walter. Hölderlins Stil als Ausdruck seiner geistigen Welt Meisenheim am Glan 1954 pp. 378-410

Höffding, Harald. Le concept d'analogie Perrin, trans. from Der Begriff der Analogie Paris: J. Vrin, 1931 Also Begrebet analogi Kopenhagen: Andr. Fred. Host & Son 1923 (Has useful bibliography)
He says analogy is "...a similarity of relations between two objects, a similarity which is not based on particular properties or parts of these objects but on reciprocal relations between these properties or parts." Analogy may lead to an hypothesis but as it does not constitute it the analogy may then be discarded.

Hoffman, Arthur. John Dryden's Imagery Gainesville: University of Florida Press 1962

Hoffmann, Hellmut. Die Metaphern in Predigten und Schriften Abrahams à Sancta Clara Düsseldorf: Express-druckerei. Thesis, Cologne 1933

Hohler, R. C. "Lucretius' Use of the Simile" Classical Journal 21 (Jan. 1926) 281-5

Holder, Alexander. "On the Structure of Henry James' Metaphors" English Studies 41 (Oct. 1960) 289-97

_____. "Review of Brooke-Rose A Grammar of Metaphor" Erasmus: Speculum Scientiarum 12 (1959) 20-23

Holder-Barell, Alexander. Development of Imagery and Its Functional Significance in Henry James' Novels New York: Haskell Press 1959. PhD dissertation Basel 1959

Holland, Virginia. Counterpoint: Kenneth Burke and Aristotle's Theories of Rhetoric New York: Philosophical Library 1959

Hollander, Lee M. The Skalds: A Selection of Their Poems, with Introductions and Notes Princeton University Press 1945 (University of Michigan 1968)

Holmes, Elizabeth. Aspects of Elizabethan Imagery Oxford: B. Blackwell 1929; New York: Russell and Russell 1966

Holmes, Elizabeth Ann. "Children's Knowledge of Figurative Language" M.A. thesis, University of Oklahoma 1959
An examination of fifth grade students' understanding of figures showed that of 3640 responses to 140 expressions, 2373 were correct, 1267 students did not know the answer. The texts examined contained figures the children did not understand and one of every five responses was a verbalized misconception. The study of figures should be stressed by teachers and by texts which are made more adequate in this regard.

Holöhr, Walter. "De metaphoris Aristophanis" PhD diss. Marburg 1923

Höltker, P. Georg. "Einige Metaphern im Aztekischen des P. Sahagun" *Anthropos: International Review of Ethnology and Linguistics* 27 (Jan. 1932) 249-59

Holz, Hans Heinz. "Das Wesen metaphorischen Sprechens" *Festschrift Ernst Bloch zum 70 Geburtstag* Rugard Gropp, ed. Berlin 1955 pp. 101-20
Metaphor makes the non-visible part of reality visible or picturable. 1) "Necessary metaphors" or "primary metaphors" unify picture (image) and meaning to render the subjective and social side of man. They are necessary because the non-sensual can only be expressed metaphorically. The metaphor determines the impression. It modifies speech. The discovery of new words in poetic speech is at the same time an indication of a deeper, more meaningful understanding and mastery of the world. Speech is both subject and object of philosophy. The picture of the metaphor and what it denotes are identical.
2) "Contingent metaphor" only denotes its object by a likeness. To this type belong figures of speech, synecdoche, metonymy, or transfer from one sphere of knowledge to another. Contingent metaphors lack the coincidence of word content and designation which belongs to the necessary metaphor.
Spatial metaphors reveal the non-spatial. Adjectival metaphors deal with qualities and are similar to analogy. Verbal metaphors are primary in the sense that the denoted can be expressed only metaphorically; they do not express a quality, but only the "type of a completion" or mode is expressed metaphorically. The non-sensual does not become object by means of determining predicates, but by the mode of the specific action, by expression which can only be fulfilled in words.

Honig, Edwin. "In Defense of Allegory" *Kenyon Review* 20 (Winter 1958) 1-19

______. *Dark Conceit: The Making of Allegory* Evanston, Illinois: Northwestern University Press 1959

Hook, La Rue van. "The Metaphorical Terminology of Greek Rhetoric and Literary Criticism" PhD diss. University of Chicago 1905

Hoppe, Dr. De comparationum et metaphorarum apud tragicos graecos usu. Programm d. Berlinischen Gymn. zum grauen Kloster 1939 pp. 1-32

Hoppe, I. Janus. Die Analogie Berlin 1873
On the logic of analogy.

Horace. Satire, Epistles, Ars Poetica H. R. Fairclough, trans. Cambridge, Mass.: Harvard Univ. Press 1961 "Ars Poetica" pp. 442-489 (cf. Haight)
Ut pictura poesis - "A poem is like a picture: one strikes your fancy more, the nearer you stand; another, the farther away...this pleased but once; that...always..." (Note: Simonides had earlier said that painting is dumb poetry, and poetry vocal painting.)

Horák, W. "Die Metapher in der tschechischen volksthümlichen Dichtung" Zeitschrift für das Realschulwesen 12 (1898) 137-42

Horgan, J. "Aspects of Cajetan's Theory of Analogy" The Irish Ecclesiastical Record 46 (1934) 114-135

Hörmann, Wolfgang. "Gleichnis und Metapher in der griechischen Tragödie" PhD dissertation München 1934

Hornback, Bert. The Metaphor of Chance Ohio University Press 1970
A consideration of some of Hardy's novels and poems in the perspective of his metaphors of time and chance.

Hornbostel, Erich M. von. "The Unity of the Senses" Psyche: An annual of general and linguistic psychology 7 (April 1927) 83-89
It is not transferred meaning that for example, a dancer becomes her dance, identifies completely with it. The senses were originally unified and only later became separate. We do actually and directly experience the unity of the senses in art e.g. hear colors or shapes.
(cf. Bouwsma's discussion of "The music is sad.")

Hornick, Lita. "The Intricate Image: A Study of Dylan Thomas" PhD diss. Columbia University 1958
Thomas superimposes two or more images on the basis of remote analogies which are not visualizable. His images are used for feelings, or meanings associated with them. His metaphors seem surreal but are rather condensed metaphors lacking sensuous concreteness.

Hornsby, R. A. "Vergilian Simile as Means of Judgment" Classical Journal 60 (May 1965) 337-44

Hornstein, Lillian H. "Analysis of Imagery: A Critique of Literary Method" PMLA 57 (Sept. 1942) 638-53
Criticism of Spurgeon's view that from the imagery used one

can tell about a person's physical history and environment. No figure is necessarily dependent on environmental experience.

Horrell, Joe. "Some Notes on Conversion of Words in Poetry" Southern Review 7 (1941) 117-131

Horsburgh, H. J. N. "Philosophers Against Metaphor" Philosophical Quarterly 8 (1958) 231-245
An attempt to show that the contemporary philosophers' attack on metaphor is misguided.

Horst, Karl-August. "Die Metapher in Calderóns Comedias" PhD diss. Bonn 1946

Hörtnagl, Hans. Bausteine zu einer Grammatik der Bildersprache Innsbruck: Universitätsverlag Wagner 1922

Hotopf, W. H. N. Language, Thought and Comprehension Bloomington: Indiana University Press 1965
On I. A. Richards' thought. For Richards metaphor may refer to the vehicle, or tenor and vehicle together; the use of metaphor allows us to experience a greater variety of feelings and to become more aware of them. Feelings are regarded as objective referrings. Hotopf thinks only language is metaphoric, not perception.

Hough, Graham. "The Allegorical Circle" Critical Quarterly 3 (1961) 99-209

Housman, A. E. The Name and Nature of Poetry Cambridge University Press 1933 (cf. Criticism by W. Greene)

Houston, Howard. Metaphors in Walden PhD diss. Claremont Graduate School 1967

Howard, William G. "Ut Pictura Poesis" PMLA 24 (1909) 40-143

Howe, G. Nature Similes in Catullus (Studies in Philosophy vol. 7) pp. 1-15 University of Carolina Press 1911

Howell, Samuel. Logic and Rhetoric in England 1500-1700 Princeton University Press 1956

Howson, John. The Metaphors of St. Paul; and Companions of St. Paul Boston: American Tract Society 1871; New York: Hurd and Houghton 1872. Reprinted from various periodicals.
In the New Testament St. Paul's metaphors are most important.

Hsia, T. A. "Metaphor, Myth, Ritual and the People's Commune" (Current Chinese Language Project: Studies in Chinese Communist Terminology no. 7) June 1961, 60 pp.

Huber, E. "Bermerkungen zu Diderots Gebrauch von Vergleich und Metapher in Le Neveu de Rameau" *Syntactica und Stilistica. Festschrift für Ernst Gamillscheg* Günter Reichenkron, ed. Tübingen: Max Niemeyer Verlag 1957 pp. 229-242
Statistics given.

_____. "Paul Valérys Metaphorik und der Französische Symbolismus" *Zeitschrift für französische Sprache und Literatur* 67 (1957) 168-201, 68 (1958) 165-186, 69 (1959) 1-21
An extensive and statistical analysis of Valéry's metaphors.

_____. *García Lorca: Weltbild und Metaphorische Darstellung* München: Fink 1967

Huber, J. P. *Zu den platonischen Gleichnissen* Passau 1879

Hübner, Walter. "Der Vergleich bei Shakespeare" PhD dissertation Berlin 1908

Hugedé, Norbert. *La métaphore du miroir dans les épîtres de Saint Paul aux Corinthiens* Neuchâtel-Paris: Delachaux & Niestlé 1957

Hughes, Glenn. *Imagism and the Imagists* Stanford University Press and Oxford University Press 1931
Contains good bibliography on imagism.
The imagists stress the use of clear images of solid, seen things. (These are juxtaposed almost like the pictures in a Chinese ideogram, a kind of visual metaphor.) (Note: Although imagists wish to present sense images their poetry is rather, highly metaphorical.) Ezra Pound says an image is that which presents an intellectual and emotional complex in an instance of time; and "It is better to present one image in a lifetime than to produce voluminous works."

Hughes, Theone. "Linguistic Approaches to Figurative Speech" *The Instructor* 77 (Dec. 1967) 58-9
The child in the primary grades should be taught to understand and use metaphors e.g. to convey emotions, qualify, compare, economize, etc. A teaching aid may be to list inanimate nouns beside animate verbs and relate them e.g. the stone nestles.

Huguet, Edmond. *Le langage figuré au seizième siècle* Paris: Hachette 1933

_____. *Les métaphores et les comparaisons dans l'oeuvre de Victor Hugo* Paris: Hachette 1904-1905. Vol. I Le sens de la forme dans les métaphores de Victor Hugo 1904, Vol. II La couleur et la lumière de l'ombre dans les métaphores de Victor Hugo 1905

Hulme, T. E. *Speculations* New York: Harcourt, Brace and Company

1924
Hulme is called the founder of the imagist movement. Artists give others a unique, new vision or image. The image is a direct, intuitive, irrational, mysterious, synthesis. Bergson is cited for support. The artist must see reality unconventionally and in ever new ways. Fresh metaphors vividly convey actual sensation and emotions. Prose is a "museum of dead metaphors."

______. Further Speculations University of Nebraska Press 1962
"Each word must be an image seen." "Method: analogies from all possible subjects." "Thought: the simultaneous presentation...of two different images." "The history of philosophy should be written as that of seven or eight metaphors." He rejects "counter" philosophers for "visual" philosophers. The poet's sincerity "may be measured by the number of his images." Imagery and metaphor alone properly represent the flux of reality. Two images in music form a new visual cord.

Hülsmann, Heinz. "Sprache und Analogie" Zur Theorie der Sprache bei Edmund Husserl München: Verlag Anton Pustet 1964 pp. 136-142

Hülsmann, Helene. "Die Metaphern in Shakespeares Romeo and Juliet" PhD dissertation Münster 1927

Humphreys, A. R. "Review of Wimsatt The Verbal Icon" The Review of English Studies 7 (1956) 102-104
Brief summary of The Verbal Icon.

Hungerland, Isabel. Poetic Discourse (University of California Publications in Philosophy, 33) Berkeley: University of California Press 1958 esp. ch. 4 "Figurative Language"
Metaphor or figures of speech are deliberate deviations from normal usage or rules of usage. Figures involve concreteness, condensation (dreams), suggestiveness, change of usual response. They cannot be exactly paraphrased or rule bound. Their classification is no substitute for detailed contextual examination. Science depends on metaphoric likeness between different fields of knowledge. Seeing-as is perceptual, or theoretical. Sound can be figurative.

Huntley, F. L. "Sir Thomas Browne and the Metaphor of the Circle" Journal of the History of Ideas 14 (June 1953) 353-64

Hussey, Christopher. The Picturesque London: Putnam 1927 (Archon Books 1967)

Hussey, George B. "The More Complicated Figures of Comparison in Plato" American Journal of Philology 17 (1896) 329-346. Also Transactions and Proceedings of the American Philological Association 26 (1895) pp. 8-11

Hutchinson, H. "Strange Similes" Living Age 291 (Nov. 11, 1916) 376-8

Hutten, E. H. "The Rôle of Models in Physics" British Journal for the Philosophy of Science 4 (1953) 284-301
The model is a kind of metaphor used to link theory and experiment. It supports, and partly constitutes theory, relates unfamiliar to familiar, specifies rules of usage and a context or universe of discourse, is a "way of speaking." It is not true or false. Mathematics cannot serve as a model as it needs interpretation. A theory needs many models for its interpretation.

Hüttig, Ernst. Der Vergleich im mhd. Heldenepos; ein Beitrag zur vergleichenden mhd. Stilistik Halle: Klinz 1930

Huxley, Julian. "Analogies: Dangerous and Otherwise: Extension of Biological Principles into Human Affairs" Yale Review N.S. 29 (March 1940) 532-55
Analogy aids discovery and hypothesis but may mislead. It can never serve as proof but can only give illumination. e.g. relating man to speechless animals is misleading.

Huysmans, Joris K. A Rebours (a novel) Paris: Fasquelle 1934 (1884)
On synaesthesia. A mouth organ is described such that one drinks a symphony of liqueurs. Curaçao corresponds to clarinet, kümmel to nasal oboe, mint and anisette to the flute, etc. One plays silent melodies on his tongue.

Hyde, Isabel. "Poetic Imagery: A Point of Comparison Between Henryson and Dunbar" Studies in Scottish Literature 11 (1965) 183-197

_____. "Primary Sources and Associations of Dunbar's Aureate Imagery" Modern Language Review 51 (Oct. 1956) 481-92

Hyman, Stanley. The Armed Vision: A Study in the Methods of Modern Literary Criticism New York: Knopf 1948
Gives account of Wilson, Eliot, Bodkin, Blackmur, Burke, Richards, etc.

Hynes, J. A. "Image and Symbol in Great Expectations" ELH 30 (1963) 258-292

Hytier, Jean. The Poetics of Paul Valéry Richard Howard, trans. New York: Doubleday 1966
Metaphor for Valéry is a shift of meaning and the forgetting of the original meaning; a natural felt happening resulting from looking at something in a certain way; a "stationary movement"; a psychological attitude; a groping. Language was originally gesture but is now metaphoric. Orators' gestures are metaphors. "Do this, do that - and there you have all

the metaphors in the world." The philosopher borrows a metaphor from the poet and then interprets all nature in terms of it.

Ibérico, Mariano. Estudio sobre la metáfora Lima: Casa de la Cultura del Peru 1965
Metaphor is an intuitive and subjective emotional similarity between two objects. It is expressive and combines diverse images into a unity, a resemblance in difference. Because of its subjective, intuitive nature it cannot be translated literally. It combines the concrete and the abstract. Every symbol is a metaphor.

Ibn Abī 'Aun (ninth century). Kitāb al-tashīhāt 'Abdul Mu'īd Khān, ed. London: Luzac 1950
On simile.

Ibn al-Sharīf, Muhamūd. al-Amthāl fī al-Qur'ān [Parables, or Metaphors, in the Qur'ān] 1964

"Idea and Image" Times Literary Supplement 2949 (Sept. 5, 1958) 497

Inowraclawer, Ascher. "De metaphorae apud Plautum usu" PhD diss. Rostock 1876

Inviolata, Barry. "St. Augustine, the Orator: A Study of the Rhetorical Qualities of St. Augustine's Sermones ad populum" PhD diss. Catholic University of America 1924
A collection of metaphors.

Ioannou, Iakobos. "On Scripture Metaphors" Biblical Review 5 (1846-1850) 55-69
Aristotle's four categories are non-figurative or inadequate in failing to include some figures. Campbell's definition is rejected. Ioannou states, "A metaphor is a figure of speech by which the name of one thing is applied to denote or describe another, because of some resembling characteristics, (conceived) inherent or belonging, whereby they are related to each other, and which may be either [essential] qualities, properties [or powers] or relations." Metaphors are classified as based on 1) true similarities 2) analogy of qualities 3) resembling relations (Aristotle's four term analogous metaphor). Metaphors assist apprehension or at the same time move and suggest emotions. They are necessary in order to speak of mental processes. They add precision. They transfer emotions of one object to another. Metaphors cannot be rendered literally without loss of meaning.

Irving, David. The Elements of English Composition London 1828 esp. "Of Metaphor" pp. 145-162
Metaphor is based on a natural comparison, looks beyond immediate connections, relates emotions and objects, renders the unfamiliar by the familiar, makes ideas visible (approaching painting), pleases and enlightens. It should not be too elevated, used in excess, forced, or mixed with other types of metaphors or the literal in the same sentence. Metaphor is a figure of thought; trope is a figure of words.

Isaacs, Neil. "The Autoerotic Metaphor in Joyce, Sterne, Lawrence, Stevens, and Whitman" Literature and Psychology 15 (1965) 92-106

Isenberg, Arnold. "The Esthetic Function of Language" Journal of Philosophy 46 (1949) 5-20

_____. "On Defining Metaphor" Journal of Philosophy 60 (Oct. 10, 1963) 609-622; 622-623 comments by Paul Welsh
Metaphor is not a condensed simile but more like resemblance in difference. But, he adds, "We do not and perhaps never shall have an explicit understanding of metaphor. For no one has come up with anything faintly recognizable as a sufficient condition for the application of the term."

Iser, Wolfgang. "Manieristische Metaphorik in der englischen Dichtung" Germanisch-romanische Monatsschrift N. F. 10 (1960) 266-287

Isidore. (See Hispalensis)

Isocrates, Evagoras. In Thesaurus Graecae Linguae Henri Estienne (Stephanus), Graz 1954 vol. 6 p. 903. Also in Works three vols. George Norlin and La Rue Hook, trans. Loeb Classical Library, New York: Putnam 1928-1945 (cf. Curran p. 30, Stanford Greek Metaphor p. 3, Berggren 1959 p. 17)
Said to be the first to use the word metaphorá. But Gorgias is said to have formulated the idea before this (Berggren).

Itzinger, F. "Index der in Ciceros Rede für Milo enthaltenen Metaphern und Angabe des Wandels der Wortbedeutung" Programm Budweis 1888

Jackson, Richard. "An Aspect of the Metaphorical Technique in the *Greguería* of Ramón Gómez de la Serna" *Romance Notes* 7 (1965) 9-11
In the *Greguería* inert objects are made human with life, personality and being from within them on the same level as man. It is an object-centered type of personification. All is on the aesthetic level, giving a change of perspective.

Jacobs, Wilhelmina and Vivian. "The Color Blue: Its Uses as Metaphor and Symbol" *American Speech* 33 (Feb. 1958) 29-46
Blue has been used metaphorically in many ways, but such use seems arbitrary.

Jaensch, Erich Rudolf. *Eidetic Imagery and Typological Methods of Investigation* Oscar Oeser, trans. New York: Harcourt, Brace and Co. 1930 (cf. Werner 1957)
He stresses pictorial rather than logical aspects of images. He says children actually see castles in air (cf. articles on "seeing-as"). An eidetic image is an intermediate stage between perception and memory image.

Jakobson, Roman. "Linguistics and Poetics" *Style in Language* Thomas A. Sebeok, ed. Cambridge: MIT Press 1960

_____. "Randbemerkungen zur Prosa des Dichters Pasternak" *Slavische Rundschau* 7 (1935) 357-374

_____. "Two Aspects of Language and Two Types of Aphasic Disturbances" *Fundamentals of Language* The Hague: Mouton 1956 pp. 55-82. Also in French in *Les temps modernes* 17 (1962) 853-880
Metaphor is based on similarity and *metonymy* on congruity. In aphasia one or both of these processes is restricted. The problem of these two polar processes awaits detailed investigation, yet they are of primal significance for all verbal behavior and for human behavior in general.

James, D. G. "Metaphor and Symbol" *Metaphor and Symbol* L. C. Knights and Basil Cottle, eds. London: Butterworth 1960 esp. pp. 96-102
"Metaphor is only the way in which the imagination works; it never adds up to a statement and doctrine." Religion contaminates it. Poetry proceeds by the use of metaphor and symbol. Metaphor is not emotive. It is the imagination of one thing in the form of another.

James, G. Ingli. "In Defense of Miss Groby: A Study in the Fluctuating Fortunes of the Metaphor" *Twentieth Century* 161 (Feb. 1957) 145-149
A Thurber character, "Miss Groby," loved figures of speech and treated them all as equally valuable. Being partial to one figure of speech over another prevents our appreciation and understanding of poetry and literature.

Jamieson, Alexander. A Grammar of Rhetoric 1818 esp. "Metaphor" pp. 153-162
Metaphor is a comparison which "clothes" thought and sentiment and brings pictures before the eyes. It should not be mixed, forced, far-fetched (as are Cowley's), used in excess, too elevated, sunk below its proper dignity, or based on much emotion. An allegory is a strained metaphor.

Jaurrieta, Carmen. "La metáfora en Ortega y Gasset" Boletín de la Real Academia Española 43 (1963) 57-149
Ortega's views are as follows: Verisimilitude has a reality of its own. Metaphor, the real aesthetic object, is a metamorphosis. Metaphor is unverified identity, subjective, sentiment based, irrational, inexplicable, and ideal. The two real images take on an ideal form. The transfer is mutual. Every metaphor is a law of the universe, a form of scientific thought, and insight. Metaphor relates spiritual and physical, and is meant to vitalize and dramatize. Even after a metaphor has been created we remain ignorant of its motive.

Jefferson, D. W. "Aspects of Dryden's Imagery" Essays in Criticism 4 (1954) 20-41

Jeffrey, Francis. Contributions to the Edinburgh Review four vols. in one, Boston: Sampson 1857
He held a view of the objective correlative, long before T. S. Eliot proposed it. Outward things and qualities represent inward abilities and emotions in an analogous way.

Jeffries, Christie. "Metaphor in Sons and Lovers" Personalist 29 (July 1948) 287-292
D. H. Lawrence's imagery is said here to reveal himself as a tormented man with warring personalities, preoccupied with daily life, showing strong regression to infancy and dominated by emotional and sadistic tendencies.

Jenkins, Philip R. "Is Our Language Vivid?" Writer 54 (May 1941) 148-149, 160
Metaphor is a contracted simile, but a flash of thought, not just comparison or ornament. By its incongruous juxtaposition it may be used to create humor. The writer should study Shakespeare's figures of speech.

Jennings, James G. An Essay on Metaphor in Poetry London: Blackie and Son 1915 (Review in Times Literary Supplement March 2, 1916 p. 102)
Metaphor illustrates, adds clarity, gives pictorial background, gives unity in diversity, delights, adds beauty, and is consciously made. It is, unlike emotion, inessential to poetry.

Jenyns, Soame. "On the Analogy Between Things Material and Intellectual" Disquisitions on Several Subjects London 1782 pp.

97-113; The Works of Soame Jenyns three vols. Charles Cole, ed. London: T. Cadell 1790 pp. 234-256
There is an analogy between all things because all have the same author. Resemblance can be: 1) physical (cheeks like an apple), 2) non-physical (brave like a lion), 3) relation between things having no resemblance in isolation (ship plows the sea); this is analogy.

Jesperson, Otto. Language: Its Nature, Development, and Origin New York: W. W. Norton 1964
Refutation of Müller's "root" or "radical metaphor" theory according to which words once represented physical objects and were metaphorically expanded to apply to mental and non-physical ones. Jesperson says that instead language went from "inseparable irregular conglomerations to freely and regularly combinable short elements."

Jewel, Bishop. Oratio contra Rhetoricam 1548

Johann, Loris̆. "O metafore v prostonarodní poesii c̆eské" Jahresbericht der k. k. tschechischen Oberrealschule in Rakonitz 1897 (source: W. Horák)

John, S. "Image and Symbol in the Work of Albert Camus" French Studies 9 (1955) 42-53

Johnson, Albert. Common English Sayings: A Collection of Metaphors in Everyday Use New York: Longmans, Green 1958

Johnson, G. W. "Stephen Crane's Metaphor of Decorum" PMLA 78 (1963) 250-256

Johnson, Lemuel A. "The Negro as a Metaphor: A Study of Esthetic and Ethical Negativism in English, Spanish and French Literatures" PhD diss. University of Michigan 1969

Johnson, Richard. "Imaginative Sensitivity in Schizophrenia" Review of Existential Psychology and Psychiatry 4 (1964) 255-264 (Part of PhD diss. University of Kentucky)
Deals with metaphor and schizophrenia. Schizophrenics are characterized by their abnormal use of metaphors, e.g. they may believe a revolving door is a devouring mouth. Johnson finds that such metaphors are a result of higher than normal psychic activity, as is the case with artists who are highly sensitive to connotative nuances. The schizophrenic, however, may believe his metaphors more than the artist believes his. In general, metaphor is consciously and cognitively apprehended and may convey more knowledge of the real world than denotative language.

Johnson, Dr. Samuel. "Essay on Cowley" Lives of the English Poets New York: Dutton 1925 [1886]
He says Cowley has wild comparisons. He defines wit as

similarity in dissimilarity and occult resemblances of things seemingly unlike. Conceits are "heterogeneous ideas yoked by violence together."

_____. "Metaphor" Dictionary [1755] New York: AMS Press 1967 vol. 2 (pages unnumbered)
"The application of a word to an use to which, in its original import, it cannot be put: as, he bridles his anger.... A metaphor is a simile comprized in a word."

Johnston, Brian. "The Metaphoric Structure of The Wild Duck" Contemporary Approaches to Ibsen Oslo 1966

Jones, A. R. "Imagism: A Unity of Gesture" American Poetry 31 (1965) 115-133

Jones, Ernest. Papers on Psychoanalysis Baltimore: Williams and Wilkins Co. 1949 esp. "The Theory of Symbolism"

Jones, F. "Some Aspects of the Image in the Poetry of Jean Cocteau" Archivum Linguisticum 15 (1963) 43-86, 174-215 esp. pp. 181 192 on metaphor.
A complete survey of Cocteau's surrealistic images.

Jones, Henry. "Misuse of Metaphors in the Human Sciences" Hibbert Journal 4 (Jan. 1906) 294-313
Metaphors of mechanism and natural cause do not apply to human relations and mental facts. Man is process. Much of the human sciences falsely rests on superficial metaphors and analogies.

Jones, William. Lectures on the Figurative Language of Holy Scripture London 1826

Joos, Heidel. "Die Metaphorik im Werk des Andreas Gryphius" PhD diss. Bonn 1956

Jordan, E. "Imagination and Its Organon Metaphor" Essays in Criticism University of Chicago Press 1952 pp. 87-142 (See Whittier)
"A metaphor is a hard solid reality on its own, its nature and essence are objective [syntheses of qualities], and it does not get its status or function from anything other than itself [not experience, psychology, religion, etc.]. It involves the real immediately...." "Art is what it is before there is experience of it."

Joseph, Sister Miriam. Shakespeare's Use of the Arts of Language New York: Hafner Publishing Co. 1947 [1966]. Also abridged version, Rhetoric in Shakespeare's Time New York: Harcourt, Brace 1962

Joyce, James. Finnegans Wake New York: The Viking Press 1947
Example of his employment of metaphor: "Every telling has a taling and that's the he and the she of it.... 'Tis endless now senne eye or erewone last saw Waterhouse's clogh. They took it asunder, I hurd thum sigh."

Juillière, Pierre de la. "Les comparaisons dans Rabelais" PhD diss. Bonn 1911

_____. Les images dans Rabelais Halle: Niemeyer 1912

Jung, Carl G. The Archetypes and the Collective Unconscious R. Hull, trans. Princeton University Press 1959
The "collective unconscious" is inborn, universal and its contents are archetypes (unconscious but universal form finding expression in many ways by diverse cultures). The wheel archetype may be an antidote for a chaotic mind. Water symbolizes the unconscious. The archetypes of shadow, anima and the wise old man are presented.

_____. Psychology and Religion in Collected Works seventeen vols. Herbert Read, Michael Fordham, Gerhard Alder, eds. New York: Pantheon Books 1953 vol. 11

_____. "On the Relation of Analytical Psychology to Poetic Art" Contributions to Analytical Psychology G. Helton, C. F. Baynes, eds. London: Kegan Paul 1928

Junker, Albert. "Gesunkenes Metapherngut im zeitgenössischen Italienischen" Syntactica und Stilistica. Festschrift für Ernst Gamillscheg Günter Reichenkron, ed. Tübingen: Max Niemeyer 1957 pp. 243-259

Kafka, Franz. "Beschreibung eines Kampfes" Gesammelte Werke Max Brod, ed. New York and Frankfurt 1954 esp. p. 42 (cf. Description of a Struggle Tania and James Stern, trans. New York: Schocken Books 1958) (cf. Hillmann) He attacks Dickens as having unnecessary, arbitrary, very disparate metaphors.

_____. Tagebücher 1910-1923 Max Brod, ed. New York and Frankfurt (cf. The Diaries of Franz Kafka two vols. Max Brod, ed., Joseph Kresh, trans. New York: Schocken Books 1948-49) He says, "Metaphor is one thing among the many that make me despair of writing." He realizes we must use them anyway.

Kahlert, Annemarie. "Metapher und Symbol in der englishschottischen Volksballade" PhD diss. Marburg: Philipps-Universität 1930

Kahlmeyer, Johannes. "Seesturm und Schiffbruch als Bild im antiken Schrifttum" PhD diss. Griefswald, Hildesheim 1934

Kainz, Friedrich. Psychologie der Sprache five vols. Stuttgart: F. Enke 1941-65 esp. vol. I Grundlagen der allgemeinen Sprachpsychologie esp. pp. 235-241, "Vergleich und Metapher" pp. 238-241

Kaiser, R. A. "Student Physiological Response to Metaphor in Reading" PhD diss. University of Pittsburgh 1967 A statistical, experimental analysis. He concludes that metaphorical description did not evoke significantly greater emotional response than do literal forms of writing, for those who understand figurative language.

Kalinowski, Georges. "La Pluralité Ontique en Philosophie du Droit, L'Application de la Théorie de l'Analogie à l'Ontologie Juridique" Revue Philosophique de Louvain 64 (May 1966) 263-280

Kallich, Martin. "Image and Theme in Pope's Essay on Criticism" Ball State University Forum 8 (1967) 54-60

Kalmus, H. "Analogies of Language to Life" Language and Speech 5 (1962) 15-25

Kames, Lord Henry Home. Elements of Criticism Abraham Mills, ed. New York: Huntington and Savage 1846 Metaphor is a condensed simile formed by an act of mind or faculty of imagination, regarding one thing as another. Figure has a principle object and accessory (cf. I. A. Richards' tenor and vehicle). Consequences cannot be drawn from a figure (McCloskey (1964) has same view). A list is given of figurative subjects and attributes. Metaphor has no cognitive function.

Kaminsky, Jack. "Review of Turbayne: The Myth of Metaphor" Philosophy and Phenomenological Research 29 (1964) 596

Kane, Elisha. Gongorism and the Golden Age: A Study of Exuberance and Unrestraint in the Arts Chapel Hill: University of North Carolina Press 1928. A revised Harvard PhD diss. "Gongorism and the Artistic Culture of the Golden Age" 1926
An unsympathetic account of Gongorism. She links it with any out of the ordinary movement including new jazz, E. E. Cummings' poetry and the Anglo-Saxon kenning (which she terms an "uncouth piling up of metaphors"). Gongorism is characterized by cultism (only high culture can appreciate it. It stresses words) or conceptism (abuse in metaphysical conceits, paradoxes, obscurity. It is concerned with ideas), figures of speech used in excess, puns, jumbled syntax, neologisms omission of letters, oxymora, acrostics, an attempt to approximate Spanish grammatical patterns to Latin languages.

Kane, P. V. A History of Sanskrit Poetics Bombay 1923 (1961, 3rd rev. ed.)

Kanner, Leo. "Irrelevant and Metaphorical Language in Early Infantile Autism" The American Journal of Psychiatry 103 (1946) 242-246. Reply by J. Despert pp. 245-246 (Summary in R. de Saussure "On Personal Metaphors" pp. 188-189
Seemingly irrelevant utterances of autistic children are metaphorical transfers of meaning by 1) substitutive analogy 2) generalization 3) restriction of whole to part.

Kanter, Fritz. "Der bildliche Ausdruck in Kleists Penthesilea" PhD diss. Jena 1914 (Borna-Leipzig, 1913)

Kanzer, Mark. "Imagery in King Lear" American Images 22 (1965) 3-13

Kaplan, Abraham. "Referential Meaning in the Arts" Journal of Aesthetics and Art Criticism 12 (June 1954) 457-474
Both emotion and reference may be involved in metaphor. Richards' view of the relation between tenor and vehicle is confused. The tenor is embodied in the vehicle. Metaphor cannot be reduced to literal statement without remainder.

_____, and Ernst Kris. "Esthetic Ambiguity" Psychoanalytic Explorations in Art New York 1952. Also in Philosophy and Phenomenological Research 8 (March 1948) 415-435

Kaplan, Bernard. "Radical Metaphor, Aesthetic, and the Origin of Language" Review of Existential Psychology and Psychiatry 2 (Winter 1962) 75-84 (Paper read at the American Psychological Association, Symposium on Metaphor, Sept. 5, 1961) (cf. Mawardi, H. Nash)

He takes a "high evaluation" of metaphor. "Radical metaphorizing is the process of taking any lived-thru or enjoyed experience in a medium which is completely foreign to that experience." It is a special act of "intentionality" which brings things into an order or "fittingness," just as we know that "ping" better represents mouse than "pong."

_____, and H. Werner. Symbol Formation See Werner entry.

Kappenberg, Hans. "Der bildliche Ausdruck in der Prosa Eduard Mörikes" PhD diss. Greifswald 1914

Kathleen, Sister. "Metaphors and Incipits in Hymns Dedicated to Gregory the Great" Annuale Mediaevale 9 (1968) 40-57

Katz, Jerrold. See Fodor.

Kaufmann, R. J. "Metaphorical Thinking and the Scope of Literature" College English 30 (Oct. 1968) 31-47
Metaphor is constitutive of a culture, social relations and creates an image of our social self. Metaphor is a communal vision, simplifies the complex, codifies values, forms the key models of history and society, becomes the literal, contradicts the self-evident and purposely distorts. All predication with "is" is a metaphor. The "is" of a metaphor could be left out also. "A conditioned repertoire of metaphors enables us to do public thinking and to derive socially usable responses out of our feelings." "The most profound social creativity consists in the invention and imposition of new, radical metaphors."

Kauvar, Gerald. "Figurative Relationships in the Poetry of Keats" PhD diss. Duke University 1966

Kayser, Wolfgang. Das sprachliche Kunstwerk. Eine Einführung in die Literaturwissenschaft München: Francke 1959

Kazemier, B. H. and D. Vuysje, eds. The Concept and the Role of the Model in Mathematics and the Natural and Social Sciences Holland: D. Reidel 1961

Keach, Benjamin. Tropologia: A Key to Open Scripture Metaphors Waterford: Bonmahon Press 1858 [1776]

Keast, William R. "Review of Wimsatt The Verbal Icon" Modern Language Notes 71 (1956) 591-597

Keith, Arthur. Simile and Metaphor in Greek Poetry from Homer to Aeschylus Menasha, Wis: Geo. Banta Publishing Company 1914. PhD diss. University of Chicago 1910
In Homer metaphors lack deep feeling and are less important than similes. Metaphors were often regarded as mythical. The sea was regarded as a mythological creature endowed with

life. Aeschylus has the most bold and vivid imagery and personification of those authors considered.

Keller, Karl. "From Christianity to Transcendentalism: A Note on Emerson's Use of the Conceit" *American Literature* 39 (March 1967) 94-8 (cf. Emerson)
Art by means of the conceit makes Emerson's transition from religion to nature, transcendentalism to aesthetics, dogmatics to pragmatics.

Kendall, Guy. "Dogma as Metaphor" *Hibbert Journal* 22 (July 1924) 734-743
Christian dogma almost universally expresses truths in metaphorical form because in no other form can the profoundest truths about reality and the relation of God to the world and to man be adequately expressed. Metaphor yields truth but it should not be taken literally.

Kennedy, George. "Fenollosa, Pound and the Chinese Character" *Yale Literary Magazine* 126 (1959) 24-36

Kenner, Hugh. *The Poetry of Ezra Pound* Norfolk, Conn.: New Directions 1951
Pound stresses intrinsic, natural poetry imitative of actual experience. Look, see, be concrete. Adopting the idea of the Chinese ideogram which involves visual, condensed juxtapositions his cantos are carefully worked out juxtapositions of images.

Kent, Roland. "Review of H. Adank 'Essai sur les fondements psychologiques et linguistiques de la métaphore affective'" *Language* 17 (1941) 73-74
Adank states that stylistics is psychological and linguistic. Kent says it is rather psychological and aesthetic.

Ker, William Paton. *Essays on Medieval Literature* London and New York: Macmillan and Company 1905 "Historical Notes on the Similes of Dante" pp. 32-51
Dante, he says, is the first modern poet to make a consistent use, in narrative poetry, of the epic simile as derived from Homer thru Vergil and the Latin poets. The use of this device in all modern tongues may be traced back to Dante.

Kermode, Frank. "Dissociation of Sensibility" *Kenyon Review* 19 (Spring 1957) 169-94
About imagery and the Metaphysical poets.

_____. *Romantic Image* New York: Random House 1957

Kern, Edith. "Concretization of Metaphor in the *Comedia dell' Arte* and *The Modern Theatre*" *Proceedings of the IVth Congress of the International Comparative Literature Association* 2 vols. Francois Jost, ed. The Hague: Mouton 1964

vol. 2, pp. 1232-42
"Reification" or "concretization of metaphor" may serve as as a basis for comedy. The denotation of action, e.g. love, is given concreteness, a concrete picture e.g. in Beckett's _Endgame_ the blind man wants his chair in the center of the room.

Kessler, Tina. "Zur Bildlichkeit der religiösen Erkenntnis" _Zeitschrift für Theologie und Kirche_ N.F. 9 (1928) 383-399

Kevin, Neil. "Our English in Ireland: Abuse of Metaphor" _Irish Ecclesiastical Record_ 53 (Jan. 1939) 19-29
The weakness of the Irish for language which is too figurative and picturesque results in mixed metaphor, sustained metaphor and so nonsense. The use of metaphor should be limited; its misuse taught in school and we should "hold them up to public ridicule." "If only we had an all-around purge of such faults in metaphor..."

Key, James A. "An Introduction to Melville's Bird Imagery" PhD diss. Tulane 1966

Khatchadourian, Haig. "Metaphor" _British Journal of Aesthetics_ 8 (July 1968) 227-243
He accepts Black's "interaction" theory and Beardsley's "logical absurdity" theory of metaphor. Metaphor is untranslatable, an analogy (not a resemblance), emotive, open-texture, a contrast of meaning or antithesis, tensive, a conscious shift on the part of the reader. There is a range of types and qualities of metaphor such that no one theory can apply to all situations. We must examine particular metaphors in context.

_____. "Symbols and Metaphors" _Southern Journal of Philosophy_ 6 (Fall 1968) 181-190
Metaphor is a transfer of name, idea or picture by means of resemblance or analogy. It is a "category-mistake" (cf. Ryle) outside of literature. It need not create images. Metaphor moves thought and feeling. Collage is an example of metaphor in the plastic arts.

King, Alec. _Wordsworth and the Artist's Vision: An Essay in Interpretation_ University of London: The Athlone Press 1966

King, Andrew A. "The Metaphor in Civil Rights Oratory: The Rhetoric of Accommodation" PhD diss. University of Minnesota 1968
The figures of F. Douglass, Booker T. Washington and Martin Luther King are examined.

King, Bishop. "Divine Predestination" in his _Essay on the Origin of Evil_ Cambridge 1758 (Refutation by A. Collins)

Metaphor is a relation of things already known in order to affect the passions and so may deceive. It heightens small things by means of greater ones. Analogy allows us to know the unknowable by means of the known.

King, Bruce. "Wallace Steven's 'Metaphors of a Magnifico'" English Studies 49 (Oct. 1968) 450-452
Juxtaposed images create a dialectic here without terse statement. Also a dialectic is created between intellect and sensation neither of which alone is adequate.

Kissane, Leedice. "Interpretation Through Language: A Study of the Metaphors in Stephen Crane's The Open Boat" Rendezvous 1 (1966) 18-22

Kitt, Johannes. De Translationibus Taciti Programm-K. Gymnasium zu Conitz 1884
On Tacitus, figures of speech and metaphor.

Kittlitz-Ottendorff. Über die Verschiedenheit der Gleichnisse in Homers Ilias und Odyssee Zeitschrift für d. Gymn. 1856

Kitzhaber, Albert. A Bibliography on Rhetoric in American Colleges 1850-1900 Denver: Bibliography Center for Research. Denver Publishing Library 1954

Klaeber, Friedrich. Das Bild bei Chaucer Berlin 1893

Klein, Ernest. A Comprehensive Etymological Dictionary of the English Language 2 vols. Amsterdam: Elsevier Publishing Co. 1966
Etymology reveals how language progresses metaphorically.

Kleiser, Grenville. Similes and Their Use New York: Funk and Wagnalls Company 1931

Kloepfer, Rolf. "Das trunkene Schiff: Rimbaud-Magier der 'kühnen' Metapher" Romanische Forschungen 80 (1968) 147-67

Klotman, Phillis Rauch. "The Running Man as Metaphor in Contemporary Negro Literature" PhD diss. Case Western Reserve University 1969

Klubertanz, George. "Problem of Analogy of Being" Review of Metaphysics 10 (June 1957) 553-579
A Thomistic theory of analogy and metaphor. "I believe that there is a place to treat of improper proportionality [i.e. metaphor] in metaphysics, but not in the analysis of the sensible being of experience."

_____. St. Thomas Aquinas on Analogy Chicago: Loyola University Press 1960

Kluge, F. Deutsche Studentensprache Strassburg 1895

Klüver, Heinrich. An Experimental Study of the Eidetic Type (Genetic Psychology Monograph v. 1 no. 2) Worcester, Mass. 1926

Knapp, Robert. "A Study of Metaphor" Journal of Projective Technique 24 (Dec. 1960) 389-395
Metaphor is divergent objects equated by means of a common attribute. He assumes the Freudian notions of a "primary [dream governing or depth] structure" and "secondary [reality coping] process." A seven scale preference gradation test is devised to classify metaphors appropriate or inappropriate to the concepts "time," "success," etc. in order to reveal "deep structure" or "primary processes." He finds that the test is acceptable.

_____, and John Garbutt. "Time Imagery and the Achievement Motive" Journal of Personality 26 (Sept. 1958) 426-434

Knauber, Charles. "Imagery of Light in Dylan Thomas" Renascence 6 (Spring 1954) 95-96, 116

Knight, D. "Development of the Imagery of Colour in German Literary Criticism from Gottsched to Herder" Modern Language Review 56 (July 1961) 354-72

Knight, G. W. Wheel of Fire: Interpretations of Shakespearean Tragedy London: Methuen 1949
A Spurgeon-like attempt to determine character by means of imagery.

Knight, Karl F. "Diction, Metaphor and Symbol in the Poetry of John Crowe Ransom" PhD diss. Emory University 1961-1962. Also The Poetry of John Crowe Ransom; a study of diction metaphor, and symbol The Hague: Mouton 1964
For Ransom metaphor is for aesthetic contemplation and to give pleasure. It makes a sensuous image of the imperceptible, shifts the values of the tenor and keeps focus on the world of direct concrete experience.

Knights, Lionel C. "King Lear as Metaphor" Further Explorations Palo Alto, California: Stanford University Press 1965 pp. 169-185. Also in Myth and Symbol N. Frye, et al., eds. Lincoln University of Nebraska Press 1963 pp. 21-38
He uses M. Foss' definition of metaphor.

_____, and Basil Cottle. Metaphor and Symbol London: Butterworth 1960 [Reviewed in Times Literary Supplement (May 12, 1961) p. 295 Reviewer thinks poetry is itself cognitive, gives insight and cannot be made literal. Also reviewed by Rau]
Contains articles by Wheelwright, Harding, James Barfield, Lewis et al.

Kobayashi, Makoto. "R. M. Rilke: Dichtung und die moderne Ausdruckswelt" Universitas (Stuttgart) 23 (1968) 713-17

Koch, S. "Psychological Science Versus the Science-Humanism Antinomy: Intimations of a Significant Science of Men" American Psychologist 16 (1961) 629-639

Koen, F. "An Intra-Verbal Explication of the Nature of Metaphor" Journal of Verbal Learning and Verbal Behavior 4 (1965) 129-133

Koestler, Arthur. Insight and Outlook New York and London: Macmillan 1949 esp. ch. 23 "Metaphor, Poetic Imagery and Archetypes"
Bisociation refers to "any mental occurrence similtaneously associated with two habitually incompatible contexts." This concept, he states, is central to his entire book. Metaphor is an emotive bisociative juxtaposition of two trains of thought moving in two different fields, one train of thought being compressed.

_____. The Act of Creation New York: Macmillan 1964
On humor and imagery in the act of creation.

Koffka, Mira. "Jean Pauls Bildersprache im 'Hesperus'" PhD diss. München 1910

Kögel, Therese. Bilder bei Mme. de Sévigné: Eine lexikographische Arbeit PhD diss. München. Würzburg: R. Mayr 1937
On metaphor and simile.

Kohfeldt, Gustav. Zur Ästhetik der Metapher" Zeitschrift für Philosophie und philosophische Kritik N.F. 103 (1894) 221-286.
Also a PhD diss. Rostock 1892
He discusses the history of metaphor from ancient to present times and discusses the aesthetic aspects of metaphor. The aesthetic involves making ideas and emotions real and adds interest rather than practical value and the literal. Metaphor brings life to literal language by making it more sensual, by unifying the real and ideal and by humanizing the literal. In metaphor images unite to create a new concretion and bring forth hidden powers of the real object. This happens in music and architecture also. Every new image becomes meaningful only in its connection to a series of old known images or pictures. Images must be comprehensible to the reader and this depends on feeling content, mood, and harmony for which there can be no formula. If there is a rule it involves subjective truth and the metaphor must arise out of the real situation. Metaphor involves intuitive observation and purely aesthetic contemplation. Successful metaphors are determined by 1) sensual aspects including imagery, sound, rhythm, 2) sensual truth forming a whole. A subjective impression must be formed which fits the overall

picture. Sound must relate to imagery, to what is seen and to rhythm, 3) freshness. The images must be new. One may say "wings of hate" instead of "wings of love." He goes on to relate metaphor to the comic. The comic also involves the surprising, strange and unexpected.

Köhler, Albrecht. "Zum metaphorischen Coquere" Archiv fur lateinische Lexikographie und Grammatik 10 (1898) 289-291

Kohler, Erika. Liebeskrieg, zur Bildersprache der höfischen Dichtung des Mittelalters Stuttgart-Berlin: W. Kohlhammer 1935

Kok, Benedictus. Die Vergelyking in die Afrikaanse Volkstaal Pretoria: J. L. van Schaik, bepk. 1942

Kolb, Philip. "An Enigmatic Proustian Metaphor" The Romanic Review 54 (1963) 187-197

Kolbe, A. von Die Gleichnisse aus dem Tierreich bei den römischen Epikern Marienwerder 1909

Kolbe, Frederick. The Four Mysteries of the Faith London 1926

_____. Shakespeare's Way London: Sheed & Ward 1930
W. Clemen states that it is the only book on Shakespeare's imagery before Spurgeon's.

Komornicka, Anna M. "Métaphores, personnifications et comparaisons dans l'oeuvre d'Aristophane" Wroclaw, Warszawa, Krakóv 1964 (cf. Sum in Pasini)

König, J. Zu den homerischen Metaphern und Gleichnissen in Bezug auf Inhalt und Vergleichungspunkt Programm 1875

Konrad, Hedwig. Étude sur la métaphore Paris: J. Vrin (1959)
Also PhD diss. Lavergne 1939 (Reviews by Bruneau, Cohen, Louis, Marouzeau)
Figures as drawn from the arts and crafts may reflect transposition of words from one sociological sphere to another. Metaphor should involve concretion as well as abstraction. Metaphor is a conjunction of two objects under a personal point of view. She discusses critically the view that metaphor is a transposition based on abstraction and resemblance, shows the relation between metaphor and irony, myth, euphemism, hyperbole, comparison, and discusses the works of Hugo, Mallarmé, S. George, and historical views of metaphor.

Koppetsch, Ewald. "Die Metapher bei André Chénier" PhD diss. Konigsberg i. Pr. 1908

Korg, Jacob. "Imagery and Universe in Dylan Thomas' 'Eighteen Poems'" Accent 17 (Winter 1957) 3-15

For Thomas 1) the universe is a machine operated by God, e.g. "brassy blood" 2) life is an explosion 3) body is the world, e.g. "Dawn breaks behind the eyes," and "syllabic blood."

_____. Dylan Thomas New York: Twayne Publ. 1965 "The Rhetoric of Mysticism" ch. 2, p. 26-55
Thomas' images are irrational; all relates to all else.

Korol'kov, B. I. "Metafora" Kratkaya literaturnaya encyclopedia Moscow vol. 4 (1967) 794-797

Kramer, W. "De vergelijking" De Nieuwe Taalgids vol. 24, p. 273ff. (Source: Stutterheim 1941)

_____. "Synaesthesie als stijlverschijnsel" De Nieuwe Taalgids vol. 24, p. 179ff. (Source: Stutterheim 1941)

Kranz, Walther. "Gleichnis und Vergleich in der frühgriechischen Philosophie" Hermes 73 (1938) 19-122

Kreczmar, Jerzy. "O przenośni u Arystotelesa" [The metaphor according to Aristotle] Prace ofiarowane Kazimierzowi Woycickiemu (Warsaw) 6 (1937) 321-336 (Source: Krzyżanowski)

Kroesch, S. "Change of Meaning by Analogy" Studies in Honor of Hermann Collitz Baltimore: Johns Hopkins Press 1930

Krondl. Quae potissimum Vergilius similitudinibus illustraverit Prerau, Pr. 1878

Kronegger, Maria. "James Joyce and Associated Image Makers" PhD diss. Florida State University 1960
On imagery, Joyce, Poe and the Symbolists.

Krummacher, Hans. Das 'als ob' in der Lyrik; Erscheinungsformen und Wandlungen einer Sprachfigur der Metaphorik von der Romantik bis zu Rilke Graz (Köln): Bölau 1965. Revised version of PhD diss., Heidelberg 1956

Krupp, D. Homerische Gleichnisse Zweibrücken 1882

Krzyżanowski, Julian. O Przenośni (La Métaphore) (Source: New York Public Library Slavonic Collection)

Kudlien, Fridolf. "Krankheitsmetaphorik im Laurentiushymnus des Prudentius" Hermes 90 (1962) 104-115

Kuhn, Thomas S. The Structure of Scientific Revolutions Chicago: University of Chicago Press 1962
Each scientific theory or school of thought depends on a root metaphor, model, or "paradigm" e.g. atomism. All other research in a certain age is thought of as unscientific. "Science students accept theories on the authority of teacher

and text, not because of evidence." The paradigm of the time permeates our thinking and even our perception and seeing. (cf. seeing-as. "Something like a paradigm is prerequisite to perception itself.") "Paradigms prove to be constitutive of the research activity." The current paradigm captivates us and we can see in no other way. But gradually it is seen to be inadequate and becomes replaced eventually by another paradigm at the total expense of the first, bringing about a scientific revolution but also a revolution in our thinking and way of seeing the world. We see in terms of ever new metaphors but the current one tends to hold our entire experience captive preventing us from thinking in any other way. Thus, we see the narrowness and dogmatism current in academic and non-academic disciplines.

Kulessa, Ignaz. "Zur Bildersprache des Apollonios Rhodios" PhD diss. Breslau 1938

Kumaniecki, Casimirus. _De elocutionis Aeschyleae natura_ Kraków Gebethner and Wolff 1935 esp. p. 80ff. (cf. _Bulletin international de l'académie polonaise des sciences et des lettres_ classe de philologie, classe d'histoire et de philosophie 1934 pp. 109-111)

Kuusi, Matti. Suomen Kansan Vertauksia. Kuvittanut Kimmo Kaivanto. Helsinki, Suomalaisen Kirjallisuuden Seura 1960, 552 pps. On Finnish metaphor, humor and figures of speech.

Kuypers, K. "De metaphora in de zelf-interpretatie van den mens" Lecture delivered to De Philologencongres of Utrecht April 1, 1937 (cf. Handelingen enz., Groningen 1937 pp. 131ff.)

Laan, J. E. van der. "Review of Stutterheim Het begrip metaphoor" Vereeniging van Leraren in Levende Talen (Groningen) 27 (1941) p. 300 (Name of journal changed to Levende talen berichten en mededeelingen)

_____. "De metaphoor" Neophilologus 27 (1942) 81-91
A summary of Stutterheim, Het begrip metaphoor. A brief history of metaphor and accounts of Brinkmann 1878, Stählin 1914, H. Werner 1919, H. Pongs 1927, A. Biese 1893.

Lacan, Jacques. "La Direction de la cure et les principes de son pouvoir" La Psychanalyse 6 (1961) 149-206
On metaphor and metonymy.

_____. "L'Instance de la lettre dans l'inconscient ou la raison depuis Freud" La Psychanalyse 3 (1957) 47-81 [Jan Miel, trans. into English Yale French Studies nos. 36-37 (Oct. 1966) 112-147]
On the use of metaphor and metonymy.

_____. "Fonction et champ de la parole et du langage en psychanalyse" La Psychanalyse vol. 1 1956. Trans. by Anthony Wilden as The Language of the Self Johns Hopkins Press 1968
A psychological and linguistic analysis of metaphor based on the work of Saussure, Freud, and Jakobson. Metaphor involves unconscious signifying, transposition or "sliding" of meaning, Freudian condensation, substitution and similarity. The manifest term may represent the distorted return of the repressed symptom.

La Fontaine, Jean de. The Fables of La Fontaine Marianne Moore, trans. New York: Viking Press 1952

Lago, M. M. and T. Gupta. "Pattern in the Imagery of Jivanananda Das" Journal of Asian Studies 24 (Aug. 1965) 637-44

Laguardia, Eric. "Aesthetics of Analogy" Diogenes 62 (Summer 1968) 49-61
A discussion of the doctrine of universal correspondence which he says "is founded on the concept of the figurative, on the potential of metaphor." The principle may be just aesthetic and so not apply to the actual world.

_____. "Figural Imitation in English Renaissance Poetry" Proceedings of IV Congress of International Comparative Literature Association 2 vols. François Jost, ed. The Hague: Mouton 1966, II, 844-54

Lāhiṛī, Śibacandra. Baṅālā kābye upamāloka (In Bengali)
On simile and Bengali poetry.

La Juillière, Pierre de. (see Juillière)

Lalande, A. Vocabulaire technique et critique de la philosophie Paris 1932

L'Allemand, Evrard. Laborintus (ca. 1279)
Traditional view of metaphor.

Lambert, Dorothy M. "The Semantic Syntax of Metaphor: A Case Grammar Analysis" PhD diss. University of Michigan 1969
A theory of metaphor is needed based on generative grammar. She presents a modified Fillmore Case Grammar explanation of metaphor. Fillmore follows Chomsky's narrow approach to deviation, yet is amenable to H. Weinrich's recent views.

Lambrechts, G. "Un Aspect du style de Shakespeare: Les métaphores ravivées" Études Anglaises 17 (1964) 364-371

Lamotte, Charles. An Essay upon Poetry and Painting with Relation to the Sacred and Profane History London 1730

Landau, Martin. "Due Process of Inquiry" American Behavioral Scientist 9 (Oct. 1965) 4-10

_____. "On the Use of Metaphor in Political Analysis" Social Research 28 (Fall 1961) 331-53
Metaphors are models which structure inquiry and provide interpretative system. They should be used consciously and their implications noticed. The metaphors of mechanism and evolutionism in American political thinking are examined.

Landow, George. "Ruskin's Version of 'Ut Pictura Poesis'" Journal of Aesthetics and Art Criticism 26 (1968) 521-28

Lane, Pinkie, "Metaphorical Imagery in the Prose Works of Sir Thomas Browne" PhD diss. Louisiana State University 1967

Lang, Henry R. "On Spanish Metaphors" American Journal of Philology 6 (1885) 74-79
Examples in Spanish given to support Brinkmann's view of metaphor.

_____. "The Face and Its Parts in the Spanish Proverb and Metaphor" Baltimore 1887. Reprinted from Transactions of the Modern Language Assoc. of America vol. 3, 1887

Lange, Klaus. "Geistliche Speise. Untersuchungen zur Metaphorik der Bibelhermeneutik" Zeitschrift für deutsches Altertum und deutsche Literatur 95 (May 1966) 81-122 (PhD diss. Kiel 1963)
About biblical metaphors.

Lange, Konrad. Das Wesen der Kunst Berlin: Grote 1901 (cf. Nyman)

Langen, Peter. "Die Metapher im Lateinischen von Plautus bis

Terentius" Neue Jahrbücher für klassische Philologie 125 (1882) 673-693; 753-779

Langer, Susanne. Problems of Art New York: Charles Scribner's 1957
She says the understanding of one thing through another is a deeply intuitive process in the human brain. The symbol in art is a metaphor.

_____. Philosophy in a New Key New York: The New American Library 1951
Largely influenced by the work of Ernst Cassirer on myth and symbolic forms. General words are derived metaphorically from words for concrete objects. ("Every new experience, or new idea about things, evokes first of all some metaphorical expression.") "Metaphor is our most striking evidence of abstractive seeing, of the power of human minds to use presentational symbols." Metaphor "is the force that makes language essentially relational, intellectual, forever showing up new, abstractable forms in reality." The two separate modes of symbolism are 1) discursive (science) and 2) presentational (art, music, myth, metaphor).

_____. Feeling and Form New York: C. Scribner's 1953

Lanham, Richard. A Handlist of Rhetorical Terms University of California Press 1969

Lanier, Sidney. "Metaphors" Southern Magazine 10 (1871-1875) 172 (cf. Eclectic Magazine of Foreign Literature, Science and Art 63 (Oct. 1864) 158-161. An article from The Saturday Review.)

_____. Music and Poetry New York: C. Scribner's 1898 esp. ch. 8 "Nature-Metaphors" pp. 95-114
Metaphors originate not in thought but in love, the principle of all emotion. Love unites duality. Nature-metaphor is a union of human with physical nature. Man himself, as matter with soul, is a metaphor. Nature-metaphor is the poet's strongest tool. "This harmonious union of soul and body, of spirit and nature, of essence and form, is promoted by the nature-metaphor..."

Lapp, J. C. "Mythological Imagery in Pontus de Tyard" Studies in Philology 54 (April 1957) 101-111

La Roche, P. Über die homerischen Vergleiche (Philologie) 1860

Larsson, Hans. Intuition and The Logic of Poetry (cf. Nyman)

Lauretano, Bruno. (Letter to author of this bibliography.)
He states that his work on metaphor involves two major theses; 1) "Conception of the metaphor as a 'synolon,' a dynamic

structure which establishes its own terms (tenor-vehicle) the very moment it asserts itself as a metaphor; thus all pseudo-rhetorical considerations of the metaphor are discouraged" 2) There is a metaphoric origin of philosophic systems though philosophers are only dimly and confusedly aware of this.

_____. Ambiguitá e metafora Napoli: Edizioni Scientifiche Italiane 1964 (Reviewed by Franconi) (cf. next entry)

The book consists of the following three main chapters.

Ch. 1, Extra-metaphorization and Logical Mistakes.

There is a largely unconscious phenomenon of extra-metaphorization. Lauretano summarizes in his epilogue the view presented in this chapter that whereas formerly the metaphorical context was the only form of thinking, today it appears as a residual and specialized form of symbolization and finds no confirmation in a general mythical Weltanschauung; rather it appears besieged by other forms of symbolization, such as logico-mathematical symbolism. In such condition, the metaphor is extinguished or is corrupted and, instead of being returned to a mythical horizon, or Weltanschauung, is transliterated and made to perform on a logico-conceptual level. This results, he says, in that "bastard and monstrous configuration which is the analogical quasi-metaphor."

A metaphor is enriched by the absorption of peripheral and extra-metaphorical meanings some of which result in ambiguity. This process often turns metaphor which is an integration of lifelike character into an unauthentic, cold, uninspired, mechanical analogy. Analogy is proper to science but when serving as the basis for metaphor used in other areas it becomes pseudo-metaphor.

Metaphor is not the coupling of unrelated terms by means of a third thing resulting from pre-existent terms nor mechanical or ornamental but an energetic unity, an active tension and vital impulse constituting the proper terms of the moment in which it constitutes itself as a metaphor and as an organic reality which makes simultaneous the integrated terms. Style is the serial linking of metaphors. He rejects the "spatialistic" interpretation of metaphor, metaphor as just a transfer of a name. In metaphor there is no interval or distance or delay between the metaphor and the terms integrated in it.

Metaphor is a perspective in which the terms emerge to the metaphorical unity and without such a perspective the terms do not exist. The terms of a metaphor are energetic, integrative, relational, constitutive, evocative tensions. He rejects the view that the terms of a metaphor are static, congealed, inactive and given.

A logical mistake ("gaffe") is taking a metaphor which is

pre-logical and displacing it from its context to another which treats it as an analogy. Metaphor does not have clarity in the sense of logical evidence. We tend to confuse pre-logical metaphor without realizing it. Lauretano thinks the two should be kept separate more than is now the case. Philosophies often begin with an original metaphor but it is dangerous to derive logical constructions from metaphors. This produces ambiguity which is "the sickness of language." Ambiguity and pseudo-metaphor are often the result of metaphors creeping into logical discourse.

Ch. 2 An interpretation of some of Machiavelli's metaphors esp. "virtu" and "fortuna." Lauretano laments that words are de-semanticized by the "vulgarization" of metaphors into pseudo-metaphors e.g. "liberty," by metaphorical enlargements (extra-metaphorization). New terms are used but may mislead by means of old metaphorical meanings.

Ch. 3 For a Lexical Reading of Plato.

Lauretano promotes lexical reading. Plato transposed his terms ambiguously e.g. "idea" once meant "to see" and relates to visions. This is an "extra-metaphorical sliding" or "boomerang effect": That is, a metaphor once displaced from its original lifelike sphere, returns from the different sphere enriched or impoverished in problematic, conceptualized or logico-analogical form. It turns around deformed, detached from its lifelike sphere still not attaining to analogical validity. It may become an unauthentic hybrid or pseudo-metaphor.

Plato produces lexical equivocations and linguistic ambiguity in his use of the term "beauty." The uses he puts to "beauty" are often not even connected. They are suspended between and oscillate between scientific and literary discourse. Lauretano concludes that the Platonic term "beauty" is really indefinable and that Plato himself realized this.

In his epilogue Lauretano states that his reductionist method presupposes an archaic or pre-logical phase which can be reconstructed only through the study of language. Metaphor derives from such a phase of symbolization by a "principle of participation" by which "all is in all" and all can be metaphorically exchanged with all. Metaphorism is still today a form of "precategorical thought." Poetry testifies to an archaic, magico-mystical _Weltanschauung_.

_____. _Ambiguità e metafora_ Napoli: Edizioni Scientifiche Italiane 1964 (Reviewed by Francioni)
The author makes two proposals: 1) consideration of metaphor as a _synolon_, a dynamic structure that establishes its own terms (tenor and vehicle) at that very moment it establishes itself; this conflicts with the rhetoric and triangular conceptions according to which metaphor results from the apposition of two terms originally given outside it;

2) indication of the incoercibly metaphorical character of philosophical activity which owing to the lack of precise linguistic conventions, oscillates perfidiously between scientific and literary language, so becoming linked to certain root metaphors assumed uncritically and subsequently "rationalized," to borrow a term from psycho-analysis. The illustrative part of the book points to the metaphorical origin of certain theories. [annotation by Lauretano]

_____. "Un ambiguo cultore dell'ambiguità" Giornale Critico della Filosofia Italiana no. 3 (1966) 425-437

_____. "Demetaforizzazione linguistica e unificazione del sapere" L'Unificazione del Sapere XX Congresso Nazionale di Filosofia, Perugia 1965. Firenze: Sansoni 1967 pp. 312-319
The aim of this article is to underline the importance, for the unification of knowledge, of making homogeneous the languages and jargons of the individual sciences, which may be achieved by the reduction process which tends to eliminate or reduce the metaphorical *quantum* of such languages and jargons. A particular scientific language is in fact sometimes characterized by a special metaphorical tendency. [annotation by Lauretano]

_____. "Eclissi e tentazioni della gnoseologia" La Cultura fasc. 2 (1966) 249-262

_____. "Linguaggio metaforico e linguaggio terminologico" Proceedings of the Fifth International Congress of Aesthetics Amsterdam 1964 The Hague: Mouton 1968 pp. 397-400
In this article, after a brief survey of the history of the problem, two main aspects of linguistic activity are distinguished: 1) the metaphorical and 2) the terminological to which Prodicos from Ceos (fifth cent. B.C.) first called attention. The metaphor is therefore lineated as the archeological survival of an archaic, mystical and pre-scientific phase of language; like the dream-state, the metaphor is derived from a principle of mystic participation, transmutability and universal metamorphosis. [annotation by Lauretano]

_____. "Le metafore antropomorfiche della teoria cibernetica" Atti del XXI Congresso Nazionale di Filosofia--Pisa 1967. Filosofia 1967 pp. 1-7 vol. 2 pp. 171-174; vol. 3 pp. 272-276
This article examines the ambiguity and metaphorical nature of many terms in cybernetics. Machinery and its performance are frequently described with anthropomorphic metaphors from the most varied fields: cognitive, perceptive, intellectual, volitional, etc. It then criticizes the use of terminology (of introspective origin and developed in a pre-scientific age) which is used to describe the performance of electronic machinery. The adoption of a strict, proper, non-metaphori-

cal terminology for cybernetics is required. [annotation by Lauretano]

_____. "Nel labirinto dei segni" Giornale Critico della Filosofia Italiana 18 (1964) 14-37. Section 1 "Realtà della metafora. La cosa irreale" pp. 14-18

_____. Le 'Oscure Sciarade' di Richards" Giornale Critico della Filosofia Italiana no. 4 (1968) 595-622

_____. "Verità e libertà" Atti del XVIII Congresso Nazionale della Società Filosofica Italiana. Palermo 1960 pp. 303-310

Lausberg, Heinrich. Handbuch der literarischen Rhetorik. Eine Grundlegung der Literaturwissenschaft 2 vols. München: Hueber 1960

Law, Helen. "Hyperbole in Mythological Comparisons" American Journal of Philology 47 (Oct. 1926) 361-372

Lawler, Lillian B. B. "Dance in Metaphor" Classical Journal 46 (May 1951) 383-91
The figurative use of the word dance is extensively exemplified, e.g. Nietzsche thought of life as a rhythmic dance. Regarding the Greek view of dance as harmony she states, "Perhaps the Greek was not actively conscious that most of these examples are actually metaphors; for to him the whole world did indeed dance."

Lawlor, J. "Mind and Hand; Some Reflections on the Study of Shakespeare's Imagery" Shakespeare Quarterly 8 (Spring 1957) 179-93

Lay, Wilfred. "Mental Imagery--Experimentally and Subjectively Considered" (The Psychological Review Monograph Supplement, no. 7, Columbia Contributions to Philosophy, Psychology and Education, vol. 4 no. 2) New York 1898

Lazarescu, I. "Review of Tudor Vianu Problemele metaphorei şi alte studii..." Studii şi Cercetări Ştiinţifice, Filologie 9 (1958) 192-193

Lázaro, Fernando. "La metafora impressionista" Rivista di Letterature Moderne e Comparate 2 (Sept. 1951) 370-376 (Also Actes du 5e Congrès intern des langues et littératures modernes pp. 475-481)

_____. "Sobre la dificultad conceptista" Estudios dedicados a Menéndez-Pidal 6 (1956) 355-386
He bases an attempt to elucidate the essence of conceptismo on Gracián's definition of conceit and on Jáuregui's distinction between dificultad and oscuridad.

Lázló, Antal. _Questions of Meaning_ (Janua Linguarum N. R., XXVII) The Hague: Mouton 1963

Lea, Kathleen M. "Conceits" _Modern Language Review_ 20 (Oct. 1925) 389-406
The 16th century conceits came from the _concetti_ of Italy. They are natural in reflecting excitement, gusto, creation, novelty and experiment. 18th century poetry however, is not conceited in this sense.

Leakey, F. W. "Baudelaire's Metaphor in the 'Fleurs du Mal'" PhD diss. London: Queen Mary College 1951

_____. "Intention in Metaphor" _Essays in Criticism_ 4 (1954) 191-98 (Adapted from his PhD diss. on Baudelaire)
Metaphors may be classified by means of their function or intention as 1) illustrative (vehicle not striking), 2)decorative (striking vehicle), 3) evocative or sensuous (tenor and vehicle reciprocal) e.g. genuine synaesthesia, 4) emotive (tenor is a state of mind; vehicle an object matching it).

Leaver, H. R. "Two Parasites; Reply to V. Cameron" _Canadian Bookman_ 15 (Dec. 1933) p. 173

Lecke, Bodo. _Das Stimmungsbild: Musikmetaphorik und Naturgefühl in der dichterischen Prosaskizze 1721-1780_ Göttingen: Vandenhoeck & Ruprecht 1967

Leckie, G. G. "Note on Symbolic Inversion" _Philosophical Review_ 52 (May 1943) 289-98

Lecky, Eleazer. _Meaning and Metaphor_ PhD diss. Cornell University 1938
Metaphors are deviations from custom and words not used in their ordinary context. The same word may be literal or figurative. There is no absolute difference between metaphor and simile. "No objective standard exists by which to measure metaphor." He awaits progress in psychology.

Lee, D. _The Similes of the Iliad and the Odyssey Compared_ (Australian Humanities Research Council. Monograph no. 10) Melbourne University Press 1964

Lee, Rensselaer. _Ut Pictura Poesis: The Humanistic Theory of Painting_ New York: W. W. Norton & Co. 1967
The 16th century theory of painting rested on the view that painting resembles poetry in imitating human action, and must resemble poetry in subject matter, purpose and human content. Painting like poetry must express human emotion, give pleasure, impart wisdom, achieve the sublime, and interpret universal human experience. This theory was undermined by Rousseau, Longinus and views of creative genius.

Leech, G. N. "Linguistics and the Figures of Rhetoric" <u>Essays on Style and Language</u> Roger Fowler, ed. New York: Humanities 1966 pp. 135-156
Figurative meaning is formal deviation in the selection of an inappropriate grammatical class or in the collocational foreground of a lexical item. But no linguistic warranty can be found for metaphor.

Lees, Jas. T. "The Metaphor in Aeschylus" <u>Studies in Honor of Basil L. Gildersleeve</u> Baltimore: Johns Hopkins Press 1902 pp. 483-496
Aeschylus uses metaphors more than any other figure and extends them. The subjects of his metaphors are listed.

Lees, Ronald. "Tyranny of Metaphor" <u>The London Quarterly and Holborn Review</u> 171 (Oct. 1946) 346-8
Metaphors are used throughout religion but if taken literally yield tyranny and error. Metaphor is not dogma but suggests a likeness only. It should not be pressed too far. Metaphor is a "good servant but a bad master."

Lefkowitz, Mary. "Metaphor and Simile in Ennius" <u>The Classical Journal</u> 55 (Dec. 1959) 123-125
Ennius is highly metaphorical.

Leger, G. "Review of Analogy Literature" <u>Bulletin Thomiste</u> 8 (1948) 577-92. The index of this journal contains entries under analogy, and metaphor.

Le Hir, Yves. <u>Rhétorique et stylistique de la Pléiade au Parnasse</u> Paris 1960

Lehmann, A. G. <u>The Symbolist Aesthetic in France 1885-1895</u> Oxford: Blackwell 1950

Leisi, Ernst. <u>Der Wortinhalt. Seine Struktur im Deutschen und Englischen</u> Heidelberg: Quelle & Meyer 1953 "Die indirekte Metapher" pp. 70-75

Leistner, Rudolf. "Über die Vergeliche in Gottfrieds von Strassburg Tristan mit Berücksichtigung des metaphorischen Elementes im engeren Sinne" PhD diss. Leipzig 1907

Leiter, Louis H. "Typology, Paradigm, Metaphor and Image in the York Creation of Adam and Eve" <u>Drama Survey</u> 7 (Winter 1968-1969) 113-32

Lemmon, Martha. "A Psychological Consideration of Analogy" <u>American Journal of Psychology</u> 51 (April 1938) 304-356
An attempt to determine how one identifies a relation between two unlike contexts. She suggests it is symbolizing, which is different from comprehending. It occurs when literal significance comes first then changes to figurative implication.

Lemos, M. G. de. "Metáfora no portuguẽs nomes des animals aplicados a pessoas" PhD diss. Coimbra 1951
Comparative study exploring proverbs and folklore in Portugal, Spain and France.

Lentricchia, Frank. The Gaiety of Language: An Essay on the Radical Poetics of W. B. Yeats and Wallace Stevens Berkeley: University of California Press 1968 esp. "Metaphor and the Constructive Imagination" 168-186
He takes a one-sided view that for Stevens metaphor merely distorts and evades reality. It is illusive and irrational but helps to humanize the world man lives in. He admits, however, that metaphor, for Stevens, sometimes reveals aspects of the world.

Leonard, Sterling. The Doctrine of Correctness in English Usage 1700-1800 New York: Russell and Russell 1962

Leonard, Vivien R. "An Introductory Study of Imagery in the Prefaces to the New York Edition of the Novels and Tales of Henry James" PhD diss. Columbia University 1966

Leondar, Barbara. "The Structure and Function of Metaphor" EdD diss. Harvard University 1968
Metaphor is a logical incongruity with double layers of meaning. It is a transgression of categories. "Fusion metaphor" is isomorphic like a map, diagram or scientific model. Tenor and vehicle are given equal prominence and it is highly tensive. An elaborate scale of gradation of figures is given ranging from what Barfield calls the "born literal" to the "achieved literal"; from no tenor or tension (of closed simile) to no vehicle or tension of the "dead" metaphor. In that order are various types of simile, metaphor and symbol graded. There is no clear line between the literal and metaphorical. About language in general she holds that ideas, words and objects are inextricably related (as do Cassirer, Croce, Whorf, Sapir and Coleridge). "I consider the identity of language and reason as one of the fundamental principles of our science."

Lerner, L. D. "The Miltonic Simile" Essays in Criticism 4 (1954) 297-308

Leroux, Pierre. "Du style symbolique" Globe April 1829 (cf. D. Evans; M. Baym 1961)
Ideas are compared and only the second idea is developed. Proper word is replaced by a metaphor, idea by its emblem. This creates the "metaphor of an idea."

LeSage, Laurence. "The Cliché Basis for Some of the Metaphors of Jean Giraudoux" Modern Language Notes 56 (1941) 435-439

Giraudoux's imagery follows definite patterns.

_____. "Jean Giraudoux's Use of the Metaphor" PhD diss. University of Illinois 1940

_____. Metaphor in the Nondramatic Works of Jean Giraudoux Eugene, Oregon: University of Oregon Press 1952
Metaphor is the key to Giraudoux's work. It reflects the secret affinities of nature and involves paradox, humor, escape, a natural spontaneity, a reduction of abstract to concrete, and picture thoughts or visions. LeSage defends the conceit.

_____. "Jean Giraudoux, Prince des Précieux" PMLA 57 (1942) 1196-1205

Lesin, [or Lesyn] B. M. and O. C. Pulinets'. "Metafora" Slovnik literaturoznavchikh termini' 1965 vol. 2 pp. 206-207

Leskov, Nikolai. "Metapher vom König Lear" Werke 3 vols. München: Biederstein 1963-1964 vol. 3 pp. 123-155

Lessing, Gotthold E. Laocoön or the Limits of Painting and Poetry W. A. Steel, trans. E. P. Dutton and Company 1961
"A poetic picture is not necessarily that which can be transmuted into a material painting...There are paintable and unpaintable facts." The poet often does more than the painter and painters sometimes imitate the poet.

Lever, Katherine. "Poetic Metaphor and Dramatic Allegory in Aristophanes" The Classical Weekly 46 (April 1953) 220-223
Characters' names have meanings. There is personification of meanings. Poverty is represented as a ragged old woman.

Levin, Samuel. Linguistic Structures in Poetry The Hague: Mouton and Company 1964 esp. ch. 4 "Coupling"

Lewin, Bertram. "Metaphor, Mind and Manikin" The Psychoanalytic Quarterly 40 (1971) 6-39

Lewis, Clarence I. An Analysis of Knowledge and Valuation La-Salle, Illinois: The Open Court Publishing Company 1946 esp. pp. 102-103

Lewis, Clive Staples. The Allegory of Love: A Study in Medieval Tradition New York: Oxford University Press 1965
Presents a theory of personification allegory.

_____. "Bluspels and Flalansferes" Rehabilitations and Other Essays New York: Oxford University Press 1939 pp. 135-58

"All our truth, or all but a few fragments, is won by metaphor." "Literalness we cannot have." We can only think and speak in metaphors but we must be conscious that they are metaphors.

Lewis, Hywel D. "Imagination and Experience" Metaphor and Symbol L. C. Knights and Basil Cottle, eds. London: Butterworth 1960 pp. 64-77

Lewis, J. C. "The Rhetoric of Faith: A Study of Donne's Use of the Conceit in the Divine Poems" PhD diss. University of Washington 1964
He holds that Donne was the first and greatest English exponent of the art of "indirect communication."

Lewis, Merrill. "Organic Metaphor and Edenic Myth in George Bancroft's History of the United States" Journal of the History of Ideas 26 (Oct. 1965) 587-92

Lewontin, R. C. "Models, Mathematics and Metaphors" Synthese 15 (1963) 222-244
Metaphorical change is "The substitution of a physical entity with an already associated set of observed or inferred attributes..." That is, "The model should be chosen before the metaphor and not by means of it...chosen by virtue of its elements of similarity to the pre-existent structure of rules." The metaphor unifies and is didactic. It makes the model more visible and able to be sensed.

Lewy, F. B. "Zur Verbalmetapher bei André Chénier und den französischen Romantikern" PhD diss. Strassburg 1913

Liddie, Alexander. "Stevens' 'Metaphors of a Magnifico'" Explicator 21 (Oct. 1962) Item 15
The poem shows how careful sense observation startles one out of theorizing.

Lieb, Hans-Heinrich. "Der Umfang des historischen Metaphernbegriffs" PhD diss. Köln University 1964
A detailed classification of definitions of metaphor, which relies heavily on Carnap's semantics. These definitions are traced historically also. (He has an unpublished work on metaphor in literature, which stresses the lyrics of Benn.)

_____. "Review of Meier Die Metapher" Zeitschrift für Romanische Philologie 82 (1966) 187-194

_____. "Was bezeichnet der herkömmliche Begriff 'Metapher'?" Muttersprache 77 (1967) 43-52 (Based on his PhD diss.)
A classification of metaphors according to general categories and an examination of the relations between the categories. Metaphors may contain a general or specific content and al-

so a wider and narrower focus. The metaphor may be classified by the number of objects (e.g. two or three) that it compares. Lieb distinguishes fourteen types of metaphor, seven for the general and seven for the specific metaphors. He also discusses metaphor as it relates to context.

Liebesny, Hugh J. "Metaphor in Language Teaching" Modern Language Journal 41 (Feb. 1957) 59-65
We speak in metaphors or pictures everyday, in slang as well as in poetry. Metaphor provides a transition from concrete to abstract, associates immaterial concepts with material things.

Liedstrand, Fritjof. "Metapher und Vergleich in 'The Unfortunate Traveller' von Thomas Nashe und bei seinen Vorbildern François Rabelais und Pietro Aretino" PhD diss. Münster, Weimar 1929

Lincke, Ernst. De elocutione Isaei PhD diss. Leipzig 1884 pp. 19-20 on metaphor.

Lindner, Albert. "Die Metaphern bei Sophokles. Versuch einer systematischen Darstellung nach onomasiologischen Gesichtspunkten" Inaug. diss. Leipzig 1957

Lindstrom, James D. "Metaphoric Structure in the Verse Fables and Horatian Imitations of Jonathan Swift: An Introduction to His Poetic Style" PhD diss. University of California at Los Angeles 1969

Lingenberg, W. Platonische Bilder und Sprichwörter Programm Köln 1872

Linn, John C. "Proust's Theatre Metaphors" Romanic Review 49 (1958) 179-190
He follows closely the associations arising from a locutional nucleus.

Lipps, Hans. "Metaphern" Deutsche Vierteljahrsschrift für Literaturwissenschaft und Geistesgeschichte 12 (1934) 352-363. Also in Die Verbindlichkeit der Sprache: Arbeiten zur Sprachphilosophie und Logik. Frankfurt/M 1944 (1958)

Lira, T. [pseudonym of Harry D. Feltenstein]

Lisca, Peter. "Nick Carraway and the Imagery of Disorder" Twentieth Century Literature 13 (1967) 18-28

Littell, P. "Wilstach's Dictionary of Similes" New Republic 9 (Nov. 25, 1916) p. 99

Littlefield, D. J. "Metaphor and Myth: The Unity of Aristophanes'

Knights" _Studies in Philology_ 65 (Jan. 1968) 1-22

Littmann, Hildegard. _Die Metapher in Merediths und Hardys Lyrik_ Zürich/Leipzig: M. Niehans 1938. PhD diss. Bern 1938: "Das dichterische Bild in der Lyrik George Merediths und Thomas Hardys im Zusammenhang mit ihrer Weltanschauung"

Litvinenk, A. S. "Termin i metafora" 1954 (Source: Korol'kov)

Liu, James. _The Art of Chinese Poetry_ University of Chicago Press 1962 esp. "Imagery and Symbolism" pp. 101-130 Definitions of imagery are given. Before Tu Fu, poetry has only simple juxtaposition. There are no genuine synaesthetic images in Chinese--only substitutions. Many original metaphorical implications of the Chinese character are now lost, the views of Pound and Fenollosa notwithstanding.

Ljasota, Jir. L. [See Lyasota]

Llie, Paul. _The Surrealist Mode in Spanish Literature_ Ann Arbor: University of Michigan 1968
Especially on Machado, Solana, Aleixandre, Lorca, Dali, Alberti.

Lloyd, G. E. R. _Polarity and Analogy_ Cambridge: University Press 1966

Locke, John. _Essay Concerning Human Understanding_ John Yolton, ed. New York: Dutton 1965 esp. Book III
All words are originally derived from names for sensible things e.g. "spirit" derives from "breath." Metaphors mislead.

Lockwood, J. F. "The Metaphorical Vocabulary of Dionysius of Halicarnassus" _The Classical Quarterly_ 31 (1937) 192-203
Metaphor is used when assistance of visual image is needed to give clarity.

Lodge, Thomas. _Defense of Poetry_ 1579

Loeb, I. "La vie des métaphores dans la Bible" Paris: Léopold Conf. 1891. Reprinted in his book _La littérature des pauvres dans la Bible_ Paris 1892

Logan, John. "The Blue Guitar: A Semantic Study of Poetry" PhD diss. in Philosophy, University of Texas 1962
Poetry has a unique cognitive role. On Stevens, Wheelwright and Langer.

Longinus. _On the Sublime_ G. Grube, trans. Indianapolis: Bobbs-Merrill 1957
Figures reinforce greatness and _vice versa_. They express passion, delight and are best if unnoticed, natural and not

used in excess.

Looby, Ruth. "Understandings Children Derive from Their Reading" Elementary English Review 16 (Feb. 1939) 58-62

Lorca [See García Lorca]

Lord, David N. Characteristics and Laws of Figurative Language New York: Franklin Knight 1855
"A metaphor is an affirmation, or representation by words, that an agent, object, quality, or act, is that which it merely resembles." In a metaphor the subject is literal and the predicate figurative. All grammatical classes of words can be metaphorized e.g. verb, preposition, adverb, etc. Names may be metaphorical. Some metaphors involve ellipsis. Exercises in metaphor are given for the student.

Lorenz, Erika. Der metaphorische Kosmos der modernen spanischen Lyrik 1936-1956 Hamburg: Cram, De Gruyter 1961
Subconscious origin of archetypes is stressed. An examination of water, earth, and sky metaphors in these poets.

_____. "José Ramón Medina und José Luis Hidalgo--durch eine Metapher gesehen" Romanische Forschungen 70 (1958) 111-125
There is revolt and agnosticism in the symbols of sea and passing time.

Lottich, Otto. "De sermone vulgari Atticorum maxime ex Aristophanis fabulis cognoscendo" PhD diss. Halle 1881 pp. 20-24 On metaphor.

Louch, A. R. "Games and Metaphors" Explanation and Human Action Berkeley and Los Angeles: University of California Press 1966 pp. 209-232
He stresses the context-bound individual case, which metaphor can render, as opposed to general theory. Sometimes man is like a chess-player writ large as R. S. Peters suggests, sometimes not. The value of game analysis is only in its metaphorical not its theoretical use.

Louis, Pierre. Les métaphores de Platon Thesis, University of Paris (Paris: Les Belles Lettres 1945)

_____. "Review of Konrad Études sur la métaphore" Revue de philologie: De littérature et d'histoire anciennes 14 (1940) 180

Love, Walter D. "Edmund Burke's Idea of the Body Corporate: A Study in Imagery" Review of Politics 27 (April 1965) 184-97
Burke's language is highly figurative and often not reducible to exact definition. D. Davie is quoted as saying that Burke spent his entire career bringing to life the metaphor of

the body politic. The body corporate is a mysterious whole, a chartered town, a church, a local government, a monastic foundation, a colonial assembly, parliament, an estate of society, etc.

Lowes, John. The Road to Xanadu: A Study in the Ways of the Imagination Boston: Houghton Mifflin 1927
On Coleridge's theory of the imagination.

Luca, Reginaldo de. "Filosofía y metáfora" Nosotros 59 (1928) 5-32

Lucas, F. L. "Simile and Metaphor" Style New York: Collier Books 1962 pp. 185-213 (London: Cassell 1955 (1960) pp. 191-218)
Every expression is metaphorical, a superimposition of two ideas. Metaphor itself is a metaphor meaning "carry across." "Idea" comes from "shape"; "spirit" from "breath" etymologically. Metaphor can give strength, clarity, speed or humor. If one has no gift for metaphor he should not write, not even prose.

Lucchetti, L. Les images dans les oeuvres de V. Hugo Veroli 1909

Lüers, Grete. Die Sprache der Deutschen des Mittelalters im Werke der Mechthild von Magdeburg Munich: E. Reinhardt 1926

Lurker, Manfred, et al. Bibliographie zur Symbolkunde 3 vols. Baden-Baden: Heitz 1968
A bibliography of works dealing with the subject of symbolism. Has an author and subject index.

Lyasota, Jir. L. "Ponyatie o kontekstual' noi (metaforicheskoy) gruppe" Uchenie zapiski dal' nevostochovo universiteta. Seriya filologicheskaya. Vladivostok 5 (1962) 93-98 (Russian and English used)

Lyly, John. Euphues: The Anatomy of Wit; Euphues & His England Morris Croll and Harry Clemons, eds. New York: Russell & Russell 1964
Introduction is on euphuism and rhetoric.

Lyons, C. R. "Bertolt Brecht's 'Baal': The Structure of Images" Modern Drama 8 (Dec. 1965) 311-23

Lyons, Helen. "Figures of Speech in Seneca's Medea" The Classical World 35 (1941-42) 256-257

Lyttkens, Hampus. The Analogy Between God and the World: An Investigation of Its Background and Interpretation of Its Use by Thomas of Aquino. Uppsala: Lundequistska bokhandeln 1952

Maass, K. Über Metapher und Allegorie im deutschen Sprichwort Leipzig 1891

Macbeth, John. The Might and Mirth of Literature London 1876 Presents 220 figures of speech. Has ornament view of metaphor.

MacDonald, Margaret. "The Philosopher's Use of Analogy" Logic and Language 2 vols. Antony Flew, ed. Oxford: Basil Blackwell 1960 Vol. I pp. 80-100

MacGill, Stevenson. Lectures on Rhetoric and Criticism Edinburgh 1838 (cf. A. Ward)
He gives four laws of association as the basis of figures of speech:
1) Association by cause/effect - metonymy
2) Association by contiguity --- synecdoche
3) Association by resemblance -- metaphor and simile
4) Association by contrariety -- irony and antithesis

MacIntyre, Alistair. "Analogy in Metaphysics" Downside Review 69 (1951) 45-6

MacIver, A. M. "Metaphor" Analysis 7 (Oct. 1940) 61-67
A criticism of Britton's "The Description of Logical Properties." "Metaphor is simply the application to one thing of a name properly (that is, in normal usage hitherto) belonging to something else, on the strength of some more or less remote resemblance connecting them." He objects to Britton's view that logical terms are metaphorical and so yield mistakes.

Mack, Maynard. "Wit and Poetry and Pope: Some Observations on His Imagery" Pope and His Contemporaries. Essays presented to George Sherburn James Clifford, ed. Oxford 1949 pp. 20-40

Mackel, Dr. Die Metapher im Unterricht (32 Jahresbericht des K. Realgymnasiums zu Perleberg über das Schuljahr 1893/94) 1894
A discussion of the great importance metaphor has in the education of students in German secondary schools. Metaphor helps present the double concepts of the real and the theoretical, existence and becoming, and also shows the nature and development of language and culture. Metaphor and comparison give one an excellent kind of concentration and understanding. The student by becoming conscious that many of our seemingly literal words are in fact metaphors can expose them as fictions. Teachers should hold weekly meetings to encourage and clarify the teaching of metaphor. Metaphor is regarded as a shortened comparison here. Metaphorical instruction can show that an object is just a fiction and is really elliptical for all of its qualities. Metaphor development progresses along with technological development by means of increased comparisons e.g. war introduces military termino-

logy e.g. "disarmed." It indicates the development of a people. The poetic metaphor is often pictorial and personification is its most important form. Poets improve the language and prevent it from stagnating, but innovation in language is usually anonymous, rather than literary. Metaphorical speech reflects the attitude of our ancestors although we are usually unaware of it. Metaphors differ in different languages. Homework and exercises in metaphor for students is outlined.

Mackey, Louis. "Aristotle and Feidelson on Metaphor: Toward a Reconciliation of Ancient and Modern" _Arion_ 4 (Summer 1965) 272-85
Aristotle's account of metaphor implicitly meets the demands of Feidelson's account as presented in the latter's _Symbolism and American Literature_. Both theories are summarized.

_____. "On Philosophical Form, a Tear for Adonais" _Thought_ 42 (Summer 1967) 238-260)
The style or way something is said partly constitutes what is said e.g. to understand Kant's philosophy we must understand his metaphors. Philosophical argument is an inadequate abstraction from a work's metaphors, style and "whole meaning." Style transcends formal structure. The basic metaphor in Plato is a circle, in Aquinas a hierarchy of arches, in Hume the spatially flat and uncentered.

Mackin, Cooper R. "Aural Imagery as Miltonic Metaphor: The Temptation Scenes of _Paradise Lost_ and _Paradise Regained_" _Explorations of Literature_ Rima D. Reck, ed. Baton Rouge: Louisiana State University 1966 pp. 32-42

MacLeish, Archibald. "Metaphor" _Poetry and Experience_ Boston: Houghton Mifflin Company 1961 pp. 65-88
Metaphor is the placing of two incongruous images side by side yielding a new meaning while retaining the old meanings. It shows us relations we had not seen and yields something only emotion can know.

Macmillan, Hugh. _The True Vine or the Analogies of Our Lord's Allegory_ London: Macmillan 1871

MacNeice, Louis. _Modern Poetry: A Personal Essay_ New York and London: Oxford University Press 1938 pp. 90-113 (London: SMC Press 1967)
Imagery and meaning are nearly inseparable. Images are 1) cerebral or metaphysical, or 2) emotional, visual or intuitive (from senses or the unconscious), or 3) both. Cerebral images can express emotion. An image can captivate us and change our lives.

Macquarrie, John. _God Talk: An Examination of the Language and Logic of Theology_ New York: Harper and Row 1967 (London:

SMC Press 1967) esp. chapt. 10 "Analogy and Paradox" Analogical language about God is paradoxical and meaningful.

Maddock, Lawrence Hill. "The Critical Image of Thomas Wolfe" PhD dissertation Geo. Peabody College 1966

Madge, Charles. "Myth, Metaphor and World Picture" Manchester Literary and Philosophical Society (Proceedings) 105 (1963) 53-63
Metaphors are primitive, physiologically based processes and satisfactions which are intersubjective because we have similar body-minds. Metaphor does not explain, and is not a symbolic process. It is the reference of one thing by the name of another, an illogical, magical, mental transformation revealing the inward, deep resemblance of things thereby giving a feeling of liberation. There is reciprocal metaphor (two way), metamorphic metaphor (A becomes B), latent metaphor (a single object, experience, work of art, may function as a metaphor), pure metaphor (those metaphors provoking the active awareness of metaphors). Metaphor may be the basis of all the arts.

_____. "Metaphor" The Concise Encyclopedia of English and American Poetry Stephen Spender and Donald Hall, eds. New York: Hawthorne Books 1963 pp. 198-202

Magdeburg. Über die Bilder und Gleichnisse bei Euripides Programm, Danzig 1884

Mahoney, John. "Keats and the Metaphor of Fame" English Studies 44 (1963) 355-357

Makarov, V. V. "Review of Tudor Vianu Problemele metaforei şi alte studii..." Studii şi Cercetări Lingvistice (Bucureşti) 9 (1958) 421-423

Malkley, Gervais de. Ars Versificaria (Ca. 1208-1213)
A traditional view of metaphor.

Mandelbaum, Maurice. "Language and Chess: De Saussure's Analogy" Philosophical Review 77 (1968) 356-357
Earlier than Wittgenstein, de Saussure spoke of language as a game and compared it with chess in his Cours de linguistique générale.

Mansart, E. A. Du Sublime et des Tropes 1883

Manser, A. R. "Images" Encyclopedia of Philosophy vol. 4, 1967 pp. 133-136
He discusses the views of image as: idea, object, mental picture, perception, meaning of words. Objections by Ryle, Price,

Wittgenstein, Sartre, etc. are presented.

_____. "Imagination" _Encyclopedia of Philosophy_ vol. 4 1967 pp. 136-139
A discussion of the nature of the imagination e.g. as a faculty, a power to form metaphors or mental images etc. The views of Aristotle, Hume, Kant, Coleridge, Ryle, Sartre, etc. are presented.

Mansfeld, Franz. _Das literarische Barock im kunsttheoretischen Urteil Gottscheds und der Schweizer..._ Halle: E. Klinz 1928. PhD dissertation Halle-Wittenberg. Friedrichs Universität
On the theory of metaphor of Gottsched, Bodmer and Breitinger.

Manso, P. "The Metaphoric Style of Joyce's Portrait" _Modern Fiction Studies_ 13 (Summer 1967) 221-36
The significance of the _Portrait_ is in the metaphoric nature of its structure and style. There is progression from 1) the incoherent simile stage (immature solopsism) to 2) the metaphoric stage (dualism) to 3) the symbolic stage (unity of all).

Marcellino, Ralph. "Some Aspects of the Metaphors of Propertius" PhD dissertation New York University 1952

Marcus, M. and E. Marcus. "Animal Imagery in 'The Red Badge of Courage'" _Modern Language Notes_ 74 (Feb. 1959) 108-11

Mardiros, Anthony. "Review of Turbayne: _The Myth of Metaphor_" _Queen's Quarterly_ 70 (1963) 281-282

Margolis, Joseph. "Figurative Language" _The Language of Art and Art Criticism_ Detroit: Wayne State University 1965 pp. 165-177
A view of metaphor as play, which may derive from the views of Kant, K. Lange, Schiller, Huizinga, et al.

_____. "Notes on the Logic of Simile, Metaphor and Analogy" _American Speech_ 32 (Oct. 1957) 186-9
Although metaphors are said to be able to be converted into similes and similes into metaphors this is often not possible. Also metaphors can be unlike figurative analogies. Metaphor is compared to open and closed similes.

Marheineke. Über die Shakespeareschen Gleichnisse. _Herrig's Archiv_ 51:173

Mariani, Gaetano. "La tecnica dell' analogia nella poesia secentista e in quella contemporanea" in _La Critica Stilistica e il Barocco Letterario_ Atti del Secondo Congresso Internazionale di Studi Italiani. Venice 1956 pp. 272-282

Marinists link extreme concrete elements.

Marías, Julián. "Philosophic Truth and the Metaphoric System" *Interpretation: The Poetry of Meaning* Stanley Hopper and David Miller, eds. New York: Harcourt, Brace and World Inc. pp. 40-53
There is no reality as such only metaphorical perspectives which constitute reality. No single metaphor can reveal reality but each one relates to ever more metaphors, a system of metaphors. Thus thinking never stops.

Marignac, Aloys de. Imagination et dialectique. Essai sur l'expression du spirituel par l'image dans les dialogues de Platon Paris: Les Belles Lettres, 1951

Marino, Giambattista. (See J. Mirollo and others on marinism.)

Marouzeau, J. "Review of Konrad: *Étude sur la métaphore*" *Revue des Études Latines* 17 (1939) 394-395

Marquardt, H. *Die altenglischen Kenningar: Ein Beitrag zur Stilkunde altgermanischer Dichtung* Halle 1938

Marques, Oswaldino. *Teoria da Metáfora & Renascença da poesia americana* Rio de Janeiro: Livraria São José 1956

Marsh, Florence. *Wordsworth's Imagery: a study in poetic vision* New Haven: Yale University Press 1952

Marsh, T. N. "Elizabethan Wit in Metaphor and Conceit: Sidney, Shakespeare, Donne" *English Miscellany: Symposium of History Literature and the Arts* 13 (1962) 25-29

Martin, Anthony. "Figurative Language" PhD diss. in Philosophy, Johns Hopkins University 1969
He presents criteria for literalness and defends a modified, classical comparison theory of metaphor.

Martin, Graham. "Metaphors in Supervielle's Poetry" *Modern Language Review* 59 (Oct. 1964) 579-82
Metaphor is a complex transfer of attributes, e.g. the sun seeming to be travelling with a train, and often involving an imagined object with a personality (a "metaphorical personality"). Supervielle uses transferred attribution and extended personification more than most poets.

Martin, Robert. "Drange on Type Crossings" *Philosophy and Phenomenological Research* 30 (Sept. 1969) 126-135 Reply by Drange pp. 136-139

Martin, Wallace and I. Fletcher. *A Catalogue of the Imagist Poets* New York: J. H. Woolmer 1966

Martino, E. "Ser y valor de la metáfora" *Humanidades* (Mérida) 13 (1961) 167-192
On "the being and value of metaphor" in classical antiquity, as related to other figures, to language and in itself. Metaphor begins as an association of images and becomes a verbal and psychological substitution. It reveals a real object in an unlimited, irreducible, unparaphrasable sense. It is not a perfect representation or unity. It means one thing by the concept of another.

Marty, Anton. *Die Frage nach der geschichtlichen Entwicklung des Farbensinnes* Wien: C. Gerold 1879 Abhang 2, "Über Befähigung und Berechtigung der Poesie zur Schilderung von Farben und Formen."

_____. *Untersuchungen zur Grundlegung der allgemeinen Grammatik und Sprachphilosophie* Halle: S. Niemeyer 1908 (Criticized by O. Funke and G. Stern)

Martyn, James, ed. *Pictures and Emblems* London 1885
Imagery of Alexander MacLaren's sermons.

Marzot, Giulio. *L'Ingegno e il genio nel seicento* Florence 1944

Marzullo, Benedetto. "Di una metafora greca della rugiada" *Maia (firenze): Rivisita di letterature classiche* N.S. 5 (1952) 277-82

Mascall, E. *Existence and Analogy* Longmans, Green (London) 1949 "The Doctrine of Analogy" pp. 175-181
Thomistic theory of analogy and metaphor. He follows Cajetan to some extent except that here an analogy of proportionality and an analogy of attribution are combined.

Masiello, R. J. "The Analogy of Proportion According to the Metaphysics of St. Thomas" *The Modern Schoolman* 35 (1958) 91-105

Matlaw, R. "Recurrent Imagery in Dostoevsky" *Harvard Slavic Studies* 3 (1957) 201-226

Matoré, Georges. "Les images gustatives dans *Du Coté de chez Swann*" (Mélanges de linguistique et de littérature romanes à la mémoire d'István Frank. Annales Universitatis Saraviensis, 6. Saarbrücken 1957 pp. 685-692)

Matt, Hildegard. "Das 'visuelle' Element in der Kunst Victor Hugos betrachtet an seinen Bildern" PhD dissertation Freiburg i. Br. 1934

Matthew of Vendôme. [See Vendôme]

Matthews, Honor. *Character and Symbol in Shakespeare's Plays* (A

Study of Certain Christian and Pre-Christian Elements in Their Structure and Imagery) Cambridge: Cambridge University Press 1962

Matthews, W. "Review of Allegory; The Theory of a Symbolic Mode by A. Fletcher" Romance Philology 20 (1967) 557-563

Maurer, Armand. "St. Thomas and the Analogy of Genus" New Scholasticism 29 (1955) 127-44

Mauron, Charles P. Des métaphores obsédantes au mythe personnel Paris: Corti 1963 (Also PhD dissertation, Paris 1963) (Translated into Italian by M. Picchi, Milan: Il Saggiatore 1966)
The obsessional réseau ("nets" or metaphors) are mortcombat, triomphe-grandeur, rire. These reveal themselves through different poems.

Mauser, Wolfram. Bild und Gebärde in der Sprache Hofmannsthals Wien 1961

Mausser, O. Deutsche Soldatensprache Strassburg 1917

Mauthner, F. Beiträge zu einer Kritik der Sprache vol. II Zur Sprachwissenschaft Stuttgart 1901 "Die Metapher" pp. 465-549 (cf. G. Weiler, Mauthner's Critique of Language London 1970)
An extensive discussion of metaphor, trope, comparison, unconscious metaphor, metaphor as related to: myth, wit, being, etymology, association, psychology, etc. He discusses Aristotle, Müller, Vico, Jean Paul, Shakespeare, Goethe, Bruchmann, Kant, Schopenhauer, etc.

Mawardi, Betty H. "Creative Use of the Metaphor in a Cognitive Impasse" Paper read in New York at the American Psychological Association, Sept. 1961 (cf. B. Kaplan, H. Nash)
Based on her PhD dissertation. An examination of the role of metaphor in creative thinking and invention. Freudian concepts are assumed. Metaphor is a word meaning one thing used to indicate something else on the basis of similarity. It stimulates and liberates the "unconscious" to be creative.

_____. "Industrial Invention: A Study in Group Problem Solving" PhD diss. Harvard University 1959

May, T. E. "Gracián's Idea of the 'Concepto'" Hispanic Review 18 (Jan. 1950) 15-41
For Gracián the concepto is the total unified act of the understanding in grasping reality transformed harmoniously to produce wit. The conceit, agudeza, is a special act of understanding, an intuition. It depends on a specific context and so cannot be given a complete general analysis. It justifies itself. Gracián, then, just describes the experience of conceits in concrete situations.

_____. "Interpretation of Gracián's Agudeza y Arte de Ingenio" Hispanic Review 16 (Oct. 1948) 275-300
The conceit is an intuitive experience of the harmonious and total resolution of extremes. It is not a formal construction of abstract data. Thus it cannot be paraphrased adequately. It must modify and transform our perception of the object. The conceit is concerned with truth and beauty. The same conceit may be taken in various ways: as profound, as humorous, etc.

Mayer, Gilbert. "Les images dans Montaigne, d'après le chapître 'De l'Institution des enfants'" Mélanges de philologie et d'histoire littéraire offerts à Edmond Huguet Paris: Boivin 1940 pp. 110-118
Mayer is a disciple of Bruneau and so shows the skill of Montaigne in metaphorical condensation and profuseness.

Mayröcker, Friederike. Metaphorisch Stuttgart: Dr. E. Walther 1964

Mays, W. "Review of Turbayne: The Myth of Metaphor" British Journal for the Philosophy of Science 15 (1964) 78-82

Mazzeo, Joseph Anthony. "Aspects of Wit and Science in the Renaissance" PhD dissertation, Columbia University 1950
On metaphor and on John Donne.

_____. "Critique of Some Modern Theories of Metaphysical Poetry" Modern Philology 50 (Nov. 1952) 88-96
Metaphysical poetry, Marinismo, Concettismo, and Gongorismo are based on a belief in universal analogy of all things (a view held by Gracián and Tesauro also) thus giving justification to even the most far-fetched conceits. Mazzeo opposes Tuve's Ramistic logic theory of conceit and Croce's baroque theory. Praz's emblem theory is opposed partly because metaphors or conceits cannot be pictured.

_____. "Dante's Conception of Poetic Expression" Romanic Review 47 (Dec. 1956) 241-58

_____. "Metaphysical Poetry and the Poetic of Correspondence" Journal of the History of Ideas 14 (April 1953) 221-34
Many images we today call "artificial conceits" were really faithful and accurate images when there was a belief in a universal analogy of all things. Such analogy has since been eliminated from our perception by Bacon, Descartes and science. The views of E. Tesauro are presented.

_____. "Notes on John Donne's Alchemical Imagery" Isis 48 (June 1957) 103-23
Donne's poetry is almost all "alchemical metaphor," occult correspondences between science and the ethical or spiritual,

physical and spiritual, microcosm and macrocosm, between virtue and the operation of elixir, etc. These correspondences are well used by Donne and show an underlying belief in the unity of all things. Donne could have believed in Hermetic philosophy though he sometimes satirizes it.

_____. Renaissance and Seventeenth-Century Studies New York: Columbia University Press 1964
The major 17th century critics of the conceit were: Gracián, Tesauro, Cardinal Sforza-Pallavicino, Pierfrancesco Minozzi, M. Pellegrini. Their views are discussed. Reality was based on universal analogy and was interpreted by means of conceits. The bestiary tradition (even plants) reveal witty significance. What we term artificial conceit today was in its time a genuine description of reality. Baudelaire, Yeats and Swendenborg also approach nature through analogy. For Mazzeo metaphor reveals a primal perception of identity.

_____. "Seventeenth-Century Theory of Metaphysical Poetry" Romanic Review 42 (Dec. 1951) 245-55
The way to surpass the imitative view of art stressing beautiful objects was by means of the conceit, the form of words created (not imitated) by the artist. The faculty of ingegno creates extreme word combinations yielding insight, beauty, wonder, the marvelous or extraordinary. Madness is required; the insane make good metaphors, take one thing for another.

_____. "Universal Analogy and the Culture of the Renaissance" Journal of the History of Ideas 15 (April 1954) 299-304

McCabe, Bernard. "Analysis of Imagery" Journal of Education 148 (Dec. 1965) 63-7
The levels of meaning of imagery may be taught to secondary school students by distinguishing the literal, metaphorical, analogical, allegorical, symbolic and surrealistic. Examples of each are given.

McCall, Marsh, Jr. Ancient Rhetorical Theories of Simile and Comparison Cambridge, Mass.: Harvard University Press 1969
An examination of the nature, scope and purpose of comparison and simile. He discusses pre-Aristotelian views, Aristotle, Rhetorica ad Herennium, Cicero, Greeks of 1st Century B.C. and A.D., the Senecas, Quintilian, Plutarch, Fronto, Trypho. The purpose of simile and comparison is usually embellishment and to give a proof. Their method of comparisons involves description, contrast, vividness, parallel, sequence, brevity, etc.

McCanles, Michael. "Univocalism in Cajetan's Doctrine of Analogy" New Scholasticism 42 (Winter 1968) 18-47 (Has bibliography on Thomistic views of analogy)

McCann, Eleanor. "Oxymora in Spanish Mystics and English Metaphysical Writers" Comparative Literature 13 (Winter 1961) 16-25. Also Clavileño (Madrid) 13 (1961) 16-25 (cf. James Simmonds Neuren Sprachen)
Diego de Estella, Saint Teresa, John of the Cross, Luis de León, Donne, Crashaw etc. used oxymora e.g. dying life, blind vision, free slave, descend to soar. These were logical developments from Spanish mystic and Thomistic beliefs about body-soul relation combined with a tendency to blend eroticism with spiritual fervor.

McCartney, Eugene. "Figurative Uses of Animal Names in Latin and Their Application to Military Devices. A Study in Semantics" PhD dissertation, University of Pennsylvania 1912

McCartney, Eugene S. "Vivid Ways of Indicating Uncountable Numbers" Classical Philology 55 (April 1960) 79-89

McCloskey, Mary A. "Metaphors" Mind 73 (1964) 215-33
Unlike literal language metaphors are not true or false, do not lead to deductions, nor is their meaning generally agreed upon. Metaphor transgresses usual logical rules and purposes, is tensive, condensed, and striking. It is like an assertion plus a quick denial.

McGarry, M. F. "The Allegorical and Metaphorical Language in the Autos Sacramentales of Calderón" (Studies in Romance Language and Literature, 16.) PhD dissertation, Washington 1937

McInerny, Ralph. "Logic of Analogy" New Scholasticism 31 (April 1957) 149-171
A Thomistic view of analogy and metaphor. For St. Thomas analogy is a logical doctrine not a metaphysical one. "A logical intention, such as analogy, is based on things, not as they exist in rerum natura, but as they are known."

_____. The Logic of Analogy The Hague: Nijhoff 1961
A Thomistic view. Analogy is a logical doctrine, a "second intention" and so not a metaphysical doctrine. He quotes the authority of Aquinas for support and shows Cajetan's mistake of trying to include real differences in something which is simply logical. Analogy tells us only about our knowledge of reality, our naming of concepts, not about reality. Metaphor is a "univocal" term used in a proposition to "suppose" for something which does not fall under its signification. It is "improper supposition." Metaphor gives insight into the confusion of human existence and by means of it we transfer what we know of sensible things to non-sensible things. Aquinas states that nothing involving matter in its definition (e.g. heat, light) can be predicated of God except metaphorically.

_____. "Metaphor and Analogy" Sciences ecclésiastiques 16 (1964)

273-289
A Thomistic view of analogy and metaphor. Metaphor is proportional similitude as Aquinas says. It is a transference from material to immaterial or a word from its normal context to a new context.

_____. "The Ratio Communis of the Analogous Name" Laval Théologique et Philosophique 18 (1962) 9-34

_____. Studies in Analogy The Hague: Nijhoff 1968
A Thomistic theory of analogy and continuation of his 1961 book, The Logic of Analogy. He still holds that analogical signification is a matter of logic. This work concentrates more on relations of equivocation, analogy and metaphor in Aristotle but is still an exegesis of Thomistic texts. Ch. 2 is on metaphor and analogy and Ch. 3 is on metaphor and fundamental ontology.

McKeon, Richard. "Aristotle's Conception of Language and the Arts of Language" Classical Philology 41 (Oct. 1946) 193-206, 42 (Jan. 1947) 21-50
On Aristotle and metaphor.

McLuhan, H. M. "Tennyson and Picturesque Poetry" Essays in Criticism 1 (July 1951) 262-282
The picturesque or natural landscape is related to Eliot's "objective correlative," or "the internal landscape." Landscapes present juxtapositions without the copula.

"The McLuhan Metaphor" New Yorker (May 15, 1965) 43-44
"One environment seen through another becomes a metaphor, for example, Andy Warhol's 'Liz Taylor."

McLuhan, Marshall, and Quentin Fiore. The Medium is the Message New York: Bantam Books 1967
A juxtaposition of pictures and words in a metaphorical way. His main insight seems to be that the medium itself e.g. a television set or a written page is itself seen and experienced and so is part of what is said or communicated. But he thinks such media yield too partial an experience. Rather than develop any of his metaphors, even that the medium is the message, he jumps from metaphor to metaphor e.g. he says we "think linearly" because we read lines. He uses the medium of his book to oppose books as a medium. The notion that the medium is the message was earlier developed in a thorough way by Wittgenstein, Croce, and others.

McMullin, Erman. "Metaphor and Reality: Review of Wheelwright's Book" Modern Schoolman 40 (Jan. 1963) 184-93

McNaughton, Ruth. "The Imagery of Emily Dickinson" M.A. Thesis University of Nebraska 1949 (cf. S. Wilson)

McPherson, Thomas. "Assertion and Analogy" Proceedings of the Aristotelian Society 60 (1959-60) 155-70

Meadows, Paul. "The Human Image and the New Partnership of Change" Personalist 48 (Fall 1967) 524-547

_____. "The Metaphors of Order: toward a taxonomy of organization theory" Sociological Theory: Inquiries and Paradigms Llewellyn Gross, ed. New York: Harper and Row 1967 pp. 77-103
Metaphor shapes our thought and allows us to impose order on the world e.g. organismic, mechanical, atomistic, human order is imposed on scientific order, etc. He discusses the assumptions involved in the following five metaphors of order: hierarchy, sequence, configuration, covariance, syntax.

Meeussen. "Review of Stutterheim Het begrip Metaphoor" Leuvense Bijdragen. Tijdschrift voor moderne philologie (Bijblad) 33 (1941) 79-81

Mehrabian, Albert. An Analysis of Personality Theories New Jersey: Prentice Hall 1968
Metaphors determine theory and guide observation, e.g. personality is treated as if it were physical or biological or an organism, putty, hydrolic fluid, etc. The metaphor chosen is our contribution not objective fact. Many metaphors are possible, not a single one, but some are better than others. "slippery metaphors" are unclear ones which should be clarified or avoided e.g. "unconscious communication," "faith."

Mehren, A. G. Die Rhetorik der Araber Kopenhagen-Wien 1853

Meier, Diederich. "Vergleich und Metapher in den Lustspielen Molières" PhD dissertation Marburg 1885

Meier, Hugo. Die Metapher: Versuch einer zusammenfassenden Betrachtung ihrer linguistischen Merkmale Winterthur: P. G. Keller 1963 (Reviews by H. Lieb, L. Söll)
A presentation of the main theories of metaphor before linguistics and in linguistic research and an attempt at a synthesis in order to establish a general theoretical definition of the concept of metaphor.

Meilakh, Boris S. "O metafore kak elemente khudozhestvennovo-myshleniya" Akademiya nauk SSSR trudy otdela novoi russkoi literatury. Moscow I (1948) 207-232
Metaphor as an element of artistic thought.

Meissner, Rudolf. Die Kenningar der Skalden: Ein Beitrag zur skaldischen Poetik Bonn-Leipzig: K. Schroeder 1921
Said to be one of the best works on kennings of the skalds. (Note: "kenning" means a teaching, lesson or doctrine)

Meissner, W. "Some Notes on a Figure in St. Thomas" The New Scholasticism 31 (1957) 68-84
A Thomistic view. An attempt "to gather pertinent texts involving St. Thomas' use of a particular example ["health"] in explaining analogy..."

Mejlach, B. S. [See Mĕilakh]

Mellon, John C. "The Analysis of Metaphorical Sentences in Sets of Action-Description Statements" Harvard 1965 (Unpublished paper)

Melmoth, William. [See pseudonym, Sir Thomas Fitzosborne]

Mendelsohn, Charles. Studies in the Wordplay in Plautus (Publications of the University of Pennsylvania, Series in Philology and Literature 12) Philadelphia: Winston 1907
I. The name-play, II. The use of single words in a double meaning.

Mendes, Chrisani. "A metáfora e Cecília Meireles" Jornal de Letras (Newspaper format) 219 (1968) 7-10

Mengel, E. F. "Patterns of Imagery in Pope's Arbuthnot" PMLA 69 (March 1954) 189-97

Menges, Matthew. The Concept of Univocity Regarding the Predication of God and Creature According to William Ockham New York: Franciscan Institute 1952

Menne, Albert. "Was ist Analogie?" Philosophisches Jahrbuch der Görres-Gesellschaft 67 (1958) 389-395
From the perspective of logic and Thomism.

Merwe Scholtz, Hendrik van der. The Kenning in Anglo-Saxon and Old Norse Poetry Utrecht: Dekker and van de Vegt en J. W. van Leeuwen 1927

Mészáros, István. "Metaphor and Simile" Proceedings of the Aristotelian Society 67 (1966-67) 127-44
Metaphor as it may be used in philosophy is an "anticipatory intuitive synthesis," which prepares the way for later discursive elaboration (e.g. as a simile). It cannot be understood by analyzing its elements - some metaphors are even nonfigurative. Metaphor is context-bound. Its truth is self-referential in that it applies only to an "as-if" subject or world.

METAPHOR [TOPIC]:

"Metáfora" Enciclopedia de la Literatura Mexico vol. 4 pp. 466-468

A likeness or comparison. It expresses the material by means of the ideal, the objective by means of the abstract and vice versa. According to Ortega metaphor is the most fertile power man has, allowing us to transcend reality and create an escape from reality. Language via metaphor is an "inexhaustible rock."

<u>Metáfora; Revista Literaria</u> Mexico. A journal published from around 1955-1958
Does not deal with metaphor.

"American Metaphor" <u>Atlantic Monthly</u> 73 (1894) 574-575

"Amusing Metaphors" <u>Chambers' Journal</u> 4 (Jan. 1887) 222-224

"Force of Metaphor" <u>Scribner's Magazine</u> 33 (March 1903) 379-80
Metaphor should surprise and shock.

"The Metaphor of Everyday Life" <u>Atlantic Monthly</u> 72 (1893) 278-87
Americans are deficient in creating good metaphors.

"On the Mixing of Metaphor" <u>Atlantic Monthly</u> 120 (Sept. 1917) 429-31
He humorously advocates mixing metaphors.

"Metaphors" <u>Times Literary Supplement</u> Oct. 14, 1926 pp. 681-682

"Metaphor" <u>The Oxford English Dictionary</u> Oxford, England vol. 6 (1933) p. 384
Related terms are metaphorally, metaphorically, metaphorist, metaphorize, metaphorous (full of metaphor).
"Metaphor is the figure of speech in which a name or descriptive term is transferred to some object different from, but analogous to, that to which it is properly applicable."

"Metaphor" Webster's <u>New International Dictionary</u> (1947) p. 1546
Metaphor is from Greek <u>metapherein</u>, to carry over or transfer (<u>meta</u>, beyond; <u>pherein</u>, to bring).
"The use of a word or phrase literally denoting one kind of object or idea in place of another by way of suggesting a likeness or analogy between them." It is an implicit or compressed simile.

"Metaphor" <u>Encyclopaedia Britannica</u> first edition, vol. 3 (1771) p. 174
"Metaphor: in rhetoric, a trope, by which we put a strange word for a proper word, by reason of its resemblance to it; or it may be defined, a simile or comparison intended to enforce and illustrate the thing we speak of, without the signs or forms of comparison [i.e. without like or as]."

"Metaphor" <u>Encyclopaedia Britannica</u> third edition, vol. 11 (1797)

pp. 475-480
"A metaphor differs from a simile, in form only, not in substance: in a simile the two subjects are kept distinct in the expression, as well as in the thought; in a metaphor, the two subjects are kept distinct in the thought only not in the expression." Rules for the use of metaphor are given such as don't mix metaphors, the terms of the metaphor should be literally applicable to the subject, etc.

"Metaphor" Encyclopaedia Britannica eighth edition, vol. 14 (1857) p. 550
A trope founded on resemblance, an abridged simile. Metaphor is more bold in saying one thing is another rather than is like another. Frequently used metaphors become common language.

["Metaphor" is not included in the 1883, 1891, 1892 (9th edition), or 1902 (10th edition).]

"Metaphor" Encyclopaedia Britannica eleventh edition, vol. 18 (1910) p. 224
Metaphor is from Greek, metaphorá, meaning "transfer of sense." "Metaphor consists in the transference to one object of an attribute or name which strictly and literally is not applicable to it, but only figuratively and by analogy." It is an abridged simile. "Continued metaphors" are simple metaphors which are extended and worked out in detail.

"Metaphor" Encyclopaedia Britannica fourteenth edition, vol. 15 (1929, 1946) p. 332
Same as the 11th edition account, but shorter.

"Metaphor" Encyclopaedia Britannica vol. 15 (1961) p. 328 (See G. W. Allen entry)
Same as 14th edition. See Boulton "Figures of Speech" for an entirely different Britannica approach, 1968 edition.

Meyer, Adolf. Wesen und Geschichte der Theorie vom Mikro- und Makro- kosmos Bern 1900 esp. p. 109ff.
Do not confuse metaphor and real situations.

Meyer, Richard. Deutsche Stilistik München: C. H. Beck 1906
Metaphor is the most important figure of speech. It replaces the usual expression by a figurative expression and gives an object or action a name from a sphere of perception other than the one from which it has its name when used in the usual sense. He mentions the views of German writers on metaphor e.g. Gerber, Vischer, Biese, Elster, etc. Metaphor serves to translate the less concrete or less familiar into the more familiar and more concrete. Metaphor serves the need to express a vivid perception in an immediate way. Metaphor should be used in moderation and only when there is a

reason for its use. When mood or perception suggest a change of expression, metaphor and metonymy are excellent to accentuate the development of thought.

Meyer, Sam. "Figures of Rhetoric in Spenser's 'Colin Clout'" PMLA 79 (June 1964) 206-18

Meyer, Selina. "Metaphor as a Means of Characterization in the Works of Friedrich Hebbel" PhD dissertation, University of Wisconsin 1933

Meyer, Theodor A. Ästhetik Berlin 1925

Meyer. "Vergleich und Metapher bei Molière" Diss. Marburg 1885 (Source: G. Kohfeldt)

Michaëlsson, E. "L'Eau centre de métaphores et de métamorphoses dans la littérature française de la première moitié du XVIe siècle. Le miroir de l'eau et de déluge" Orbis Litterarum (Copenhagen) 14 (1959) 121-173

Mielke, Hans. "Die Bildersprache des Aischylos" PhD dissertation Breslau (Teildr.) Ohlau i. Schl. 1934

Migliorini, Bruno. "La metafora reciproca" In Homenaje al R.P.F. Restrepo S. I. Bogotá: Libr. Voluntad Boletín del Instituto Caro y Cuervo Thesaurus 5 (1950) 33-40
Examples given of "reciprocal metaphor" or when the sea is referred to as a field and then the fields as wave-tossed seas; Calderón calls stars, "flowers of the night" and flowers, "stars of the day." He quotes Esnault, "A semantical equation, if it seems particularly just, can be read in two senses: if A is B, B is A; both are permutable." Colors may be described with auditory expressions and vice versa. Often reciprocal metaphor is based on similarity of two concrete objects.

_____. "Metafora" Enciclopedia Italiana 23 (1934) p. 23
Metaphor is a transferring of a term from that idea to which it properly belongs to another idea which has some resemblance to the first. Metaphor is merely an abbreviated analogy. All language is metaphoric in its origins. "Live metaphors" are those in which next to the transferred meaning the real meaning can be perceived. We can enliven dead metaphors by inquiring into their etymology. Mixed metaphors should be avoided.

Miles, Josephine. The Pathetic Fallacy in the Nineteenth Century New York: Octagon Books 1965
Ruskin and the imagist, Amy Lowell, reject the pathetic fallacy, the attribution of feelings to things, because it falsifies objective qualities. Wordsworth and others accept it however, for qualities and beauty are thought to be influenced by minds.

_____. "The Problem of Imagery" Sewanee Review 58 (1950) 522-526

Miller Analogies Test. A test based on ability to complete analogies. See similar psychological tests.

Miller, Donald W. "Scene and Image in Three Novels by Elizabeth Bowen" PhD dissertation, Columbia University 1967

Mincoff, Marco. "Imagery and Imaginative Figures" The Study of Style naouka i izkoustvo pp.98-127

Mindel, Joseph. "Uses of Metaphor: Henry Adams and the Symbols of Science" Journal of the History of Ideas 26 (Jan. 1965) 89-102
H. Adams attempted in his search for absolute certainty to explain social and historical processes metaphorically in terms of laws of natural science such as the phase rule, dissipation of energy, laws of thermodynamics, geology, astronomy, etc. He took his metaphors literally, without being conscious of it, to construct a science of history which forms absolute laws of human behavior.

Miner, E. "Pound, Haiku and the Image" Hudson Review 9 (Winter 1956-1957) 570-84

Minkowski, Eugène. "Métaphore et symbole" Studia Estetyczne 4 (1967) 309-316. Also Cahiers internationaux de symbolisme no. 5 (1964) 47-55
Human sciences need metaphor and a symbolic consciousness. "Psychosomatic medicine is based entirely on the works of metaphor." There is an intimate union of the expounder and that which is expressed.

Minozzi, Pierfrancesco. Gli Sfogamenti dell'ingegno Venice 1641

Mirollo, James. The Poet of the Marvelous: Giambattista Marino New York: Columbia University Press 1963 (Includes translations of Marino's work.)

Mizener, Arthur. "Some Notes on the Nature of English Poetry" Sewanee Review 51 (1943) 27-51 esp. p.34
Contrasts between metaphorical style of various periods are a clue to their different philosophical outlooks.

_____. "The Structure of Figurative Language in Shakespeare's Sonnets" Southern Review 5 (1940) 730-747

Mohr, W. Kenningstudien: Beiträge zur Stilgeschichte der altgermanischen Dichtung Stuttgart: W. Kohlhammer 1933

Molhova, Jana. "On Metaphor" Zeitschrift für Anglistik und Amerikanistik 8 (1960) 289-294
Metaphor is an intentional and emotive transfer based on sim-

ilarity and the possession of at least one common feature. Nouns, verbs, and adjectives are in that order most subject to metaphor. Types of transfer are classified.

Monboddo, Lord James Burnet. Of the Origin and Progress of Language 6 vols. Edinburgh 1773-1792 (Menston, England: The Scholar Press Ltd. 1967)
Metaphors are short similes.

Mondin, Battista. The Principle of Analogy in Protestant and Catholic Theology The Hague: Nijhoff 1963 (Thesis, Harvard University)

Monro, D. H. Argument of Laughter University of Notre Dame Press 1963
Many types of humor defined by Monro seem to describe metaphors and tropes also e.g.
1) any breach of the usual order of events
2) importing into one situation what belongs to another
3) anything masquerading as something it is not
4) word play, puns
5) nonsense
6) forbidden breach
7) novelty, freshness, unexpectedness, escape.
etc.

Monson, Charles H. "Metaphors for the University" Educational Record 48 (Winter 1967) 22-29
The university has been termed: bargaining table, mother (alma mater), active monastery, maze to escape from, work of art, or chamber orchestra, baseball team, theatre, mould, bread leavening, antiseptic, hospital, marketplace, beehive, large home, department store, extinct dinosaur, zoo, etc. Insight may be given by expanding and becoming more aware of the rôle such metaphors play in our thinking.

Montagnes, Bernard. La Doctrine de l'Analogie de l'Être d'après Saint Thomas d'Aquin Louvain and Paris 1963

Montes, José Ares. Góngora y la Poesía Portuguesa del Siglo XVII Madrid: Editorial Gredos 1956 esp. Ch. X "Metáforas e imagenes".

Moog, Willy. "Die homerischen Gleichnisse" Zeitschrift für Äesthetik und allgemeine Kunstwissenschaft 7 (1912) 104-128, 266-302, 353-371

Moogan, G. C. The Parables and Metaphors of Our Lord Marshall, Morgan, and Scott 1943

Mooij, J. J. A. "Review of Wheelwright, 1962" (Review of Metaphor and Reality and The Burning Fountain) Foundations of Language 3 (1967) 108-111

Moore, Sebastian. "Analogy: A Reaction and a Challenge" Downside Review 76 (1958) 125-48

_____. "Analogy and the Free Mind" Downside Review 76 (1958) 1-28

Moore, Thomas V. "The Temporal Relations of Meaning and Imagery" Psychological Review 22 (1915) 177-225, 24 (1917) 318-322

Mora, José F. "Metáfora" Diccionario de Filosofia Buenos Aires: Editorial Sudamericana 1965 vol. 2 pp. 188-192
A summary of the theories of various writers on metaphor.

Moraux, Paul. "Review of Hans Newiger: Metapher und Allegorie: Studien zu Aristophanes" Erasmus 11 (1958) 242-45

Morawski, C. "De metaphoris Tullianis observationes selectae" Eos: commentarii Societatis Philologae Polonorum 16 (1910) 1-7 In Latin.

Morel, Louis M. De vocabulis partium corporis in lingua graeca metaphorice dictis Genevae: excudebat J. G. Fick 1875
Partly concerns transfer of names of parts of body to nature.

_____. Essai sur la métaphore dans la langue grecque. Les noms d'animâux pris métaphoriquement Genève: Georg 1879 [1869]
(Partial summary in S. Brown World of Imagery pp. 184-186)

Morelle, Jean. "Étude sur les adjectifs de couleur en grec ancien. Leur valeur évocatrice, leur emploi métaphorique" Thèse de licence, Univ. de Liége 1943

Morgan, Edwin. "Review of Brooke-Rose: A Grammar of Metaphor" Review of English Studies N. S. 11 (1960) 340-342
A fairly detailed critical account.

Morier, Henri. "Métaphore" Dictionnaire de poétique et de rhétorique Paris: Presses Universitaires de France 1961 pp. 258-260
Metaphor is an abbreviated comparison without using like or as. It is a comparison of thought not of language and involves an imagistic transfer. It renders all types of emotion and is necessary for understanding.

Morozov, M. M. "The Individualization of Shakespeare's Characters Through Imagery" Shakespeare Survey 2 (1949) 83-106

Morris, C. B. "Metaphor in El Burlador de Sevilla (by Tirso)" Romanic Review 55 (Dec. 1964) 248-55
Make metaphor alive by means of a larger dramatic context.

Morse, Samuel. "The Motive for Metaphor--Wallace Stevens: His Poetry and Practice" Origin V 2 (Spring 1952) 3-65

Mortenson, P. "Image and Structure in Shelley's Longer Lyrics" *Studies in Romanticism* 4 (Winter 1965) 104-10

Morton, Richard. "Notes on the Imagery of Dylan Thomas" *English Studies* 43 (1962) 155-164

Moseley, Thomas A. E. *The 'Lady' in Comparisons from the Poetry of the 'dolce stil nuovo'...* George Banta 1916. PhD diss. Johns Hopkins University 1915
On simile.

Moses, Paul J. "Die Häufigkeit der metaphorischen Bezeichnung in der Phonetik" 1948 (Source: Fónagy)
"One talks about dark voices, high voices, black bassos, using synesthesia, a connection between sensations of different senses which is independent of association established by experience."

Moses, William. "The Metaphysical Conceit in the Poetry of John Donne" PhD diss. Vanderbilt University 1941

Mourgues, Odette de. *Metaphysical, Baroque and Précieux Poetry* Oxford: Clarendon Press 1953

Moynihan, William T. "The Poetry of Dylan Thomas: A Study of its Meaning and Unity" PhD diss. Brown University 1962

_____. *The Craft and Art of Dylan Thomas* Ithaca: Cornell University Press 1966

Mrozkowski, Przemyslaw. "Shakespeare's 'As ifs'" *Kwartalnik Neofilologiczny* (Warsaw) 15 (1968) 3-29
On pretending.

Muir, Kenneth. "Shakespeare's Imagery--Then and Now" *Shakespeare Survey* 18 (1965) 46-57

_____. "Imagery and Symbolism in Hamlet" *Études Anglaises* 17 (1964) 353-363

_____. "Fifty Years of Shakespeare Criticism: 1900-1950" *Shakespeare Survey* 4 (1951) 1-25
On the literature on metaphor and imagery in Shakespeare.

Müller, Bodo. *Góngoras Metaphorik; Versuch einer Typologie* Wiesbaden: F. Steiner 1963

Müller-Graupa, Edwin. "Verbale Tiermetaphern" *Philologische Wochenschrift* 63 (1943) 43-48, 91-95, 167-168

_____. "Verbale Tiermetaphern" *Beiträge zur Geschichte der deutschen Sprache und Literatur* (Halle) Supplement, 79 (1957)

456-491

Müller, [Gustav], of Köthen. Zur Konkordanz lateinischer und deutscher Metaphern. Programm Köthen: P. Schettler 1881 pp. 1-12

Müller, Friedrich Max. Lectures on the Science of Language 2 vols. New York: Charles Scribner's & Co. 1871 esp. Ch. 8 "Metaphor" (Criticized by Jesperson p. 425ff., C. Ward p. 155ff., Barfield (1828) p. 67, Bloomfield Language p. 240, Cassirer Essay on Man pp. 128-29, Urban Language and Reality p. 732. Also cf. Wheelwright)
"All words expressive of immaterial conceptions are derived by metaphor from words expressive of sensible ideas ["roots"]..." e.g. "Spirit" derives etymologically from "to draw breath," "mind" from "air." Language develops by metaphorical extension of meaning. There was once a metaphorical or mythic period in which words were unconsciously being metaphorically extended to new uses. Unconscious metaphor creates myth and can lead to a "disease of language." "Radical metaphor" is the automatic, normal extension of everyday language. "Poetic metaphor" is the conscious, artificial combination of remote terms. Metaphor is "a transferring of a name from the object to which it properly belongs to other objects which strike the mind as in some way or other participating in the peculiarities of the first object."

______. "Metaphor as a Mode of Abstraction" Fortnightly Review 46 (1886) 617-632
A modification of his earlier views. Metaphor is not just conscious transfer but "a new side of abstraction and generalization." The word is gradually generalized until it becomes a metaphor. "Radical metaphor" is now thought of as "diaphora" or "transformation," not just a transfer. It is unconsciously apprehended; the two terms are not distinct. "Poetic" or "verbal metaphor" is a conscious transfer of distinct terms. "Fundamental metaphor" is personification. "Grammatical metaphor" is grammatical imperfection e.g. metonymy. He classifies poetic metaphors in terms of transitions involving material-immaterial, cause-effect, part-whole, man-animal, sign-signified, and things generally associated.

______. Science of Thought New York: Charles Scribner's 1887 esp. pp. 322-5 and 480-512
Metaphor is divided into fundamental metaphor and grammatical metaphor.

Müller, Josef. Das Bild in der Dichtung. Philosophie und Geschichte der Metapher München, Selbstverlag. vol. I Theorie der Metapher (1903) vol. II Die griechische Metapher (1906)
An important work on metaphor in poetry. He discusses the history of metaphor, Western theories of metaphor, the aesthetic

metaphor, rules for metaphor, and metaphor in India, China, Japan, Assyria and Egypt.

Müller, Maria. Verhüllende Metaphorik in der Saga; ein Beitrag zur Kulturpsychologie Altislands Würzburg: Triltsch 1939

Müller, Richard. Die deutsche Klassik; Wesen und Geschichte im Spiegel des Strommotives Bonn: H. Bouvier 1959, 193 pp.
On German literature of the 18th century and metaphor.

Müller, Ruth. "Die Metaphorik in der Dichtung Daniel von Czepkos; eine Studie zur Persönlichkeit des Dichters an Hand der Bilder seines Werkes" PhD diss. München 1956

Muncie, Wendell. "The Psychopathology of Metaphor" Archives of Neurology and Psychiatry 37 (1937) 796-804
A Freudian approach.
Metaphor is "displacement," transference of psychical from latent to manifest content. The psychopath shows metaphor disorder and uses it as escape from reality and as autistic gratification. e.g. "one patient wanted to be an airplane pilot, in order to get the proper 'perspective on the world'."

Munro, D. H. "Review of Turbayne: The Myth of Metaphor" Australasian Journal of Philosophy 40 (1962) 388-90

Murry, John Middleton. "Metaphor" John Clare and Other Studies London and New York: Peter Nevill Limited 1950 pp. 85-97
Also in Selected Criticism 1916-1917 Richard Rees, ed. London: Oxford University Press 1960 pp. 65-75. Also in The Symposium 2 (April 1931). Also in his Countries of the Mind second series, London: Oxford University Press 1931
"Metaphor is as ultimate as speech itself, and speech as ultimate as thought. If we try to penetrate them beyond a certain point, we find ourselves questioning the very faculty and instrument with which we are trying to penetrate them." Metaphor should be true and have the effect of a revelation.

_____. The Problem of Style London: Oxford University Press 1956
Metaphor is not ornament or comparison nor can it be logically analyzed. It is a unique mode of apprehension which expresses emotion, gives a name for things without names, gives precision to language, and notes the affinities which all things have.

Müsken, Annemarie. "Jean Paul und die Metaphorik" PhD diss. Bonn 1946

Musurillo, Herbert. "Sunken Imagery in Sophocles' Oedipus" American Journal of Philology 78 (1957) 36-51
He presents Sophocles' five dominant images and six minor ones. There is no single dominant image and Oedipus has no single interpretation - just complex images.

Myers, Charles Mason. "The Circular Use of Metaphor" Philosophy and Phenomenological Research 26 (March 1966) 391-402
"Explicative metaphor" may give an empirical hypothesis or an analysis of a concept. The explication may be conceptual, empirical, or an irreducibly metaphysical explanation but is circular if the pre-analytic experience is confused with the post-analytic. The explicandum must have clarity. Metaphors often disguise their circularity.

_____. "Metaphors and Mediately Informative Expressions" Southern Journal of Philosophy 6 (Fall 1968) 159-166
"Philosophic metaphors" or "perspectival metaphors" distort ordinary language, but are "systematically leading," when expanded, to give insight. They are open to interpretation, cannot be taken literally and are not true or false yet they are useful. P. Henle's iconic theory of metaphor is discussed.

_____. "Review of Turbayne: The Myth of Metaphor" Philosophical Review 73 (1964) 549-552

_____. "Metaphors and the Intelligibility of Dreams" Philosophy and Rhetoric 2 (Spring 1969) 91-99
We do not know we can dream contradictory things such as a circle with three sides yet experience suggests that we do. To account for this it is suggested that dreams have metaphorical import.

_____. "Inexplicable Analogies" Philosophy and Phenomenological Research 22 (March 1962) 326-333
On Thomistic analogy. Inexplicable analogies are possible. There is evidence for denying that the existence of a similarity between two things implies they have a property in common. Orange is similar to red and yellow, but not analyzable into them. Thus the theologian's inability to explicate the analogy between human and divine attributes does not rule out the possibility that they are analogous.

Myers, Gerald. "Review of Warren Shibles, Philosophical Pictures" Philosophy and Rhetoric 3 (1970) 67-68
A brief account of the notion of a "picture."

Myers, Henry A. "The Usefulness of Figurative Language" Quarterly Journal of Speech 26 (1940) 236-243
Logic is inferior to rhetoric. Thought is metaphorical and metaphor gives essential and constitutive models for science, philosophy and culture. Metaphor is not ornament but conveys meaning (not literally true) produced by the faculty of the imagination. Metaphors or models should be examined to see if they correspond point by point and in value. We should reduce metaphors to similes to check the point by point correspondence and see if the terms related are of equal value.

Nair, K. K. [Pseudonym is K. Chaitanya] Sanskrit Poetics Bombay: Asia Publishing House 1918 (New York 1965) esp. ch. 4 "Poetic Figures." Has extensive bibliography. (cf. De)
The basic position of Sanskrit poetics, Nair thinks, is that figures, including metaphor, are dispensable but emotion (rasa) and experience are not. The rasa must be realized. Figures are termed alamkaras (literally: ornaments); metaphor is rupaka; simile is upama. The various terms and critics are treated in some detail. Some reduce all figures and poetry to metaphor.

Nash, Harvey. "Freud and Metaphor" Archives of Psychiatry 7 (1962) 25-29 (cf. Mawardi, B. Kaplan)
In Freudian theory metaphor not only illustrates but also constitutes the object. Freud's metaphors are sometimes clear but often blurred and inconsistent thus needing correction. A list is given of the metaphors Freud uses in explaining his theory.

_____. "The Role of Metaphor in Psychological Theory" Behavioral Science 8 (1963) 336-345 (Paper read at Sept. 1964 meeting of the American Psychological Association.)
Metaphor involves the linking of a familiar experience with a novel one. Metaphor is a legitimate method of generating and guiding theory. Good operational ideas often spring from highly personal metaphors which are then redefined operationally. We should be conscious of our metaphors and not confuse them with identity. Examples of some metaphors are heat seen as fluid, society as an organism, human behavior as like animal behavior; and mass, work and force as anthropomorphic terms.

Nash, Ogden. "Very Like a Whale" Saturday Evening Post 206 (May 12, 1934) p. 62
A poem. A spoof on metaphor when taken literally. It recommends a restricted use of metaphor and simile.

Nashāt, Maḥmūd. Adāt-i tashbīh dar zabān-i Fārsi; yā tashbīh bi i 'tibār-i adāt. Tihrān 1340 (1961)
On metaphor and symbolism in Persian poetry.

Nassar, Eugene P. Wallace Stevens: An Anatomy of Figuration University of Pennsylvania Press 1965

Nassau-Noordewier, Michael. Metaphorae Aristophaneae PhD diss. Leiden, Delft 1891

Naumann, Walter. "Hunger und Durst als Metaphern bei Dante" Romanische Forschungen 54 (1940) 13-36

Navratil, Leo. Schizophrenie und Sprache: Zur Psychologie der Dichtung München: Deutscher Taschenbuch Verlag 1966

Nazaryan, Armand Grantovich. Obraznye sravneniya frantsuzskovo yazyka Moscow 1965
On the French language, terms, phrases and similes.

Needham, K. "Synonymy and Semantic Classification" PhD diss. Cambridge University 1964
An attempt to rest the interaction view on a literal descriptive view.

Nelson, Kenneth M. "A Religious Metaphor" Reconstructionist 31 (1965) 7-16
About the metaphor "call it sleep."

Nemerov, Howard. "On Metaphor" Virginia Quarterly Review 45 (1969) 621-36
Metaphor is a compressed story, condensed myth, compressed fable, and implicit resemblance. Metaphor (a "carrying across") is itself a metaphor. Images and names are metaphors e.g. DNA, Hamlet. Poetry is naming done by story telling.

Nemetz, Anthony. "Literalness and the Sensus Litteralis (medieval treatment of figurative language)" Speculum 34 (Jan. 1959) 76-89
[Note: Speculum refers to a mirroring. cf. universal analogy]
It is a mistake to think the medieval "sensus litteralis" means "literal." It meant only what words or concepts signify and includes poetry as well as science. It is just "human sense" or "natural sense."

_____. "Metaphor: The Daedalus of Discourse" Thought 33 (1958) 417-442
"A word is used metaphorically when it is either immediately or contextually evident that its meaning can only be grasped by the simultaneous use of at least two modes of verification." "The reason...a metaphor says one thing and means another is that...there is an assumed union of two modes or levels of truth or causality which necessitates a similar union in the levels of psychic activity to which corresponds the verbal substitution of terms indicating a union of levels in the subject matter." "Metaphor is an expression which is based on the simultaneous use of two meanings of truth." The triadic character of metaphor is: levels of truth, levels of subject matter and levels of consciousness.

_____. "Metaphysics and Metaphor" Philosophy of Knowledge Roland Houde and Joseph Mullally, eds. Philadelphia: Lippincott 1960 pp. 317-328

Nes, Dirk van. "Die maritime Bildersprache des Aischylos" PhD diss. Utrecht, Groningen 1963

Neuenschwander, Paul. "Der bildliche Ausdruck des Apuleius. Ein Beitrag zur Geschichte der Metapher im Lateinischen" PhD diss. Zürich 1913

Newiger, Hans Joachim. Metapher und Allegorie: Studien zu Aristophanes (Zetemata. Monographien zur klassischen Altertumswissenschaft. 16) München: Beck 1957 (Review by Moraux)

Newman, Arnold Eugene. "The Romantic Image in the Poetry of Hart Crane" PhD diss. University of Wisconsin 1965

Newton, Francis. "Recurrent Imagery in Aeneid IV" Transactions and Proceedings of the American Philological Association 88 (1957) 31-43

Nicholes, E. L. "Simile of the Sparrow in The Rainbow by D. H. Lawrence" Modern Language Notes 64 (March 1949) 171-174

Nicolson, Marjorie. The Breaking of the Circle: Studies in the Effect of the 'New Science' upon 17th Century Poetry Evanston: Northwestern University Press 1950 (Revised 1960)
An analogy accepted literally in one age as a basic postulate is abandoned as a mere metaphor in the next age as a result of the shift in the way of looking at the world (cf. view by Thomas Kuhn). She deals here with the collapse of the divine analogy of the 17th century.

Nielsen, Niels Jr. "Przywara's Philosophy of Analogia Entis" Review of Metaphysics 4 (June 1952) 599-620
There is an analogy between being and becoming that is an identity in difference involving tension, and that analogy is directed beyond itself to a transcendence of either one. (There is a tension between essence and existence.) He combines the views of Aquinas, Husserl and Heidegger.

Niemeyer, K. A. E. Die Gleichnisse bei Quintus Smyrnaeus Zwickau, Programm 1883-1884

Nietzsche, Friedrich. "On Truth and Lie in an Extra-Moral Sense" Werke in drei Bänden Karl Schlechta, ed. München 1960
The translation from sense perception to image and from image to language is metaphorical. Language is made of nothing but metaphors and man has a fundamental drive to create them, but he is usually not aware that he uses them. We divide things metaphorically and arbitrarily into genders and speak metaphorically of nerve stimulus transformed into a percept or percept copied into a sound. We do not know things in themselves but only metaphors of the things. "And what therefore is truth? A mobile army of metaphors, metonymies, anthropomorphisms: in short a sum of human relations which became poetically and rhetorically intensified, metamorphosed, adorned, and after long usage seem to a nation fixed

canonic and binding; truths are illusions of which one has forgotten that they are illusions; worn-out metaphors which have become powerless to affect the senses." The intentional adherence to illusion in spite of our awareness of it is a kind of "lie in an extra-moral sense." In terms of his general philosophy Nietzsche asserts in his works: (cf. Vaihinger p. 341 ff.) Conscious fictions, regulative fictions, untruths regarded as truths, insanity, living errors, illusion, delusional concepts, metaphor, the ideal, falsification, as-if's; myths or lies must be used in science as well as in life. "We need blindness sometimes and must allow certain articles of faith and errors to remain untouched within us--so long as they maintain us in life." i.e. They must serve a justifiable use or purpose if they cannot be intelligibly explained. Art is the conscious creation of an aesthetic illusion and rests on a primitive will to or longing for illusion. "The construction of metaphors is the fundamental instinct of man." Illusions of beauty make life worthwhile. The nature of science and action is to be veiled in illusion. "Our greatness lies in the supreme illusion." Our intellect operates with conscious symbols, pictures, rhetorical figures, with metaphors. "To know is merely to work with one's favorite metaphors." To think is to create "pictures." e.g. "Cause" is a "picture" we read into nature. Both language and thought are based on unreal or falsifying operations. Nietzsche speaks of "Education, which sanctifies so many lies." A child's games are conscious self-deceptions. "We are still continually seduced by words..." "We distort by simplifying, abstracting, isolating." Nietzsche calls his philosophy "perspectivism" because all we can have is perspectives, perspective falsifications, and perspective vision. "The most erroneous assumptions are precisely the most indispensable for us." Still many fictions are unintelligible and should be exposed as such. His work Antichrist attacks all imaginary entities, the religious world of fiction and the dualistic fictions. Nietzsche presents the following as fictions: Substance, external world, man, fictional "unity" of psychical faculties, consciousness, soul, pure logical thinking, thing, subject, means-end, active-passive, language and its grammar, drama is a fictional transfer of one's character, truth is called the most expedient form of error, freedom of will, circle, straight line, surface, bodies, atoms, divisible time and space, cause-effect, rest, motion, logic, shape, content, matter, number, identity, laws of nature, ego character, blame, praise, reward, punishment, wisdom, goodness, will, purpose, subject-object, (our senses distort, the whole of physics is a false but temporarily servicable arrangement.)

Nikiforova, O. I. "Vospriyatis metafory" (Source: Korol'kov)

Nodelman, Perry M. "Art Palace to Evolution: Tennyson's Metaphors of Organization" PhD diss. Yale 1969

Noel, Roden. "On the Use of Metaphor and 'Pathetic Fallacy' in Poetry" Fortnightly 5 (1866) 670-684

Norton, Dan and P. Ruston. A Glossary of Literary Terms New York: Rinehart 1957 p. 36
"Figurative language is language which deviates from the literal or standard construction, order, and significance, in order to achieve special meaning or effect."

Norwood, W. D. Jr. "C. S. Lewis, Owen Barfield, and the Modern Myth" Midwest Quarterly 8 (April 1967) 279-91
We take a model or metaphor for the universe (e.g. the machine). As long as it is unrecognized as a metaphor it remains superstition. Lewis holds that any picturable description of reality is metaphoric. Man contributes to the seeing of the world. (cf. seeing-as) (Norwood's PhD diss., Texas 1965, contains discussions of mythic and archetypal themes.)

Nosek, Jiří. "English Colloquial Metaphor and the Syntax" Philologica Pragensia 10 (1967) 175-181
Metaphor is dissociated from syntax. A verb may be inherently metaphorical. Metaphor is not intrinsically tied up with one particular member of a sentence to the exclusion of the others.

_____. "Metaphor in Modern Colloquial English" Zdeněk Stříbrný, I. Poldauf & J. Nosek, eds. Prague Studies in English XII. (Acta Universitatis Carolinae Philologica 5) Praha: U. Karlova 1967 pp. 41-62

_____. "Review of Brooke-Rose: A Grammar of Metaphor" Philologica Pragensia 46 (1964) 327-328

Notopoulos, J. A. "Homeric Similes in the Light of Oral Poetry" Classical Journal 52 (April 1957) 323-8

Nováková, Julie. Umbra. Ein Beitrag zur dichterischen Semantik (Deutsche Akademie der Wissenschaften zu Berlin: Schriften der Sektion für Altertumswissenschaft, 36) Berlin 1964

Nowottny, Winifred M. T. "Review of Wimsatt: The Verbal Icon" Modern Language Review 50 (1955) p. 571

_____. The Language Poets Use London: Athlone Press 1965 Ch. 3 "Metaphor" Ch. 4 "Metaphor and Poetic Structure"
"A metaphor is...a set of linguistic directions for supplying the sense of an unwritten literal term." (This is why metaphor can 'say' things not provided for in the existing literal vocabulary of our language.) Metaphor is speaking of

X as though it were Y, a four term analogy, a model or diagram. It dissolves the distinction between subject and object, fact and fiction, determines what can be said in poetry, but is not "a peephole on the nature of transcendental reality." He distinguishes between metaphoric thought and metaphoric language.

Nunes, José. "A Metáfora no Linguagem" Revista Lusitana: Arquivo de estudos filologicos e etnologicos relativos a Portugal 24 (1922) 286-294

Nussbaum, Eugenie. "Metapher und Gleichnis bei Berthold von Regensburg" Wien: Selbstverlag 1902 PhD diss. Zürich 1902

Nyman, Alf. Metafor Och Fiktion Lunds Universitets Årsskrift N.F. Avd. 1, Bd. 18, nr. 6, Lund: Gleerup 1922
A Kantian view of metaphor. From this perspective he examines fiction, e.g. that of Victor Hugo. He discusses especially the views of Hans Werner, Gottsched, Kant, Konrad Lange, Karl Groos, Fr. Paulhan, Vaihinger, Albalat, Vischer, T. Meyer Sterzinger, Wilhelm Wundt, Hans Larsson and Elster. He uses key Kantian terms such as synthesis, constitutive, intuition, as-if, fiction, hypothetical, schema, appearance-reality, aesthetic, logic, imagination, sensation, concept, apperception, condition, synthesis of representations. By use of the Kantian scheme he hopes to provide a firm basis for metaphor and avoid being misled by metaphor.

Paul-Louis Courtier and Gottsched wanted to rid language of metaphor. Thomas Thorild regarded the poetic image as untruthful, and as a distortion of reality. Eugene Dühring rejects the metaphor as superstition. Kreutzfeld (1777) derives poetic image from illusions.

T. Meyer, Schopenhauer, Albalat say that language and meaning have little to do with visualizing and imagery. Nyman says they fail to see the as-if nature of the relation between image and object.

Kant distinguishes between imagery as play and imagery as illusion. As play it keeps our spirit in pleasant fluctuation on the border between truth and falsehood. Images are true in the form of playful appearances (cf. Schiller's play-theory). For Kant logic deals only with concepts, not with sensation. Sensation and imagination cause representation to spread over several conceptions allowing more than can be said with words (and is thus not reducible to the literal). He speaks of experience through an attribute which the power of imagination associates and which stirs up a host of sensations and secondary conceptions for which there are no direct expressions. The image thus allows a free and wide view over a boundless field of related conceptions involving fantasy, imagination, and feeling yielding the "aesthetic idea" which can be rendered in no other way.

Paulhan and K. Lange approach the problem from the point

of view of appearance and reality and hold that beauty is based on conscious self-deception, illusion or lie. Art should create illusory reality and let us live in an illusory but nevertheless satisfying reality. We simultaneously affirm and deny the reality of art. Both affirmation and denial are needed. This is Lange's "pendulum-theory," an oscillation between image and object. Paulhan (in "La logique de la contradiction") holds a logical contradiction view (cf. Beardsley) which leads to a division of the ego.

Paulhan thinks rhetoric (metaphor and simile) involves contradiction which is essential to our spiritual life. Tension of contradiction of the two terms of a metaphor make it esthetically effective. It is a unity in difference. Without tension and contradiction metaphor becomes dead and unpoetic.

For Lange a poetic image is two simultaneous images or two images in quick succession. Metaphor is a perspective and is multi-meaning. (Nyman agrees that the aesthetic experience is that form of viewing things which allows man to absorb the greatest number of ideas in the shortest amount of time without tiring.) Following Kant it is asserted that the aesthetic principle is an intuitive synthesis. A metaphor or image of any kind serves to bring together a greater number of conceptions than we can manage to press together in a more colorless expression. We rise to a higher view or synthesis to take an overview of the multitude of conceptions and contexts and relationships.

Nyman agrees with Lange that every poetic effect does have a pendulum effect or contradiction but suggests that this does not account for the aesthetic effect of metaphor. Why, for example, does one oscillation cause mysticism and another comedy? Lange and Sterzinger are said to confuse a _condition for_ synthesis with the synthesis itself.

For Nyman metaphor is a multi-meaning perspective, an intuitive state of mind. He agrees with Kant's views as presented above. The image, metaphor, or scientific fiction _constitutes_ a conscious deviation from reality, in the interest of knowledge or reality. The as-if viewing digresses from reality to get closer to reality, to greater intuitiveness. There is a simultaneously fictional and synthesizing nature of fiction. There is an as-if or analogical apperception. The relation between image and object is an as-if or hypothetical not a real identification. Vaihinger is cited for support of this.

According to Nyman the psychological experiments of Plüss and Groos which concern the degree of imagery awakened by metaphor and simile, deal with only a passing moment. They overlook specific circumstances and the aesthetic value of an image or metaphor. Psychological images solely as inner states ignore the function of context. One may have clear images but not appreciate their aesthetic qualities.

Comprehension, visualness, explanation, fictional understanding, all are entwined in each other and reveal the deepest function of metaphor, i.e. intensification of intuitiveness achieved through consciously false representations. The intended reality is adjusted and grouped in accordance with the intuitive (schema) brought forth by the image. It fuses into a new representation. Synthesis is the main characteristic of aesthetic metaphor. Metaphor is fused or in synthesis while with simile the two elements are yet to be synthesized. Nyman points out that his view applies to Victor Hugo whose metaphors synthesize thought and emotion by means of intuition to clarify, concentrate and give insight.

Nyman agrees with Hans Larsson's Poesiens Logik (Stockholm 1922) and Intuition according to which poetic devices are first of all logical and then an intuitive means of intensification or synthesis of representation around which is laid a forcefield of emotion.

Nyrop, K. Das Leben der Wörter Leipzig 1903

Ochse, Horst. Studien zur Metaphorik Calderóns (Freiburger Schriften zur romanischen Philologie, 1) München: W. Fink 1967 Also PhD diss. Freiburg.

O'Dea, Richard. "Vehicle and Tenor in 'Macbeth'" Coranto: Journal of the Friends of Libraries (U.S.C.) 5 (1967) 26-28 Macbeth thinks in images, not ideas. When Macbeth finally links tenor and vehicle in "The world is a stage" metaphor, his soul becomes annihilated.

Odegard, Douglas. "Review of Max Black Models and Metaphors" Philosophy 39 (Oct. 1964) 349-356

Odell, George C. D. Simile and Metaphor in the English and Scottish Ballads PhD diss. Columbia College 1892

Ogden, Charles K. and I. A. Richards. The Foundations of Aesthetics New York: International Publishers 1929 On his theory of opposites and synaesthesia. [cf. I. Richards]

_____. Bentham's Theory of Fictions New Jersey: Littlefield, Adams 1959 Many words or concepts are fictions and ought to be analyzed into statements based on real entities. Language not referring directly to materially real entities is metaphorical, a fiction. Psychological terms are metaphorically derived from words for physical objects. Legal terms are often fictions spoken of as if they refer to objects. Other fictions are power, right, time, motion, mind, political terms, quality, obligation, condition, certainty, impossibility, surface (i.e. surface without depth), line (without thickness) and all predicative language and every psychological description is fictional. Fictions are said to hold us captive. They "are mightly pretty things," are cultivated by long acquaintance and by thinking that fictions of language name things. "To language, then--to language alone--it is that fictitious entities owe their existence; their impossible, yet indispensable existence." Bentham holds that language needs fictions for communication but that we should not take fictions or metaphors literally. Fictions may have only a verbal reality and still we may speak of them as if they are real. Those most related to our senses are termed archetypes. They seem to be like pictures or models for the fiction. (For example, obligation is rendered by the emblematical or archetypal image of a man lying down with a heavy body pressing upon him.) The reference of fictions is fixed to actual objects by means of archetypation and phraseoplerosis (completing the elliptical fiction). These are in effect logical analyses or analyses of fictions. Since fictions unlike non-fictions cannot be defined by genus and difference they must be expounded by paraphrasis (the exposition of fiction in terms of real objects). In general, metaphors and fictions are misleading.

Bentham wrote, "But above all, the pestilential breath of fiction poisons the sense of every instrument it comes near."

_____, and I. A Richards. The Meaning of Meaning London: Routledge and Kegan Paul 1952 [1923] esp. p. 213 for definition of metaphor.

Ogilvie, J. T. "From Woods to Stars: A Pattern of Imagery in Robert Frost's Poetry" South Atlantic Quarterly 58 (Winter 1959) 64-76
An examination of imagery in Frost's poems. "The drift in Frost's poetry from an empirically operative intuitiveness toward an insistent didacticism is reflected, interestingly enough, by a shift in imagery pattern. Woods, symbolic of the introspective life, are gradually displaced by the heavenly bodies of outer space, symbolic of more impersonal, intellectual considerations."

Olivero, Frederico. "A Study on the Metaphor in Dante" Il Giornale Dantesco 28 (1925) 61-84, 176-179
The main object of Dante's art is to beautify sensation and thought and strengthen emotion. His images are logically consistent. For Dante every idea becomes an image and he speaks to us through metaphors. "The metaphor discloses to us the inmost character of the subject." By imagery one passes from perception to cognition. Poetry works mainly through metaphors.

_____. The Representation of the Image in Dante...1936 (250 copies printed) (Source: University of California Library, Berkeley)

Olken, Ilene. "Colette: Aspects of Imagery" PhD diss. University of Michigan 1960
Colette's images are classified as 1) sensory 2) transpositions including synaesthesia 3) animal traits in imagery 4) imagery of conflict. Colette relies almost entirely on the physical concrete symbol for psychological explanation. It is a persuasive animateness based on primitivism--a transposed statement of primitive drives.

_____. "Aspects of Imagery in Colette: Color and Light" PMLA 77 (1962) 140-148. Also PhD diss. University of Michigan

Olscamp, Paul J. "Philosophical Importance of C. M. Turbayne's The Myth of Metaphor" International Philosophical Quarterly 6 (March 1966) 110-31
A review and criticism of reviews of Turbayne's book. He discusses at length reviews by C. M. Meyers, C. K. Grant, J. Kaminsky, F. Sparshott, A. Mardiros, W. Mays, D. Weeks, J. Davis, D. Munro.

_____. "How Some Metaphors May Be True or False" Journal of Aesthetics and Art Criticism 29 (1970) 77-86
He discusses the views of Wheelwright and Aristotle and proceeds to show that Wheelwright's epiphoric or comparison

metaphor is either true or false. Olscamp renders "Man is a wolf" logically as $(x)\ [Mx \supset (\exists F)\ (\exists G)\ (M_1F \cdot W_1G \cdot FR_1G)]$. This reads "For any x if x is a man then there are properties F and G (e.g. visciousness) such that F is a property of men and G is a property of wolves and F resembles G." This leaves open the possibility that there are other resemblant or non-resemblant properties. He believes that metaphors are partly based on comparison and are elliptical similes. The comparison as an assertion of resemblance can be either true or false.

Olsen, Elder. "The Imagery of Marianne Moore" PhD diss. Pennsylvania State University 1957

_____. "William Empson, Contemporary Criticism, and Poetic Diction" *Critics and Criticism: Ancient and Modern* R. S. Crane, ed. Chicago: University of Chicago Press 1952 (1965) esp. p. 81

O'Malley, Glenn. *Shelley and Synesthesia* Evanston, Ill.: Northwestern University Press 1964
"No other poet matches Shelley's care and ingenuity in working synesthesia into the fabric of his verse." He uses synesthesia to render a harmony of the senses and intersense analogies, to equate moral discernment with sensory perception, to coordinate spiritual and sensuous experience, to imply a visionary spiritual order, to provide emblems and visions.

O'Neill, Joseph. "The Metaphorical Mode: Image, Metaphor, Symbol" *Thought* 31 (1956) 79-113
True metaphor is an analogy of extrinsic proportion (Thomistic view). Metaphor may also be an unconscious, imaginative, emotive and intuitive analogy of two different spheres of being. All thinking is metaphorical.

O'Neill, Martin S. "Some Remarks on the Analogy of God and Creatures in St. Thomas Aquinas" *Mediaeval Studies* 23 (1961) 206-15

Ong, Walter J. "Metaphor and the Twinned Vision" *The Sewanee Review* 63 (April 1955) 193-201. Also in his *The Barbarian Within* New York: Macmillan 1962 pp. 41-48
A Thomistically inspired view that metaphor is based on similarity and is a "twinned vision" i.e. just as all judgement can only be in terms of subject and predicate (two things) not one thing alone. Metaphor is unity in diversity and is best if its terms are far-fetched or unexpected and then united.

_____. "Wit and Mystery: A Revaluation in Medieval Latin Hymnody" *Speculum* 22 (1947) 310-341. Reprinted in his *The Barbarian Within* New York: Macmillan 1962 pp. 88-130
He discusses conceits used to express mysteries of the Catholic faith.

Oppenheimer, Robert. "Analogy in Science" The American Psychologist 11 (March 1956) 127-135

Oppian. Halieuticks William Diaper and John Jones, eds. Oxford 1722
He says the "regular gradation of created Beings from man down to the lowest vegetable" explains the basis of metaphor. All the links of the chain are similar and so joy and grief can be read in trees and plants. Moral precepts can be gained from observing animals.

Oroz, Rodolfo. "El uso metafórico de nombres de animales en el lenguaje familiar y vulgar chileno" Atenea 37 (1932) 1-30
About animal metaphors as designations of stupidity (pavo, borrico), ugliness (mono, sapo), etc.

Orpinela, Robert. "Professor Ryle on Category Mistakes" M.A. thesis Berkeley: University of California 1961

Ortega y Gasset, José. Obras completas 9 vols. Madrid: Revista de Occidente 1964 (1947) (cf. Jaurrieta, Arroyo, et al.)

1) Vol. 6 "La metáfora"
In metaphor there is in reality non-identity between two terms which leads to a subjective (sentiment), ideal identification. This identification constitutes one's self and his perception (cf. seeing-as). The aesthetic object is metaphor. Metaphor is an annihilation of real relations to push to an ideal, subjective , aesthetic object.

2) Vol. 3 "El 'Tabu' y la metáfora"
The metaphor is probably the most fertile power man has. Only the metaphor offers escape from reality, masking one object with another. It is rooted in taboo, the necessity to avoid certain realities or names. Metaphor also is used to adorn the real object.

3) Vol. 2 "Las dos grandes metáforas" (en el segundo centenario del nacimiento de Kant) In 1916 he gave a course in Buenos Aires dealing with three great metaphors (Source: J. Marías).
Metaphor is constitutive in poetry but supplementary in science. Both kinds of metaphor are needed. Metaphor is a new naming, transposition of names, a rushed association. In science metaphor is analytic, in poetry it is synthetic and more than the sum of its parts. Metaphor allows us to grasp what is beyond our conceptual potential as well as reality, and to relate subject-object, mind-body. Even seeing is metaphorical.

Ortiz, Ambrosio. "Uso tropologico en el lenguaje chileno, de nombres del reino vegetal" Boletín de Filologia (Santiago de

Chile) 5 (1947-49) 137-262
A rich study and classification of metaphors.

Osborn, Michael M. "Archetypal Metaphor in Rhetoric: The Light-Dark Family" Quarterly Journal of Speech 53 (April 1967) 115-26
Archetypal metaphors such as light or darkness are selected more often in rhetorical discourse than are non-archetypal ones such as ivy, Edsel, etc. Four sources of archetypes discussed are: light and darkness, sun, heat and cold, and the cycle of the seasons. He recommends a "microscopic venture, concerned with tracing fine distinctions according to the imagery appropriate in each art form."

_____. "The Function and Significance of Metaphor in Rhetorical Discourse" PhD diss. University of Florida 1963
An attempt to combine the lingusitic and psychological aspects of metaphor as well as the perspective of rhetoric which takes account of speaker and audience. Metaphor is the interaction of mental events or thoughts which depend on a lingusitic occurrence. Metaphor allows us to express what cannot be expressed in ordinary language. It reveals feeling. Its phases are 1) error phase 2) recoil or puzzlement-recoils phase 3) resolution phase. The link between the terms of a metaphor are 1) contextual (linguistic) 2) communal 3) perceptual 4) situational 5) emotional 6) private. "Poetic metaphor" is tentative, exploratory, often private, constitutive or self-explanatory. "Rhetorical metaphor" is the natural illustrative influence coming out of a speaker's subject. It is not private. He states "Students...need to become more familiar with analogical forms of reasoning...and metaphoric association in particular.... An expanded training program would appear desirable."

_____. "Main Sources of Metaphor in American Public Address, and Their Relation to Axiology" (Paper unpublished under this title.)

_____, and J. W. Bowers. "Attitudinal Effects of Selected Types of Concluding Metaphors in Persuasive Speeches" Speech Monographs 33 (1966) 147-155
Metaphor is termed "puzzlement-recoil" because of the effort required in transferring its denotation. The use of intense metaphors at the conclusion of speeches has a different effect than does literal language.

_____, and D. Ehninger. "The Metaphor in Public Address" Speech Monographs 29 (August 1962) 223-234
Metaphor is a communicative stimulus as well as a mental response. Stimulus is defined as the identifying of an idea or object through a sign which usually denotes a different one.

The response is an interaction of one thought or "interpretant" from the usual denotation of the sign, with another thought from its denotation in the given context. Metaphors influence the speaker as well as the audience. Metaphors are distinguished on the basis of tension and distance between tenor and vehicle.

Osgood, Charles E. "The Principle of Congruity in the Prediction of Attitude Change" Psychological Review 62 (1955) 42-55

_____, and G. J. Suci and P. H. Tannenbaum. The Measurement of Meaning Urbana: The University of Illinois Press 1957

_____, and James Snider. Semantic Differential Technique Chicago: Aldine 1969

Ouy, Achille. "Le raisonnement par analogie et l'automorphisme" Mercure de France 306 (June 1949) 357-61
On metaphor and analogy.

Owen, S. G. "Ovid's Use of the Simile" Classical Review 45 (July 1931) 97-106

Owens, Joseph. "Analogy as a Thomistic Approach to Being" Mediaeval Studies 24 (1962) 303-22

Pacernick, Gary B. "Logic of Metaphor: An Aesthetic Approach to the Poetry and Poetics of Hart Crane" PhD diss. Arizona State University 1969
The "logic of metaphor" is the basis of Crane's symbolism. The poem is the symbol of emotional and spiritual experience which communicates through an irrational "short-hand logic" to the reader. Eight poems are discussed regarding Crane's search for the "imaged word."

Page, Alex. "Faculty Psychology and Metaphor in Eighteenth-Century Criticism" _Modern Philology_ 66 (Feb. 1969) 237-47
A brief tracing of the views of metaphor of Johnson, Pope, Longinus, Robert Dodsley, Horace, Joseph Warton, etc. Page thinks of metaphor as functional imagery which is creative, suggestive, complex, far-ranging, honest.

Pagnini, Marcello. "Imagism" _Studi Americani_ II (1965) 181-95
Literary approach to imagism.

Painter, Jack W. "A Semiotic Approach to Some Problems and Theories in the Interpretation of Metaphors" PhD diss. Emory University 1961
An attempt to show "that a semiotic [semantic, syntactic, pragmatic] metalanguage is precise and useful in discussions of metaphor interpretation." An attempt at an essay in applied logic.

Paiva Boleo, Manuel de. _A metáfora na língua portuguesa corrente_ Coimbra: Coimbra Editora 1935

Palley, Julián. "The Metaphors of Jorge Guillén" _Hispanica_ 36 (1953) 321-324
Metaphor is a type of image, a transfer from one thought or image to another to produce a third. Guillén, a poetic ancestor of the highly metaphorical Góngora, uses many concretized abstraction types of metaphor. Guillermo de Torres' four types of metaphor are presented.

Palmer, Humphrey. _The Concept of Analogy_ Oxford: Blackwell 1971

Pandey, Arvind. Rītikālīna kāvya memlakshanā kā prayoga (In Hindi) 1966
On Hindi poetry and metaphor.

Pap, Arthur. "Types and Meaninglessness" _Mind_ N.S. 69 (1960) 41-54

Pappenheim, E. _Die Tropen der griechischen Skeptiker_ Gymnas. Köln Programm 1885

Paradkar, Moreshwar. _Similes in Manusmrti_ Delhi: Motilal Banarsidass 1960

Pardee, W. Hearne. "Images of Vision (Proust)" Yale French Studies 34 (1965) 19-23
"Our examination of Proust's abstract visual imagery has shown it to dramatize his philosophy in concrete terms, in his attempts to distill a superessential light from the visual world." e.g. his use of crystal and sapphire which reflect light with new brilliance.

Parisi, Attilio. Il linguaggio figurato in A. Persio Flacco Cherasco: Raselli 1913

Park, Roy. "Ut Pictura Poesis: The Nineteenth-Century Aftermath" Journal of Aesthetics and Art Criticism 28 (Winter 1969) 155-164

Parker, Alexander. "Metáfora y símbolo en la interpretación de Calderón" International Congress of Hispanists Oxford: Dolphin Book Co. 1964 pp. 141-160
His ideological metaphors develop into symbols visible in the action and characters.

Parker, Richard. Aids to English Composition New York 1845

Parkhurst, Helen H. Beauty: An Interpretation of Art and the Imaginative Life New York: Harcourt, Brace 1930
Metaphor is the intuitive resemblance or juxtaposition of two dissimilar realms or objects. It unites and explores incongruities, opposites, and antitheses (examples are given including mythical animal combinations such as mermaids). There are plastic metaphors e.g. Blake's sketch of a child gazing into the eyes of a horse. The two terms yield a mysterious and emergent new concept. Metaphor is the essence of poetry and fiction. Any supreme insight is a metaphor.

Parry, Milman. "The Homeric Metaphor as a Traditional Poetic Device" Transactions and Proceedings of the American Philological Association (An abstract of a paper read) 62 (1931) p. 24
The traditional, or "fixed metaphor," of Homer and others is a metaphor used over and over as a synonym, empty of meaning but as a help to the verse. "Winged words" is used 123 times in the first book of the Iliad.

_____. "The Traditional Metaphor in Homer" Classical Philology 28 (Jan. 1933) 30-43

Parsons, Elsie. "Riddles and Metaphors Among Indian Peoples" Journal of American Folk-lore 49 (1936) 171-174

Parsons, Wilfrid. "A Study of the Vocabulary and Rhetoric of the

Letters of St. Augustine" PhD diss. Catholic University of America 1923

Pasini, Gian F. "Lo Studio delle metafore" Lingua e Stile 3 (1968) 71-89
A linguistic or structural approach to the theory of metaphor. Pierre Guiraud is quoted as saying in his La Semantica that the study of metaphors postulates implicitly the notion of structure. He outlines and criticizes the views of Jean Taillardat, Gérald Antoine, Henry Wells, H. Hempel, Stephen Ullmann, Anna Komornicka, C. Brooke-Rose, Roman Jakobson, T. Pavel. He presents Hempel's view of metaphor from "Essence et origine de la métaphore" according to which metaphor considered according to its origins can be divided loosely into four types: 1) Practical Metaphor--metaphors used because ordinary language is inadequate or to create euphemisms 2) Rhetorical Metaphor--It proposes to act on the will of the listener 3) Affective Metaphor--satisfies emotive need. It is necessary wherever it appears 4) Poetic Metaphor--This is the highest kind of metaphor. It has no rational end. Pasini states that Hempel's classification only reproduces, in an indirect way, the old distinction of rhetoric between proper style and figurative style. A. Komornicka's theory is said to be based on Aristotle's views and is presented as follows: The origin of metaphor may be studied under three aspects: 1) Temporal--analysis of the surroundings and social conditions that caused the birth of the metaphor, its evolution, rejuvenation, etc. 2) Semantic--a) variations of rapport between word image and word object involving relations between abstract and concrete. b) variations of thematic content of the two terms of the metaphor 3) Formal--metaphors obeying either principles of grammar or syntax. Metaphors have natural, spontaneous origin or derive from an individual poetic vision or are learned or literary. Four functions Komornicka gives to metaphor are: 1) denominative, or to name 2) expressive 3) epistemological, having knowledge as an objective. It cannot be phrased in any other way and reveals new aspects 4) esthetic function. Its end is the cosmos and it creates the illusion that is at the base of all literary fiction and constitutes the essence of our receptivity to any work of art. It can be comic, pathetic or lyrical. Roman Jakobson's views are regarded as being based on non-demonstrated territory and as being unsystematic. Drawing largely on the work of Pavel, Pasini synthesizes his survey partly as follows: 1) Aristotle's definition of metaphor and subsequent definitions have made no substantial progress but can be integrated and clarified by linguistic structure, which presents it as a neutralization or syncretism of the lexicon. 2) Metaphor cannot be regarded as mere ornament or merely based on a distinction of proper style and figurative style. As a basis of the linguistic study of tropes should be the consciousness of their functional necessity. 3) Pavel's dis-

tinction between syncretism and commutation allow the possibility of tracing the limits of habitual and new metaphors better than do other methods. 4) In the interior of an author's work metaphors can constitute a system.

Patterson, H. Temple. "The Origin of Hugo's Condensed Metaphors" *French Studies* 5 (1951) 343-348
Hugo owes his condensed metaphors to Louis-Sébastian Mercier who stressed metaphor and the unity of nature. Examples of condensed metaphor are: *le dogue liberté*, *le lion océan*, *la borne Aristotle*, *homme-chien*, *échelle-cièl*.

Pauer, Karl. "Die Bildersprache des Euripides" PhD diss. Breslau 1935 (Possibly Bauer, Karl)

Paul, Anthony. *Figurative Language* PhD diss. Johns Hopkins University 1969 (Also a condensation of Part I was read at the 1968 Annual Meeting of the Western Division of the American Philosophical Association.)
He defends a modification of the classical simile theory of metaphor. Figurative language can be literally translated. Figures are based on literal language. Metaphor and models are not indispensable in science. He discusses metaphor theories. Literal involves familiarity and frequency.

Paul, Hermann. *Prinzipien der Sprachgeschichte* Halle 1886 (Tübingen 1960) esp. section 68, 69

Paul, Jean. [pseudonym for Johann Paul Richter]

Paulhan, Fr. *La double fonction du langage* Paris 1929 (cf. Nyman)

Pavel, Toma. "Notes pour une description structurale de la métaphore poètique" Cercetări de Lingvisticǎ. Cluj, Romania. *Poetics-Poetyka...* Donald Davie, et al., eds. The Hague: Mouton 1962 pp. 185-207 (cf. Pasini)
A linguistic and structural account of metaphor partly based on the work of Hjelmslev and the Copenhagen school of linguistics. Metaphor is a "neutralization" or "syncretism" involving "coalescence" or "implication." In metaphoric syncretism "extensive" refers to the figurative term and "intensive" to the proper term. In syncretism the figurative term loses its denoted meaning and acquires that of the proper term. The denoted meaning of the figurative term does not disappear completely, but becomes connotative and contributes to the construction.

Pavy, David. "Verbal Behavior in Schizophrenia: A Review of Recent Studies" *Psychological Bulletin* 70 no. 3 (Sept. 1968) 164-178. Has an excellent bibliography.
"Deviant verbal behavior is one of the principle diagnostic indices of the syndrome of schizophrenia." Various tests of

the schizophrenic's metaphors are examined and found inadequate. He suggests an approach stressing attention and employing Chomsky's generative grammar.

Peacham, Henry. The Garden of Eloquence. Scholars' Facsimiles and Reprints Gainesville, Florida 1954 [1577, 1593]
Said by William Crane to be "The most extensive and accurate treatment of figures obtainable in English." It is based on Susenbrotus' and Sherry's work. The contents of the various editions differ. Metaphor is an "artificial translation of one word from the proper signification, to another not proper, but yet like." It is based on the faculties of memory, (remembered similarity) and judgement. It pleases; clarifies; persuades; is easily remembered; moves judgement, emotions and wit; extends language. It should not be far-fetched, superficial, ugly or inappropriate.

Peacock, Markham Jr. The Critical Opinions of William Wordsworth Baltimore: Johns Hopkins Press 1950
For Wordsworth poetry should imitate ordinary man. The Imagination is a truthful, real, permanent likeness of inherent essential properties which are naturally and automatically seen or found but not created by us. By imagination the sensible represents abstract and intellectual existing complexes. It allows us to transcend reality. The fancy on the other hand is a temporary voluntary combination of inessential properties and does not transcend itself. It yields surprise, play, humor, emotion by means of profusion and rapidity to beguile the temporal part of our nature.

Pear, T. H. "Imagery and Mentality" British Journal of Psychology 14 (1924) 291-299

Peckham, Morse. "Metaphor: A Little Plain Speaking on a Weary Subject" Connotation (Farleigh Dickinson University) I, no. 2 (1962) 29-46

Pecz, Wilhelm. Beiträge zur vergleichende Tropik der Poesie. I. Systematische Darstellung der Tropen des Aeschylus, Sophocles und Euripides miteinander verglichen und in poetischer und kulturhistorischer Rücksicht behandelt (Berliner Studien für klassische Philologie und Archaeologie 3) Berlin: Calvary & Co. 1886
Gives brief bibliography of literature on tropes up to 1886.

_____. "Die Tropen des Aristophanes verglichen mit den Tropen des Aeschylus, Sophokles und Euripides" Ungarische Revue 13 (1893) 198-205

_____. "Die Tropen der Ilias und der Odyssee" Neue Jahrbücher für das klassische Altertum, Geschichte und deutsche Literatur 15 (1912) 665-670

Pederson-Krag, Geraldine. "The Use of Metaphor in Analytic Thinking" The Psychoanalytic Quarterly 25 (1956) 66-71
Metaphors or models may in theories, clarify or confuse, eg. Freud likened mind to protoplasm, to a continent inhabited by warring nations, and he personified the ego. "As we try to emulate Freud and clarify our concept of what is happening in a patient's psyche, we may find ourselves betraying whatever insight we have gained by too faithful adherence to the implications of our metaphors."

Pelc, Jerzy. "Semantic Functions as Applied to the Analysis of the Concept of Metaphor" Poetics, Poetyka, Poetyka I. D. Davie, et al. editors. The Hague: Mouton and Company 1961 pp. 305-339
A linguistic analysis of the concept of metaphor. The semantic function of the sign is applied to the analysis of metaphor. Various tropes are similarly analyzed.

Pellegrini, Camillo. (1598-1663) Del Concetto Poetico 1898 (1639). (cf. Sarmiento 1935)
Opposes Gracián's interpretation of the conceit. He gives five kinds of acutezze mirabile: serious, gay, pleasing, ridiculous, and mixed. Seven sources of the acutezza are: the unexpected, the incredible, trickery, agreement, imitation, enthymeme, the assumption and derision. He also gives ten types of imperfection. Acutezza is an inferior trope.

Pellegrini, Matteo [also written Peregrini, Pelligrine] I Fonti dell'ingegno ridotti ad arte Bologna 1650

_____. Delle Acutezze Genova: C. Ferroni 1639
He gives 22 topoi and derives conceits from each. Jokes may be derived, as Quintilian says, from the topics in the same way as arguments.

Pelliot, Paul. "Review of C. A. S. Williams: A Manual of Chinese Metaphor" Toung Pao 21 (1922) 426-439

Pénido, Abbé. Le rôle de l'analogie en théologie dogmatique Paris: Vrin 1931

Pepper, Stephen. World Hypothesis Berkeley: University of California Press 1942 (Reviews in Philosophical Review 52 (1943) 602-604; 590-601. Journal of Philosophy 33 (1936) 575-77, 42 (1945) 85-101)
The "root-metaphor" method is an "analogical method for generating world theories. The method in principle seems to be this: A man desiring to understand the world looks about for a clue to its comprehension. He pitches upon some area of common-sense fact and tries [to see] if he cannot understand other areas in terms of this one. The original area becomes then his basic analogy or root metaphor." He discusses four

basic root-metaphors: 1) Formism, 2) Mechanism, 3) Contextualism and 4) Organicism. His order of preference is 3,2,4,1.

_____. "The Root Metaphor Theory of Metaphysics" Journal of Philosophy 32 (July 4, 1935) 365-374. Also abstract in 32 (1935) p. 155
The root metaphor is a small concept or hypothesis applied to a larger range of events. We usually think in such metaphors. But no single metaphor is adequate, several are needed. He opposes single, dogmatic (i.e. self-righteous) philosophies unaware of their root metaphors. Root metaphors have their own logic and are not bound by universal principles e.g. principle of non-contradiction.

_____. "Philosophy and Metaphor" Journal of Philosophy 25 (March 1928) 130-132
We cannot object to metaphor, for every philosophy is a metaphor and science is metaphorical. "Both philosophers and poets live by metaphor." It takes great genius to create new dynamic metaphors.

Percy, Walker. "Metaphor as Mistake" Sewanee Review 66 (Winter 1958) 79-99
To know is to symbolize, as Cassirer says, and to conceive a thing under the wrong name is to know it better also. It results in an authentic poetic experience, one absent before the mistake was made. Naming is a metaphorical symbolic process. "The 'wrongness' of metaphor...is the very condition of our knowing anything at all." The thrill and insight of metaphor can hardly be surpassed.

Peregrini. (See Pellegrini)

Perelman, Ch. and L. Olbrechts-Tyteca. The New Rhetoric: A Treatise on Argumentation John Wilkinson and Purcell Weaver, trans. University of Notre Dame Press 1969. (Paris: 1958) Chapters on analogy and metaphor.
A rhetoric based on Thomistic thought. Metaphor is a condensed analogy, the fusion of an element of the phoros (the two terms of four term analogy which support the theme or topic) and one from the theme. The fusion is complete in itself, not merely reducible to the analogy. Metaphor is not imagery.

_____. "Analogie et métaphore en science, poesie et philosophie" Revue Internationale de Philosophie 23 (1969) 3-15

Pérès, J. "L'image" Revue Politique et Littéraire 74 (Sept. 19, 1936) 628-35

Peretts, Varvara Pavlovna (Adrianova). Ocherki poeticheskovo stilia drevnei Rusi. Moskva, Izd-vo Akademii nauk SSSR 1947

On Russian literature to 1700, figures of speech and metaphor.

Perkins, David. "Johnson on Wit and Metaphysical Poetry" ELH 20 (1953) 200-217
Johnson had a higher estimation for the metaphysical poets and imagery than is usually thought.

Perrin, Norman. "Parables of Jesus as Parables, as Metaphors, and as Aesthetic Objects: A Review Article" Journal of Religion 47 (Oct. 1967) 340-6 (Review of R. Funk Language, Hermeneutic...)
He supports Funk but thinks the Great Supper is not just metaphor but also historically supported parable.

Perry, Bliss. A Study of Poetry Boston and New York 1920 esp. p. 74-97

Petersen, Leiva. Zur Geschichte der Personifikation in griechischer Dichtung und bildender Kunst Würzburg: Triltsch 1939. PhD diss. Frankfurt/Würzburg 1939

Petrich, Hermann. "Drei Kapitel vom romantischen Stil. Beitrag zur Charakteristik der romantischen Schule, ihrer Sprache und Dichtung, mit vorwiegender Rücksicht auf Ludwig Tieck" Leipzig 1878

Petrie, Hugh. "Seeing and Seeing As" American Philosophical Association Bulletin Western Division 68th Annual Meeting. May 1970 p. 15 (abstract)
Those who think perception is theory-laden must still appeal to objective facts. On Wittgenstein's analysis such objectivity is accounted for in terms of given or primitive language-games. Seeing is a primitive language-game. Seeing-as presupposes these primitive language games. "Seeing-as marks the transition between two areas of thought marked off by two different language-games." Observation is theory-laden; all perception involves cognition.

Petrović, Mihailo. Metafore i alegorije Belgrade 1967 (srpska kn'izhevna zadruga) He also cites on p. 187: Vreme u alegorijama, metaforama i aforizmima. Letopis matitse srpske 1927

Petsch, Robert. Die lyrische Dichtkunst, ihr Wesen und ihre Formen Halle: M. Niemeyer 1939

Petter, H. "John Updike's Metaphoric Novels" English Studies 50 (April 1969) 197-206

Pettet, E. C. "Hot Irons and Fever: A Note on Some of the Imagery of King John" Essays in Criticism 4 (1954) 128-144

Pettit, Henry. "Apposite Metaphor in Pope's Essay on Criticism" Books Abroad 35 (1961) 225-230. Also Langue et Littérature 1961 ca. p. 321
The images of Pope's poem form a unifying pattern of imagery of nature, imagery of fallibility, or imagery of aspiration.

Petz, Gorlielmos. "Ta Metaphorika Schemata Ton Aristophanons" Athēna 5 (1893) 241-284, 6 (1894) 426-441 (In Greek)
On Aristophanes' metaphors.

Phelan, Gerald. St. Thomas and Analogy Marquette University 1941
A Thomistic view. He rejects metaphor because it is "improper proportionality" and he supports the analogy of proper proportionality. True analogy or likeness arises from participation in the act of existence which is common to all things e.g. God's being: God's essence:: man's being: man's essence. Every being exercises an act of existence in proportion to its essence.

Phelps, Leland. "Gottsched to Herder: The Changing Conception of Metaphor in Eighteenth-Century Germany" Monatshefte für deutschen Unterricht; deutsche Sprache und Literatur 44 (March 1952) 129-34
A rationalistic rule-governed view of metaphor is held by Gottsched, Adelung, Breitinger and Lessing. Hamann, Herder and the author support a more mystical approach according to which metaphor reveals truth.

Philbrick, Frederick. Understanding English: An Introduction to Semantics New York: Macmillan 1942

Phillips, Allen. "Borges y su concepto de la metáfora" Movimientos literarios de vanguardia Iberoamérica Mexico 1965 pp. 41-53

_____, and F. Warnke. "Oxymoron" Encyclopedia of Poetry and Poetics A. Preminger, ed. Princeton University Press 1965 pp. 595-596

Phillips, W. L. "The Imagery of Dreiser's Novels" PMLA 78 (1963) 572-585

Picard, Jacques. "Les Trois modes du raisonnement analogique" Revue Philosophique de la France et de L'Étranger 104 (1927) 242-82

Pierson, W. "Die Metaphern des Persius" Rheinisches Museum für Philologie 12 (1857) 88-98

Pinsker, Sanford. The Schlemiel as Metaphor: Studies in the Yiddish and American Jewish Novel PhD diss. University of Washington 1967

Piro, Sergio. Il Linguaggio Schizofrenico Milano: Feltrinelli Editore 1967
Has excellent bibliography on schizophrenic language and metaphor.

Platt, A. "Homer's Similes" Journal of Philology 24 (1896) p. 28 ff.

Plüss, Theodor. Das Gleichnis in erzählender Dichtung. Ein Problem für Philologen und Schulmänner. Festschrift zur 49. Versammlung deutscher Philologen und Schulmänner in Basel im Jahre 1907 pp. 40-64

_____. "Das anschauliche Vorstellen beim poetischen Gleichnis" Zeitschrift für Aesthetik 9 (1914) 186-204
He found that the reaction to simile and comparison indicates that its purpose is not to arouse visual images but to create a "gesamtvorstellung" (whole representation) common to both terms.

Pongs, Hermann. Das Bild in der Dichtung I, Versuch einer Morphologie der metaphorischen Formen 1927. II, Voruntersuchungen zum Symbol, Marburg: N. G. Elwert 1939 (1960). (Reviews by Fink, Seidler, Laan 1942)
A lengthy work on metaphor. In this work he considers the origin and nature of metaphor, figurative inner speech form, (including dreams) poetic imagery, objective and subjective simile, the notion of as-if, analogy, animation, the I-(self-, or ego-) metaphor, mythical metaphor, cosmic metaphor, magical metaphor (e.g. Droste, Brentano, Tieck), wonder metaphor, expressionistic metaphor, visionary imagery, metaphors of chaos (e.g. Döblin), metaphors of many of the major German writers, psychological theories of metaphor of Stählin, Sterzinger, Henning, Kainz, Werner, etc. The metaphor is the expression of a cosmic sentiment. Different levels of the metaphor evolve according to their structure. At the highest level it is a complex unity born of the fusion of several antitheses of superior unities. The two meanings form a new higher unity. Metaphor is an aesthetic phenomenon based on illusion. It surpasses logical and psychological interpretations.

The "poetic image" is not differentiated from metaphor. It is regarded as a name-giving, language-forming force, a grasping of something unnamed or unknown by means of a non-literal name. The poetic image is regarded as the most important expression of the basic human faculty of creativity. It comes from spontaneous, emotive, creative forces within the individual in a dialectic interaction with the world. The poetic image follows a natural evolutionary-morphological pattern of growth in each age and in each individual poet.

There are two principles or polar attitudes towards the world which determine the various types of metaphor, namely, subjective-objective, the masculine-feminine principle in nature, or animation-objective empathy.

Objective empathy is a reaching into objective relations which does not change them but fills them with a sort of emotive comprehension. Metaphor merges these two poles, and the relations between them determine the various kinds of metaphor.

Pongs regards the Greek metaphor (e.g. of Aristotle) as a strictly logical, proportional analysis of the external world, a transfer of names according to analogy. The German metaphor, on the other hand, corresponds to the true creative force. It derives from emotion not intellect and fuses the subjective and objective world from which emerges an image with its own measure of reality. This is the emotive metaphor. Prosaic, everyday metaphor is more like the Greek metaphor. Poetic metaphor is not a transfer of names but a change of essence or being. An entire poem creates a world other than the real one. The poetic metaphor depends on the entire context of the poem.

Pongs' analysis of images or metaphor is not of style but of the attitudes or world-views from which emerge different archetypes of image creation.

He presents two basic types of metaphor 1) _the mythic_, which originates from the subjective pole, animates, personifies, and brings life to the external world, and 2) _the magical_, or _mystic_ metaphor, which derives from a view of the world which does not impose itself on the phenomena of nature, but grasps their essence through "objective empathy."

The mythical metaphor. a) In sensual, common poetry the world is animated not in a spiritual but rather in an animating, instinctive manner, e.g. hammer and anvil perform the sex act, or one can see the fat earth, the field between the hill's thighs. This is a crude form of personification and mythologizing. b) Demonicizing forms. Nature is animated out of passionate forces in the individual and is not merely humanized. There is here tension between the individual and nature, e.g. "The moon shines 'sleepily' behind the mist." c) A truly mythic metaphor is possible when the tension between spirit and nature is resolved. Their resolution or unity allows for the creation of ideal figures, God-like images of the phenomena of nature, e.g. streams are personified as Gods as in
"Calmly Night stepped on land,
And is leaning, full of dreams, against the
mountain well."

The individualizing mythic metaphor is extended into a "Mythic-cosmic metaphor."

The magical-mythic metaphor. This is like the mythical metaphor but stresses receptivity to hidden meanings within the phenomena. The individual stands back and abandons himself to the world and finds meaning in it, not through assimilation by animation, but through uncovering inherent qualities either in single objects or in the entire universe by means of objective empathy.

Magical metaphor. A primitive view of the world as magical spirits or forces everywhere affecting our lives. Mythic metaphor produces a humanized figure with personal characteristics created as a projection of the poet's spontaneous mood of the moment whereas the magical metaphor reveals archetypal features of nature, depersonalized or abstracted.

This attitude is expanded into a "revelation metaphor" where the universe is full of such spiritual forces and everything is interrelated, including the experiences of the human soul, as in the poetry of Eichendorff.

Mystical metaphor. This relates to the revelation metaphor. It may express the unity of a transcendental God and the world of experience. It may render pantheism. In modern poetry lacking certainty of the existence of a higher being we find mystical metaphor in the poetry of things. Inexpressible divine forces are revealed by means of metaphor or poetic imagery.

_____. "L'Image poétique et l'inconscient" Psychologie du langage Mlle G. Bianquis, trans., H. Delacroix, et al., eds. 1933 pp. 120-63. Also in Psychologische Studien 2 (1906) 120-163
Images are the product of the essence of a poets' soul to the extent that it implies a radical conflict between life and spirit. Great poets do not attempt to hide life as they perceive it in their unconscious, but attempt to make it comprehensible, to give it a significative sense and form. He discusses metaphor as unconscious escape (Freud), as taboo (Ortega), and metaphor as liberation of repressed desires which seek release in images where the conflict both reveals and conceals itself, and a "collective unconscious." The poet's unconscious image may evade reality but then be justified by means of his artistic consciousness.

_____. "Metapher und Bild" Dichtung im gespaltenen Deutschland Stuttgart: Union Verlag 1966 pp. 53-65
A discussion of the history and various views of metaphor. It is noted that even the word metaphor is a metaphor, i.e. something "carried across" (meta-) from the physical realm to the spiritual realm. He discusses the theories of Leo Weisgerber, Hermann Paul, Karl Vossler, Heinz Werner, Karl Bühler, Walter Porzig, Hans Lipps, Josef Derbolav and others.

_____. "Metaphor" Das kleine Lexikon der Weltliteratur H. Pongs, Stuttgart: Union Verlag 1967 pp. 1267-1269
A discussion of some of the main writers on metaphor. F. Brinkmann is criticized for overlooking the fact that the possibility for different images is unlimited, and therefore, can never be systematized by the implied subjects only. Heinz Werner's, Die Ursprünge der Metapher finds the source of metaphor in tabu e.g. sexual tabu. But Freud had already discussed this in his Totem and Tabu. For Freud there was an unconscious covering up in images in order not to re-

veal inner wishes. Walter Killy, in "Wandlungen des lyrischen Bildes" Goethe bis Benn (1956) presents the view that metaphors of a great individual are affected by the time in which he lives and by outside events. This may fall back on societal prerequisites of Marxism. Pongs cites in this regard Stalin's "Marxism and the Question of Linguistics" 1951. Pongs summarizes his book, Das Bild in der Dichtung as follows: In the tradition of Jean Paul, Pongs tries to Germanize the metaphor as a creative construction which in turn reaches out for another name--a "reaching into the unknown." A morphology of the metaphor developed over the years, of two poles, masculine and feminine poles of creation--always connected with the original rhythm which is manifested in sounds, construction and figures of speech.

Ponomariff, C. V. "The Image Seekers: An Analysis of Imaginist Poetic Theory 1919-1924" Slavic and East European Journal 12 (1968) 275-96

Pope, Alexander (Supposed author). [Peri Bathos by Martinus Scriblerus, pseud.] The Art of Sinking in Poetry Edna Steeves, ed. New York: King's Crown Press 1952 (cf. Swift) To sink a metaphor is to draw one term from the lowest things and the other from the highest e.g. "The King talks big." The metaphor can be run down by going too far with it. Other possibilities are examined.

Pörner, Martin. "Die Entwicklung des bildlichen Ausdruck in der Prosa Klemens Brentanos" PhD diss. Greifswald 1911

Porter, B. H. "Some Newfoundland Phrases, Sayings and Figures of Speech" American Speech 41 (Dec. 1966) 294-7

Porter, Charles. "Figures of Speech, Divergent Thinking, and Activation Theory" Ed.D diss. North Texas State University 1969
The relation between figures of speech and divergent thinking is high. The more figures of speech one uses the greater is his divergent thinking. Figures of speech are not just ornaments of thinking.

Porzig, Walter. Aischylos, die attische Tragödie Leipzig: Wiegandt 1926 esp. pp. 55-72

_____. "Beiträge zur Geschichte der deutschen Sprache" 1934 (Source: Pongs, "Metapher und Bild")
There is an inner dynamic of metaphor. The verb is used in an extended sense and so bursts into another field of meaning. Metaphor connects members of two different fields and holds them in a tension thus making the metaphor powerfully expressive.

Pöschl, Viktor. Bibliographie zur antiken Bildersprache bearbeitet von Helga Gärtner und W. Heyke Heidelberg: Carl Winter, Universitätsverlag 1964

Poteat, E. M. "Body of Christ as Metaphor or Fact" Religion in Life 25 (Summer 1956) 378-85

Pott, A. F. "Metaphern, vom Leben und von körperlichen Lebensverrichtungen hergenommen" (Zeitschrift für vergleichende Sprachforschung 2 (1853) pp. 101-127)

Potter, George Reuben. "A Protest Against the Term 'Conceit'" Renaissance Studies in Honor of Hardin Craig Stanford University Press 1941 pp. 282-291
"Conceit" meant an idea, power of understanding, etc. and came to mean an artificial device. Its use is confused today and requires a subtle analysis of the concept.

Pound, Ezra. Introduction to Ernest Fenollosa's Article 'The Chinese Written Characters' The Little Review Anthology Margaret Anderson, ed. (1914-1929) Hermitage House 1953
"The poet...must prepare for new advances along the lines of true metaphor that is interpretative metaphor, or image, as diametrically opposed to untrue, or ornamental metaphor." (cf. G. Hughes) An example of his imagist poetry (besides the cantos):

In a Station of the Metro

The apparition of these faces in the crowd;
Petals on a wet, black bough.

This abrupt juxtaposition omits the copula "is" and transcends grammar by images.

Pozzo, G. M. "Metáfora" Enciclopedia Filosofía 3 (1957) p. 551

Prado, C. G. "Review of Analytical Philosophy of Knowledge" Dialogue 8 (1969) 503-507
Danto presents a view of intentionality (that knowing and perceiving are always "of" something) and a relation of man and the world, which are only able to be represented by means of metaphors e.g. "The space between us and the world" which is not "a space within the world." Prado calls these "crisis metaphors." The space between us as knowers and the world is based on such metaphors and cannot be given literal interpretation or rendered in any other way. Crisis metaphors give unique insight.

Pratt, W. C., ed. The Imagist Poem New York: Dutton 1963

Praz, Mario. "The Flaming Heart: Richard Crashaw and the Baroque" The Flaming Heart New York: Doubleday 1958 pp. 204-263
An examination of the conceit in its various forms. "Seventeenth-century men saw instances of argutezza [agudeza, wit]

in every aspect of the universe...Everything was subservient to wit"; "Emblems, devices, anagrams, riddles, puzzles were accounted sublime achievements of art..." He discusses Tesauro, Donne, Shakespeare, Sforza-Pallavicino, Marino, Crashaw and others throughout the book in relating Italian to English notions of the conceit.

_____. Studi sul concettismo Firenze: G. C. Sansoni 1940
Stresses emblems.

_____. Studies in Seventeenth-Century Imagery 2 vols. in one. Rome: Edizioni di Storia e Letteratura 1964 (London: Warburg Institute. I 1939, II 1947) Chapt. I is "Emblem, Device, Epigram, Conceit." Contains an extensive bibliography on emblems.

Predmore, R. L. "Flesh and Spirit in the Works of Unamuno" PMLA 70 (Sept. 1955) 587-605

Preis, Paul. Die Animalisierung von Gegenständen in den Metaphern der spanischen Sprache Tübingen: E. Göbel 1932

Prescott, Frederick. The Poetic Mind New York: Great Seal Books 1961
Metaphor is a resemblance, a "rapid confusion" of two objects, a fusion. It is not a condensed simile but is older and more primitive. The poet recognizes metaphoric resemblances but does not try to explain them.

Pressler, Karl-Heinz. "Die Einwirkung des Sportlebens auf den Englischen Sprachschatz im Bereich der 'Live Metaphorical Expressions'" PhD diss. Mainz 1951

Preston, Keith. "Studies in the Diction of the Sermo Amatorius in Roman Comedy" PhD diss. Chicago 1916

Preuss, Alfred. Die metaphorische Kunst Vergils in der Aeneis Programm d. königlich evang. Gymnasium Graudenz 1894 pp. 1-29

Pride, Armistead Scott. "Criticisms of the Metaphor in England, 1660-1740" M. A. Thesis, University of Chicago 1932

Prior, M. E. "Imagery as a Test of Authorship" Shakespeare Quarterly 6 (Fall 1955) 381-6

Proffer, Carl. The Simile and Gogol's Dead Souls The Hague: Mouton 1967

Provenzal, Dino. Dizionario delle immagini Milano: Hoepli 1953
10,000 similes from Manzoni to the contemporaries.

Przwara, Erich. _Analogia Entis_ Munich: Kösel und Pustet 1932

_____. _Polarity_ A. Bouquet, trans. London: Oxford University Press 1935
(A translation of _Religionsphilosophie Katholischer Theologie_ Munich 1927)

Puttenham, George. _The Arte of English Poesie_ Gladys Willcock and Alice Walker, eds. Cambridge 1936

Quayle, Thomas. Poetic Diction: A Study of Eighteenth-Century Verse London: Methuen 1924
A detailed discussion of compound epithets and personification among other subjects, e.g. anger-kindling (cf. kenning).

Quincey, J. H. "The Metaphorical Sense of Lekuthos and Ampulla" Classical Quarterly 43 (1939) 32-44

Quinlan, M.J. "Swift's Use of Literalization as a Rhetoric Device" PMLA 82 (Dec. 1967) 516-521
Swift contrasts metaphorical and literal terms to obtain ironic disparity.

Quintilian. Institutio Oratoria four vols. H. Butler, ed. and trans. Cambridge: Harvard University Press 1920 esp. vols. I, III
There is metaphorical thought as well as metaphorical speech. Metaphor is a shortened simile, a deviation from proper meaning to stir emotions, produce a picture, clarify, adorn, achieve sublime knowledge. Metaphors should not be far-fetched or ugly. They may be classified on the basis of transfer of animate with inanimate, part with whole, rational with irrational. If continued metaphor may become an allegory.

Quṭb, Sayyid. al-Taṣwīr al-fanni fī al-Qur'ān 1963
On metaphors in the Koran.

Rabuse, Georg. "Dantes Bilder und Vergleiche" Orbis Litterarum 15 (1960) 65-94

Radtke, Gustav. De Tragicorum Graecorum Tropis. Partic. II De metaphoris ex verbis nauticis et ex venaticis petitis. Programm Krotoschin 1867

_____. "De Tropis apud Tragicos Graecos" PhD diss. Berol. Lange 1865

Radyserb-Wjela, Jan. (1882-1907, comp.) Metaforiske hrona abo prěnoški a přirunanki w rěči hronjolužiskich Serbów. Budyšin, Wudal a nakl, Ernst Muka 1905

Raeder, Hans F. E. "Die Tropen und Figuren bei R. Garnier, ihrem Inhalt nach untersucht und in den römischen Tragödien mit der lateinischen Vorlage verglichen" PhD diss. Kiel (Wandsbeck)

Ragsdale, J. D. "Invention in English Stylistic Rhetorics: 1600-1800" Quarterly Journal of Speech 51 (April 1965) 164-7

Raimondi, Ezio. "Ingegno e metafora nella poetica del Tesauro" Il Verri 2 (August 1958) 53-75
About metaphor and humor in Tesauro's Cannochiale Aristotelico.

Raina, M. L. "Imagery of 'A Passage to India': A Further Note" English Literature in Transition 1880-1920 10 (1967) 8-9

Raines, Charles. "Yeats' Metaphors of Permanence" Twentieth Century Literature 5 (1959) 12-20

Rainolde, Richard. (See Reynolds)

Raleigh, Sir Walter. Style New York and London: Edward Arnold and Company 1879 pp. 56-61
"Poets, it is said, anticipate science...Every writer and every speaker works ahead of science, expressing analogies and contrasts, likenesses and differences, that will not abide the apparatus of proof.... The finest instrument of these discoveries is metaphor, the spectroscope of letters."

Rambo, E. F. "On Homer's Similes" Classical Journal 28 (Oct. 1932) 22-31

Ramsay, Sir William. Teaching of Paul in Terms of the Present Day 1914 esp. chapt. on "Metaphor and Truth"
He states that all of St. Paul's language about priesthood and sacrifice is purely illustrative and metaphorical. His point is that metaphors must not be pressed beyond the point or scope of the implied comparison.

Ramsey, Ian T. Models and Mystery New York, London, and Toronto: Oxford University Press 1964 (Review by Gill)
Models and metaphors give us a unique insight into reality. No single metaphor can exhaust a subject matter. In a metaphor two ideas cooperate in an inclusive meaning-giving "mystery" generating an insight or "disclosure" which is geared to the context of that insight and arises out of it. "A metaphor is always a signpost of some disclosure." "What is not verbally odd is void of disclosure power." He applies his views especially to science and religion.

_____. Religious Language New York: Macmillan 1963
In his chapter "Models and Qualifiers" he discusses God and His attributes e.g. the attributes "impassible," "immutable," "perfection," "simplicity," "first cause," "infinitely wise," etc. Paradigms, characteristic situations, models or specific ordinary language contexts are found in an attempt to elucidate these notions e.g. we usually have a model or picture of what a "cause" is though we may not be conscious of it.

Ramsey, Warren. "Uses of the Visible: American Imagism, French Symbolism" Comparative Literature Studies 4 (1967) 177-91

Randolph, Vance and George P. Wilson. Down in the Holler: A Gallery of Ozark Folk Speech Norman: University of Oklahoma Press 1953
Sound, grammar and semantic deviation of slang and dialect are metaphorical deviations which are aesthetic, amusing or give insight. e.g. "I aim to print the news, all of 'em, no matter whose ox is gored," "fine as frog hair," "useless as brains in a preacher's head," "the cucumberest year," "the back-comin'est feller."

Rank, Otto. "Myth and Metaphor" Art and Artist C. F. Atkinson, trans. New York: Knopf 1932 pp. 207-31
The spatial metaphors (similes) of Homer aim at fixing a collective pristine age of his people. The temporal metaphors of Proust try to recall a personal past of the individual. Myth is one gigantic metaphor.

Rankin, James. "A Study of the Kennings in Anglo-Saxon Poetry" Journal of English and Germanic Philology 8 (1909) 357-422, 9 (1910) 42-84
A classification and location of the sources of Anglo-Saxon kennings to determine authorship. Kennings are given from Vulgate and Apocryphal Gospel of Nicodemus, hymns, late Latin poetry, and prose. Terms for religious conceptions are found to comprise four fifths of the kennings in Anglo-Saxon poetry. Kenning is used here loosely to refer to a metaphorical, periphrastic complex.

Ransom, John Crowe. "The Concrete Universal: Observations on the Understanding of Poetry" _Kenyon Review_ 17 (Summer 1955) 383-407 esp. pp. 400-402 "The Motive for Metaphor." He discusses among other things Wallace Stevens' "The Motive for Metaphor." A poet's theology is metaphorical and he knows it is metaphorical.

_____. "The Inorganic Muses" _Kenyon Review_ 5 (1943) 278-300

_____. _The New Criticism_ New York: New Directions 1941 I. A. Richards' "tenor" and "vehicle" are criticized as being too logical and being themselves metaphors. Metaphor is more spontaneous. It is not just ornament but is true "dense" discourse as the world is "dense" with cross-relations.

_____. "Poetry: A Note in Ontology" _Critiques and Essays in Criticism_ Robert Stallman, ed. New York: Ronald Press Co. 1949 esp. p. 30. Also in _The World's Body_

_____. "Positive and Near-Positive Aesthetics" _Kenyon Review_ 5 (Summer 1943) 443-444

_____. "William Wordsworth: Notes Toward an Understanding of Poetry" _Kenyon Review_ 12 (Summer 1950) 498-519 Ransom classifies metaphors as importers that introduce "foreign objects" into the situation adding to "local texture of irrelevance" that he thinks essential to poetry. A vehicle must have a good logical excuse to get in and its objective content must have the same sense with respect to its affects as the tenor into which it is introduced, so that it both extend the concretion and fortify our feelings toward the original object.

_____. _The World's Body_ New York: Scribner 1938 Religion, myth, the conceit and metaphysical poetry are born of metaphors e.g. the conceit is a metaphor which is clearly intended. Metaphor represents _Dinglichkeit_ (thinginess), the remarkable nature that objects are. The poet discovers a partial analogy which should be considerable, and completes it.

Rappold, J. _Beiträge zur Kenntnis des Gleichnisses bei Aischylos, Sophokles und Euripides_ Leipzig: G. Fock 1887

Rasch, Wolfdietrich. _Die Erzählweise Jean Pauls. Metaphernspiele und dissonante Strukturen_ München: C. Hanser 1961

Rau, Catherine. "Review of Philip Wheelwright's _Metaphor and Reality_" _Journal of Aesthetics and Art Criticism_ 21 (Winter 1962) 232-234 She says that Wheelwright's claims are more matters of the heart than the head.

_____. "Review of L. Knights and B. Cottle, eds. Metaphor and Symbol" Journal of Aesthetics and Art Criticism 20 (Spring 1962) 324-326

Raumer, Sigmund von. Die Metapher bei Lucrez Programm des königlich bayer. Gymnasiums zu Erlangen 1893

Read, C. "The Function of Relations in Thought" British Journal of Psychology 4 (1911) 342-385

Read, Sir Herbert. Collected Essays in Literary Criticism London: Faber & Faber 1941

_____. Icon and Idea New York: Schocken Books 1965 (1969) esp. "The Vital Image," "The Constructive Image"
The imaginative (art and visual) are prior to language and the conceptual.

_____. English Prose Style London: G. Bell 1928 (New York: Pantheon 1952) esp. pp. 25-34
"Metaphor is the synthesis of several units of observation into one commanding image...by a sudden perception of an objective relation."

_____. "Surrealism and the Romantic Principle" Criticism: The Foundations of Modern Literary Judgement Mark Schorer, J. Miles, G. McKenzie, eds. New York: Harcourt, Brace 1948

_____. (ed.) Surrealism London: Faber & Faber 1936.

_____. The Tenth Muse New York: Books for Libraries Press 1969 (1967) esp. "The Image in Modern English Poetry"

Reed, J. L. "The Proverbs Test in Schizophrenia" British Journal of Psychiatry 114 (1968) 317-321
On metaphorical proverbs.

Rees, G. O. "Animal Imagery in the Novels of André Malraux" French Studies 9 (1955) 129-141

_____. "Types of Recurring Similes in Malraux's Novels" Modern Language Notes 68 (June 1953) 373-7

Regnaud, Paul. Origine et Philosophie du Langage Paris 1888 (Source: Adank p. 162)
Metaphor is an essential process of language. By extension words mean new things.

Rehbold, Hilde. "Die Bildersprache W. von der Vogelweide" PhD diss. Köln 1953

Reichardt, Konstantin. "Studien zu den Skalden des 9. und 10.

Jahrhunderts" *Palaestra* no. 159 Leipzig: Mayer & Müller 1928 pp. 1-254

Reichenbach, Hans. *Experience and Prediction* University of Chicago Press 1938
He distrusts all metaphor and rejects the metaphorical language of metaphysics.

Reichling, A. *Het Woord* Nijmegen 1935 (cf. Stutterheim 1941, 1968)
A language element is a formal semantic unit. The sound form is a unity and the meaning content also. A word keeps its form and meaning unity but the ways it is used may differ. The metaphor is a linguistic phenomenon, signifying a unity of form (Gestalt) and meaning. In usage, the word retains its identity, and does not cease to be its meaning. The meaning is a unity whose identity makes actualized distinctions necessary in a disjunctive way. The idea of "transfer" disappears in his theory.

Reinert, Otto. "Sight Imagery in the 'Wild Duck'" *Journal of English and Germanic Philology* 55 (July 1956) 457-62
Although *The Wild Duck* is Ibsen's worst play its imagery is impressive. Imagery of sight and blindness "combines the rich suggestiveness of metaphorical language with the insistent and solid actuality of naturalism. The sight imagery never becomes intrusive; the ironies do not call attention to themselves by breaking through the surface of commonplace idiom. But they are there..."

Reinhardt, Karl. "Personification und Allegory" *Vermächtnis der Antike, Gesammelte Essays zur Philosophie und Geschichtsschreibung* Carl Becker, ed. Göttingen 1960 pp. 7 ff

Reis, Edgardo Moutinho dos. A metáfora em 3 obras de Eça.... Tese, Lisboa (Source: C. Mendes p. 10)

Reverdy, Paul. Quoted in Herbert Read, *Collected Essays in Literary Criticism* Faber 1950 pp. 98-99 (Also this is André Breton's statement in the "First Surrealist Manifesto")
"The image is a pure creation of the spirit. It cannot emerge from a comparison but only from the bringing together of two more or less distant realities.... No image is produced by comparing (always inadequately) two disproportionate realities. A striking image, on the contrary, one new to mind, is produced by bringing into relation without comparison two distant realities, whose relations the spirit alone has seized."

Rew, Cecil L. "Imaginative Comparisons in the Fiction of Anatole France: An Attempt at Classification" *French Review* 18 (Dec. 1944) 100-8

A. France is a master of metaphor and uses only about one to every 28 pages. A fourth of them are concerned with physical characteristics of men, women and children especially those of color and expression of eyes, e.g. eyes are cat-like, dog-like, wolf-like, like velvet, flame, flowers, etc. His metaphors materialize ideas and move from the abstract to the concrete.

Reynolds, Henry. *Mythomystes: wherein a short survey is taken of the nature and value of true poesy and depths of the ancients above our modern poets* 1632

Reynolds, Richard. *The Foundacion of Rhetorike* New York: Scholars' Facsimiles and Reprints 1945 (1563)

Rhys-Davids, Mrs. "Buddhist Parables and Similes" *The Open Court* 22 (Sept. 1908) 522-535
"The generic Pali term for illustration, *upamā* is nearly parallel to the Greek analogon [analogy]; *upa*, towards, *mā*, to think." The Buddhist imagery is true to natural scenes of everyday life. They are deeply felt and reveal ethical and philosophical doctrine. Simile and metaphor are regarded as condensed fables and parables, and the former may be expanded into the latter.

_____. "Similes in the Nikayas: A classified index" *Journal of the Pali Text Society* 1906-1907, pp. 52-151. Also (1908) pp. 180-187

Ribot, Théodule. *Essay on the Creative Imagination* Albert Baron, trans. Chicago: Open Court 1961 esp. pp. 28-29
Says processes underlying metaphor are relevant to industrial, scientific and commercial invention.

Ricard, Robert. "*Wit* et *agudeza*" *Révue de Moyen Age Latin* 4 (1948) 283-285

Rice, Philip B. "A Modern Poet's Technique: Guillaume Apollinaire" *Symposium* 2 (1931) 468-483
A study of Apollinaire's metaphors. Shows the effect of relating new to old, modern to traditional.

Richards, Ivor A. "Between Truth and Truth" *The Symposium* 2 (April 1931) 228-29

_____. *Coleridge on Imagination* Bloomington: Indiana University Press 1960
A discussion of Coleridge's theory of fancy and imagination as well as of his theory of psychology, the coalescence of subject and object, inner sense and outer object. *Fancy* just assembles independent ideas. *Imagination* works through the fancy but is a mutual modification and unifying of many

ideas. In its normal state the mind uses both types according to Coleridge.

_____, and C. K. Ogden. Foundations of Aesthetics London: George Allen & Unwin 1922
Says synaesthesia is the one affective theory that can serve as the basis of an aesthetic. Beauty is a harmony and equilibrium of our impulses. [cf. Ogden]

_____. "The Interactions of Words" The Language of Poetry Allen Tate, ed. Princeton University Press 1942
Words only work together, interact inseparably and so one cannot analyze a poem completely nor should we look at it too closely. A poet may be just expanding expressions, increasing their interactions. Since a poet is engaged in one kind of task his work should not be analyzed as if he were doing another. "To read the poem rightly would be to hear and come."

_____. Interpretation in Teaching New York: Harcourt, Brace 1938
"In metaphor, more narrowly defined, we cross sorts to make new occasional sorts; but the sorting operation is fundamental. In metaphor there is a cross-grouping and a resultant tension between the particular similarity employed and more stable habitual classifications, which would be absent here." "However we describe the condition of the topic [of metaphor]....we find ourselves therein employing devices of metaphor.... We only substitute another metaphor--recognized as such or not--for the one we are eluding. There is no escape." "What we have to do is to watch them [metaphors] at work tricking us and our fellows into supposing matters to be alternatively much simpler and much more complex than they are." "The conduct of even the plainest, most 'direct' untechnical prose is a ceaseless exercise in metaphor." Metaphor requires and mainly involves practice. "The higher the abstraction the fewer the different varieties of metaphor that can be made to or from it. But the modes of comparison between concretes are inexhaustible. They become the more numerous the more we know about the concretes." "Supply a special enough setting and anything may be linked in metaphor with anything." "Whether, or to what extent, writing may be without metaphors, in some limited sense, is a difficult question." "What a metaphor expresses could not be expressed in direct language." "Tenor and vehicle are like two men acting together. We do not understand them better by supposing that they somehow fuse to become a third man who is neither." "Metaphor" may stand for the vehicle only or for both tenor and vehicle. In the former a term is a metaphor, in the latter it is a sentence. A diagram is given to illustrate this.

_____. Principles of Literary Criticism New York: Harcourt,

Brace 1952
By "imagination" we often mean merely the use of metaphor. A metaphor illustrates, diagrams, renders the abstract by means of the concrete, brings disparity together into a unity, controls feeling, and expands experience to make it more whole. It is not based on logical relations.

_____. "The Places and the Figures" Elizabethan Poetry: Modern Essays in Criticism Paul J. Alpers, ed. New York: Oxford University Press 1967 pp. 78-89

_____. Practical Criticism New York: Harcourt, Brace 1954
"A better understanding of metaphor is one of the aims which an improved curriculum of literary studies might well set before itself." A metaphor is a shift, carrying over of a word from its normal use to a new use. "Prose or sense metaphor" is a shift based on a similarity between the old and the new object. "Emotive metaphor" is a shift based on similarity between feelings of the new and the old situation.

_____. "Science and Poetry" Criticism: The Foundations of Modern Literary Judgement Mark Schorer, J. Miles and G. McKenzie, eds. New York: Harcourt, Brace 1948 pp. 505-523
Richards' view and change of view. He has an aspect theory involving giving many definitions of the same thing.

_____. The Philosophy of Rhetoric New York: Oxford University Press 1936
"When we use a metaphor we have two thoughts of different things active together and supported by a single word or phrase whose meaning is a result of interaction." "All thinking is sorting." "It [metaphor] is a borrowing between and intercourse of thoughts, a transaction between contexts. Thought is metaphoric, and proceeds by comparison." "As it [philosophy] grows more abstract we think increasingly be means of metaphors that we profess not to be relying on." "The metaphors we are avoiding steer our thought as much as those we accept." "No images...need come in at any point." "The processes of metaphor in language...are superimposed upon a perceived world which is itself a product of earlier or unwitting metaphor." "Most sentences in free and fluid discourse turn out to be metaphoric." Metaphor is analyzed into "tenor" and "vehicle," terms Richards created and is well-known for. "Tenor" is "the underlying idea or principle subject which the vehicle or figure means," or the plain meaning. The "vehicle" is the figure. Tenor and vehicle can interact and give insight to one another. The tenor can become the vehicle and vice versa. Context and emotion contribute to the metaphorical link. "We can find no word or description for any of the intellectual operations which, if its history is known, is not seen to have been taken, by metaphor, from a description

of some physical happening." "However stone dead...metaphors seem, we can easily wake them up."

Richardson, J. "Facade of Bawdry: Image Patterns in Chaucer's Shipman's Tale" ELH 32 (Sept. 1965) 303-13

_____. "Function of Formal Imagery in Ovid's Metamorphoses" Classical Journal 59 (Jan. 1964) 161-9

Richter, Johann Paul Friedrich. Vorschule der Ästhetik; nebst einigen Vorlesungen in Leipzig über die Parteien der Zeit Stuttgart: Cotta 1813 [cf. "Jean Pauls Metaphorik in Siebenkäs" (Source: Vonessen)] (cf. Müsken)

Rickels, Milton. "The Imagery of George Washington Harris" American Literature 31 (May 1959) 173-87

Rickert, Edith. New Methods for the Study of Literature Chicago: University of Chicago Press 1928 esp. pp. 24-72
On imagery.

Ricks, Christopher. "Johnson's Battle of the Pygmies and Cranes" Essays in Criticism 16 (July 1966) 281-9

_____. Milton's Grand Style Oxford: Clarendon Press 1963 esp. "The Unsuccessful Metaphor," "The Successful Metaphor."

Riddel, Joseph. "The Never-Ending Meditation: A study of myth, metaphor, and the poetry of order in the works of Wallace Stevens" PhD diss. University of Wisconsin 1960

_____. The Clairvoyant Eye: The Poetry and Poetics of Wallace Stevens Baton Rouge: Louisiana State University Press 1965
An analysis of Stevens' poetry and an account of his theory of imagination. He concentrates on a detailed analysis of individual poems. "My thesis...is that Stevens' total work constitutes metaphysically the act of creating oneself... and living (figuratively, but in a very real sense, actually) in poetry." The world as fiction and the "harmonium" are also discussed.

Ridenour, George. The Style of Don Juan New Haven: Yale University Press 1960

Rieger, P. "Die Bildersprache des Sophokles" PhD diss. Breslau-Carlowitz 1934

Rieser, Max. "Analysis of the Poetic Simile" Journal of Philosophy 37 (April 1940) 209-17
In simile the poet "compares only the impressions which both of them [objects] have left in his sensibility. Not the objects themselves.... The link is not factual but emotional."

Other figures are based on simile.

_____. "Brief Introduction to an Epistemology of Art" Journal of Philosophy 47 (1950) 695-704
"The real poetic comparison is based not on realistic similarity but...valuational equivalence..." It is based on feeling or emotion. It may or may not be pictorial. Even music or an entire drama may be metaphorical.

_____. "Language of Poetic and Scientific Thought" Journal of Philosophy 40 (August 1943) 421-435
"The ultimate result of the poetic creation will then be a valuational synthesis while science issues in fact-analysis. In the process of living the valuational approach is the ultimate one"; "On the expressive level things are not defined by their objective functions but by their values, and are understood valuationally, which is a grasp sui generis."

_____. "Metaphor and Expression in the Plastic Arts" Journal of Aesthetics and Art Criticism 17 (Dec. 1958) 194-200
Metaphor is imagistic, direct and non-linguistic, thus e.g. paintings are metaphoric. Even in language metaphor is direct and non-lingusitic. It is not a comparison but a valuational kindred world of feelings. It possesses an explanatory function.

Riffaterre, Michael. "Describing Poetic Structures: Two Approaches to Baudelaire's Les chats" Yale French Studies nos. 36-37 (1966) 200-242 (Entire issue is on Structuralism) (Also in Structuralism Jacques Ehrmann, ed., New York: Doubleday 1970 pp. 188-230)
A discussion of Baudelaire's 'Les chats' and of its critique by Jakobson and others. Jakobson analyzes by means of the two metaphoric poles of 1) selection (similarity) and 2) combination (contiguity). Riffaterre discusses whether unmodified structural lingusitics is relevant to the analysis of poetry in giving a detailed analysis of this work by Baudelaire.

_____. "Le style des Pléiades de Gobineau. Essai d'application d'une méthode stylistique" (Société de publications romanes et françaises, 57.) Genève, Paris 1957 pp. 171-189

Riniker, Rudolf. Die Preziosität der französischen Renaissancepoesie Zürich: Müller, Werder & Cie. 1898
On metaphor and conceits in the poetry of Cl. Marot, Saint-Gelais, Ronsard, Belleau, Magny and Desportes.

Rippley, La Vern. "The House as Metaphor in E. T. A. Hoffman's Rat Krespel" Papers on Language and Literature 7 (1971) 52-60

Ritzler, Paula. "Zur Bedeutung des bildlichen Ausdrucks im Werke

Heinrich von Kleists" Trivium 2 (1944) 178-194

Rivers, William Napoleon. "A Study of the Metaphors and Comparisons of Théophile Gautier" PhD diss. Ithaca: Cornell University 1932

Robb, James. "Patterns of Image and Structure in the Essays of Alfonso Reyes" Thesis. Catholic University of America; Washington D. C. 1958

Robbe-Grillet, Alain. "Dehumanizing Nature" The Modern Tradition: Backgrounds of Modern Literature Richard Ellmann and Charles Feidelson Jr., eds. New York: Oxford University Press 1965 pp. 362-378

_____. For a New Novel: Essays on Fiction Richard Howard, trans. New York: Grove Press 1965 esp. 53-59 on metaphor. An existentialistic account of metaphor seemingly based on the notion of "man-in-the world." Metaphor is not just comparison but a sympathetic relation between man's inner states and objects such that they become entwined and inseparable. Inner states are in the world as if waiting to be discovered. (cf. personification) In "Dehumanizing Nature" he said, "Symbol or metaphor is always useless, adding nothing new to the description of the reality of the material universe."

Robbins, Samuel. "A New Objective Text for Verbal Imagery Types" Psychological Review 27 (1920) 38-49

Roberts, Graves. "The Epithet in Spanish Poetry of the Romantic Period" University of Iowa Studies in Spanish Language and Literature vol. 6 (1936) PhD diss. University of Iowa 1934

Robertson, Mysie. L'épithète dans les oeuvres lyriques de Victor Hugo Paris: Champion 1927

Robillard, Hyacinthe-Marie. "Justification philosophique et théologique de l'analogie métaphorique" Revue Dominicaine 65, I (June 1959) 281-88

_____. "Analogie métaphorique, vie liturgique et catéchèse chrétienne" Revue Dominicaine 65, I (May 1959) 225-40

Robinson, Benjamin Willard. "Some elements of forcefulness in the comparisons of Jesus, with comparative tables of metaphors from the Deutero-Isaiah and Paul" (Reprinted from Journal of Biblical Literature vol. 23, pt. 2, pp. 106-179) PhD diss. University of Chicago 1904

Robinson, Charles. "The Tropes and Figures of Isaeus, A Study of His Rhetorical Art" PhD diss. Princeton University 1901 esp. pp. 52-53 on metaphor.

Robson, Ernest. "On the Metaphor in Horace, Od. I, 5 (A Brief Note)" The Classical Review 14 (1900) p. 414

Rodale, Jerome Irving. The Phrase Finder 3 vols. in one. Emmaus, Pennsylvania: Rodale Press 1957 pp. 898-1124 for "Metaphor Finder"

Roddey, Gloria. "The Metaphor of Counsel: A Shift from Objective Realism to Psychological Subjectivism in the Conceptual Cosmology of Puritanism" PhD diss. University of Kentucky 1970

Rodríguez-Alcalá, Hugo. "Metaforismo, 'criaturalismo' y sátira en la obra novelística de Francisco Ayala" Revista Hispánica Moderna 25 (1959) 291-303. Also in his Ensayos de norte a sur Seattle: University of Washington Press 1960 pp. 61-77

Roedig, Charles F. "Baudelaire and Synesthesia" Kentucky Foreign Language Quarterly 5 (1958) 128-135

Rohovit, D. Dean. "Metaphor and Mind: A Reevaluation of Metaphor Theory" American Image: A Psychoanalytic Journal for the Arts and Sciences 17 (1960) 289-309
A Freudian interpretation. In metaphor one term may be unconscious latent content (vehicle), the other, conscious manifest content (tenor). Clinical tests show that psychotic patients' metaphors can reveal their problems by revealing latent content. The mechanisms of metaphor are the Freudian ones of "displacement," "condensation," etc.

Röhrich, Lutz. Gebärde, Metapher, Parodie. Studien zur Sprache und Volksdichtung Düsseldorf: Schwann 1967
This is a study of gesticulation, metaphor, parody; a study of language and folk poetry. He discusses metaphorical language in sayings, fairy tales, anecdotes, pranks and in popular poetry. Contains metaphorical illustrations.

_____. "Liebesmetaphorik im Volkslied" Folklore International: Essays in Traditional Literature, Belief and Custom in Honor of Wayland Debs Hand. D. K. Wilgus, ed. Hatboro, Penn.: Folklore Associates 1967 pp. 187-200

Romagnoli, Ettore. "Origine ed elementi della commedia d'Aristofane" Studi Italiani di Filologia Classica 13 (1905) 83-268 esp. "Le metafore e le immagini" pp. 241-265

Romilly, Jacqueline de. La crainte et l'angoisse dans le théâtre d'Eschyle Paris: Les Belles Lettres 1958 pp. 42-52 on metaphor.

Ronnet, Gilberte. Étude sur le style de Démosthène dans les discours politiques Paris: de Boccard 1951 pp. 149-192 on metaphor and simile.

Rooth, Erik. "Review of Stutterheim Het begrip metaphoor" Theoria 8 (1942) 188-190

Roppen, Georg. Strangers and Pilgrims; an essay on the metaphor of journey New York: Humanities Press 1964
Peer Gynt at the end of his life finds an onion, peels it. It serves as a metaphor the layers representing the events of his travels and the identities he has assumed. But there is no kernel left after it is peeled. His travels are not a metaphor of himself after all. Still the metaphor of journey is a basic and inextricable form of the imaginative life of man.

Rosaldo, Renato. "Metaphors of Hierarchy in a Mayan Ritual" American Anthropologist 70 (1968) 524-36

Roschatt, Alois. Die Metaphern bei den attischen Rednern Programm d. königlichen Studienanstalt, Straubing 1886

Rose, H. J. "Metaphor, Ancient and Modern" Studies in Honor of Gilbert Norwood E. White, ed. (The Phoenix Journal of the Classical Association of Canada, Suppl. I; University of Toronto Press 1952) pp. 239-247

Rosenberg, Albert. "Bishop Sprat on Science and Imagery" Isis 43 (1952) 220-2
"The...attention paid to Bishop Sprat's comments on a proper prose style has tended to obscure his equally important pronouncements concerning science as a source of imagery."

Rosenberg, Marvin. "A Metaphor for Dramatic Form" Journal of Aesthetics and Art Criticism 17 (1958) 174-180. Also Aesthetic Inquiry Monroe C. Beardsley & Herbert Schueller, eds., Belmont, California: Dickenson 1967

Ross, James F. "Analogy as a Rule of Meaning for Religious Language" International Philosophical Quarterly 1 (1961) 468-502. Reply by Ross 2 (1962) 658-62

______. "A Critical Analysis of the Theory of Analogy of St. Thomas Aquinas" PhD diss. Brown University 1958

______. "Logic of Analogy" International Philosophical Quarterly 2 (1962) 633-42

Ross, Ralph. Symbols and Civilization New York: Harcourt, Brace & World 1962 esp. ch. 2 "Language and Thought," pp. 11-26 on metaphor.

Rothstein, Eric. "Allusion and Analogy in the Romance of Caleb Williams" University of Toronto Quarterly 37 (1967) 18-30

Rousset, Jean. "La Poésie baroque au temps de Malherbe: la métaphore" Bulletin de la société d'etudes du dix-septième siècle (XVII ème siècle) no. 31 (April 1956) 353-370 Metaphor and the Baroque are characterized by disguise, ostentation and fluidity or changing forms. "Multiple metaphor" or "metaphor in action" is an accumulation of related symbols throughout a poem. Some users of prolonged metaphor are in the spirit of Montaigne regarding the world and spirit as fluid and unstable, or use fantasies or visions to "paint the intangible," to depict in painting feelings, sensations, moral qualities. Malherbe's metaphors become increasingly sterile and immobile. Du Perron stated that the metaphor is a small similitude, an abbreviated similitude, which must pass quickly without being dwelled upon; when it is too prolonged it is vicious and degenerates into an enigma. In the 17th century the positivistic attitude and new science prevailed. Most opposed metaphor and regarded it as superfluous and misleading distortion. The notion of universal analogy and correspondences between all things provides a metaphysical basis of some uses of metaphor. Pierre Nicole stated that the metaphor is a sign of the weakness of nature which shies away from simple and pure truth. It is a mask, a comedy, which does not attain to true beauty. The rebirth of lyricism with Romanticism revived the metaphor and universal analogy (e.g. Hugo, Baudelaire, Claudel). Mlle de Gournay defends metaphor stating that it is essential to poetry and is the main interest and source of poetry. She distinguishes between the metaphor which simply compares two similar objects, and the higher form which juxtaposes two dissimilar objects. The latter illustrates the art of discerning conformity in opposites. The metaphor views two objects together, representing one by the other although they may be greatly separate. The artist seems to transform subjects into his own nature, discerning secret identities everywhere.

Rowland, Beryl. "Melville's Bachelors and Maids: Interpretation Through Symbol and Metaphor" American Literature 41 (Nov. 1969) 389-405

_____. "Forgotten Metaphor in Three Popular Children's Rhymes" Southern Folklore Quarterly 31 (March 1969) 12-19

_____. "Mill in Popular Metaphor from Chaucer to the Present Day" Southern Folklore Quarterly 33 (June 1969) 69-79

Rowley, B. A. "The Light of Music and the Music of Light, Synaesthetic Imagery in the Works of Ludwig Tieck" Publications of the English Goethe Society 26 (1957) pp. 52-80

Rowntree, C. M. "Press Metaphors" (G. K.'s) Weekly Review 12 (Oct. 25, 1930) p. 102

Royce, Joseph. "Metaphoric Knowledge and Humanistic Psychology"

Challenges of Humanistic Psychology James Bugental, ed. New York: McGraw-Hill 1967 pp. 21-28
Metaphorism is an intuitive symbolic way of knowing, yielding universal insight. It is involved in science and religion as well as art and is a legitimate way of knowing. It is a method, then, which may help unite psychology (which is too empirical) with other disciplines.

______. _The Encapsulated Man: an interdisciplinary essay on the search for meaning_ Princeton: Van Nostrand 1964
Our philosophic commitments give us limited or encapsulated images of reality.

Różewicz, Tadeusz. _Rzecz Poetycka_ Wydawnictwo Łódzkie 1960 (cited in Stanley Hopper and David Miller, eds. _Interpretation: The Poetry of Meaning_ New York: Harcourt, Brace & World 1967)
On metaphor.

Rubinstein, E. "1 Henry IV: The Metaphor of Liability" _Studies in English Literature 1500-1900_ 10 (1970) 287-295

Rugoff, Milton A. _Donne's Imagery: A Study in Creative Sources_ New York: Russell and Russell 1962 (c. 1939)

Ruin, H. "Métaphore et Catharsis" In _Deuxième congrès internationale d'esth. et de science de l'art_ II, Parigi 1937 pp. 205-209
Metaphor is not just for clarity but is mysterious and helps us to understand the world by giving us a vision and profound sense of liberation. Metaphor reflects the particular in the general and identifies subject and object.

Ruiz, Mario. "An Inquiry into the Metaphorical Process of Miguel de Unamuno" PhD diss. Stanford University 1967
Ruiz says the interaction between vehicle and tenor is based on the simultaneous resolution of three basic processes necessary to any metaphor: 1) a substitution of the vehicle by the tenor 2) a condensation within the vehicle of all the needed meanings to be transferred to the tenor and 3) an interaction between vehicle and tenor through which the condensation will dissolve and inundate the tenor with unspoken feeling.

Ruskin, John. _Modern Painters_ five vols. New York: D. D. Merrill Co. 1873 esp. "The Pathetic Fallacy" vol. 3 pp. 152-167; vol. 2, section 2, on imagination and fancy pp. 142ff.
The pathetic fallacy, the metaphorical attribution of feelings to things, is a false description based on violent feelings. Metaphor should be bloody, stem accurately from passion and not be used "in cold blood." Ruskin gives an extensive account of the "faculty" of imagination. It has the three operations: penetrative, associative and contemplative. The

penetrative imagination is not concerned with combining but rather with apprehending things. Artificial fancy and imagination are distinguished . The perfect function of the imagination is the intuitive perception of ultimate truth.

Rutledge, Robert. "The Development of the Poetry of William B. Yeats as Reflected in His Metaphors" PhD diss. George Washington University 1966

Ryan, Columba. "The Reach of Analogical Argument" Dominican Studies 4 (1951) 102-18

Ryba, Bohumil. "Quelques contributions à l'exégèse des métaphores de Sénèque relatives aux rapport du corps et de l'âme" Listy filologické 54 (1927) 65-71

Ryder, F. G. "Season, Day, and Hour: Time as Metaphor in Goethe's Werther" Journal of English and Germanic Philology 63 (July 1964) 389-407

Ryle, Gilbert. "A Puzzling Element in the Notion of Thinking" Proceedings of the British Academy 44 (1958) 129-144. Also in Essays on Rhetoric Dudley Bailey, ed. New York: Oxford University Press 1965 pp. 268-281

_____. "Categories" Proceedings of the Aristotelian Society 38 (1937-38) 189-206 Reprinted in Logic and Language Second series. Antony Flew, ed., Oxford: Blackwell 1953 pp. 65-81

_____. The Concept of Mind New York: Barnes and Noble 1949 (cf. Orpinela, Berggren 1959)
Discussion of category-mistakes. It is a "category-mistake" to speak of mind as an entity in the same way as we speak of a physical entity. If the mind is not in space it cannot be described as being spatially "inside" (a metaphor) anything else or having things going on statically "inside" itself. "The phrase 'in the mind' can and should always be dispensed with." Other examples of "category-mistake" are given drawn from mental descriptions.

_____. "Systematically Misleading Expressions" Logic and Language First series. Antony Flew, ed. Oxford: Blackwell 1960 pp. 11-36
Differences of logical forms of sentences are disguised by the grammatical form between certain phrases. The task of philosophy involves systematic restatement and the avoidance of systematic language errors, e.g. grammar misleads us into thinking "existence" is a quality. Also subject universals (e.g. "unpunctuality") are misleading in being used analogously to subject particulars. These orders result in type-crossings (or metaphors).

Sabbagh, T. La métaphore dans le Coran Paris: Adrien-Maisonneuve 1943 (Thesis, University of Paris)
L'isti'ārah is the Arab word for metaphor. Beginning with Western definitions of metaphor and a look at Arab rhetoric, a detailed examination and classification is given of comparisons and metaphors in the Koran.

Sacerdos, Marius Plotius. (ca. 149-153 A. D.) Art of Grammar. Grammatici Latini 7 vols. Heinrich Keil, ed. Leipzig 1855-80 esp. VI, 460
Tropes are "metaplasms." A metaplasm or figure of speech is a word altered in its composition for the sake of meter or ornamentation.

Şăineănu, Lazăr. La Création Métaphorique en Français et en Roman, Images tirées du monde domestique (Beihefte zur Zeitschrift für romanische Philologie) Halle: M. Niemeyer 1905 Part I, 1910 Part II
On animal metaphors.

St. John, Edward P. "Is Analogical Thinking Characteristic of Children?" Religious Education 19 (Dec. 1924) 390-392
Knowledge begins from sense and is analogically extended to refer to new experience. By analogical thinking we do not discover truth but just name it after it is discovered. Jesus only used analogy with adults, those who were used to thinking about religion.

St. John, Mary C. "A Discussion of Greek Metaphor" Vassar Journal of Undergraduate Studies 8 (1934) 23-36
"The command of metaphor involves a fine sense of relationships between dissociated fields and perceptions, the substitution of suggestion for bold statement..." New metaphors are increasingly hard to create. The metaphors of the Greek writers, Aeschylus, Sophocles and Euripides are examined. Aeschylus is the most metaphorical writer. To understand them a knowledge of their metaphors is essential.

Saintsbury, George. A History of Criticism and Literary Taste in Europe from the Earliest Texts to the Present Day 3 vols. Edinburgh and London: William Blackwood 1934 esp. vol. I, p. 206

Sala, Marius. "Asupra metaforei reciproce" Fonetică şi Dialectologie 3 (1961) 203-209. Also "Sur les métaphores réciproques" Revue de Linguistique (Bucarest) 5 (1960) 311-317
He follows Migliorini "La metafora reciproca." He speaks of the return of a metaphor to its original pre-metaphorical meaning e.g. "hackney" used as "old woman." Sala takes as the point of departure the linguistic view of B. Migliorini and discusses a type of reciprocal metaphor of Rumanian terms such that the terms involve each other reciprocally in the metaphor.

Samborn, Kate. "Professional Metaphors" _Victoria Magazine_ 31 (1863-1880) 213-217
Much of our thinking and language is determined by our profession and then applied metaphorically to other areas. e.g. the last words of one chief justice to his friends were "Gentlemen of the jury , you may retire."

Sambursky, S. A. "A Democritean Metaphor in Plato's _Kratylos_" _Phronesis_ 4 (1959) 1-4

Samson, Richard. _Creative Analysis_ New York: Dutton and Company 1963 (Exercise book to accompany A. Upton's _Design for Thinking_)

Sanderson, David R. "Metaphor and Method in Mill's _On History_" _Victorian Newsletter_ 34 (1968) 22-25

Sanford, Wendy. _Theater as Metaphor in Hamlet_ Cambridge, Mass: Harvard University Press 1967

Santayana, George. _Scepticism and Animal Faith_ New York: Scribner's 1923 esp. p. 153

Sarbin, Theodore. "Anxiety: Reification of a Metaphor" _Archives of General Psychiatry_ 10 (1964) 630-638. Read before the symposium entitled "Anxiety Revisited" at the Western Division Meetings of the American Psychiatric Association, San Francisco, California, Sept. 26, 1963
He questions the traditional view that anxiety is an internal state or state of mind. Rather it denotes distal events and so the concept, anxiety, should not be used as a construct. It is a myth or metaphor which was mistakenly taken literally. Szasz is cited as pointing out that similarly the metaphor of mental illness evolved into a myth. "Anxiety as a mental state follows from certain historical mistakes occasioned by literal interpretations of metaphors"; "The mentalistic and multi-referenced term anxiety has outlived its usefulness." There is no ultimately true metaphor but only some which are more pragmatically useful than others. He speaks of "cognitive strain" (an adjusting of man in his proximal (e.g. sensations) and distal ecology (e.g. social, spatial etc.). "Instead of focusing on anxiety as a mentalistic or as a physiological signaler of internal psychic struggles, the therapist will focus on the difficulties presented by a patient in coming to terms with his world"; "For nearly half a century, a romantic mystique has evolved around the professional enterprise stimulated by Freud's colorful metaphors. Experienced clinicians recognize that the mystique is not justified,-- and that when therapy is successful, it is not due to the purging of anxiety. Rather, it is because the patient has learned how to minimize, with his finite cognitive capacities, the strains produced in his efforts to find himself in a com-

plex, changing, and often contradictory world."

_____. "A Metaphorical Analysis of Anxiety" Paper presented at the 1967 Western Psychological Association Meeting. He discusses how metaphors become myths, and states that we use familiar objects to develop concepts in less familiar areas.

_____, and Ki-Taek Chun. "An Empirical Study of 'Metaphor-to-Myth' Transformation" Paper presented to Division 24, American Psychological Association, Sept. 3, 1969, Washington D.C. Metaphors in psychology become reified leading to category-mistakes. They tend to be unconsciously taken literally and so made into a myth e.g. myths of "anxiety," "schizophrenia," "mental illness" etc. This reification process is experimentally tested as a function of title and content transparency of scientific reports.

Sarmiento, E. "On Two Criticisms of Gracián's Agudeza" Hispanic Review 3 (Jan. 1935) 23-35
An examination of Croce, C. Peregrini, Coster and Gracián on the conceit. Coster and Croce misunderstood, and Peregrini disagrees with, Gracián.

_____. "Gracián's Agudeza y Arte de Ingenio" Modern Language Review 27 (1932) 280-292, 420-429
A summary of and commentary on Gracián's book. Sarmiento states that the conceit must be approached sympathetically if one is to understand the Spanish mind. The Spaniard characteristically expresses even deep emotion by a twisted metaphor or exaggerated comparison. But Sarmiento thinks neither conceit nor metaphor can be the principle of all art. He regards metaphor as emotional transference. The conceit attempts to go a step further and is too rational for poetry. The conceit is trivial, lacks significance, beauty and symbolism. Conceits are at times only mystical elations or feelings of unity of all things.

Sarv, I. Rahvapärane võrdlus kui kõnekäänu eriliik Tartu 1960
On simile.

Saussure, Ferdinand, de. Course in General Linguistics Charles Bally, Albert Sechegaye, Albert Reidlinger, eds. Wade Baskin, trans. New York: Philosophical Library 1959

Saussure, Raymond de. "On Personal Metaphors in Psychiatric Cases" Word: Journal of the Linguistic Circle of New York 2 (1946) 188-190. A discussion of L. Kanner.
Critique of Kanner article 1946. Kanner assumes erroneously that the child always uses his language for social purposes. The child's autistic thinking may not be a retreat from the outside world. Words may be used as defense mechanisms.

Sauvage, C. "Cette prison nommée la vie: Vigny's prison metaphor" Studies in Romanticism 9 (1970) 99-113

Sauvage, G. M. "Analogy" The Catholic Encyclopedia New York: Appleton 1907 p. 450 (cf. Boyle)

Sawhill, John. The Use of Athletic Metaphors in the Biblical Homilies of St. John Chrysostom Princeton University Press 1928 (PhD diss.)

Sayce, Richard A. Style in French Prose: A Method of Analysis Oxford: Clarendon Press 1952 (1965) esp. pp. 57-68 and 69-80

_____. "La métonymie dans l'oeuvre de Racine" Actes du Premier Congrès International Racinien (Uzès) 1961. (1962 pp. 37-41)

Scanlon, Sister Aloyse. "The Sustained Metaphor in The Only Jealousy of Emer" Modern Drama 7 (1964) 273-277
On Yeats.

Scheer-Schäzler, Brigitte. A Taste for Metaphors: die Bildersprache als Interpretationsgrundlage des modernen Romans Wien: Verband der österreichischen Neuphilologen 1968

Schiavina, Enzo. "Realtà e linguaggi figurativi" Lingua e Stile 2 (1967) 67-74
A discussion of figurative language and imagery from the point of view of P. Francastel, La réalite figurative: Éléments structurels de sociologie de l'art (Paris 1965). Francastel stresses a sociological theory of art whereby artistic, material and mental activities of society are complementary. Francastel opposes pure formalism or pure content views in favor of a dialectic approach. His approach involves plastic thought which seeks insight. Plastic thought involves not being reducible to anything else. It is defined as autonomous and self-regulative. He states, "A work of art is never the substitute of anything else; it is in itself the thing, simultaneously the signifier and the signified.... The work of art is not the double of another form that can exist, but is truly the product of one of the systems across which humanity conquers and communicates its wisdom in realizing its works." Plastic art need not be translated into verbal art in order to reveal social influence. Figurative images and verbal images do not coincide. The plastic image is more direct than the verbal allowing it to give information not otherwise obtainable. Reduced to the verbal sign an image means nothing. The image does not identify with either the concrete real or the subjective imaginary. It is the product of a technical construction, of a fabrication. The image is not in a single, fixed relation but is as variable as the number of spectators observing it. It has an essential ambiguity. The image is

ultimately situated in the spirit of those who are users of the object.

Schicker, Stephen. "The Rainbow Beneath the Ground: A Study of the 'Decent into Hell' Metaphor in William Blake's 'The Marriage of Heaven and Hell,' Gerard De Nerval's 'Aurelia' and Arthur Rimbaud's 'Une Saison en Enfer'." PhD diss. Syracuse University 1969

Schier, Rudolf. "Von der Metapher zur figuralen Sprache: Abgrenzung der Begriffe" Dargestellt an Georg Trakls 'Gesang des Abgeschiedenen'. *Der Deutschunterricht* 20 (1968) 49-68

Schiff, Julius. "Naturwissenschaftliche Gleichnisse in Goethes Dichtungen, Briefen und literarischen Schriften" *Die Naturwissenschaften* 20 (1932) 223-240

Schiller, Jerome. *I. A. Richards' Theory of Literature* Yale University Press 1969 "Emotive Language and Metaphor" pp. 48-88

Schipper, Edith W. "A Note on Metaphor" *Journal of Aesthetics and Art Criticism* 27 (Winter 1968) 199-201
She opposes Beardsley's verbal-opposition theory but holds the object-comparison theory he rejects. Metaphor is a contextually determined transfer of descriptive characteristics.

Schlanger, Judith. "Metaphor and Invention" Yvonne Burne, trans. *Diogenes* 69 (Spring 1970) 12-27
In *Héloïse* Rousseau states that everyone uses figurative expressions except fools and geometricians. Schlanger denies even these two exceptions. Scientific invention uses metaphor. Metaphor involves transference from several areas or levels of knowledge and from different technical areas, renders the not yet known in terms of the known, and involves a moment of mystery while the right term appears. "The acquisition of a piece of knowledge requires a word-circuit." "Knowledge is acquired against culture." Knowledge has always been an interchange of models. There is no absolutely final, single or correct analogue or model. Not all metaphors are used in the same way. Each model influences or gives place to others, and is part of a multiplicity of models. Certain metaphors tend to predominate and become dogmatic as they become prevalent. Metaphors help popularize the technical. They give brevity and clarity by means of analogy. They do not just illustrate but become concepts. The new concept becomes part of scientific knowledge. "The invention of the formula becomes woven into the fabric of knowledge." Metaphor is an essential kind of new naming and new conceptualizing. The scientist often cannot formulate or conceive of his intuition without a metaphor to render it. The intuition is often something transcending traditional framework and types. Scientific inspiration is close to poetic inspiration. Inventive thought is impure as

it must be metaphorical. Examples are given from biology.

Schlauch, Margaret. The Gift of Language New York: Dover 1955 (First published as The Gift of Tongues) esp. 229-246 Types of metaphorical change of meaning of language are: 1) pejorative 2) ameliorative 3) narrowing 4) expansive. We often rejuvenate dead metaphors, use physical terms for psychological ones, employ synaesthetic transfer.

_____. Modern English and American Poetry London: C. A. Watts 1956
12 kinds of metaphor are 1) corporeal (from a resemblance to the body e.g. red-head) 2) synaesthesia 3) activity transfer 4) latent (etymological meaning) 5) semantic rejuvenation e.g. manunkind 6) sense transfer of one physical object to another e.g. green rustling 7) pathetic fallacy (unsuccessful attribution of feelings to nature) 8) use of concrete to express abstract 9) pure repetition 10) juxtaposition a) inanimate and animate b) human and non-human 11) conceits 12) images as symbols i.e. sustained images.

Schlegel, A. W. "Die Gemählde" in his Athenäum 3 vols. 1798-1800 Stuttgart: Cotta-Verlag 1960 vol. 2
On synaesthesia. He says, "Pictures become poems, poems music, and in like manner stately church music may once more rise heavenward as a cathedral."

Schlotthaus, Werner L. "Ingeborg Bachmann's Poem 'Mein Vogel': An Analysis of Modern Poetic Metaphor" Modern Language Quarterly 22 (June 1961) 181-91
The new technique of montage or struktur "correlates realistically unrelated spheres of meaning and builds up a figurative sense which establishes itself thru the inappropriateness of the meanings and the reader finds himself presented with a highly original interpretation of the condition humaine." There is also metaphor which involves omitting.

Schmidt, Harald. "Die Rolle der Analogie in der Sprache" PhD diss. Erlangen 1955
French language figures of speech and metaphor.

Schmidt, Oskar. Metapher und Gleichnis bei Lucian PhD diss. Zürich 1899

_____. Metapher und Gleichnis in den Schriften Lucians Winterthur: Geschwister Ziegler 1897

Schnabel. Walter. Montaignes Stilkunst, eine Untersuchung vornehmlich auf Grund seiner Metaphern Breslau, Oppeln: Priebatsch 1930 (PhD diss. Breslau 1930) Also in Sprache und Kultur der germanisch-romanischen Völker vol. 6, 1930, 141 pgs.
He classifies metaphors by subject content e.g. theatre, music, etc.

Schneider, Fritz. Gleichnisse und Bilder bei Horaz Nürnberg: Buch und Kunstdruckerei B. Hilz 1914

Schneider, K. L. Der bildhafte Ausdruck in den Dichtungen Georg Heyms, Georg Trakls und Ernst Stadlers. Studien zum lyrischen Sprachstil des deutschen Expressionismus. Heldelberg 1954

Schnemann, J. "See und Seefahrt nebst dem metaphorischen Gebrauche dieser Begriffe in Shakespeares Dramen" Pr. schol. Thom. Lipsiae 1876

Schoeck, Richard J. "Mathematics and the Languages of Literary Criticism" Journal of Aesthetics and Art Criticism 26 (Spring 1968) 367-376
Literary criticism often employs metaphors unconsciously e.g. house of literature, stream of development, body of the work, etc. Other metaphors consciously used might achieve more accuracy e.g. from vector analysis or topology or other mathematical notions.

Schoff, Gretchen. The Major Prose of Dylan Thomas PhD diss. University of Wisconsin 1966

Schon, D. A. Displacement of Concepts London: Tavistock 1963 (1959) "Analogy and Metaphor" pp. 35-52, "The Life of Metaphors in Theory" pp. 191-199
His "displacement of concepts" is Cassirer's "radical metaphor"--a transmutation or process of thought with a unique emergent concept. It has a special use in hypothesis and theory development but plays a central role in all thought.

Schorer, Mark. "Fiction and 'Matrix of Analogy'" Kenyon Review 11 (Autumn 1949) 539-60. Reprinted in Critiques and Essays on Modern Fiction J. W. Aldridge, ed. New York: Ronald 1952 pp. 83-98
In novels metaphors unify; interpret; structure; give style its special quality; express, define, and evaluate themes; provide counterpoint; reveal the character of any imaginative work of art. Style is conception, and rhetoric exists within the poetic.

Schottmann, Hans Heinrich. "Metapher und Vergleich in der Sprache Friedrich Hölderlins" (Abhandlungen zur Kunst- Musik- und Literaturwissenschaft 14) PhD diss. Bonn, Friedrich-Wilhelms Universität 1959

Schuchardt, Hugo. Liebesmetaphern (Romanisches und Keltisches, 13) Berlin: R. Oppenheim 1886

Schultes, Henry. Flowers of Fancy, exhibited in a collection of similes taken from various authors London: Longman, Rees,

Orme, Brown and Green 1829

Schultz, Irmgard. "Metaphern der Form im bildhaften französischen Argot" Volkstum und Kultur der Romanen 14 (1941) 244-313

_____. Die Tiere in der Namengebung der südfranzösischen Mundarten. Ein Beitrag zum Studium der Metaphern (PhD diss. Partly printed.) Frankfurter Quellen und Forschungen zur germanischen und romanischen Philologie 1938

Schulz zur Wiesch, Emil. "Der Vergleich in Shelleys lyrischen Gedichten" PhD diss. Marburg. Bochum-Langendreer 1932

Schulze. De imaginibus et figurata elocutione Aeschyli Halberstadt Programm 1854

Schürmeyer. "Vergleiche und Metaphern in den Dramen Racines" PhD diss. Marburg 1886 (Source: Kohfeldt)

Schwartz, Elimar. "De metaphoris e mari et re navali petitis quaestiones Euripideae" PhD diss. Kiel 1878

Schwartz, Herbert. "Analogy in St. Thomas and Cajetan" The New Scholasticism 18 (1954) 127-44

Schwerd, Karl. Vergleich, Metapher, und Allegorie in den "Tragiques" des Agrippa d'Aubigné Leipzig: G. Böhme 1909

Schwob, M. and G. Guieysse. "Etude sur l'argot français" Mémoires de la Société de Linguistique de Paris Sept., 1899 Paris pp. 33ff.

Schwyzer, H. "Wittgenstein's Picture-Theory of Language" Inquiry 5 (1962) 46-64

Scoggins, James. Imagination and Fancy: Complementary Modes in the Poetry of Wordsworth University of Nebraska Press 1966

Scott, A. F. "Metaphor" Current Literary Terms: A Concise Dictionary of Their Origin and Use London and New York: Macmillan and St. Martin's Press pp. 178-179

Scott, P. G. "Dancing as a Metaphor in Clough and Newman" Notes and Queries N.S. 15 (Nov. 1968) 417-18

Scudamore, W. "The Material Metaphor" (G K's) Weekly Review 24 (Jan. 21, 1937) 384-85

See, Fred G. "Metaphoric and Metonymic Imagery in Nineteenth Century American Fiction: Harriet Beecher Stowe, Rebecca H. Davis and Harold Frederick" PhD diss. University of California-Berkeley 1967

Seewald, Johannes. *Untersuchungen zu Stil und Komposition der Aischyleischen Tragödie* Greifswald: Dallmeyer 1936 III, 3 is on metaphor.

Seidler, Herbert. *Allgemeine Stilistik* Göttingen: Vandenhoeck and Ruprecht 1953 esp. pp. 281-315 "Das sprachliche Bild." Also *Die Dichtung, Wesen, Form, Dasein* (Kröners Taschenausgabe, vol. 283) Stuttgart 1959 esp. pp. 205-223 "Das sprachliche Bild."
An extensive analysis of metaphor, simile and comparison relying heavily on Pongs, *Das Bild in der Dichtung*. He gives a short bibliography on metaphor as well as on synaesthesia.

_____. "Review of Pongs *Das Bild in der Dichtung*" *Zeitschrift für deutsche Philologie* 80 (1961) 438-442

Seiffert, August. "Funktion und Hypertrophie des Sinnbilds" 1957 (Source: Pongs 1967)

Selig, Karl-Ludwig. "Gracián and Alciato's *Emblemata*" *Comparative Literature* 8 (1956) 1-11
The 21 emblems of Alciato used by Gracián are the most significant of Gracián's bent toward the enigmatic, recondite and erudite--all qualities of the *agudeza*.

Selva, Juan. "La metáfora en el crecimiento de nuestra habla" *Boletín de la Academia Argentina de Letras* (Buenos Aires) 10 (1942) 131-167

Semler, C. *Gleichnisse Homers aus Natur und ihre Bedeutung für den Unterricht und die Erziehung* 1891 Programm

Senger. "Der bildliche Ausdruck in den Werken Heinrich Kleists" (Source: Stutterheim 1941)

Serrano Poncala, Segundo. *La Metáfora* Caracas, Venezuela: Universidad Central de Venezuela 1968

Sewell, Elizabeth. *The Human Metaphor* Notre Dame 1964
Man's self and his life become one term of an ultimate metaphor of which the mysterious inner and outer cosmos is the other. The unknown can be explored by this metaphor. The mind "figures" and embodies itself in its figures. Metaphor is one of the vital and basic powers of all human thinking.

Sforza-Pallavicino, Cardinal. *Trattato del dialogo e dello stile* Rome 1646

Shakespeare, William. (See the numerous commentaries on his imagery e.g. M. Joseph)
"The poet's eye, in a fine frenzy rolling,
Doth glance from heaven to earth, from earth to heaven

And as imagination bodies forth
The forms of things unknown, the poet's pen
Turns them to shapes, and gives to airy nothing
A local habitation and a name."
A Midsummer Night's Dream v.i. 12.7
Shakespeare himself was one of the most metaphorical of writers.

Shamota, Alla Mykolaivna. Perenosne znachennya slova v movi Khudozhn'oi literatury. Kyiv, Nauk. Dumka 1967
On metaphor.

Sharkey, James. "The Directionality of the Metaphor of Light as an Indicator of the Baroque" PhD diss. University of North Carolina at Chapel Hill 1969
Baroque literature is formed on the analogical use of metaphor. He explores the metaphor of light and its analogical use in order to indicate the logical substructure of the Baroque.

Sharp, Robert L. "Observations on Metaphysical Imagery" Sewanee Review 43 (Oct. 1935) 464-78
The conceits of the Metaphysical Poets were an attempt to respond to a demand for metaphors more original than those of the Elizabethans. The latter thought in metaphors spontaneously. The conceit is not harmful and cannot be rule-bound. Conceits are condensations and ellipses. They need not be visualizable.

Sharpe, Ella Freemann. "Psycho Physical Problems Revealed in Language: An Examination of Metaphor" International Journal of Psychoanalysis 21 (1940) pp. 201-213
A Freudian approach. Metaphor conceals ideas and emotions. It is a transfer from the physical to the psychical in the individual and etymologically. Thus we should look for the physical origin of the patient's metaphors e.g. "I missed the point" may suggest breast withdrawal in infancy!

Shawcross, Donald. "A Metaphoric Approach to Reading Milton" Ball State University Forum 8 (1967) 17-22

Sheehan, Donald. "Wallace Stevens' Theory of Metaphor" Papers on Language and Literature 2 (1966) 57-66
Stevens is said to have two contradictory views: one sees reality as 1) metaphor or 2) as unknowable thing. Actually Stevens holds that to see the world both ways is to be capable of knowing.

Sheen, Fulton J. "Knowledge by Analogy" Catholic World 140 (Dec. 1934) 352-4. From his Philosophy of Science Milwaukee: Bruce Pub. 1934
Goodness, truth, beauty apply to God by analogy as they have

"formal perfection." Other names without this perfection can apply only metaphorically e.g. "God is *fire*." Traditional Thomistic view of analogy of proper proportionality.

Shelley, Percy B. "Defense of Poetry" *The Complete Works of Percy B. Shelley* 10 vols. Roger Ingpen and Walter Peck, eds., New York: Gordian Press 1965 vol. 7 pp. 107-140
Says about poets: "Their language is vitally metaphorical; that is, it marks the before unapprehended relations of things and perpetuates their apprehension." He defends the view that physical objects and actions can be presented in terms of mind.

Shepherd, Emma. "The Metaphysical Conceit in the Poetry of Edward Taylor" PhD diss. University of North Carolina 1960

Sherry, Richard. *A Treatise of Schemes and Tropes* Gainesville, Florida: Scholar's Facsimiles and Reprints 1961 [1550]
Metaphor (or *translatio*) "is a word translated from the thing that it properly signifies into another which may agree with it by a similitude." It is the main part of speech. It persuades, pictorializes, affects the emotions, and pleases. Transfers are between body-mind, reasonable-unreasonable, living-inanimate, etc. Similar figures are defined such as synecdoche, metonymy, pun, catachresis, etc.

Sherwin, P. F. "Detached Similes in Milton's Epics" *Modern Language Notes* 36 (June 1921) 341-8

Shibles, Warren. *Models of Ancient Greek Philosophy* London: Vision Press 1971
A presentation of the root metaphors of the major ancient Greek philosophers. The accounts given here are most of the major models of ancient Greek philosophy. It will be seen that a model functions very much as a metaphor does and it may be expanded and explored in a similar way. Each philosophy is seen to have one or more basic "root metaphors." One need not take as the ultimate concern of studying these early philosophers the task of piecing together their fragmented writings (much of which is hearsay) to find out what they "really said." Rather the task may be to determine what the various things we have taken them to say mean to us. We want to know how such models have given and may still give us insight into ourselves and our environment. This task is only begun here. But in any case no such models are taken to be the ultimate ones.

_____. *An Analysis of Wilbur Marshall Urbans's Discussion of Metaphor in His Theory of Language and Symbolism* M.A. thesis University of Colorado 1963 (cf. An Analysis of Metaphor)

_____. *An Analysis of Metaphor* The Hague: Mouton 1971
The purpose of the book is to determine the nature of meta-

phor, more specifically, to see in what sense, if any, metaphor can be termed a meaningful unit of discourse. To analyze these problems W. M. Urban's theory of metaphor as it was presented in his book, Language and Reality, is contrasted with the substitution theory of metaphor as held by Carnap, Stern, Buchanan and others. Wittgenstein's views are related to these subjects also. It is concluded that in opposition to the substitution theory, metaphor is not reducible to literal statements without loss of meaning. Metaphor occurs when two contexts are related and this relationship must be "intuited" (a technical definition of this is given) for the metaphor to be understood. Because it must be intuited, the metaphor is not reducible to literal statements. We are also given a more precise definition for the term, "literal." "Literal" is interpreted in terms of a contextual theory of meaning which regards a term as appropriate to a particular context. It is also shown how these conclusions might be employed in establishing a basis for the use of metaphor in philosophical reasoning. It is shown that by the use of metaphor we may gain distinctive insights into solutions of philosophical problems. The book is derived mainly from his 1963 dissertation.

_____. Philosophical Pictures Dubuque, Iowa: Kendall-Hunt 1969
This book is a collection of pictures taken with the lens of language. It consists of thirteen articles four of which have previously appeared in philosophical journals. The general aim of the essays is to present an analysis of certain philosophical problems and suggest some approaches for their solution. Topics such as cause, time, good, right, free-will, language, and meaning are considered. These approaches are called "pictures" or "models." Philosophy is seen to be a matter of taking a model or metaphor which one thinks is especially fruitful, expanding it, exploring it, and thereby gaining in-sight.

_____. Wittgenstein, Language and Philosophy Dubuque, Iowa: Kendall-Hunt 1969 [1970]
A critical interpretation and exemplification of Wittgenstein's ordinary-language philosophy. It is seen that, although it is not usually recognized, his philosophy centers around the use of metaphor in philosophical reasoning. Metaphor reveals disguised jokes, misleading statements but can give insight as well. Zen poetry is presented as serving much the same function. Includes an analysis of Alice in Wonderland.

Shipley, Joseph T., ed. "Metaphor" Dictionary of World Literature New York: Philosophical Library 1953 pp. 268-269; and 1943 pp. 377-378
Metaphor is "the substitution of one thing for another, or the identification of two things." Metaphor is the obverse of the joke. Metaphor unites, the joke separates what had

seemed one. Metaphors are classified according to H. Parkhurst _Beauty_ 1930.

Shklovskii, Viktor. Iskusstvo kak priem (Art as Artifice) _Poetika_ 1919 (Source: Dorfles "Myth and Metaphor"; cf. V. Erlich _Russian Formalism_)
He had a concept of _ostrannie_ or estranging of a certain word in a context by its becoming divorced from the context. The ordinary is thus made to seem strange so that you notice what you habitually ignored. It is an omnipresent principle of imaginative literature.

_____. _Khod Konya_ Moscow-Berlin 1923

Shook, Margaret. "Visionary Form: Blake's Prophetic Art and the Pictorial Tradition" PhD diss. University of California at Berkeley 1967

Shorey, P. "Logic of the Homeric Simile" _Classical Philology_ 17 (July 1922) 240-59

Short, R. W. "Henry James's World of Images" _PMLA_ 68 (Dec. 1953) 943-60

Showerman, G. "Life and the Simile" _Sewanee Review_ 20 (July 1912) 333-41

Shroeder, J. W. "That Inward Sphere: Notes on Hawthorne's Heart Imagery and Symbolism" _PMLA_ 65 (1950) 106-119

Shuford, Haywood. "The Logic of 'As If'" _Philosophy and Phenomenological Research_ 27 (March 1967) 401-407

Sickel, C. F. _Bruchstücke einer Einleitung in die homerischen Gesänge_ (Gleichnisse) Halle 1838

_____. _Uber die homerischen Gleichnisse_ Halle 1847

Sidney, Sir Phillip. _The Defense of Poesie_ (ca. 1582) in _Literary Criticism: Plato to Dryden_ Gilbert, ed. New York 1940 pp. 406-461
Metaphor is a union of history and philosophy.

Siebold, Erika von. "Synästhesien in der englischen Dichtung des 19. Jahrhunderts. Ein ästhetisch-psychologischer Versuch" (Englische Studien, 53) 1919-1920 pp. 1-157, and 196-334

Sihler, E. G. _A Study of Metaphor and Comparison in Plato_ PhD diss. Johns Hopkins University 1882

Silberer, H. "On Symbol-forming" _Organization and Pathology of_

Thought D. Rapaport, ed. New York: Columbia University Press 1951 pp. 208-233

Silver, Isidore. "Ronsard's Homeric Imagery" Modern Language Quarterly 16 (1955) 344-359

Silz, Walter. "Heine's Synaesthesia" PMLA 57 (1942) 469-488 Has useful bibliography. Heine speaks of green grasses telling each other green tales; and green spring enters dreams as a green echo. His synaesthesia is really only the non-psychological literary use of metaphor, or striking and ludicrous juxtaposition. (cf. Liszt to his Weimar orchestra: "O bitte, meine Herren, ein bisschen blauer!")

"New Similes Each Year" The Literary Digest 92 (Feb. 26, 1927) p. 29

Simmonds, James. "Some Traditional Oxymora in Vaughan's Secular Verse" Die neuren Sprachen 11 (1962) 569-573 (About E. McCann "Oxymora...")

Simon, H. A., and A. Newell. "The Uses and Limitations of Models" Theories in Contemporary Psychology M. H. Marx, ed. New York: Macmillan 1963 pp. 89-104
A metaphor or analogy determines the kind of theory i.e. categories, assumptions and hypotheses, underlying observation and description.

Simon, John K. "The Scene and the Imagery of Metamorphosis in As I Lay Dying" Criticism 7 (Winter 1965) 1-22

Simon, Yves. "Order in Analogical Sets" New Scholasticism 34 (1960) 1-42

Singleton, Marvin. "Deduced Knowledge as Shandean Nub: Paracelsian Hermetic as Metaphoric Bridge in Tristram Shandy" Zeitschrift für Anglistik und Amerikanistik 16 (1968) 274-84

Sister, M. Metaphern und Vergleich im Koran PhD diss. Friedrich-Wilhelms Universität, Berlin: Reichsdruckerei 1931

Skard, Sigmund. "The Use of Color in Literature" Proceedings of the American Philosophical Society 90 (1946) 163-249 (Has valuable bibliography on synaesthesia, pp. 204-241)
On synaesthesia

Skelton, Robin. The Poetic Pattern London 1956 esp. "The Poetic Image" pp. 90-105

Skinner, B. F. Verbal Behavior New York: Appleton-Century-Crofts 1957 esp. p. 92

Sklovsky, Viktor. (See Shklovskii)

Slattery, Michael P. "Two Notes on Fonseca" _Modern Schoolman_ 34 (March 1957) 193-202. First note is "Fonseca on Metaphor" pp. 193-197
He calls Fonseca the Portuguese Aristotle. In the Renaissance scholastic philosophers asked if metaphor describes anything really present and intrinsic in a subject e.g. "Is the field really smiling?" Fonseca said, "Yes." Most others disagreed.

_____. "Poets and Philosophers" _Franciscan Studies_ 17 (Dec. 1957) 373-90
Metaphors are controlled misuses of terms to express the real. In religion they are needed to express God's revelation of himself in material things. Metaphor underlies both poetry and philosophy and serves to unite them. It allows one to say what cannot otherwise be said.

Slawinska, Irena. "Metaphor in Drama" _Poetics, Poetyka_ I. D. Davie et al., eds. The Hague: Mouton and Co. 1961
Metaphor and imagery appear in language and develop themes but also in gestures and that which accompanies language such as silence, way of moving, background (e.g. sing to wall), etc.

Slote, B. "Transmutation in Crane's Imagery in 'The Bridge'" _Modern Language Notes_ 73 (Jan. 1958) 15-23

Smart, Alastair. "Pictorial Imagery in the Novels of Thomas Hardy" _Review of English Studies_ 12 (1961) 262-280

Smart, J. J. C. "A Note on Categories" _British Journal for the Philosophy of Science_ 4 (Nov. 1953) 227-28 (Sum. in A. Baker)
Ryle's test for category difference is based on whether a term will fit in a sentence frame e.g. "I listen _(hard)_." In this way achievement words e.g. "win" are separated from task words e.g. "run." Smart objects that this test will never conclusively show terms to be of the same category and that it may result in every term being of a different logical category than every other term.

Smith, Adam. _Lectures on Rhetoric and Belles Lettres_ London: Thomas Nelson 1963
There can be four kinds of metaphor: 1) idea borrowed from corporeal object and applied to an intellectual object e.g. "lust of fame," 2) transfer from intellectual to corporeal object, 3) interaction between two corporeal objects, 4) interaction between two intellectual objects.

Smith, Arvid Johannes Magnus. _On Names of Things as Designations for Human Beings in English, A Sematological Study_ Lund: H.

Ohlsson 1910 (Recently by Gale Press)
A classification based on a likeness of two objects or acts. The connecting link of the metaphor is sometimes emotional. Metaphors are often merely condensed adjectives. Likenesses are based on outward characteristics, action, purpose, use, position, parallel between physical and mental, etc.

Smith, Charles J. "The Contrarieties: Wordsworth's Dualistic Imagery" *PMLA* 69 (1954) 1181-1199

Smith, Charles Sidney. *Metaphor and Comparison in the Epistulae ad Lucilium of L. Annaeus Seneca* Baltimore: J. H. Furst Company 1910 (PhD diss. Johns Hopkins University 1910)

Smith, Charles Willard. *Browning's Star-Imagery: The study of a detail in poetic design* Princeton University Press and Oxford University Press 1941 (Octagon Press 1965)

Smith, David J. "Blake's 'The Divine Image'" *Explicator* 25 (1967) Item 69

Smith, Edward, ed., Similes and Comparisons of Shakespeare (from the text of the Chiswick edition of 1826) Philadelphia 1882 (Only 99 copies printed.)

Smith, J. Norton. "Lydgate's Metaphors" *English Studies* 42 (1961) 90-93. Reply by Claes Schaar pp. 232-234. Rejoinder by Smith p. 224. (cf. C. Schaar "Usk's 'Knot in the Hert'" *English Studies* 37 (1956) 260-261.)

Smith, John. *The Mystery of Rhetorick Unveiled* London 1721
Metaphor or *translatio* is an artificial translation of a word from its proper sense to another not proper but similar one or from one species to another. It can be drawn from any content but should be noble and not far-fetched.

Smith, Marion B. "Marlowe's Imagery and the Marlowe Canon" PhD diss. University of Pennsylvania 1940
Attempt to support Spurgeon's view of Imagery.

Smith, Nila B. "Reading: Concept Development" *Education* 70 (May 1950) 548-558

Smythies, J. R. "On Some Properties and Relations of Images" *The Philosophical Review* 67 (July 1958) 389-394
Opposes Ryle's view that there are no images. Says we do see images. Images are spatial entities that may bear either spatial or causal relations or both, to physical objects.

Snell, Bruno. *Der Aufbau der Sprache* Hamburg: Claassen 1952
"Metapher" pp. 159-160

One form of metaphor is that whereby a noun designates an object and its function, e.g. a fleet foot, a good head, a clear eye. Another form depends on characteristics, e.g. neck of the bottle, sea of misfortune, gold of stars. The meaning of metaphor extends beyond the object designated by a word.

_____. "From Myth to Logic: The Role of the Comparison" The Discovery of the Mind: The Greek Origins of European Thought Bruno Snell; T. Rosenmeyer trans. New York: Harper 1953 (1960) 191-226. (A translation of Die Entdeckung des Geistes.)

Söhngen, Gottlieb. Analogie und Metapher: Kleine Philosophie und Theologie der Sprache Freiburg-München: Alber 1962
A discussion of analogy, image, synaesthesia and metaphor in literature, philosophy, science and religion. Relevant to synaesthesia is our tendency to reduce all senses to the visual sense and to images. He speaks of translation of objects into words or word images, of one realm of word and being into another e.g. synaesthesia, the translation of concepts through perceptions into image-words, translation from one language into another. Metaphor means translation and these are a few types of translation. The secret of Goethe's language is the exchange of metaphorical and unmetaphorical expressions, which is done in such a way that the metaphorical expressions are felt to be non-metaphorical, and the other way round, so that everything appears to be said properly. Both metaphorical and literal language are intrinsic. He discusses metaphor in Aristotle, Kant, Aquinas and the Bible. Philosophy can be based on metaphor. There is metaphysics in metaphor and vice versa. Religion is based on metaphor and analogy e.g. the view that nature mirrors a divine world. Image and concept fuse to form a functional unity in metaphor. The image is less concrete than functional and points to a concept. In poetry concepts become images. In scholarly writing the images become concepts. Metaphors are not analogies but usually are based on analogies. "The Church is the body of Christ" is regarded as the significant metaphor of the New Testament. The metaphorical function of language is perhaps the original force creating the view of the world. He cites Johann Auer and Söhngen in replacing the notion of analogy in theology with that of "models."

Sojcher, Jacques. "La métaphore generalisse" Revue Internationale de Philosophie 23 (1969) 58-68

Solard, Alain P. "Étude sur la métaphore chez certains poètes baroques (1585-1650)" PhD diss. Los Angeles: University of California 1963
On the metaphors of Desportes, Sponde, La Creppède, Racan, Viau, Saint-Armant, etc. The 16th century analogous universe (like a system of mirrors), becomes modified by the "new

science" in the 17th century. Metaphor no longer reflects the analogy of the world.

Söll, Ludwig. "Review of Meier Die Metapher" Archiv für das Studium der neueren Sprachen und Literaturen 203 (1966) 204-207

Soltis, Jonas. Seeing, Knowing and Believing: A Study of the Language of Visual Perception London: George Allen & Unwin Reading, Mass: Addison-Wesley Publishing Company 1966
On Hanson's notion of "seeing-as."

Sonn, C. R. "An Approach to Wordsworth's Earlier Imagery" ELH 27 (1960) 208-222

South, Malcolm H. "Animal Imagery in Volpone" Tennessee Studies in Literature 10 (1965) 141-150

Souza, Ma. Georgina de. "A Linguagem Metafórica na Lirica Expressionista de Georg Trakl" (Source: C. Mendes p. 10)

Spacks, Patricia Meyer. "Collins' Imagery" Studies in Philology 62 (Oct. 1965) 719-736

_____. "Horror-Personification in Late Eighteenth-Century Poetry" Studies in Philology 59 (1962) 560-578

Spamer, A. "Krankheit und Tod als Metapher" Niederdeutsche Zeitschrift für Volkskunde 20 (1942) 1-17

Spangenberg, C. "De T. Lucretii Cari tropis" PhD diss. Marburg 1880

Sparshott, F. E. "Review of Turbayne: The Myth of Metaphor" The University of Toronto Quarterly 32 (1963) ca. p. 106

Specht, Ernst. Der Analogiebegriff bei Kant und Hegel (Kantstudien 66) Köln: Kölner Universitätsverlag 1952

Spencer, Benjamin T. "Antony and Cleopatra and the Paradoxical Metaphor" Shakespeare Quarterly 9 (Summer 1958) 373-8

Spencer, Herbert. Philosophy of Style New York: Appleton-Century Co. 1933 (1889)
Metaphor is not a simile. It should not be obscure.

Spencer, John. Things New and Old J. G. Pilkington, ed. London: R. D. Dickinson 1868 (1658)
Contains an added "treasury of similes" by Robert Cawdray.

Speranski, W. "Essai sur l'origine psychologique des métaphores"

Revue Philosophique 44 (1897) 494-507, 605-621
Metaphor involves imagination and feeling. Often an intellectual analysis of metaphor cannot be given e.g. "May the wind blow until its cheeks explode" (*King Lear*). Two types of metaphor are a) characteristics of one object attributed to another based on similarity of qualities b) identification of a little known object to a familiar one. The first involves the number and intensity of similarities; the second yields myth. Originally language and myth were one because primitive man could not perceive qualities in abstraction. Like myth, poetry gives abstract ideas concrete form. Metaphors are spontaneous and come forth naturally. They cannot be taken literally nor can they be adequately reduced to literal language. They are somewhere between myth and literal language. Both plastic art and metaphor please because they distort and create illusion but are yet based on the natural succession of associations by resemblance. Types and categories are abstractions, are fictions or metaphors. So also historical analysis modifies actual fact. The illusion should not be too evident nor too intense. (Irony is a type of metaphor because a non-literal quality is attributed.)

Sperry, R. W. "Neurology and the Mind-Brain Problem" *Basic Readings in Neuropsychology* Robert Isaacson, ed. New York: Harper & Row 1969 pp. 403-429. Also in *American Scientist* 40 (1952) 291-312
On seeing-as and images.

Spevack, Marvin. "Hamlet and Imagery: The Mind's Eye" *Die Neueren Sprachen* 15 (1966) 203-12

Spicer, Julia. "The Epithet in the Parnassian School of French Poetry" *Studies in Spanish Language and Literature* vol. 7 University of Iowa 1938

Spire, André. *Plaisir poétique et plaisir musculaire: essai sur l'evolution des techniques poétiques* New York: S. F. Vanni 1949

Spitzer, Leo. "Kenning und Calderóns Begriffsspielerei" *Zeitschrift für Romanische Philologie* 56 (1936) 100-102

______. *Romanische Stil-und Literaturstudien* Marburg a. Lahn 1931 (Kölner Romanistische Arbeiten 1-2)

Spivack, Bernard. *Shakespeare and the Allegory of Evil: The History of a Metaphor in Relation to His Major Villains* New York: Columbia University Press 1958

Spoerri, Theophile. "La Puissance Métaphorique" *Paul Valéry. Essais et Témoignages Inédits* Neuchâtel 1945 pp. 177-198

Spratt, Thomas. The History of the Royal Society of London for the Improving of Natural Knowledge London: Printed for J. Knapton et al. 1667 (1734) pp. 112-113. (cf. Jones, "The Attack on Pulpit" JEGP 30 (1931) 188-217. Jones "Science and Language in England of the Mid-Seventeenth Century" JEGP 31 (1932) 315-331. Francis Christensen "John Wilkins and the Royal Society's Reform of Prose Style" MLQ 7 (1946) 179-187; 279-290. Basil Willey, The Seventeenth Century Background New York: 1953 p. 221ff. William Wimsatt & Cleanth Brooks, Literary Criticism: A Short History New York: 1957 pp. 226 ff.)
Spratt states about metaphors: "They are in open defiance against reason...they give the mind a notion too changeable, and bewitching to consist with right practice." Spratt rejects metaphorical speech and wishes to legally ban it from the language. He prefers the model of mathematics.

Spurgeon, Caroline F. E. "The Use of Imagery by Shakespeare and Bacon" Review of English Studies 9 (Oct. 1933) 385-396

_____. Shakespeare's Imagery Cambridge University Press 1935 (1952) (cf. Hornstein)
An analysis of all of Shakespeare's imagery and some of the imagery of his contemporaries in order to determine his personality, temperament and thought and how the imagery relates to the themes and characters of his plays. "I use the term 'image'...to cover every kind of simile, as well as every kind of what is really compressed simile...metaphor." "Analogy...which is the fact underlying the possibility and reality of metaphor, holds within itself the very secret of the universe."

Spurgeon, Charles H. The Art of Illustration New York 1894

Srzednicki, J. "On Metaphor" The Philosophical Quarterly 10 (July 1960) 228-37
"A metaphor arises when an utterance, which by reason either of its very construction or its context, would be apparently unintelligible in a straightforward manner, is found to contain, despite this, a point of similarity." It may be based on analogy or emotion. Extension of its meaning is considered.

Stadler, I. "On Seeing-As" Philosophical Review 67 (Jan. 1958) 91-94. A response to Fleming on seeing-as.

Stählin, Wilhelm. Zur Psychologie und Statistik der Metaphern PhD diss. Würzburg 1913. Also Archiv für die gesamte Psychologie 31 (1914) 297-425 (See Laan)

Stallknecht, Newton P. "On Metaphor" The Yale Review 51 (Summer 1962) 637-642
A review of Max Black, Models and Metaphors; Robert Boyle,

Metaphor in Hopkins; and Philip Wheelwright, _Metaphor and Reality_. Particular examples often give more insight than does theory.

Standley, Fred L. "Rabbit, Run: An Image of Life" _Midwest Quarterly_ 8 (1967) 371-86

Stanford, William Bedell. _Greek Metaphor, Studies in Theory and Practice_ Oxford: Blackwell 1936
Metaphor is a "stereoscope of ideas," a double or second meaning. It is a term for an object or concept used in such context or universe of discourse that it must refer to another object or concept--a merging and emerging yet with original meanings retained, an integration of diversity in which neither term can overpower. It is synthetic, intensive, illogical, dogmatic, intuitive, conscious, living, open-meaning, is unlike the simile, and cannot be paraphrased. He thinks metaphors are based on an original unity of perception (cf. Buck) and so opposes Müller's "root" theory of metaphor. He states about synaesthetic metaphors, "They are the expressions of genuine experience, not the conceits of a petty wit." Metaphor is hard to define, thus "This is metaphorical" is often used merely as a disclaimer. No single word _per se_ is a metaphor. Classical views of metaphor are examined. Aristotle's analogical-genus view is rejected as a mechanical exercise in logic. Classical writers also ignore the emotive link of metaphor. Stanford agrees with Coleridge that words are living things in themselves, and adds that there is a primeval connection between the shape, sound and meaning of words. "A great book on literary metaphor has still to be written in English."

______. "Synaesthetic Metaphor" _Comparative Literature Studies_ 6-7 (1942) 26-30
Synaesthetic metaphor begins with Homer e.g. "lily-voices of the cicadas." Stanford regards many such metaphors to be clever rather than true synaesthesia which involves an unusual actual experience. He cites examples of true, and clever synaesthesic metaphors.

Stankiewicz, Edward. "Linguistics and the Study of Poetic Language" _Style and Language_ Thomas Sebeok, ed. Cambridge: MIT Press, and John Wiley 1960 pp. 69-81
As with Jakobson, he asserts that metaphor is based on semantic similarity, and metonymy or contiguity. It is a metalinguistic problem.

Stauffer, Donald. _Shakespeare's World of Images: The Development of His Moral Ideas_ Bloomington: Indiana University Press 1966 [1949]

Steadman, J. M. _The Bee-Similes of Du Bartas and Vergil: A Study_ *in Literary Imitation* (Romanica. Festschrift für Gerhard Rohlfs, Halle) 1968 pp. 446-448

Steadman, John M. "Eliot and Husserl: The Origin of the 'Objective Correlative'" *Notes and Queries* N.S. 5 (June 1958) 261-262
Eliot's phrase 'objective correlative' is probably from Husserl's "objectives Korrelat" but the meaning is entirely different.

Stech, S. "Zur Gestalt der etymologischen Figur in verschiedenen Sprachen" *Zeitschrift für vergleichende Sprachforschung auf dem Gebiete der indogermanischen Sprachen* 81 (1967) 134-152

Steele, R. B. "The Similes in Latin Epic Poetry" *Transactions and Proceedings of the American Philological Association* 44 (1918) 83-100

Stein, Arnold. "Structures of Sound in Donne's Verse" *Kenyon Review* 13 (1951) 20-36, 256-270
Sound and sense work together to create a metaphor of reality. Sound functions as a contributing metaphor. Counterpoint is used metaphorically.

Stein, Gertrude. *Selected Writings of Gertrude Stein* Carl Van Vechten ed. New York: Modern Library, Random House 1962

Steinhoff, William R. "Metaphorical Texture of Daniel Deronda" *Books Abroad* 35 (Summer 1961) 220-4
"George Eliot wrote of *Daniel Deronda*: 'I meant everything in the book to be related to everything else there.' In the metaphorical texture we see the same reconciling of opposites--the movement from province to universe, self to altruism, narrow to wide, inner to outer, darkness to light, and death to life--that is revealed in character and action."

Stelzner, Hermann. "Analysis by Metaphor" *Quarterly Journal of Speech* 51 (Feb. 1965) 52-61
Metaphors structure inquiry, establish relevance and provide an interpretative system. We should be conscious that we are using them, to avoid being misled. In discussions of oral communication the mechanical metaphor is being replaced by the biological one.

Stephen, Thomas. *Troposchematologia maximam partem ex indice rhetorico Farnabii deprompta* Dublin (cited in S. Brown, *World of Imagery* p. 161)

Stern, Emil. "Metapher und Subjektivität" *Euphorion* 5 (1898) 217-226
Metaphor is more than fancy or ornament added to an already complete language. All thinking is metaphoric. Metaphor re-

lates the unfamiliar with the familiar, the external and internal, and makes our internal life more concrete. Metaphors are sometimes assimilations such as that of old images entering into new ones without objective thought resulting in a new blend. It may lead to visions, fantastic illusions or hallucinations which are abnormal or outside of our normal spiritual life. Assimilation is regarded as an ability to read false things into a situation. The poet may describe a tree as looking like an old man and at some moment actually "see" the old man. This, however, is basically a comparison rather than a metaphor. An illusion metaphor is not assimilation but an image will not only influence but rather replace another image. This type of metaphor coincides with a momentary image of a subjective ego. It cannot be taken from some exotic distant source. One can tell about an author by the metaphors he uses.

Stern, Gustaf. Meaning and Change of Meaning Indiana University Press 1931
"Figures of speech are intentional transfers which involve emotional (incl. aesthetic) factors. They are intended to serve the expressive and purposive functions of speech better than the 'plain statement'." Metaphor is a fusion of two disparate notions. This is one of the most extensive linguistic-psychological analyses of metaphor or change of meaning.

Stern, L. William. Die Analogie im volkstümlichen Denken Berlin 1893 esp. pp. 151-162 on metaphor.

Sternheim, Carl. Chronik von des zwanzigsten Jahrhunderts Beginn 2 vols. Leipzig: Kurt Wolff 1918. Also in his novel Europa München: Musarion Verlag 1919 cf. Gesamtwerk Wilhelm Emrich, ed. Berlin 1963-1964 V "Prosa II" (Prosa 10/18)
He distrusts metaphor.

Sterzinger, Othmar. "Die Bestandteile des poetischen Bildes unter dem Gesichtspunkte seiner Schöpfung" (unverified)

_____. "Die Gründe des Gefallens und Missfallens am poetischen Bilde" Archiv für die gesamte Psychologie 29 (1913) 16-91
Figurative substitution may involve 1) oscillation between two images 2) simultaneity or 3) melting or fusion of them. The object is no longer seen as such. Images of different senses fuse. Substitution is a main factor in aesthetic pleasure.

Stevens, N. E. "Universal and Provincial Figures of Speech in the Old Testament" Methodist Review 110 (May 1927) 427-35

Stevens, Wallace. The Collected Poems of Wallace Stevens New York: Knopf 1954 esp. "Metaphors of a Magnifico," "The

Motive for Metaphor," "Thinking of the Relation Between the Images of Metaphors," "Metaphor as Degeneration." (cf. M. Turner, S. Morse, Nassar, Riddel, Benamou, Betar, Bevis, Carruth, Sheehan, King.)

_____. "Effects of Analogy" Yale Review N.S. 38 (Sept. 1948) 29-44. Also in The Necessary Angel.
Some images are emotional analogies. There are personifications, animalizations, emotional images, voluntary and involuntary images. 1) Every image is the elaboration of a particular of the subject of the image. Every image is a restatement of the subject of the image in the terms of an attitude. Every image is an intervention on the part of the image-maker. Analogy is the thing stated and the restatement. The basic books of the human spirit are vast collections of such transcendence achieved by words, by analogies. Poetry is a transcendent analogue composed of the particulars of reality created by the poet's attitude or sense of the world, as he intervenes and interposes the appearances of that sense.

_____. The Necessary Angel New York: Vintage Books, Random House 1942 (1951) (cf. Sister Egan)
There is a subtle relation between imagination and reality, real and ideal. Imagination created metaphors and both are real. Fact is all the imagination includes. There is a natural balance between imagination and reality (suggesting that metaphors are natural not far-fetched). "Imagination is the only genius." It is an activity like seeing things. It sees the normal in the abnormal. The "fancy" selects among objects already fixed and supplied by association whereas the imagination is more of a metamorphosis or process developing. Metaphor is an "escape" from reality's pressure, it yields revelation, order in chaos or disorder. All things resemble each other. Metaphor is resemblance not identity. Our age is determined by its metaphors which change under the pressure of reality to yield new knowledge. The poet gives life to "supreme fictions" to which we constantly turn and without which the world cannot be conceived.

_____. Opus Posthumous New York: Knopf 1957
"Things seen are things as seen."
"Metaphor creates a new reality from which the original appears to be unreal."
"There is a nature that absorbs the mixedness of metaphors."
"Reality is a cliché from which we escape by metaphor. It is only au pays de la métaphore qu'on est poète."
"Some objects are less susceptible to metaphor than others. The whole world is less susceptible to metaphor than a tea-cup is."
"There is no such thing as a metaphor of metaphor. One does not progress through metaphors. Thus reality is the indispensable element of each metaphor."

"A poet's natural way of thinking is by way of figures." Philosophers often feel horror of metaphor. To others it is natural."
"One is always writing about two things at the same time in poetry and it is this that produces the tension character of poetry."
Since no fact is a bare fact "the artist exhibits affinities in the actual structure of objects by which their significance is deepened and enhanced. What I desire to stress is that there is a unity rooted in the individuality of objects and discovered in a different way from the apprehension of rational connections." Stevens delights in that perceived event which is "out of place."

______. Three Academic Pieces Mass: Cummington Press 1947. Also in The Necessary Angel esp. "The Realm of Resemblance."

Stevenson, Charles. "Metaphor" Ethics and Language New Haven: Yale University Press 1960 (1944) pp. 71-76
A word or sentence has a literal or descriptive meaning determined by the rules governing its usage in a particular context. To say it is metaphorical or not literal is to say the context and hearer's expectations of the intention is such that the descriptive disposition is not realized in the usual way. But still metaphor implies a correct or literal usage in order for it to deviate from it. The literal meaning of a metaphor is not its interpretation. The interpretation refers to what the metaphor only suggests and there are an unlimited number of suggestions. "No sentence can ever descriptively mean exactly what another suggests." The metaphor retains the emotive value its descriptive statement had and because the literal meaning is not realized in an ordinary way, it intensifies the emotive meaning. "An adequate explanation of the emotional effects of metaphor lies in a little-charted region of psychology--where a psychophysical explanation is barely to be hoped for..."

Stewig, John W. "Metaphor and Children's Writing" Elementary English Review 43 (Feb. 1966) 121-123 (Review by Zale 43 (Oct. 1966) 660-2)
Children in the intermediate grades should be taught the various aspects of metaphor and become conscious of their metaphors. He discusses C. S. Lewis' views of metaphor.

Steyns, D. "Étude sur les métaphores et les comparaisons dans les oeuvres en prose de Sénèque le philosophe" (Recueil de travaux publiés par le Faculté de Philosophie et Lettres de l'Université de Gand, vol. 33) A. van der Haeghen 1906

Stirling, J. System of Rhetoric Containing All Tropes and Figures Necessary to Illustrate the Classics London 1764 (1795)

Stitz, Anton. Die Metapher bei Tacitus I. II. Jahresber. d. Obergymn. Krems 1883, pp. 1-32 and 1884, pp. 1-28

Stock, H. R. Die optischen Synästhesien bei E.T.A. Hoffmann Munich 1914

Stogdill, Ralph M. The Process of Model-Building in the Behavioral Sciences Columbus, Ohio: Ohio State University Press 1970 Eight writers discuss model-building from various fields from industrial engineering and psychology to management science. They point out the over-theoretical nature of model-building and attempt to give concrete guides and methods of teaching model-building. They also attempt to show the operation of the creative intellect in this process.

Stone, George W., ed. "Report of the Language Committee of the School and College Conference on English, 1940" Issues, Problems, and Approaches in the Teaching of English New York: Holt, Rinehart and Winston 1964 esp. p. 29

Storch, Rudolf. "Metaphors of Private Guilt and Social Rebellion in Godwin's Caleb Williams" ELH 34 (1967) 188-207

Storz, Gerhard. "Metapher" Im Lauf der Zeit. Arbeiten ein. Feuilletons, Frankfurt: Max Brück pp. 207-13. (Unverified)

_____. Sprache und Dichtung München: Kösel-Verlag 1957 "Das Bild in der Dichtung" pp. 119-186

Stössel, Christian. "Die Bilder und Vergleiche der altprovenzalischen Lyrik nach Form und Inhalt untersucht" PhD diss. Marburg 1886

Strandberg, Victor H. "Theme and Metaphor in Brother to Dragons" PMLA 79 (1964) 498-508

Strang, Barbara. Metaphors and Models Newcastle-Upon-Tyne University Publishers 1965
Models and metaphors contribute to the clarification of the nature of language. Language has been thought of as a family tree with branches and common stock, waves, structures, layers, and Chomsky's notion of a "generative" grammar. Some of these mislead. "There will always be a need for redescription in terms of different metaphors, models and theories."

Strassmann, Margard. "Die Bildlichkeit in der Lyrik Clemens Brentanos" PhD diss. Köln 1952

Straub, Joannes. "De tropis et figuris, quae inveniuntur in orationibus Demosthenis et Ciceronis" Aschaffenburg, 1883 PhD diss. Würzburg 1883

Strich, Fritz. "Das Symbol in der Dichtung" Der Dichter und die Zeit. Eine Sammlung von Reden und Vorträgen Bern 1947 pp. 13-39

Sturm, Sara and H. G. Sturm. "Astronomical Metaphor in 'La Estrella de Sevilla'" Hispania 52 (May 1969) 193-197

Stutterheim, Cornelius F. P. "Het begrip 'metaphoor' bij de Arabische rhetores" Tijdschrift voor Taal en Letteren 37 (1939) 438-450
The notion of metaphor according to Arab rhetoricians.

_____. Het begrip metaphoor Amsterdam: H. J. Paris 1941 PhD diss. Amsterdam 708 pages. (Reviews by Rooth, Meeussen, Laan)
He asserts that this book treats of the idea ("notion") not the phenomenon of the metaphor. The term metaphor is itself a metaphor. The idea of metaphor is comprised of many elements with different rapports; just as these qualities or elements vary greatly, so do the metaphors they form. Thus the evolution of metaphor is not that of a single entity. Stutterheim's view rests heavily on the linguistic theory of Reichling. Stutterheim concludes that 1) a theory of the metaphor must be preceded by a theory of the word, establishing a meaning of "word," "name," "object," etc. 2) "Metaphor" may sometimes refer to a word designating an unfamiliar reality (based on analogy); a word designating a reality about which man knows nothing; or a word which does not designate any reality (i.e. nothing). 3) In an interpretation of linguistic phenomena, psychological immanence cannot be maintained. 4) Only Reichling's theory explains why, e.g., in the "veil of truth" "veil" is the metaphor and "truth" the personification. 5) For different causes, a theory of the metaphor must be preceded by a study of the problem of identity. 6) The interpretation of the concept "metaphor" is the interpretation of metaphors. The concept of metaphor is complex and has a dual nature. The term is at once a rhetorical term and a world-view. It is viewed as an exterior ornament and as a creative expression of a personality; as a word without meaning but also as the unique bridge leading to the enigma of reality; as a lie of man but also as a revelation of God. He describes the concept of metaphor as uniting us to the distant past, but as also reaching to the future through its unresolved problems.

The author attempts to write only on the "concept (begrip) metaphor" which he defines as "the sum of all judgements which in the course of time have been made on the metaphor." He does not expound a theory of his own.

Part I of the book explains the methodology behind the entire work; Part II gives a historical survey of the metaphor in rhetoric, linguistics and philosophy; Part III is a systematic inventory of recent views, up to 1940, of metaphor in the fields of rhetoric, linguistics, and philosophy.

In the sections on philosophy he states that metaphor is dealt with only implicitly. In philosophy, metaphor is referred to in connection with the critique of knowledge, the critique of language and the nature of philosophical systems. Modern agnosticism and nominalism are directly linked to a certain view of language and especially to a view of metaphor. Metaphor is often polysemous and symbolic, and can yield an entire mystical philosophy or view of life. Metaphor is abused or venerated. In philosophic literature the concept of the metaphor lies deeply embedded in a context. Metaphor is synonymous with such terms as myth, hypostatization, fiction.

In regard to the critique of language, language is seen to have three functions: expression, communication, representation. Some say expression is achieved especially through metaphors. Language criticism usually supports the expressive function of language and of the metaphor. Views vary in regard to the communicative function. The transfer of meaning to sound is metaphorical, as is the listener's transfer from speaker's sound and meaning to his own. The views of the realist and nominalist are discussed. The author believes that there is a comparison of transcendental reality with something else, and that it is not the case that only the concrete thing and sensations are real.

In the critique of language the metaphor is a word we transfer from the realm of a first reality to that of a second in order to represent it (inadequately); or it is a word transferred to nothing (since either the second reality cannot be known or does not even exist) and then it degenerates into mere sound. According to many critics language does not possess a communicative function. Language is often seen to create the illusion that the mere existence of a word means there is a corresponding reality. Language possesses this illusion insofar as it is metaphoric.

The critique of language recognizes expression as the sole language function. It holds that: 1) language is a most important means of non-understanding; 2) thought is speech; 3) language (and therefore thought) is thoroughly metaphoric; 4) language (and especially metaphor) creates the illusion of logicity, of intelligibility, of knowledge and the existence of metaphysical reality.

In philosophy the metaphor is often only a term of abuse. A word is called a metaphor only when it stands for a metaphysical reality about which one has only inadequate knowledge, or when it stands for nothing. The critique of language tends to regard the metaphor as a linguistic hallucination: the metaphor roots in the imagination; it cannot be expressed language.

Metaphor is the result of a synthesis which the critique of language rejects in principle. It comprises all figures of speech, of rhetoric, illusion, hypostatization, and myth. It goes beyond the realm of language and thought. It is thus thought to lack the required scientific precision but possess great emotive value.

_____. "Metafoor" Moderne Encyclopedie der Wereld Literatuur vol. 5, 1968
A word can be used in such a way that it retains its "sense-unity," but because of a resemblance is applied to a different object than that mentioned when used in a non-metaphorical way. "Sense-differences" and "sense-unity" both apply to the object of a non-metaphorical word, but when a metaphorical word is used only a single distinction is applicable in the situation. This theory applies to usual metaphors. With original or new metaphors the resemblance may be only experienced and created in a unique moment of poetical inspiration, and that gives an object a characteristic that it did not have before. But this word theory does not explain the way a metaphor works. Each metaphor is different from another and so must be examined separately. A successful metaphor can be an adequate means of expression of a frame of mind, and can make us participate in a reality more essential than that of everyday life. When we try to analyze a metaphor we destroy it. Probably we experience at the same time an identity and non-identity without its striking us as 'illogical' on this level of consciousness. Identity corresponds to the "sense-unity" and non-identity to "sense-difference." The tension between the two may determine the reason for our accepting or rejecting a metaphor. One may see metaphor in every work of art, e.g., a play as an extended metaphor.

_____. "Psychologische Interpretatie van Taal-verschijnselen" Nieuwe Taalgids 31 (1937) pp. 265 ff.

Sucre, Guillermo. "La metáfora del destino" Borges, El Poeta Universidad Nacional Autónoma de México 1967 pp. 40-56
Borges at first held (e.g. in "Las Kenningar"), similar to the Ultraístas, that the essential thing about poetry was metaphor, the search for something novel. Later, e.g., in "La Metáfora," he broke away from this view to hold that metaphor is a metaphysical necessity, is a special vision of the world, must relate to reality and not lose the emotion which engendered them. His poems tend to imitate actual speech. All true metaphors have existed forever, those we can still invent are false, and it is not worth the trouble to invent them. The voice of the poet when it is authentic has to be the voice of the universe. The world is thought of as a book, one more secret and unusual than the Bible or Koran. Borges states that perhaps the history of the universe is the history of the diverse intonation of various metaphors. He aspires to situate art in a superior order in which is implied the destiny of man, the history of the universe. The Ultraístas had only a purely technical, literary conception of metaphor whereas Borges conceives of it as a metaphysical necessity.

Suerbaum, Ulrich. Die Lyrik der Korrespondenzen. Cowleys Bildkunst und die Tradition der englischen Renaissancedichtung (Beiträge zur englischen Philologie, 40.) Bochum-Langendreer 1958

Sunesen, Bent. "Some Notes on Kinesthetic Imagery" Orbis Litterarum 9 (1945) 17-28

Susenbrotus, Johannes. Epitome troporum ac schematum grammaticorum et rhetoricorum 1540
Contains many tropes. Peacham based his work on this.

Svanascini, Osvaldo. "La metáfora in el superrealismo" Boletín de la Academia Argentina de Letras 16 (1947) 765-707, and 18 (1949) 61-147

Svennung, Josef. Catulls Bildersprache; vergleichende Stilstudien (Uppsala Universitets årsskrift 1945 no. 3) Lundequistska bokhandeln; Leipzig: O. Harrassowitz 1945

Swaim, Kathleen M. "Swift's Narrative Art: A Study of the Imagery and Structure of Gulliver's Travels" PhD diss. University of Pennsylvania 1966

Swanson, J. W. "On Models" British Journal for the Philosophy of Science 17 (1966) 297-311
A model is the imputation of structure. There is a non-symmetrical identity of structure between model and theory. An experimental rendering of M. Black's "filter" or "net" view of metaphor is given in terms of a "Rational Preference Rating (RPR)." The RPR's and commonplace knowledge of the model are transferred to the theory.

Sweet, Albert. "A Semantic Explication of Metaphysical Analogy" PhD diss. Emory University 1960-61

Swift, Jonathan (supposed author). The Art of Sinking in Poetry Edna Steeves, ed. New York: Russell & Russell 1968 (cf. Pope)

Szasz, Thomas. The Myth of Mental Illness New York: Hoeber-Harper 1967 esp. on game-models (part V).
The metally ill, especially the hysteric, can be treated as if he were playing games, putting on an act. Behavior is treated as if it were games played. A physical account is rejected. (cf. pretending)

Tagger, Theodor. [pseudonym is F. Bruckner] Das neue Geschlecht: Programmschrift gegen die Metapher. Berlin: H. Hochstim 1917 (cited in Stanley Hopper, Interpretation: The Poetry of Meaning p. 121)

Taillardat, Jean. Les images d'Aristophane; études de langue et de style Paris: Société d'édition Les Belles Lettres 1962 (1965) (Part in Greek)
Stress on content of metaphors. Figures are grouped on the basis of the concept they are to express. Different images may reveal the same concept. One identifies an image; observes its tone, class and social level; regards its originality or newness. The latter is difficult to determine for ancient authors. To be original, an image 1) must be unique, 2) must not be of a coarse tone, 3) must not enter a series wherein exchanging metaphors alternate, 4) renews a used image (a rejuvenation).

Takeda, S. Kant und das Problem der Analogie 1969

Tappert, Wilhelm. Bilder und Vergleiche aus dem Orlando innamorato Bojardos und dem Orlando Furioso Ariostos Marburg: N. G. Elwert 1886

Tarbet, David W. "The Fabric of Metaphor in Kant's Critique of Pure Reason" Journal of the History of Philosophy 6 (July 1968) 257-270
Kant's metaphors reveal his philosophy, habits of association, and personality. He uses extensively such metaphors as the flight or "dove" metaphor, military or battle metaphor, legal metaphor, etc.

Tarrant, Dorothy. "Greek Metaphors of Light" The Classical Quarterly 10 (Nov. 1960) 181-187 (vol. 54 of the continuous series)
Light is a metaphor of knowledge and used intersensually e.g. Sun is truth, and Plato's use of light in the Republic and Symposium.

_____. "Metaphors of Death in the Phaedo" Classical Review 2 (June 1952) 64-6 (vol. 66 of the continuous series)

Tate, Allen. "Hardy's Philosophic Metaphors" Southern Review 6 (1940) 99-108

_____. "Longinus" Lectures in Criticism Elliott Coleman, ed. Baltimore: Johns Hopkins University 1949 esp. p. 68

_____. "Tension in Poetry" Collected Essays Denver, Colorado: Alan Swallow 1959 (Also contains "Hardy's Philosophic Metaphors.")

Tate, J. "On the History of Allegorism" Classical Quarterly 28

(1934) 105-114

Taupin, R. L'Influence du symbolisme français sur la poésie américaine Paris: H. Champion 1929

Taylor, Archer. "A Metaphor of the Human Body in Literature and Tradition" Corona: Studies in celebration of the 80th birthday of Samuel Singer, Arno Schirokauer & Wolfgang Paulsen, eds., Duke University Press 1941 pp. 3-7

_____. Proverbial Comparisons and Similes from California Berkeley: University of California Press 1954

Taylor, Warren. "Tudor Figures of Rhetoric" PhD diss. University of Chicago 1937

Teale, Edwin W. "If You Want to Know What It's Like, Ask Wilstach" American Magazine 111 (May 1931) pp. 82 and 134
About Wilstach's Dictionary of Similes.

Temkin, Owsei. "Metaphors of Human Biology" Science and Civilization Robert Stauffer, ed. Madison: University of Wisconsin Press 1949 pp. 169-194
Metaphors are used in biology (e.g. atomic view of cell), and biological concepts are used metaphorically to apply to other areas of knowledge. Metaphors should not be confused with real similarities although they are often stimulating if they are.

Terrie, Henry L., Jr. "The Image of Chester in The Ambassadors" English Studies 46 (1965) 46-50

Terry, Arthur. "A Note on Metaphor and Conceit in Siglo de Oro" Bulletin of Hispanic Studies 31 (1954) 91-97
Before 1600 metaphors were based on Aristotle's ten categories of predication e.g. quality, quantity, relation, etc. For Gracián metaphor gives real correspondence and truth as based on universal analogy. "Ingegnio" is a metaphysical intellect able to perceive these analogies.

Tesauro, D. Emanuele. Il Cannocchiale Aristotelico Torino, 1670 (1654) (Bad Homburg: Gehlen 1968) (cf. E. Raimondi; Mazzeo 1964)
Introduction has summary and useful bibliography. The world must be investigated or overcome by wit (ingegno). God is a witty creator and wrote the book of nature in metaphors or conceits (acutezze). The world is mysterious, universal correspondence and analogy. Conceits are real laws of nature not just ornaments. To observe nature is to read off the metaphors of divine wisdom. Good metaphor needs a little mystery or obscurity (cf. I. T. Ramsey). The insane are especially gifted at making metaphors. He gives 8 types of

metaphor: 1) Proportion 2) Attribution 3) Equivocation 4) Animation 5) Hyperbole 6) Concise 7) Opposition 8) Deception. He applied categories of logic to metaphor: 1) simple clever figurative words corresponding to logical concepts 2) clever propositions or figurative sentences corresponding to judgements 3) clever arguments corresponding to syllogisms.

Thale, J. "Image and Theme: The Mill on the Floss" University of Kansas City Review 23 (Mar. 1957) 227-34

Thavenius, Jan. Diktens Bildspråk, En bibliografisk översikt Lund: Studentlitteratur 1966
A short bibliography on imagery.

Thomas, Dylan. The Collected Poems of Dylan Thomas New York: New Directions 1957 [1939]
"Death is all metaphors" (in "Altarwise by Owl-Light"). "Man be my metaphor" (in "If I Were Tickled by the Rub of Love"). Dylan Thomas is said to be the most metaphorical of poets.

_____. Letter to Henry Treece. H. Treece Dylan Thomas London 1956. Also "A Battle of Images" The Modern Tradition Richard Ellmann and C. Feidelson, Jr., eds. New York: Oxford University Press 1965 pp. 157-158
"A poem by myself needs a host of images, because its center is a host of images. I make one image--though 'make' is not the word; I let, perhaps, an image be 'made' emotionally in me and then apply to it what intellectual and critical forces I possess--let it breed another, let that image contradict the first, make, of the third image bred out of the other two together, a fourth contradictory image, and let them all, within my imposed formal limits, conflict. Each image holds within it the seed of its own destruction, and my dialectical method, as I understand it, is a constant building up and breaking down of the images that come out of the central seed, which is itself destructive and constructive at the same time. What I want to try to explain--and it's necessarily vague to me--is that the life in any poem of mine cannot move concentrically round a central image; the life must come out of the center; an image must be born and die in another; and any sequence of my images must be a sequence of creations, recreations, destructions, contradictions. I cannot...make a poem out of a single motivating experience...Out of the inevitable conflict of images--inevitable, because of the creative, recreative, destructive and contradictory nature of the motivating center, the womb of war--I try to make that momentary peace which is a poem."

Thomas, Lucien-Paul. Góngora et le góngorisme considerés dans leurs rapports avec le marinisme Paris 1911

Thomas, Owen. Metaphor and Related Subjects New York: Random House 1969
An initial sketch of an attempt to base metaphor on the linguistic notion of a "generative grammar" in accordance with Chomsky's work. Metaphor is regarded as a linguistic contradiction or the statement that one thing is another which it is not.

Thomas, Robert. "Zur historischen Entwicklung der Metapher im Griechischen" PhD diss. Erlangen, Friedrich-Alexander Universität 1891

Thompson, P. R. "Haiku Question and the Reading of Images" English Journal 56 (April 1967) 547-551
The Haiku helps one become sensitive to metaphors and images.

Thomson, J. F. "The Argument from Analogy and Our Knowledge of Other Minds" Mind 60 (July 1951) 336-350
The demands for justification of knowledge of other minds is mistaken. It is the projection of a small error in a context to the entire context. For example, the evidence for grief is in the grief situation. "It is only required that we should be able to put ourself [metaphorically] in what is, sufficiently for the purpose at hand, his [another's] situation."

Thornton, Weldon. Allusions in Ulysses Chapel Hill: University of North Carolina 1961. A list of allusions in Ulysses. An allusion is a type of metaphor which has an almost inexhaustible number of points of comparison.

Thrall, Wm. F., A. Hibbard, and C. Holman. A Handbook to Literature New York: Odyssey Press 1960

Thurber, James. "Here Lies Miss Groby" New Yorker 18 (March 1942) 14-15
A humorous treatment of figures. Miss Groby loved figures of speech most of all and probably never could detach herself enough from these to understand any great literature.

Tigner, S. S. "Plato's Philosophical Uses of the Dream Metaphor" American Journal of Philology 91 (April 1970) 204-212

Tilden, Nancy Lee. "An Analysis of Metaphor" PhD diss. University of California 1952
Metaphors are meaningful, cognitive, non-literal, non-assertive (i.e. not true or false), non-emotive namings and juxtapositions of "whole-meanings," i.e., all the connotations of a situation. What is named cannot be translated into literal language, and does not allow us to transcend or attain the unknowable, as is sometimes thought. Metaphor can name new kinds of experience,

and in that capacity serves as a valuable tool for philosophy. Her view is a modification of a "cognitive theory" and "emotive theory" of metaphor, both of which are discussed.

Tilghman, B. R. *The Expression of Emotion in the Visual Arts: A Philosophical Inquiry* The Hague: Nijhoff 1970
On Wittgenstein's notion of seeing-as.

Tindall, William. *The Literary Symbol* Indiana University Press 1962 esp. p. 206
A discussion of metaphor, symbol, allegory and similar terms in relation to literature. "Metaphor, an analogy in which the elements compared are at once similar and dissimilar, may take the form of an equation of stated elements or an image by which one term is presented while the other remains implicit. Unlike allegory, the metaphysical metaphor generally consists of a complete equation. It may range from convenient expression...to essential embodiment..." He concludes the work with the quotation from Valéry, "A symbolist work has no certain meaning."

Todasco, Ruth Taylor. "The Humanism of Henry James: A Study of the Relation Between Theme and Imagery in the Later Novels" PhD diss. Texas Technological College 1965

Todorov, Tzvetan. "Tropes et figures" In *To Honor Roman Jakobson: Essays on the Occasion of His 70th Birthday* 3 vols. The Hague: Mouton 1967 vol. 3, pp. 2006-2023

Tomkins, Muriel W. "Critical and Philosophical Theories of Metaphor and Their Implications for the Teaching of English: A Perspective on Canadian High School Textbooks" PhD diss. Harvard University 1968
The modern school texts and school aids in the U.S. and Canada examined follow an inadequate 18th century theory of metaphor. She gives a number of aids for teaching metaphor in high school, e.g., relate slang to metaphor, relate metaphor to other figures, distinguish types of metaphor, etc.

Toperoff, Sam. "Whitman's Raft Metaphor" *Emerson Society Quarterly* 38 (1965) 130-132
On Whitman's "Crossing Brooklyn Ferry."

Torre, Guillermo de. *Literaturas europeas de vanguardia* Madrid 1925 (Summarized in Palley)
He gives four kinds of metaphor relations: 1) sense to sense 2) static to dynamic 3) animate to inanimate (called "metagogia" or the pathetic fallacy) 4) metaphors having heavenly or geographic elements.

Toulmin, Stephen. *Philosophy of Science* New York: Harper 1953

Influenced by Wittgenstein he gives an account of how laws, theories, maps, models and metaphors function in science. He stresses their actual functioning in the specific contexts, including linguistic contexts, from which they arise. He states, "The adoption of a new theory involves a language-shift." Models provide a new way of looking. He discusses "seeing-as."

_____. Foresight and Understanding Bloomington: Indiana University Press 1961

Trawick, Buckner. "The Moon Metaphor in Browning's 'One Word More'" Notes and Queries 6 (1959) p. 448

Trickett, Rachel. "The Augustan Pantheon Mythology and Personification in Eighteenth-Century Poetry" Essays and Studies N.S. 6 (1953) 71-86

Trier, Jost. Venus. Etymologien um das Futterlaub Köln/Graz 1963 Chapt. on "Homologie und Metapher" pp. 175 ff. (Source: L. Söll)

Tripāthī, Rāmamūrti. Vyañjanā aura navīna kavitā 1957 (Series: Nagari Pracharini Sabha, Benares. Sāstra vijñāna granthmālā, 2)
On Hindi poetics and metaphor.

_____. Lakshanā aura usakā Hindī kāvya meṃ prasāra. (Same series as above, no. 6)

Trowbridge, Hoyt. "Joseph Warton on the Imagination" Modern Philology 35 (1937) 73-87

Tryphon. Quoted in L. Spengel, Rhetores Graeci Leipzig 1856 (Frankfurt 1966) vol. 3, p. 192
"Metaphor is from an object of reference which has already a proper name applied to it to another which also has already a proper name applied to it. Catachresis is from an object of reference having a proper name applied to it to another object without any proper name of its own."

Trzynadlowskiego, J. "Od mitu do metafory" Prace Polonistyczne 4 (1946) 157-177

Tschiževskij, Dmitrij. "Umkehrung der dichterischen Metaphern, Topoi und anderer Stilmittel" Die Welt der Slaven Vierteljahrsschrift für Slavistik (Wiesbaden) 6 (1961) 337-354
Reversals of figures of speech involve meanings or images being reversed, interchanged or replaced by their opposites. The reverse of personification is shown by comparing a drunkard with a wine barrel. In some ages snake refers to Satan

but sometimes to wisdom. The author traces throughout world literature some reversals of bee when used metaphorically. Sometimes these reversals are brought about by new knowledge or lack of knowledge of the object. Some reversals are connected with deep philosophical motifs such as with the contrast of light and dark or day and night. Reversals of content occur to express serious new thoughts (which are occasionally representative of the philosophy of an era), to provide irony, merely as a game, to attempt to say something poetic requiring ambivalence and so expressing something having a special value.

Tuch. De Aeschyli figurata elocutione Wittenberg Programm 1869

Tumlirz, Karl. Die Lehre von den Tropen und Figuren nebst einer kurzgefassten deutschen Metrik. Zum Gebrauche für den Unterricht an höheren Lehranstalten. Prague: H. Dominicus 1832

Tupper, James W. "Tropes and Figures in Anglo-Saxon Prose" PhD diss. Johns Hopkins University 1897
The Anglo-Saxon metaphor was originally confined to one word. The elaborated metaphor is rare as is the sustained metaphor. He cites Gerber's classification of metaphor into 1) Picture-figures 2) Phonetic figures 3) Figures of thought. A metaphor is a name transfer to a different object based on resemblance.

Turbayne, Colin Murray. The Myth of Metaphor New Haven: Yale University Press 1962 (Reviews by D. Munro, J. Davis, W. Mays, A. Mardiros, F. Sparshott, J. Kaminsky, C. Grant, C. M. Myers, Olscamp.)
He attempts to show "the remedy provided by becoming aware of metaphor; and second, that the metaphysics that still dominates science and enthralls the minds of men [i.e. mechanism] is nothing but a metaphor, and a limited one." Metaphors can be acceptable if one is conscious of them. He treats natural events "as-if" they compose a "universal language," and explores this metaphor.

Turčány, Viliam. "Rým a metafora" (Vzťahy medzi zložkami v básnickej skladbe) Litteraria z Historickej Poetiky II (Bratislava) 8 (1965) 76-155

Turcato, Bruno. "Struttura ed evoluzione delle prime metafore lorchiane" Quaderni Ibero-Americani 27 (Dec. 1961) 129-142
"Metafora pura" is grammatical metaphor, antonym or apposition. "Metafora funzionale" is extra-grammatical, structural and dependent on its ramification in the poetry as such.

Turnbull, George. Treatise on Ancient Painting 1740
His theory of universal analogy is applied to painting.

_____. Principles of Moral Philosophy London 1740
The imagination like a stereoscope superimposes the analogous worlds of nature and moral truth to produce the real three-dimensional universe. Language comes from sensible objects and pictures moral concepts. The study of metaphorical words coincides with philosophy for they reveal the proper material images for exhibiting moral sentiments in an agreeable form.

Turner, Joseph. "Maxwell on the Method of Physical Analogy" British Journal for the Philosophy of Science 6 (1955-56) 226-38

Turner, Myron. "The Imagery of Wallace Stevens and Henry Green" Wisconsin Studies in Contemporary Literature 8 (1967) 60-77

Tuve, Rosemond. Elizabethan and Metaphysical Imagery Chicago: University of Chicago Press 1947 (1961) esp. pp. 121 ff.
An image is the accurate transliteration of a sense impression. It should give us immediate sense experience.

_____. "Imagery and Logic: Ramus and the Metaphysical Poets" Journal of the History of Ideas 3 (Oct. 1942) 365-400

_____. Images and Themes in Five Poems by Milton Cambridge, Mass: Harvard University Press 1957

_____. "Imitation and Images" Elizabethan Poetry: Modern Essays in Criticism Paul J. Alpers, ed. New York: Oxford University Press 1967 pp. 41-62

Tyler, Parker. 'Metaphor in the Jungle' and Other Poems Prairie City, Illinois: James A. Decker or Village Press 1940

Uhrhan, Evelyn E. "Linguistic Analysis of Góngora's Baroque Style" PhD diss. University of Illinois 1950 (Abstracted in H. R. Kahane and A. Pietrangeli, Descriptive Studies in Spanish Grammar Universtiy of Illinois Press 1954 pp. 179-241) "The purpose of this study is to determine according to the methods of descriptive linguistics, the principles of syntax which characterize the Baroque style of Góngora and thus the principles of Spanish Baroque style." She analyzes the Soledad Primera of Góngora and gives the following principles of Baroque style (in order of frequency): Substitution, Coupling, Separation, Transposition, Asymmetry, Modification.

Ullmann, Etienne de. "La transposition sensorielle chez Leconte de Lisle" Le Français Moderne 14 (1946) 23-40

_____. "L'art de la transposition dans la poésie de Théophile Gautier" Le Français Moderne 15 (1947) 265-286

Ullmann, Stephen de. "Composite Metaphors in Longfellow's Poetry" Review of English Studies 18 (April 1942) 219-228 Contains a useful bibliography on synaesthesia. Synaesthesia was regarded as illusion, a type of thought, sense transfer, a revealing aspect, a conceit, a literary device. Examples are transubstantiation, blue sounds, vowel colors, etc. Longfellow's composite metaphors of this sort are natural, spontaneous and convincingly effective.

_____. The Image in the Modern French Novel Cambridge: Cambridge University Press 1960

_____. "L'image littéraire: quelques questions de méthode" Langue et littérature 1960 pp. 41-60

_____. "The Nature of Imagery" Language and Style Oxford 1964 pp. 174-201

_____. The Principles of Semantics: A Linguistic Approach to Meaning 2nd ed. London 1957 (1st ed. 1951) Metaphors are transfers based on substantial meaning or emotive similarity and are conscious and deliberate transfers serving aesthetic purposes. A distinction is made between 1) conceptual synaesthesia (actual sensation) and 2) imaginal synaesthesia (imagined sensation).

_____. "Romanticism and Synaesthesia: A Comparative Study of Sense Transfer in Keats and Byron" PMLA 60 (1945) 811-827

_____. Style in the French Novel Cambridge 1957 esp. 189-209 and 210-262 (New York: Barnes and Noble 1964) He quotes Proust, "I believe that metaphor alone is able to give a kind of eternity to style." Metaphor is an objective or emotive association between two terms. It is often not clearly distinguishable from other figures. It may be classified in terms of relations between concrete and abstract. He discusses the imagery of Giono, Bazin, Sartre. Imagery has novelty, expressiveness, sensuousness.

_____. "Synaesthesia in the English Decadents" Egyetemes Philologiai Közlöny (Budapest) 63 (1939) 173-181. A summary of the article in English is on p. 181.
A supplement to his article on Oscar Wilde's synaesthesia (Englische Studien vol. 72, 1938). Synesthesia was a literary device devoid of intersensorial association. It gave atmosphere, illustrated emotions to suggest illusions of opium-smokers. It led to the eccentricity of its use, however.

Ungewitter, Otto. Die landwirtschaftlichen Bilder und Metaphern in den poetischen Büchern des Alten Testaments Progr. Königsberg 1885

Upton, Albert. Design for Thinking Stanford: Stanford University Press 1961 esp. 75-81 on "Metaphor"
A transfer from one "universe of discourse" to another which creates a new "meta-universe of discourse." It is based on a four term, genus related, analogy or proportion. He illustrates: "The Lord is my shepherd" (A:B::C:D)

Animal Husbandry:		Religion:
Metaphorical Universe		Contextual Universe
A. The Shepherd		C. The Lord
tends (the ratio)	=	encourages (the ratio)
B. The Sheep		D. The Psalmist

(The meta-universe term or relevant relation is "promotes the welfare of," which includes the two ratios.)

_____. "Linguistic Approach to Problems of Analysis and Interpretation" Journal of Communication 14 (June 1964) 118-22
Metaphor and similarity form the basis of all behavior and are methods of framing hypotheses in science. Metaphorical analysis develops reading and writing skills. The student is required to interpret a passage in terms of a nine place diagram of metaphor (See Design for Thinking entry for diagram).

_____. "Reading and Intelligence" Claremont College Reading Conference Yearbook 28th yearbook (1964) 137-43
In reference to his diagram of metaphor in his Design for Thinking he mentions six exercises for the interpreter of a metaphor: 1) underline the metaphorical term 2) name the universe of discourse from which the terms are borrowed 3) select a name parallel in style or level of abstraction to the above 4) name four terms of the analogy 5) formulate in language appropriate to each universe of discourse the relation

obtaining between the things mentioned above 6) formulate in terms sufficiently abstract to include these two previous formulations as special cases, the relation represented by the equality sign which here means abstract similarity.

_____, and Richard Samson. Creative Analysis New York: E. P. Dutton 1963
Exercises in metaphor and analogy based on Upton's Design for Thinking.

Upton, Anne. Workbook for Design for Thinking Palo Alto, California: Pacific Books 1961

Urbach, O. "Betrachtung über das Metaphorische" Die Literatur; Monatsschrift für Literaturfreunde 43 (Oct. 1940) 14-17
Metaphor in the narrowest sense is a picture of an object. Every trope is a transference, an exchange of the most readily available, actual name with an expression less actual and further removed. In a novella Tieck presents a critic who wants to avoid everything metaphorical because when one compares one object with another he is already lying. We use metaphorical license. Science rests on metaphorical concepts. Behind every term are countless images, often misleading, that can lead us to make false comparisons. Valéry suggests that thinking, thoughts, sentences expressing thoughts are metaphors, that is, "the broken pieces of some unknown games...that take place in the interior of the soul?" Goethe says "The human being never understands how anthropomorphic he is." He tries to personify what he does not understand and tries to personify nature. Only when an image or metaphor is not one we are accustomed to does it seem funny to us. Biese (1893) spoke of the metaphorical in the child's imagination: "The childish imagination works ceaselessly to give life to what is lifeless, to transform that piece of wood into a dog or another animal or a human." A child e.g. shares its cake with dolls. Metaphor connects something unknown until now to his already established world of notions. The metaphorical is regarded as the active application of the creative imagination. Metaphor incarnates the spiritual and spiritualizes the physical, internalizes the external and vice versa. Metonymy interchanges time and space, cause and effect, material and object. Paul Valéry is quoted as saying that the essence of consciousness is the constant emptying, getting rid of everything that appears in it; all things become interchangeable. For Valéry truth is the word, for all things are interchangeable, interconnected and therefore are metaphors. Biese said that what is intelligent and clever is based mainly on skillful and surprising analogies. Nietzsche's writing illustrates such surprising comparison. For Urbach, metaphor governs our whole thinking. The myths of the ancients are often hard to understand because we are no longer able to understand the metaphorical elements in them e.g. when the

Greeks thought of the world as water or fire. Our modern notions of force and matter are no less metaphorical. These notions too seduce us into making myths. Plato's "Ideas" and Leibniz's monads are metaphors which they never got beyond. But often what is meant by the metaphors can only be indicated indirectly and perhaps metaphors reveal a truth in themselves. He agrees with Biese that all thinking and writing is metaphorical.

Urban, Wilbur M. Language and Reality New York: Macmillan 1961 (1939) (Review by Britton, de Laguna) (cf. Shibles 1963, 1971) The understanding of metaphor depends on a theory of language. Language passes through three stages: 1) adherent, onomatopoeic or copy stage, 2) analogical or metaphorical, 3) symbolic. Knowledge appropriate to each is: 1) by acquaintance, 2) by description, 3) by interpretation. Meaning exists only in a speech community in which meanings are acknowledged. Words are authenticated in discourse. They are true insomuch as they are communicated because communication implies acknowledgement of meanings. Verification is provided by meaningful discourse. "Radical metaphor" is the unconscious, natural, analogical method of speech construction by means of which words gain new meanings and uses (2nd stage above). Metaphor is the primary law of speech construction involving a detachment from the adherent stage. It is a transfer. The "radical metaphor" is intuitive and self-authenticating. It leads to the symbolic stage (3rd above), the "fundamental metaphor" which is a form of symbolism (cf. Cassirer's "symbolic forms"). The symbol creates various universes of discourse ("symbolic forms") or acknowledged speech communities. (It has an insight-giving function.) Throughout the three stages the word becomes more abstract, symbolic and less close to reality. The metaphor of the universe of discourse of metaphysics is called the "fundamental metaphor." It is presupposed by the other universes of discourse and represents fundamental, all-encompassing aspects of an experience, e.g. "man is a machine."

Metaphor comes about when words from different universes of discourse are combined in a sentence. Each term is seen intuitively in the light of the other. Intuition is regarded as expression. Intuition is required to represent objective and subjective values. Reality is only known by language. Symbols are intuitive and not consciously designed. By literal is only meant that an expression belongs in a certain universe of discourse. It is literal in its universe of discourse.

Ushenko, A. P. "Metaphor" Thought 30 (Autumn 1955) 421-39 In metaphor tenor and vehicle are related by a "ground" on the basis of analogy to form a "resultant" in its "bearings" (i.e. context). "In actual employment of metaphors the objectionable part of their excessive meaning happens to be the effectively repressed [because of their contextual determination]." Dead metaphor lost its force by becoming detached from its context. The <u>use</u> of metaphor is what is acceptable about metaphor. Metaphor is not an isolatable figure of speech and so cannot be paraphrased. It is "alive" not fixed. It gives recurring novelty, does not wear out when reread. It is a non-paraphrasable "metamorphosis." He discusses Aristotle's, and I. A. Richards' theories of metaphor in detail.

Väänänen, Veikko. "Métaphores rajeunies et métaphores ressuscitées" <u>VIII Congresso internazionale di studi romanzi</u> 1956. Atti, vol. 2. Firenze 1959 pp. 471-476

Vaihinger, Hans. <u>The Philosophy of "As If": A System of the Theoretical, Practical and Religious Fictions of Mankind</u> C. K. Ogden, trans. New York: Barnes & Noble 1968 [1924] A discussion of types of fictions or "as-ifs" such as: abstractive, schematic, paradigmatic, utopian, type-fictions, symbolic or analogical, juristic, personificatory, summational (general ideas), heuristic, ethical, mathematical, unjustified transference, the concept of infinity, atoms, scientific fictions, etc. He presents also a history and theory of fictions. For historical confirmation he discusses especially Kant, Forberg, Lange and Nietzsche. He states, "The real tragedy of life is that the most valuable ideas are from the point of view of reality, worthless." According to his principle of fictionalism, "An idea whose theoretical untruth or incorrectness, and therewith its falsity, is admitted, is not for that reason practically valueless and useless; for such an idea, in spite of its theoretical nullity may have great practical importance." "The object of the world of ideas as a whole is not the portrayal of reality--this would be an utterly impossible task--but rather to provide us with an <u>instrument for finding our way about more easily in this world</u>." "The immense work of modern science reduces all existence, which in the last analysis is absolutely incomprehensible, to an entirely subjective and purely fictional standard." "Truth is really merely the most expedient type of error." Vaihinger combines Kantianism with pragmatism in developing his theory of <u>as if</u>. We often become captivated by our fictions or models: "Yet, though the contradictions in ideas to which we have grown accustomed are no longer noticed, they are at once recognized in new constructs." "It is an error to suppose that an absolute truth, an absolute criterion of knowledge and behavior, can be discovered. The higher aspects of life are based upon noble delusions." Man has a tendency to take his fictions as dogmas. By "fiction" he means ideas, schemes, hypotheses, as-if's, substitutes, pictures, equations, etc. We should be conscious of our fictions and distinguish between those which are counterfactual and impossible (though helpful) and those which are possible and so hypotheses. He gives the following examples of fictions: nominalism or the view that all general ideas are fictions, Greek mythology, Plato's myths, Kant's "thing-in-itself" and his "regulative ideas," religious and theological ideas, ideals, Herbart's associationism, Forberg's religion of as-if, Nietzsche's theory of fictions, thought, the mind-body distinction, all mental processes, classifications, abstractive or neglective fictions e.g. synecdoche, Adam Smith's view that all human behavior is motivated by egoism, zero, inertia, infinity, the normal average man, time, linguistic "roots," "branches" of languages, schematic drawings, the imaginary or postulated city, isolated man, isolated state, paradigmatic fictions, imaginary cases, rhetorical fictions, type fictions, substance, Aristotle's notion of potential existence, society as an organism, soul, energy, psychic activity, gravitation, force, cause, concepts of theological metaphysics, theology, conservation of energy, freedom, mathematical circles, diety, immortality, infinite perfection, ideals, imagination, vital force, mathematical points without extension, lines without breadth, surfaces without depth, spaces without content, constant velocity, consciousness in general, three dimensional space, duty to one's self, self-caused, negative numbers, irrational numbers, imaginary numbers, Cartesian co-ordinates, thing-in-itself, inner-outer applied to mental-physical, differentials in Calculus, matter, atoms, the Alpha body as the immovable central point of absolute space, the center of gravity, action at a distance (he states, "Theoretical mechanics is for the most part a tissue of such purely arbitrary ideas" and "All mathematics, indeed, is only a device, which tells us nothing about what actually exists."), thing, attribute, energy, Linnaean system of classes, most of the phrases of social intercourse are fictions e.g. "Yours truly," names, and the assumption that names must denote or refer to objects, violence, social contract, man, sugar, white, Parmenides' Being as a sphere, the medieval notion of *suppositio*, treatment of a, b, c, etc. as numbers, etc.

_____. "Aus Zwei Festschriften, Beiträge zum Verständnis der Analytik und der Dialektik in der *Kritik der reinen Vernunft*" *Kantstudien* 7 (1902) 99-119
He states that Kant is a metaphorician (*Metaphoriker*).

Valentine, C. W. "The Function of Images in the Appreciation of Poetry" *British Journal of Psychology* 14 (Oct. 1923) 164-191
Images do have such a function but not with all poems. It may not be appropriate to look for images in a poem containing metaphors. Images come *in the reading of* a poem (cf. Hester).

Valesio, Paolo. "La linguistica come metaforismo" *Arte, critica filosofia* (Studi di estetica I) Luciano Anceschi, ed. Bologna: R. Patron, 1965 pp. 327-335
In addition to pure linguistics and applied linguistics there should be a third sector, that of "linguistics as metaphorism." Insomuch as literary criticism and philosophy use linguistic terms pseudo-linguistically or non-technically they use them metaphorically e.g. "style." Such metaphorical uses are imprecise and lead to confusion. The metaphor is born when one assigns to a given word a new semantic content, associated in more or less strict fashion with the original semantic content. There is a fundamental meaning and added meaning.

Van Buren, James. "The Servant-Son Metaphor in the Poetry of George Herbert" PhD diss. Kansas State University 1967

Van Deusen, Marshall. A Metaphor for the History of American Criticism University of Uppsala Essays and Studies on American Language and Literature no. 13. Uppsala: Lundequistska 1961

Van Ghent, Dorothy. "Image-Types and Antithetical Structures in the Works of Keats" PhD diss. University of California 1942

Van Steenburgh, Elston W. "Metaphor" Journal of Philosophy 62 (Nov. 18, 1965) 678-88
With perspective metaphor one thing is a perspective of or seen as another. It is pictorial and cannot be literally paraphrased. It is cognitive since it relates qualities. Precinding metaphor, or system metaphor, is not perspectival since it presents only one thing plus an unknown such as "substratum" or "god."

_____. "A Philosophical Analysis of Metaphor Applied to George Berkeley's Theory of Meaning" PhD diss. University of Michigan 1960
Metaphor is a compressed simile involving a clash of literal meanings. All but its psychological effects can be reduced to literal statement. "Philosophical metaphor," however, cannot be paraphrased or observed or ostensively defined. Nevertheless no final definition of metaphor can be given.

Varinot, A. Dictionnaire des métaphores françaises Paris: Arthus-Bertrand 1818

Veca, S. "Metafora presupposizione e struttura in Kant" Aut Aut 103 (1967-1968) 33-49

Vela, Arqueles. Análisis de la Expresión Literaria Mexico 1965 ch. 18 "Metáfora y enigma" pp. 101-119
Poetry is produced by transpositions of reality to make intelligible internal processes. We use metaphor transforming real elements into metaphoric equivalents yielding results more complex than daily speech. The metaphoric nature of language is created in the process of moving from objective intellectual communication (or search for causes) to that which expresses the internal world, in an attempt to give form to the intensity of experience in order to bring it to life again by means of words. Metaphors express emotion and when they fail we resort to more primitive forms such as the caress or cry. In rendering the world we proceed from representation to comparison to the third phase of alteration of the sense of the words in the creative poetic act which is effected by the image. The expressive materials which compose the image leave behind their own meanings, corresponding

to objective experiences, acquiring a new meaning emanating from the fusion of the determining elements of the metaphoric composition, although in the complexity of the transposition some materials retain their original attributes. The origin of metaphor is not in an attempt to conceal or deform thought (as Ortega says) but rather the origin is in the esthetic beginnings of knowing profoundly the power of the word and its shades of meaning. Metaphor is too diverse to classify or establish a nomenclature for. The terms of a metaphor fuse in too many ways involving too many diverse inner states to allow classification. Whereas metaphor fuses and integrates elements, symbol eliminates them thus producing enigma (See title of article. Enigma refers to symbol). The symbol veils its attributes in enigmas. Its meaning is not as immediately evident in expressive connotations as it is in metaphor. Metaphor more than symbol constitutes part of the properties and attributes it represents. The conceit is the image of objective experience reflected in the individual conscience. Poetry represents the world neither as it is nor as it looks but as it is lived.

Veldtrup, Josef. "Betrachtungen zum Problem der Metapher" Deutschland: Die literarische Zeitung der Deutschen Akademie für Sprache und Dichtung 2 (Jan. 1951) 1ff. (Source unverified)

Vendler, Helen. "Yeats' Changing Metaphors for the Other World" Modern Drama 7 (1964) 308-321

Vendôme, Matthew of. Ars Versificatoria Les Arts Poétiques du XIIe et du XIIIe siècle E. Faral, ed. Paris 1924 pp. 109-193 on tropes and figures.
A traditional view which is like Ad Herennium, Quintilian, Bede, Isidore. Vendôme says he follows Isidore's views.

Venturi, Luigi. Le similitudini dantesche ordinate illustrate e confrontate; saggio di studi di Luigi Venturi Firenze: G. C. Sansoni 1874
On similes in Dante.

Vercel, Roger. "Lexique comparé des métaphores dans le théâtre de Corneille et de Racine" Caen: A. Olivier 1927. Thèse complémentaire, Univ. de Caen

Verdenius, W. J. "The Metaphorical Sense of aipus" "Mnemosyne 6 (1953) p. 115

Vesey, G. N. "Seeing and Seeing-As" Proceedings of the Aristotelian Society N.S. 56 (1956) 109-124
All seeing is seeing-as. "I saw it, but I didn't see it as anything," seems self-contradictory. A judgement is involved in our seeing something.

Vetter, Harold. Language Behavior and Psychopathology Chicago: Rand McNally 1969 esp. pp. 141-164
A presentation and analysis of language deviations in psychiatric patients. Most psychotherapy relies on language as a means of effecting a cure. But not enough research has been done in this area. The chapter "New Word Coinage in the Psychopathological Context" presents research on neologisms; and "Language Behavior and Blindness" deals in part with synaesthetic imagery in relation to the experience of the blind. The book contains a useful bibliography.

_____, ed. Language Behavior in Schizophrenia Springfield, Illinois: C. Thomas 1968 esp. pp. 58-74, 153-181. Has useful bibliography.
Includes the following articles: 1) Thomas Eliseo, "Figurative and Literal Misinterpretations of Words by Process and Reactive Schizophrenics" 2) David Forrest, "Poesis and the Language of Schizophrenia."

Vianu, Tudor. "Quelques observations sur la métaphore poétique" Poetics, Poetyka... 2 vols. Donald Davie et al., eds. The Hague: Mouton and Co. 1961 vol. 1, pp. 297-304
The metaphor is the product of a substitution for the precise term, a term to designate an object. The solution of the problem of interpretation, however, is not merely the discovery of the term substituted for. Metaphor is not merely a guessing-game for the precise term. The metaphor is diffuse in meaning, has many levels, e.g. latent and expressed content, is concrete and figurative at the same time, is cumulative in building up images, and it does not have limited meaning--which is its most important trait. Allegory may be transformed into a scientific or philosophic statement. But metaphor has no conclusion. It may be interpreted in a never-ending number of ways. Poetry would cease to exist if the profound meaning of poetic interpretation were reducible to a chain of notions or a philosophic proposition. Scholastic interpretations of great metaphorical works sometimes fall into this error. An entire poetic work may be considered a metaphor e.g. The Divine Comedy, Faust, King Lear.

_____. Problemele metaforei şi alte studii de stilistică (Reviews by V. Makarov, I. Lazarescu, I. Dumitrescu, L. Gáldi) Has three studies of verb tenses. All articles were previously published in Limba Romînă but the study of metaphor pp. 9-17 is new.

_____. Los problemas de la metáfora Traducida por Manuel Serrano Pérez. University of Buenos Aires 1967
Selections from the first part of Problemele metaforei şi alte studii de stilistică

Vico, Giambattista. The New Science T. Bergin and M. Fisch, trans. Ithaca: Cornell University Press 1968 (cf. Dorfles 1969, Edie 1969)
There are three kinds of language 1) wordless or visual thinking, gesture 2) "heroic" language of similitudes and metaphors 3) human language of conventional institutionalized expressions. Metaphor is a real, authentic and cognitive method which constitutes our world and life. It is an element of interpersonal communication having historical perspective of earlier or pre-conscious insight. It is not just a linguistic formula. Language and metaphor partly constitute and determine thought. "Every metaphor...[preconsciously formed] is a fable in brief." Words are carried over from the physical to apply to the mind and spirit.

Vigfusson, Gudbrand and F. Y. Powell, eds. and translators. "On the Figures and Metaphors (kenningar) of Old Northern Poetry" Corpus Poeticum Boreale 2 vols. New York: Russell & Russell 1965 (1883) vol. 2 pp. 447-486
A list of the metaphors and kenningar which are used, e.g. the breast is mind's house, memory's sanctuary, the lurking-place of thought, the shore of the mind, the bark of laughter, the hall of the heart.

Vinsauf, Geoffrey of. Poetria Nova and Documentum de Modo et Arte Dictandi et Versificandi Edmund Faral, ed. pp. 287-8 (Documentum... Roger Parr, trans. Milwaukee, Wisc: Marquette University Press 1968)
He gives about 65 figures of speech.

Vio, Tommaso de (called Cardinal Gaetano). The Analogy of Names and the Concept of Being A. Bushinski, trans. Pittsburgh: Duquesne University Press 1953

Viravsky. Uber die Metaphern bei Homer und Apollonius von Rhodus Gymnas. Programm, Taus 1878

Virtanen, Reino. "Proust's Metaphors from the Natural and the Exact Sciences" PMLA 69 (Dec. 1954) 1038-59
Study of about 300 scientific metaphors.

Vischer, Friedrich T. von. "Das Symbol" Philosophische Aufsätze Edward Zeller, ed. Leipzig 1887 pp. 153-193
He gives the relation between metaphor and symbol.

_____. Aesthetik, oder Wissenschaft des Schönen 6 vols. Stuttgart 1846-1857

Vogt-Terhorst, Antoinette. Der bildliche Ausdruck in den Predigten Johann Taulers Breslau: M. & H. Marcus 1920
About metaphors esp. transcendental and religious ones.

Voigt, Hermann. "Gleichnisse und Metaphern in Shakespeares Dramen und in seinen Quellenschriften" PhD diss. Strassburg 1908

Voigt, Walter. *Die Bildersprache Thomas Wolfes, mit besonderer Berücksichtigung der Metaphorik des amerikanischen Englisch* München: M. Hueber 1960

Volkmann, Richard. *Die Rhetorik der Griechen und Römer in systematischer Übersicht* Leipzig: Teubner 1885 (Also Hildesheim: Olms 1962)

Volkov, N. N. "Chto takoe metafora" 1927 (Source: Korol'kov)

Voltaire, François de. "Métaphore" *Oeuvres Complètes* 1785 vol. 48 pp. 387-391
Metaphor is a mark of genius, a lively and subtle representation of objects, emotions, truth by means of its sensible character. It should be unmixed and used with restraint. Metaphor is used in the Orient without restraint or art.

Vonessen, Franz. "Die Ontologische Struktur der Metapher" *Zeitschrift für philosophische Forschung* 13 (1959) 397-419
Logic is based on unnoticed metaphors. Logicians banish metaphor from their interests. Their logic is too static to deal with metaphor. But actually no concept lacks the vivid visual element. In metaphor it is not that one set concept is replaced by or related to another. Words are not metaphorical, only contexts and sentences are. The metaphorical function is gained from the whole of the judgment. It is gained from the speakers, the subject of the statement and the word use. No statement is completely literal nor can a metaphor be replaced by the literal. No metaphor alone is comprehensible but is based on a "collective metaphor" (i.e. a *Sprachbild*) that appears to be uninterpreted and unnoticed. A *Sprachbild* consists of certain essential image structures which imperceptibly govern all chance expressions. Certain immediately comprehensible philosophical metaphors can only be grasped in connection with other figurative expressions. Mental phenomena are often rendered metaphorically. They complement one another [or perhaps they are circular?]. Metaphor: *Sprachbild*:: detail: whole picture. The whole is effective and lively in detail even when it remains unknown or unnoticed. The imagination creates and reveals reality by using the *Sprachbild* as the naturally given method of uncovering the essential structures of the world. If individual metaphors are poor and similes weak it is because our understanding of the essence, our ability to see the whole, is never sufficient. There is some deep necessity in the creation of metaphors, e.g. language and world view have to be in masculine and feminine form. The reality of phenomena arises from the union of the two possibilities.

Etymological hints, unintentional idioms, consciously intended and artful metaphors of poets are all in agreement. They all reveal the same essence of being. The philosophical task is to explore the realm where the possibility of simultaneous difference and comparability exists. The goal is a study of "symbolic imagination" and a new way of looking at things. He cites Binswanger's view that metaphor is best worked out as the actual language of phenomenology. The precedence of the realm of the senses is said to be effectively called in question by his studies. Schelling is cited as regarding metaphor as a tautology rather than as transference. A metaphor does not say something different than what it means.

Vonessen, Marielene. "Die Kunstmetapher in der Frühromantik" PhD diss. Köln 1950

Vooys, C. G. N. de. "Iets over de metaphoor" De Nieuwe Taalgids vol. 4, pp. 45ff. (Source: Stutterheim 1941)

Vossler, Karl. Symbolische Denkart und Dichtung Berlin 1934
Vossler believed that it is metaphor which must be the only concern of the linguist in his investigation of semantic change.

_____. Gesammelte Aufsätze zur Sprachphilosophie München 1923

Wäber, Gottfried. "Die Bedeutung der Proustschen Metapher" Die Neueren Sprachen 14 (Sept. 1965) 431-437

Wackernagel, Wilhelm. Poetik, Rhetorik und Stilistik Akademische Vorlesungen 1836 (Halle: L. Sieber 1906; Halle: Waisenhauses 1873 esp. pp. 394-396)
He mentions Quintilian and Cicero on metaphor. Metaphor is presented as an abbreviated simile. In metaphor an abstract idea is exchanged for its concrete counterpart. Metaphor can reside in any word and any part of speech. Parable results from a simile that has been expanded to an even more sensuous vividness.

Waern, Ingrid. 'Ges Ostea', the Kenning in Pre-Christian Greek Poetry PhD diss. Uppsala: Almquist and Wiksell 1951

_____. "Zur Synästhesie in griechischer Dichtung" Eranos: Acta Philologica Suecana 50 (1952) 14-22

Wagner, Christoph T. "Die vielen Metaphern und das eine Modell der Plotinischen Metaphysik" PhD diss. Ruprecht-Karl Universität, Heidelberg 1957

Wagner, Linda W. "Metaphor and William Carlos Williams" University Review 31 (Oct. 1964) 43-9
"Symbolic metaphor" is the "polysemous" use of a noun i.e. it has its many meanings which interrelate and support each other. Metaphor is a juxtaposition as is montage. It renders the abstract concrete. Karl Shapiro is wrong in saying that William Carlos Williams does not use metaphors in his poetry.

Wahl, Jean. "Poésie et philosophie" Revista di Estetica 1 (1956) 108-111

Wajid, R. A. "Metaphor and Aesthetic Distance" Darshana International 7 (Jan. 1967) 61-67
Metaphor helps create aesthetic and psychical distance. It permits combinations which disregard practical logic. Although metaphor cannot be completely analyzed in terms of aesthetic distance the tenor and vehicle should have both continuity and distance. Context and content of the specific metaphor needs to be examined.

_____. Reply to Hester's "Metaphor and Aspect Seeing" Journal of Aesthetics and Art Criticism 26 (Spring 1968) 389-390
Hester ignores the paradoxical nature of metaphor. He is overconcerned with imagery, which is a block to a grasp of metaphor. Even Pound's imagistic poetry does not picture. Metaphor is seeing an object in terms of its negation.

Wakeman, George. "Live Metaphors" Galaxy 2 (1866) 272-280
Mainly on slang metaphors. Slang is "live metaphor." "It is

the result of the strong, rude unconscious mind of the crowd, creative, actually performing the process of using things to tell thoughts." Slang is ready-coined wit. Proverbs often serve as arguments, though one proverb often contradicts another.

_____. "Metaphors of the People" *Galaxy* 9 (May 1870) 695-700

Wald, Henri. "Métaphore et concept" *Revue de métaphysique et de morale* 71 (1966) 199-208
Ideas cannot develop without metaphors. All language is metaphorical. Metaphor is constitutive as well as expressive. It transfers between abstract and concrete, creates philosophical categories and abstractions. He quotes Lucian Blaga, Jakobson, Vianu, Biese, Aristotle.

Walker, John. *A Rhetorical Grammar* Boston 1822 (Hildesheim, Germany: Olms, 1969)
Metaphor is a word or expression departing from its normal sense to another it resembles. It is a comparison without the sign of a comparison. Philosophers as well as poets use them.

Walker, T. C. "Les métaphores et les comparaisons dans l'oeuvre poétique de Baudelaire" M.A. thesis, Indiana University 1927

Wallace, Karl. "Books on Rhetorical Theory 1500-1700" *Francis Bacon on Communication and Rhetoric* Chapel Hill: University of North Carolina 1943 pp. 231-55

Wallace, Robert and James Taaffe. "Form and Metaphor" *Poems on Poetry* New York: E. P. Dutton and Company 1965 pp. 195-222
A collection of poets' poems on poetry. "In metaphor poetry comes closest to magic, a force not of additions but multiples, a field theory that explores the world's unexpected converging unity in diversity."

Walpole, Hugh R. *Semantics: The Nature of Words and Their Meaning* New York: N. Norton 1941 esp. ch. 7 pp. 141-158

Walsh, Dorothy. "The Poetic Use of Language" *Journal of Philosophy* 35 (Feb. 3, 1938) 72-81
"Logic is not a science of language." Logic *says* nothing, is a diagram not a statement, is incomplete, general, doesn't mean what it says, and is a radical departure from ordinary language. Poetry on the other hand "does represent the ideal of linguistic precision." Poetry is flexible, fluid, rich in multiple possibilities, is metaphorical (as is all language), (metaphor identifies poetry and reality), is complete in itself, means what it says, is a thing to be said, is completely verbalized, a reality created by language such that what is said cannot be separated from how it is said. Poetry

is sensitive to the pictorial part (not just sense image) of language and it yields significant suggestion, since reality cannot be completely rendered by language anyway, and it also yields mystery.

Walzel, Oscar. "Der Dichtung Schleier aus der Hand der Wahrheit" Euphorion 33 (1932) 83-105
About metaphor of St. Thomas Aquinas.

Wann, Harry Vincent. The Tradition of the Homeric Simile in Eighteenth Century French Poetry Terre Haute, Indiana: Indiana State Teachers College Press 1931 (PhD diss. University of Michigan 1930)

Warburg, Jeremy. "Review of Brooke-Rose A Grammar of Metaphor" Modern Language Review 55 (1960) 97-98

Warburton. A Critical and Philosophical Commentary on Mr. Pope's "Essay on Man" London 1742
He says the poet converts poetical ornament into philosophic reasoning and develops a simile into an analogical argument.

Ward, Aileen. "The Unfurling of Entity: Metaphor as a Topic in Modern and Traditional Criticism" PhD diss. Radcliffe 1953
"For a metaphor to have real metaphoric meaning it must represent a conscious perception of likeness in things unlike, and then express this double perception in language consciously molded to convey this double awareness." It asserts an identity without stating the basis of connection. It creates a new unique cognitive meaning but is not true or false, or translatable. It recreates language to make it abstract and recaptures emotional and "perceptual wholes" of reality. She opposes Müller's "root" theory of metaphor. Basically metaphor is context bound and gains its meaning from the specific poem, or work. Metaphor is regarded as the basic aspect of language and thought and not just a figure of speech. It has no standards of correctness. She attempts to give historical support to the view that metaphor which was once thought of as a narrow device of rhetoric is now significant in relation to thought and language.

Ward, Herman. "Skaldskapur Roberts Frost" Andvari (Reykjavik) 5 (1963) 97-107

Warfel, Harry. Language: A Science of Human Behavior Cleveland: Howard Allen Inc. Publishing 1962 "The Metaphor System" 94-101, "The Limits of Metaphor" 119-120
Metaphor is a form of substitution in which a word, phrase or sentence from a subject-matter replaces that in another. It clarifies, makes abstract ideas visible in order to test them, gives insight and organizes experience. As a slogan it can mislead. Metaphor may become parable, fable or allegory.

Vocabulary operates as a metaphorical system. Types of metonymy and synecdoche are given.

Warren, Austin. Richard Crashaw: A Study in Baroque Sensibility Ann Arbor: University of Michigan Press 1957 [c. 1939] Contains useful bibliography.

Washietl. De similitudinibus imaginibusque Ovidianis PhD diss. Wien 1883

Wasserman, Earl R. "The Inherent Values of Eighteenth Century Personification" PMLA 65 (1950) 435-463
Personification is based on universal analogy and is a natural means of expression of man's most sublime, and profound emotions and abstractions. It is the boldest form of metaphor making the transition between sense and intellect by bringing moral ideas and abstractions before the eyes as visions and persons (e.g. old man Time). Good personification particularizes and constitutes its meaning, partakes of the reality it renders intelligible. (cf. seeing-as)

_____. "Metaphors for Poetry" The Subtler Language Baltimore, Maryland: Johns Hopkins Press 1959 pp. 169-188
The notion of concordia discors, harmony of contraries, and universal analogy were replaced by scientific views and psychology. Poetry lost its basis in an analogical world and now we have only metaphors instead, "metaphors for poetry."

_____. "Nature Moralized: The Divine Analogy in the Eighteenth Century" ELH 20 (March 1953) 39-76
The tendency to discover similitudes is one of the radical principles of the human spirit. Trees represented characters of man; from owls one learned to be manly. Renaissance numerology, herbalism, alchemy, astrology, emblems, political theory were based on universal analogy. Mirroring, and perceived, objective, natural, universal analogy served as a basis of art, mind-body correlates, internal-external (cf. T. S. Eliot's "objective correlative") but became replaced by a subjective, associational, mental, creative psychology.

Watson, George. "Hobbes and the Metaphysical Conceit" Journal of the History of Ideas 16 (Oct. 1955) 558-62 (cf. T. Gang)
Hobbes rejects the poetic conceit as nonsense because it is not confined to the senses. It is a philosophic objection and is irrelevant to the literary device of conceit.

Watson, Goodwin. "What Does One Learn from Analogy and Under What Conditions?" Religious Education 19 (Dec. 1924) 384-90
To have an analogy one must already have the experience. Religious insights must be hinted at, suggested but cannot be portrayed.

Watt, Richard. "Hölderlin's Imagery: The Development of Some Major Themes as Image Patterns in His Lyric Poetry" PhD diss. University of Michigan 1967
Hölderlin's imagery develops from the concrete to the abstract, particular to universal, revealing his idealism. Images unify and give a pattern to his poetry.

Watts, Albert F. The Language and Mental Development of Children Toronto: George Harrap and Company 1944, London: D. C. Heath 1946 esp. ch. 8 "Metaphor and Analogy"
Four levels of metaphor are 1) naïve identity 2) descriptive identity (aware of as-if nature) 3) analogy 4) proverb. Metaphor, analogy and proverb confuse children under age eleven and should be avoided. They lead to category mistakes, hasty analogy, etc. Thus proverb and analogy tests are ineffective below age eleven. Much of the child's supposedly metaphorical language is not intended. He notes also that proverbs contradict one another.

Way, Agnes. "The Language and Style of the Letters of St. Basil" PhD diss. Washington: Catholic University of America 1927

Weber, Edwart. Die Bedeutung der Analogie für die Beschäftigung Henri Estiennes mit der Vulgärsprache Marburg: H. Michaelis-Braun 1939

Weber, Max. Gleiche Metaphern im Deutschen und Lateinischen aus Ciceros Briefen gesammelt Programm Frankenthal 1887

Webster, Edward, and L. Allen. An Experiment in Imaginative Writing Sidney: W. A. Gullick 1918 (New South Wales, Teachers College, Sidney)
On similes and rhetoric.

Webster, T. B. L. "Personification as a Mode of Greek Thought" Journal of the Warburg and Courtauld Institute (London University) 17 (1954) 10-21

Wecklein, N. Das Gleichnis bei Aeschylus; Studien zu Aeschylus Berlin 1872

Wecter, D. "Burke's Theory Concerning Words, Images and Emotion" PMLA 55 (March 1940) 167-81

Weekley, Ernest. "National Sports and National Metaphor" Living Age 309 (April 16, 1921) 46-56
Certain metaphors characterize a nation. These are clues to the habits, tastes, and pursuits of the people of that nation. He presents metaphors drawn from sports.

Weeks, Donald. "A Pendentive to a Dome" (Cited in Aschenbrenner paper on metaphor.)

Wegener, Philip. Untersuchungen über die Grundfragen des Sprachlebens Halle 1885 (cf. S. Langer)

Weigandt, Max. "De metaphorarum usu quodam Ciceroniano" PhD diss. Rostock 1910 "De Platonis usu metaphorarum" pp. 61-73

Weimer, David. The City as Metaphor New York: Random House 1966 On Whitman, James, Crane, Dreiser, Cummings, Fitzgerald, W. C. Williams, Auden.

Weinrich, Harald. "Münze und Wort. Untersuchungen an einem Bildfeld" Romanica. Festschrift für Gerhard Rohlfs Herausgeben von Heinrich Lausberg und Harald Weinrich. Halle: Niemeyer 1968 pp. 508-521

_____. "Semantik der kühnen Metapher" Deutsche Vierteljahrsschrift für Literaturwissenschaft und Geistesgeschichte 37 (August 1963) 325-344 (Summary in Heinrich Henel in Demetz book) "A metaphor...is a word in a context by which it is determined in such a way that it signifies something other than what it means." It is a contradiction. Bold metaphors such as oxymora, which are highly contradictory are better than feeble ones.

Weise, Kurt. "Synaesthesien bei Balzac" Archiv für das Studium der Neueren Sprachen 172 (1937) 173-187

Weise, O. Charakteristik der Lateinischen Sprache Leipzig and Berlin 1909 esp. "Der Volkscharakter im Spiegel der Metapher"

Weisgerber, Leo. Die sprachliche Gestaltung der Welt Düsseldorf: Pädagogischer Verlag Schwann 1962

_____. Die geschichtliche Kräft der deutschen Sprache Düsseldorf: Schwann 1959
Metaphor is the drawing in of new experiences into familiar intellectual or spiritual modes of procedure. Language is regarded as a humanizing of the world (cf. personification). Thus we say "the foot of the mountain."

Weiss, Arnold. "Metáfora e imagen en la 'Epístola moral a Fabio'" Clavileño 13 (1952) 13-16

Weiss, Paul. Nine Basic Arts Carbondale, Illinois: Southern Illinois University Press 1961 esp. pp. 163-166
Nearly every word even in science is a metaphor. Metaphor is a word proper to one context applied in another. It is false if taken literally. It functions like a counterfactual conditional.

Welby, Victoria. "Meaning and Metaphor" Monist 3 (1893) 510-525
The use of a word in a striking and familiar passage gives

a complexion to its use everywhere else. Figures unconsciously influence us. Do not use "imagery which has no longer either sense or relevance, or which tends to call up a false mental picture," e.g. "inner-outer." Figures can convey truth. Terms for mental events are derived metaphorically from terms for physical events.

Wellek, Albert. "Das Doppelempfinden in der Geistesgeschichte" Zeitschrift für Aesthetik und allgemeine Kulturwissenschaft 23 (1929) 14-42

_____. "Das Doppelempfinden im abendländischen Altertum und Mittelalter" Archiv für die gesamte Psychologie 80 (1931) 120-166

_____. "Das Doppelempfinden im 18. Jahrhundert" Deutsche Vierteljahrsschrift für Literaturwissenschaft und Geistesgeschichte 14 (1936) 75-102

_____. "Renaissance- und Barock- Synästhesie. Die Geschichte des Doppelempfindens im 16. und 17. Jahrhundert" Deutsche Vierteljahrsschrift für Literaturwissenschaft und Geistesgeschichte 9 (1931) 534-584

_____. "Zur Geschichte und Kritik der Synästhesie-Forschung" Archiv für die gesamte Psychologie 79 (1931) 325-384

Wellek, René and Austin Warren. "Image, Metaphor, Symbol, Myth" Theory of Literature 3rd ed. New York: Harcourt, Brace and World 1956 chapt. 15 pp. 186-211
Metaphor is not just ornamentation or visual. It has four elements 1) analogy 2) double vision 3) sensuous image revealing the imperceptible 4) animistic projection. The setting, e.g. raging sea, may be a metaphorical background. Metaphor may be ritual as in Homer's "fixed metaphors." Thinking is metaphoric. An often used metaphor is a symbol (from Greek: "throw together"). Each age has its own metaphoric method e.g. Baroque metaphors consist of paradox, oxymora, catachresis.

Weller, Hermann. "Zu einigen Metaphern des Rig--Veda" Zeitschrift für Indologie und Iranistik 5 (1927) 178-184

Wells, Henry W. Poetic Imagery New York: Columbia University Press 1924
"Metaphor is the recognition of a succession of one concept by another dissimilar in kind but alike in some strong ungeneric characteristic." It makes the abstract visible, expresses passion, relates the old and new, relates two or more senses, relates beautiful ideas. One should always examine the specific content of the metaphor. A single metaphor can sum up a whole person or situation or be the basis or main guide for

one's entire life. Even music may be metaphorical. The degree of stress on the minor or major term of metaphor produce 1) "inverse metaphor" (major term stressed) 2) "direct metaphor" or 3) "implied image" (where image is in doubt). In his discussion he divides poetic imagery into eight types: decorative, sunken, violent or fustian, radical, intensive, expansive, exuberant and humorous. Five types of the last category are wit, irony, Gothic humor, incongruity, and fancy. He characterizes authors in terms of the imagery most stressed as follows: Sidney--decorative, Daniel--sunken, Kyd--violent, Donne--radical, Spencer--intensive, Bacon--expansive, Marlowe--exuberant, and Nash--humorous.

Welsh, Paul. "On Explicating Metaphors" Journal of Philosophy 60 (Oct. 1963) 622-623 (Reply to A. Isenberg 1963)
Not every metaphor can be analyzed by resemblance in difference, connotations, or resemblance. Some metaphors create the resemblance, or work by felt appropriateness.

Wenger, Philip. Untersuchungen über die Grundfragen des Sprachlebens Halle 1885 pp. 45-54

Wentersdorf, Karl P. "Herrick's Floral Imagery" Studia Neophilologica 36 (1964) 69-81

_____. "The Imagery of Wyatt" Studia Neophilologica 37 (1965) 161-173

Werner, Hans. "Metaphern und Gleichnisse aus dem griechischen Theaterwesen" PhD diss. Zürich, Aarau 1915

Werner, Heinz. Comparative Psychology of Mental Development New York: International Universities Press 1957 [1948] esp. "Syncretic Character of Primitive Organization" and "Synchretic and Diffuse Organization in Imagery."
Has good bibliography on imagery. He speaks of "physiognomic perception," or "synchresis" by means of emotion or as a result of brain damage, schizophrenia, synaesthesia, privation, drugs and primitive mentality. There is a primordial unity of the sensory and the imagination, a synaesthetic, undifferentiated perceptual experience. Primitives who have "visions" are highly regarded by their tribesmen. Image is a stage toward becoming reflective and is based on feelings and fantasy. Jaensch's views on eidetic imagery are discussed.

_____, ed. On Expressive Language Worcester: Clark University Press 1955

_____. Die Ursprünge der Metapher Heft II Der Arbeiten zur Entwicklungspsychologie. Leipzig: Verlag von Wilhelm Engleman 1919 (cf. Freud Totem and Tabu, Laan)

An influential book on metaphor. The development of metaphor is examined in terms of ethnological, cultural and psychological events, tabu, irony, flattery, music, etc. He concentrates on various types of metaphor such as condensed metaphor, pseudo-metaphor, etc. The metaphor is born out of deception, out of concealing ambiguity, out of contrary strivings to conceal and reveal at the same time. (A similar view is held by Ortega later.)

_____, and B. Kaplan. Symbol Formation New York: Wiley 1963
A significant and extensive psychological examination of the symbolic process. In one experiment sentences are represented metaphorically by lines drawn, resulting in spatial metaphors or metaphors with minimal or intermediate distance between sentence and line, and alluding metaphors. This reveals how thought and language are metaphorically represented. Visual imagery and the schizophrenic's use of deviant language is also presented.

Westendörpf, K. Der soziologische Charakter der englischen Bildersprache Leipzig 1939

Whaler, James. "Animal Simile in Paradise Lost" PMLA 47 (June 1932) 534-553

_____. "Compounding and Distribution of Similes in 'Paradise Lost'" Modern Philology 28 (Feb. 1931) 313-327

_____. "Grammatical 'Nexus' of the Miltonic Simile" Journal of English and Germanic Philology 30 (July 1931) 327-34
No other poet than Milton "more consciously and with more skill refines similes." A detailed analysis of similes.

_____. "Miltonic Simile" PMLA 46 (Dec. 1931) 1034-74

Whalley, George. "Metaphor" Encyclopedia of Poetry and Poetics Alex Preminger, ed. Princeton University Press 1965 pp. 490-495
"Essential metaphor" depends on context, a non-predicative, "resonating," "energy system." The "is" of a metaphor tends to destroy the comparison, emendation, substitution. Grammatical construction does not identify the metaphor. Metaphor can fall into many grammatical patterns. Metaphor is not just interaction but is like "nuclear-fission." Resemblance is inadequate or irrelevant if we take into account the actual sensation metaphors induce. Metaphors are untranslatable without cognitive loss and they escape analysis. There is also the danger of being too inclusive in defining metaphor. The "radical" form of metaphor is "A is B" (identity) or A-B ("parataxis," juxtaposing without copula e.g. "sphinx-woman.") Metaphor is the problem of all thought and knowledge not just that of language.

______. Poetic Process London: Routledge & K. Paul 1953 "Metaphor" pp. 139-163
Metaphor is a four term relation. It transmits and is an equivalent of feeling, translates visual into verbal, renders the complexity of reality, gives immediacy, is a primitive relation, is replaceable by the literal, and distorts the senses to give paradox and insight. Metaphors are often better if mixed and inconsistent. A "ringing metaphor" is one which illuminates and has "resonance" through the whole poem. (It has a trans-sensory character.) A "sone" is a group of words resonating in the process of metaphor. The sublime is contained in sense experience and image. An image, however, is not a determinate entity. T. S. Eliot's "objective correlative" Whalley calls a "pointing metaphor" because it starts and ends in sensory experience.

Whately, Richard. Elements of Rhetoric New York: Harper 1863

Wheeler, Benjamin. Analogy and the Scope of Its Application in Language Cornell University Press 1887
A classification of products of the action of analogy in language. "The operation of analogy in language is in every case ultimately conditioned and determined by the natural quest of the mind for unity to replace multiplicity, system to replace anomalous diversity, and groups to replace monads."

Wheeler, E. "Color Similes" Current Literature 29 (Sept. 1900) 277-8

Wheelwright, Philip. The Burning Fountain, revised ed., Indiana University Press 1968 (Review of his works by Mooij, Cohen, Green (1966), Rau)
Although all language is metaphorical "steno-language" unlike "expressive language" tries to be literal, to attain fixed, limited meaning. Expressive (metaphorical) language is emotive yet referential. It is untranslatable. Four types of imagination are 1) Confrontative (particularizes) 2) Stylistic (which distances) 3) Compositive (fuses into unity) 4) Archetypal (object is seen in the light of a higher, more universal or more general concept). Aspects of semantic expressive language are: 1) referential congruity (imitation), 2) conceptual variation 3) plurisignation (multi-signification defying simple analysis, yielding a concrete universal or indirection) (subtle suggestion and opposition) "The power of metaphor outruns every expository maneuver," 4) soft-focus (a revealing vagueness) 5) paralogical dimensionality (e.g. emotive or causal incongruity) 6) assertorial lightness (meaningful assertion not true or false) 7) paradox (e.g. oxymoron). The most essential aspect of metaphor is semantic tension among the heterogeneous elements it brings together in its one-in-many, many-in-one relations. Tension is created by a merging of simile and plurisignation. "Radical metaphor,"

or metaphor which contributes to the growth of language, was once tensive but became dead or latent with constant use and familiarity. It may be rejuvenated by replacing the term in certain revealing contexts. Metaphor leads to myth, which is a metaphor taken as identity and which gives a valid perspective of the world. Expressive or metaphorical language reveals reality better than does steno-language.

_____. Heraclitus Princeton University Press 1959

_____. "The Archetypal Symbol" Perspectives in Literary Symbolism Joseph Strelka, ed. University Park: Pennsylvania State University Press 1968 pp. 214-43

_____. Metaphor and Reality Bloomington: Indiana University Press 1962
"Thought is not possible to any significant degree without language, nor language without metaphoric activity whether open or concealed." Metaphor is an open perspective of reality and part of reality is constituted by the way in which we conceive it. Reality cannot be limited to a single perspective. It is always changing. He discusses the various types of tension involved in metaphor. "The test of essential metaphor is not any rule of grammatical form but rather the quality of semantic transformation that is brought about." The tension of a metaphor should arise naturally from associations tending to coalesce. Imagery can involve a metaphor in the act of perception itself e.g. playing a guitar as if seeming to listen to the moon.

_____. "Notes on Mythopoeia" Sewanee Review 59 (1951) 574-592

_____. "On the Semantics of Poetry" Kenyon Review 2 (1940) 263-83

_____. "Poetry and Logic" Symposium 1 (1930) 440-457
Logic is an inadequate verbal atomism containing invariant symbols. Poetry on the other hand is more adequate. Poetry is expressive, objective, contains value, relates poet to audience, is aesthetic. Even scientific, verifiable beliefs require imaginative assent.

_____. "Poetry, Myth and Reality" The Modern Critical Spectrum Gerald Goldberg and Nancy Goldberg, eds. New Jersey: Prentice-Hall 1962 pp. 306-320 (Also in The Language of Poetry A. Tate, ed. Princeton University Press 1942 pp. 3-33)
Primitive language is metaphorical and so has multiple reference which it must have to express the mythic mystery. Thus primitives employ paradox freely.

_____. "The Semantic Approach to Myth" Myth: A Symposium Thomas Sebeok, ed. Bloomington: Indiana University Press 1958 pp. 154-168

_____. "Semantics and Ontology" Metaphor and Symbol L. C. Knights and Basil Cottle, eds. London: Butterworths Scientific Publications 1960 pp. 1-9
Epiphor: an antecedent resemblance or implicit analogy justifying the metaphor. Diaphor: an induced resemblance. It is novel, untranslatable, paradoxical and irreducible. Both types of metaphor partially constitute real objects. Block or steno-language of science is distinguished from more adequate, metaphorical, tensive language.

_____. "Symbol, Metaphor and Myth" Sewanee Review 58 (1950) 678-98
A review of I. Lee, ed. The Language of Wisdom and Folly; M. Foss, Symbol and Metaphor; R. Chase, Quest for Myth; Jung and Kerényi, Essays on a Science of Mythology; G. Reichard, Navaho Religion. He states that the "expressive symbol" is common to all of these.

Whitbread, L. "Medieval English Metaphor; The Surgings of Care Taken as Hot or Cold" Philological Quarterly 17 (Oct. 1938) 365-70

White, Mary Alice. "A Study of Schizophrenic Language" Journal of Abnormal and Social Psychology 44 (1949) 61-74
Gives 28 characteristics of schizophrenic language. It has more nonsense words than normal, more phrases, more mixed word arrangements, fewer personal sentences, etc.

Whittier, Duane. "Jordan's Metaphysic of Language and Aesthetic Meaning" PhD diss. University of Illinois 1961

Whorf, Benjamin L. Collected Papers on Metalinguistics Washington D. C.: Foreign Service Institute, Department of State 1952
Metaphor arises out of synaesthesia, a primitive, non-linguistic mode of experience. His general view of language is that language partly determines and constitutes reality.

Widmer, K. "Iconography of Renunciation: The Miltonic Simile" ELH 25 (Dec. 1958) 258-69

Wiehe, R. E. "Two Images in Vaughan" English Studies 45 (Dec. 1964) 457-60

Wiener, Meïr. "Die Orientalische Metapher" Der Jude: Eine Monatsschrift 6 (1921) 167-74

Wier, M. C. "Similes of Apollonius Rhodius Compared with Those of Virgil and Homer" School Review 10 (May 1902) 384-6

Wietfeld, Albert. "Die Bildersprache in Shakespeares Sonetten" PhD diss. Göttingen 1914

Wilhington, R. "Plays Upon Language" Atlantic Monthly 166 (1940) 506-508

Wilkins, Eliza. "A Classification of the Similes of Homer" Classical Weekly 13 (March 1920) 147-150, 154-159

Wilkinson, L. P. Horace and His Lyric Poetry Cambridge: Cambridge University Press 1951 esp. p. 124 ff.

Williams, Aubrey. "Submerged Metaphor in Pope" Essays in Criticism 9 (1959) 197-201

Williams, Charles A. S. A Manual of Chinese Metaphor (Statistical Dept. of the Inspectorate General) Commercial Press 1920 (Review by Pelliot)
A collection of Chinese metaphors. Chinese word symbols are sometimes painted pictures, but more often metaphorical. Abstract words are rendered by natural, concrete objects. The metaphor is usually expressed in terms of four characters.

Williams, K. M. "Animal Rationis Capax: A Study of Certain Aspects of Swift's Imagery" ELH 21 (Sept. 1954) 193-207

Williamson, George. "The Rhetorical Pattern of Neo-Classical Wit" Modern Philology 33 (1935) 55-81

_____. "Strong Lines" English Studies 18 (1936) 152-159 (Reprinted in Seventeenth Century Contexts London 1960 pp. 120-131)
On the conceit.

Willis, George. The Philosophy of Speech London: George Allen and Unwin Limited 1919 esp. ch. 4, "Metaphor"
Mainly an outline of Aristotle's theory of metaphor.

Willis, Richard. De Re Poetica 1573

Wilson, Francis. Yeats's Iconography New York: Macmillan 1960

_____. "Patterns in Yeats's Imagery: The Herne's Egg" Modern Philology 55 (Aug. 1957) 46-52

Wilson, Harry. "The Metaphor in the Epic Poems of Publius Papinius Statius" PhD diss. Johns Hopkins University 1896

Wilson, Suzanne. "Structure and Imagery Patterns in the Poetry of Emily Dickinson" PhD diss. University of Southern California 1959 (cf. McNaughton)

Wilson, Thomas. Arte of Rhetorique (1553) George Mair, ed. Oxford 1909

Wilss, Wolfram. "Der bildliche Ausdruck im Leitartikel der Tages-

presse" Muttersprache: Zeitschrift zur Pflege und Erforschung der deutschen Sprache 71 (1961) 97-108
A light account and a listing of some examples.

_____. "Die Metapher im publizistischen Text" Sprachpflege: Zeitschrift für gutes Deutsch in Schrift und Wort 10 (1961) 101-102

Wilstach, Frank Jenners. A Dictionary of Similes Boston: Little, Brown, and Co. 1934 (1924 Adler Press) (Review by Teale, Gilman, Littell, and next 2 entries.)
Some examples are: Innocent as the wayside fly, Indifferent as rain, Lovely as day, Lovely as light.

a.) (No author) "Helps for the Unimaginative Writer" Literary Digest 100 (March 23, 1929) 23-4 (on Wilstach)

b.) (No author) "Trailing the Simile Through the Centuries" Current Opinion 63 (August 1917) p. 120 (on Wilstach)

Wimsatt, W. K., Jr. "Poetic Tension: A Summary" New Scholasticism 32 (Jan. 1958) 73-88
A Thomistic inspired view. Poetry is essentially tensional between poetic and moral or religious values, between speaker and audience, as well as between the metaphor's two terms. It is a dramatization, a kind of mystical vision, and involves mystery.

_____. "Review of Foss, Symbol and Metaphor" Review of Metaphysics 4 (Dec. 1950) 279-90
Besides Foss he mentions views of W. Stanford and Beardsley. "A copresence of likeness and difference is necessary for the indefinite radiations of meaning, the solidity and concreteness, for which metaphor is prized."

_____. "Verbal Style: Logical and Counterlogical" PMLA 65 (March 1950) 5-20

_____. "Rhetoric and Poems: The Example of Pope" English Institute Essays D. Robertson Jr., ed. 1948 New York: Columbia University Press 1949 pp. 179-207

_____, and Beardsley. The Verbal Icon University of Kentucky Press 1954 esp. pp. 119-30 (Reviews by Keast, Humphreys, Davidson, Bacon, Nowottny)
A collection of essays. "The verbal image...is not merely a bright picture but also an interpretation of reality in its metaphoric and symbolic dimension." It is a "verbal icon."

_____, and C. Brooks. Literary Criticism: A Short History New York: Knopf 1965
Because poetry and painting were regarded as being very close the painter had to know literature and the author had to know

painting. One must know the visual symbols by which human emotion is portrayed. Various critics' views are presented.

Winchester, George. "Report of the Language Committee of the School and College Conference on English 1940" Issues, Problems and Approaches in the Teaching of English New York: Holt, Rinehart and Winston 1964 esp. p. 29 (Also quoted in General Education Progressive Education Association, Curriculum Commission, New York: Appleton-Century Co. 1950.)

Windfuhr, Manfred. Die barocke Bildlichkeit und ihre Kritiker. Stilhaltungen in der deutschen Literatur des 17. und 18. Jahrhunderts. Stuttgart: Metzler 1966

Winkler, Walter. Metapher und Vergleich im Schaffen der Annette von Droste--Hülshoff PhD diss. Zürich: Winterthur, P. G. Keller 1954

Winter, Ronald. "Notes sur le dynamisme de la métaphore" Bulletin des Jeunes Romanistes no. 2 (Dec. 1960) 41-48
Metaphor is an alternance between two poles. Out of the two poles of a metaphor a new value, a magical, illogical, synthesis of intellect and emotions, true and objective, is created overthrowing the established order. Music also is metaphorical e.g. in fugue and counterpoint.

Wisdom, John. "Philosophy, Metaphysics and Psychoanalysis" Philosophy and Psychoanalysis Blackwell 1957 esp. pp. 248-82
Metaphor allows one to look at his behavior in various lights. Its explanatory power is in its paradoxical juxtaposition of different cases. It is context-bound and so can explore the individual case. See also his Paradox and Discovery.

Wittgenstein, Ludwig. Philosophical Investigations 3rd ed. New York: Macmillan 1968 (1953) esp. p. 216; no. 531, no. 533, no. 77. Also passages on "seeing-as."
He says little about metaphors as such but his implied theory of metaphor is represented and modified by V. Aldrich, M. Hester, and W. Shibles.

_____. Blue and Brown Books New York: Harper 1958 esp. pp. 162-182 on "seeing-as."
The seeing-as experience (in a visual puzzle such as a double duck-rabbit picture) takes place only at the moment of seeing the change e.g. from duck to rabbit. We do not see the duck as a rabbit. To see-as is not necessarily to have an image. Seeing-as is a direct experience, a language game. It does not involve an internal mental process, for example, of "interpretation." It is not a psychological state but a behavior. This is perceptual seeing-as. (Note: He says "Seeing-as is not a part of perception," but this may just mean that it *is* perception.) There is also non-perceptual seeing-as but he does not really discuss it.

Wittich, E. Homer in seinen Bildern und Vergleichungen Stuttgart 1908

Wohlberg, Joseph. "Structure of the Laodamia Simile in Catullus 68b" Classical Philology 50 (Jan. 1955) 42-6
An attempt "to show that Catullus did construct the simile along definite, formal lines with strict attention to contrasts and common elements."

Wolf, Gunther. "Über die Geschichte der Staatsschiffmetapher" Geschichte in Wissenschaft und Unterricht 10 (Nov. 1959) 696-698

Wood, Chauncey Derby. "Chaucer's Use of Astrology for Poetic Imagery" PhD diss. Princeton 1964

Woodhouse, A. S. P. "Imagination" Encyclopedia of Poetry and Poetics Alex Preminger, ed. Princeton University Press 1965
A presentation of the various views held about the nature of the imagination e.g. as creative, image producing, image combining, vision producing, etc.

_____. "Collins and the Creative Imagination" Studies in English by members of University College, Toronto 1931

Woods, M. J. "Gracián, Peregrini and the Theory of Topics" Modern Language Review 63 (Oct. 1968) 854-63
An attempt to show that an acquaintance with the classical theory of topics of Cicero, etc., is necessary to understand Gracián's and other theories of 17th century wit (conceit, metaphor). Gracián's work on the conceit is based mainly on circumstantial topics thereby ignoring classificatory ones. Peregrini stressed Aristotle's "categories."

_____. "Topical Theory in the Sixteenth Century: Some Spanish and Italian Views" Modern Language Review 63 (1968) 66-73

Woodworth, Robert S. "A Revision of Imageless Thought" Psychological Review 22 (1915) 1-27

Woolmer, J. Howard. A Catalogue of the Imagist Poets New York 1966
Contains Wallace Martin, "The Forgotten School of 1909 and the Origins of Imagism" pp. 7-38, and Ian Fletcher "Some Anticipations of Imagism" pp. 39-53

Wordsworth, William. (See Peacock, Zall)
On imagination and imagery.

Wragg, Otis. "Functional Approach to Literary Criticism" English Journal 54 (Dec. 1965) 801-5 Reply by Robert Hoffman 55 (April 1966) 477-9

Wright, Elizabeth C. Metaphor, Sound and Meaning in Bridges' "The Testament of Beauty" University of Pennsylvania Press 1951

Wu, Joseph. "Chinese Language and Chinese Thought" Philosophy East and West 19 (Oct. 1969) 423-34 (cf. Fenollosa) Connectives are minimized, the concrete is stressed, and objects are regarded as events, in Chinese which juxtaposes picture symbols. Chia-chieh is a way of using language, esp. metaphors, to suggest a new meaning. Hui-i is the way logical or ideographic aggregates combine two or more characters to suggest a new meaning.

Wunderer, C. "Gleichnisse und Metaphern bei Polybios" (Source: Stutterheim 1941)

Wünsche, A. Die Bildersprache des Alten Testaments. Ein Beitrag zur aesthetischen Würdigung des poetischen Schrifttums im Alten Testament. Leipzig 1906

Wundt, Wilhelm. Völkerpsychologie. Eine Untersuchung der Entwicklungsgesetze von Sprache, Mythus und Sitte 2 vols. Leipzig 1922 vol II, "Die Sprache" [1903]

Yasuda, Kenneth. The Japanese Haiku Rutland, Vermont: Charles Tuttle 1957 esp. pp. 50-53
Simile, personification and metaphor are regarded as interferences to the Haiku poet and should be avoided. The Haiku poet stresses the "naked poem."

Yeats, William B. "The Completed Image" The Modern Tradition Richard Ellmann and C. Feidelson Jr. eds. New York: Oxford University Press 1965 p. 190

Yelton, Donald. "Symbol and Metaphor in Conrad's Fiction" PhD diss. Columbia University 1962
Conrad's metaphors and symbols are related to those of the French symbolists.

_____. Mimesis and Metaphor: An Inquiry into the Genesis and Scope of Conrad's Symbolic Imagery The Hague: Mouton 1967
An examination of the expressive and unifying effect of metaphor in its thematic context in eight works of Conrad. Conrad is seen to explore new fictional modes, to use suggestive metaphors but still to adhere to the Aristotelian notion of mimesis or imitation as a basis of the arts.

Yndurain, Francisco. "Gracián--un estilo" in Homenaje a Gracián Charles V. Aubrun, et al. (Zaragoza 1958) esp. pp. 182 ff.
On Gracián's metaphors. They are intellectual, lack felt sensory experience, are bookish.

Yoder, Audrey. Animal Analogy in Shakespeare's Character Portrayal New York: AMS Press 1947

Yuasa, Nobuyuki. "A Study of Metaphor is Spenser's Amoretti" Studies in English Literature (Tokyo: Hosei Univ.) 37 (1961) 163-186

Zale, Eric. "Metaphor and Children's Writing" Elementary English 43 (Oct. 1966) 660-2
An emotional attack on Stewig's article. Zale states that all of us know what a metaphor is. He disagrees with Stewig's view that the man "who does not consciously use metaphor talks without thinking."

Zall, Paul. Literary Criticism of William Wordsworth Lincoln, Nebr: University of Nebraska Press 1966
Contains the 1815 Preface on imagination and fancy and other prefaces and critical accounts.

Zardoya, Concha. "La técnica metafórica de F. García Lorca" Revista Hispánica Moderna 20 (Oct. 1954) 295-326
A very detailed classification.

Zaubitzer, Hannelore. "Clownmetaphern bei Baudelaire, Mallarmé und Michaux" Die Neueren Sprachen 15 (Oct. 1966) 445-56
On Baudelaire's Le Vieux Saltimbanque.

Ziemendorff, Ingeborg. "Die Metapher bei den weltlichen Lyrikern des deutschen Barock" (Germanische Studien Heft 135 (1933) 144 pgs.) Berlin: E. Ebering 1933. PhD diss. Berlin 1932

Zimmer, Heinrich. Philosophies of India Joseph Campbell, ed. New York: Pantheon Books 1951 esp. p. 363 ff. (Cambridge, Mass: MIT Press 1965)

Zimmermann, Eléonore. "'Vision' in Poetry" The Disciplines of Criticism Peter Demetz, Thomas Greene, Lowry Nelson, Jr., eds. New Haven: Yale University Press 1968

Zipf, George. The Psycho-Biology of Language: An Introduction to Dynamic Philology Boston: Houghton Mifflin Co. 1935 esp. pp. 289-291 (Cambridge: MIT Press 1965)
The first time a word is used instead of another it is a metaphor, after this the figure is included in the word's meaning. The most frequent usage is the primary meaning.

Žirmunskij, Viktor. Voprosy Teori Literatury Leningrad 1928 "On Classic and Romantic Poetry" pp. 175-182

Zoll, Allan R. "Toward a Theory of Baroque Lyric Metaphor" PhD diss. University of Michigan 1969
A theory of metaphor which tries to account for Renaissance and 17th century ideas of epistemology, metaphysics and the functions of language. Aristotle, Ramus, St. Thomas are discussed.

Zwiazek Polskich Artystów Plastyków. Metafory (Metafory: malarstwo, rzeźba, grafika) Warsaw: Centralne Biuro Wystaw Artstycznych. An art catalog. (Introduction by Ryszard Stanislawski)

INDEX

Section I Extensive Works on Metaphor

(To be consulted as a supplement to this index)

Bauer, Jakob. _Das Bild in der Sprache_

Beardsley, Monroe C. _Aesthetics_

Berggren, Douglas. "An Analysis of Metaphorical Meaning and Truth"

Biese, Alfred. _Die Philosophie des Metaphorischen_

Brinkmann, Friedrich. _Die Metaphern_

Brooke-Rose, Christine. _A Grammar of Metaphor_

Gerber, Gustav. _Die Sprache als Kunst_

Gracián, Baltasar y Morales. _Agudeza y arte de ingenio_

Hester, Marcus. _The Meaning of Poetic Metaphor_

Lauretano, Bruno. _Ambiguità e metafora_

Leonard, Barbara. "The Structure and Function of Metaphor"

Meier, Hugo. _Die Metapher_

Müller, Josef. _Das Bild in der Dichtung_

Osborn, Michael. "The Function and Significance of Metaphor in Rhetorical Discourse"

Pongs, Hermann. _Das Bild in der Dichtung_

Shibles, Warren. _An Analysis of Metaphor_

Stanford, William. _Greek Metaphor_

Stutterheim, Cornelius. _Het begrip metaphoor_

Tilden, Nancy. "An Analysis of Metaphor"

Urban, Wilbur. _Language and Reality_

Vianu, Tudor. _Problemele metaforei si alte studii stilistica_

Ward, Aileen. "The Unfurling of Entity: Metaphor as a Topic in Modern and Traditional Criticism"

Werner, Heinz. _Die Ursprünge der Metapher_

Wheelwright, Philip. _The Burning Fountain_; _Metaphor and Reality_

(The following might also be consulted: Aristotle, J. Brown, Buck, Curran, Fónagy, S. George, Groesbeck, Leondar, Nyman, A. Paul, Richards, Stählin, Tomkins, Turbayne, Wells. See also entries under, "metaphor, bibliography of")

INDEX

SECTION II. GENERAL TERMS AND NAMES

[Abbreviations: R (review), m (metaphor)]
[Accents are omitted]

Schwerd, Spivack, (history of) J. Tate, Tilden, Vianu, (as m) Warfel

Allen, L. (see E. Webster)

allusion (as m) Thornton

analogia entis Aalders, Nielsen, Przwara

analogy (archetypal) Abrams, (scientific) Achinstein, (in Plato) J. Anderson, (mathematical) J. Anderson, (scientific) Arber, Ashe, Ballard, Bennet, (as structural m) Berggren, (scientific) Bonner, (misleading) Bouwsma, Buchanan, (scientific) Bunge, (argumental) K. Burke, Burrell, (argumental) J. Butler, Canguilhem, (argumental) Carney, (false) Chase, (archetypal) Cheyne, (tests) Church, (types) Church, (anti-) A. Collins, Conger, (unconscious) Crain, Damon, G. Davies, (religious) Debaisieux, (4 term) Delaney, (true) Demetrius, Dooyeweerd, Edel, Emmet, (scientific) Farber, (scientific) Finzi-Contini, Flanigan, Foote, R. Frost, (Aristotle) Goldthwait, G. Graham, (physiological) G. Graham, Gregory, (as logical) Gregory, Grenet, (Aquinas) Habbel, Hagner, (body politic) Hale, (of feeling) Hampshire, F. Harrison, (definition) M. Hesse, Hoffding, Hoppe, Horgan, Heinz Hulsmann, Huxley, Kalinowski, Kalmus, Kroesch, Leger, Lloyd, MacDonald, Macmillan, Macquarrie, (of mind) Madge, Mariani, Mascall, Masiello, Maurer, McCabe, McInerny, McPherson, Menges, Menne, Mondin, Montagnes, S. Moore, C. Myers, Oppenheimer, Ouy, Penido, Percy, Phelan, (in reasoning) Picard, Rhys-Davids, J. Ross, Rothstein, Ryan, St. Augustine, E. St. John, G. Sauvage, H. Schmidt, Schon, Schorer, Sheen, H. Simon, Y. Simon, Sohngen, Specht, Spurgeon, L. Stern, W. Stevens, Sweet, Perelman Takeda, Terry, Tesauro, Thomson, J. Turner, Vio, Goodwin Watson, Watts, E. Weber, B. Wheeler, Yoder

analogy, universal Aish, Aquinas, Ashe, Barton, Baudelaire, (based on m) Baumgartner, Beinhauer, Biese, Bozon, B. Brown, K. Burke, Cheyne, Cicero, D. Clark, (based on Physics) Crain, Croce, Curran, Dallas, (secret affinities in nature) Danielou, (harmony of nature) C. Davies, J. Edwards, Emerson, M. Evans, (scientific) Farber, Fordyce, F. George, Hulme, (as law) Jaurrieta, Jenyns, Korg, Laguardia, Lauretano, Leger, Lyttkens, Mazzeo, Murry, speculum or mirroring) Nemetz, Nicolson, Oppian, Patterson, Praz, Richards, Rousset, (feeling of unity of all) Sarmiento, Sohngen, Solard, W. Stevens, Terry, Tesauro, Turbayne, Turnbull, Urbach, Wasserman

anglo-saxon (literature) Bode, (poetry) Collins, (m) Gummere, Rankin, Tupper

Anouilh, Jean (imagery of) Calin

anthropomorphism Nietzsche, Urbach

antimetaphor Allemann

Antoine, Gerald   Pasini

anxiety   (as m) Sarbin

ape   (as m) Curtius

Apollinaire, Guillaume   (m) Rice

Apollonius of Rhodes   (similes) Goodwin, Kulessa, Viravsky, Wier

Apuleius, Lucius   Neuenschwander

Aquinas, St. Thomas   (analogy) J. Anderson, Blanche, Burrell, Cajetan, Flanigan, Frye,(analogy) Habbel, F. Harrison, Klubertanz, Lyttkens, Mackey, Masiello, Maurer, McInerny, W. Meissner, Montagnes, Nielsen, M. O'Neill, Phelan, J. Ross, H. Schwartz, Sohngen, Walzel, Zoll

archetypation   (Bentham) Ogden

archetype   Abrams, (as unconscious) Black, Bodkin, Durand, G. Foster, (as repeated image) Friedman, Frye, Gunter, Jung, Lorenz, Norwood, Ogden, Pongs, Wheelwright

architect   (as m of the static) Edelman

Aretino, Pietro   Liedstrand

Aristide, Aelius   Boulanger

Aristophanes   Holohr, Komornicka, Lever, Littlefield, Lottich, Moraux, Nassau, Newiger, Pecz, Petz, Romagnoli, Taillardat

Aristotle   Bauer, Berg, Burrell, E. Cope, Croce, Curran, D'Alton, Davie, Delaney, Eucken, Feltenstein, Frye, Goldthwait, Gracian, W. Greene, Hangard, F. Harrison, Hatzfeld, M. Hesse, Holland, Ioannou, Kreczmar, Mackey, Manser, Mauthner, McCall, McInerny, McKeon, Olscamp, Pasini, Pongs, Slattery, Sohngen, Stanford, Terry, Tesauro, Ushenko, Vaihinger, Wald, G. Willis, Woods, Yelton, Zoll

rnheim, Rudolf   Dorfles

rnold, Matthew   Greenberg

rt   (of psychopaths) Basaglia, (metaphorically described) Battcock, (as particular) Denbigh, (as metaphorical) Dorfles, (languages of) Goodman, (m) Madge, Speranski

s-if   J. Austin, S. Baker, Biese, (proportional metaphor as) Cajetan, Dauthendey, Ferre, Hillmann, Nietzsche, Nyman, Shuford, Szasz

spect-seeing   Aldrich

Bazin, Rene   S. Ullmann

Beardsley, Monroe   Khatchadourian, Nyman, Schipper, Wimsatt

Beckett   Kern

Bede, The Venerable   Vendome

Beecher, Henry W.   A. J. Graham

Belleau, Remi   Riniker

Benn, Gottfried   Lieb, Pongs

Bentham, Jeremy   Ogden

Bergamin, Jose   Beinhauer

Berggren, Douglas   Isocrates

Bergson, Henri   Brehier, Fiser, Hersch, Hulme

Berkeley, George   Davie, Van Steenburgh

Berthold von Regensburg   Nussbaum

bestiary   Mazzeo, Parkhurst

Biese, Alfred   Laan, R. Meyer, Urbach, Wald

Bildsphare   Deutschbein

Binswanger, P.   F. Vonessen

Bismarck, Otto von   Blumner

bisociation   Koestler

Black, Max   Erwin, Khatchadourian, (R) Odegard, (R) Stallknecht, Swanson

Blackmur, Richard   Hyman

Blaga, Lucian   Wald

Blake, William   (m) Corrigan, (synaesthesia) Downey, Ellmann (archetype) Frye, (m) Gorrigan, Parkhurst, Schicker, Shook, D.J. Smith

Bloch, Oscar   (see D. Diderot)

blue (m) Jacobs

Boas, Franz (m) Dorfles

Bobrowski, Johannes (m) Behrmann

Bodkin, Maud Hyman

Bodmer, Johann (m) Blackall, Mansfeld

body (see m, body)

Boileau-Despreaux, Nicolas Hatzfeld

boomerang effect (see extra-metaphorization)

Borges, Jorge (m) Gertel, (m) Girardot, A. Phillips, Sucre

Bourdeille, Pierre de (see Brantome)

Bowen, Elizabeth Miller

Bowers, J. W. (see Osborn)

Boyle, Robert (R) Hess, (R) Stallknecht

Brantome (Pierre de Bourdeille) (m) Coupland

breath (m) Abrams, Lucas, F. Muller

Brecht, Bertold C. Lyons

Breitinger, Johann (m) Blackall, Mansfeld, Phelps

Brentano, Clemen Pongs, Porner, Strassmann

Breton, Andre (m, metamorphosis) Balakian, Reverdy

Bridges, Robert Wright

Brinkmann, Friedrich Beinhauer, Carpenter, Laan, Lang, Pongs

Britton, Karl MacIver

Bronte, Charlotte Ericksen

Brooke-Rose, Christine (R) Draper, (R) Holder, (R) Morgan, (R) Nosek, Pasini, (R) Warburg

Brown, Kenneth (imagery) Bigsby

Browne, Sir Thomas Huntley, Lane

Browning, Robert (touch images) Bonnell, C. W. Smith, (moon m) Trawick

Bruchmann, K. Mauthner

Bruckner, Ferdinand (see Theodor Tagger)

Bruneau Mayer

Buchanan, Scott Shibles

Buck, Gertrude Stanford

Buddhism Rhys-Davids

Bühler, Karl (proverbs) Church, Pongs

Burch, George (Thomism) J. Anderson

Burke, Edmund Love, Wecter

Burke, Kenneth Egan, Holland, Hyman

Burnet, Lord James (see Monboddo)

Byron, George (m) Elledge, Ridenour, S. Ullmann

Caesar, Julius Dannehl

Cajetan, Cardinal F. Harrison, Horgan, Mascall, McCanles, McInerny, H. Schwartz

Calderon Brinkmann, E. Hesse, Horst, McGarry, Migliorini, Ochse, A. Parker, Spitzer

Cameron, V. Leaver

Campbell, George Ioannou

Campbell, N. R. M. Hesse

Camus, Albert John

Carew, Thomas (conceit) Alden

Carlyle, Thomas (m) G. Carter

Carnap, R. Lieb, Shibles

Carraway, Nick Lisca

Carroll, Lewis Ferdiere

cartoon (m) Goodman

Carus, Titus Lucretius (see Lucretius)

Cassirer, Ernst Langer, Leondar, Percy, Schon, Urban

catachresis Black, Sherry

category (m) Speranski, (Aristotle) Terry, (Aristotle) Tesauro

Catullus Howe, Svennung, Wohlberg

Celan, Paul Allemann

Chaitanya, Krishna (pseudonym for K. Nair)

Chambers, Leland (see Gracian)

Chapman Carpenter

Charisius Diomedis

Charlemagne Alcuin

Chartier, Emile (see pseudonym, Alain)

Chase, R. (R) Wheelwright

Chaucer (m) Baum, Klaeber, Richardson, Rowland, Wood

Chenier, Andre Koppetsch, Lewy

Chomsky, Noam Barone, Ellis, Hillman, Lambert, Pavy, Strang, O. Thomas

Chrysostom, St. John Degen, Sawhill

Chun, Ki-Taek (see T. Sarbin)

Churchill, Winston H. Fowler

Cicero Bauer, Capella, Itzinger, McCall, Morawski, Straub, Wackernagel, M. Weber, Wiegandt, Woods

concordia discors Wasserman

concrete universal Frye, Wheelwright

Conrad, Joseph (*Lord Jim* as m) Cook, R. Evans, Graver, Guetti, Yelton

Corneille (m) Arendt, Cretin, Vercel

correspondence, universal (see analogy, universal)

Coster, Adolphe Sarmiento

Cottle, Basil (see L. Knights)

counterpoint (as m) A. Stein

Courtier, Paul-Louis Nyman

Cowley, Abraham (conceits) Alden, Jamieson, S. Johnson, Suerbaum

Crane, Hart R. Day, Ellmann, Fuller, Newman, Pacernick, Slote

Crane, Stephen G. Johnson, (m) Kissane, Marcus, Weimer

Crane, William Peacham

Crashaw, Richard R. Harrison, McCann, Praz, Warren

criticism (partial listing) Atkins, Bate, Brooks, (music) Roger Brown, Frye, Gibbons, Hagstrum, Hook, Hyman, Kames, Lalande, (new criticism) Ransom, H. Read, Richards, Saintsbury, Van Deusen, A. Ward, Wragg, Zoll

Croce, Benedetto Leondar, Mazzeo, M. McLuhan, Sarmiento, Schiavina, Urban

cultismo (cf. culturanismo) Coster, (cultism) E. Kane

culturanismo (cf. cultismo) Atkinson, Borges

Cummings, E. E. Babcock, Friedman, E. Kane, Weimer

cybernetics Deutsch, Lauretano

Czepkos, Daniel von R. Muller

Dali, Salvador Llie

dance (as m) Lawler, (as m) P. Scott

Daniel, Samuel Wells

Dante Alighieri Applewhite, (m) H. Austin, Beck, Brandeis, Dunbar, (m) Fergusson, Ker, Mazzeo, Naumann, Olivero, Rabuse, Venturi, Vianu

Danto, Arthur Prado

Dario, Ruben Garcia-Giron

Das, Jivanananda Lago

Dauthendey, Max (as-if) Biese

Davidson, Donald (m) Bradford

Davie, Donald Love

Davis, J. Olscamp

Davis, Rebecca H. See

Day-Lewis, Cecil (R) L. Cranfield, H. Harris

death (as m) Spamer, Steinhoff, Tarrant, (as all m's) D. Thomas, (fiction) Vaihinger

defense mechanism (as m) Freud

delectation De

Deloney, Thomas Hablutzel

Democritus Sambursky

Demosthenes Adami, Baden, Ronnet, Straub

Derbolav, Josef Pongs

Descartes, Rene (mixed m) Edelman, Harriman, Mazzeo

design (as m) Embler

Desportes, Philippe Riniker, Solard

Dewey, John Dorfles, Groesbeck

diagram (as m) Frye, Leondar

Dickens, Charles   Hynes, Kafka

Dickinson, Emily   McNaughton, S. Wilson

Diderot, Denis   E. Huber

Dinglichkeit (thinginess)   Ransom

Dionysius of Halicarnassus   Greilich, Lockwood

Doblin, Alfred   Pongs

Dodsley, Robert   Page

dogma   (as m) Keller, (as m) Kendall

Donatus, Aelius   (on m) Charisius, Diomedis, Hispalensis

Donne, John   (conceits) Alden, (m) Allen, Bethell, (and D. Thomas) Chaneles, Empson, (Petrarchism) Guss, J. Lewis, T. Marsh, Mazzeo, McCann, W. Moses, Praz, Rugoff, A. Stein, Wells

Doppelempfinden   A. Wellek

Dostoevsky, Fedor   Matlaw

Douglass, F.   Andrew King

Drange, Theodore   Erwin, (R) R. Martin

dreams, as metaphorical (cf. m, Freudian theories of)   Boulton, Courcelle, Downing, Freud, (dream-like) Haworth, Hungerland, Knapp, Lauretano, C. Myers, (sleep) Nelson

Dreiser, Theodore   W. Phillips, Weimer

Droste-Hulshoff, Annette   Balkenhol, Pongs, Winkler

Dryden, John   (m) Compton, (image) R. Frazer, Hoffman, Jefferson

Du Marsais, Cesar   Diderot

Du Perron   Rousset

Duhem, Pierre   M. Hesse

Duhring, Eugene   Nyman

Dunbar, William   Hyde

Duns Scotus Burrell

Edwards, Jonathan Baumgartner

Edwards, Paul Gill

ego (see m, Freudian theories of)

Ehninger, D. Osborn

Eichendorff Pongs

Eichs, Gunter (Naturmetaphorik) Hesehaus

eighteenth century Atkins, (painters) Bodmer, (personification) Chapin, (synaesthesia) Erhardt-Siebold, (image) R. Frazer, (m) S. George, Lea, (German literature) R. Muller, Pride, Quayle, Spacks, Tomkins, Trickett, Wann, Wasserman, A. Wellek, Windfuhr

Eisenstein, Sergei Ellmann

Ekstein, Rudolf (see Elaine Caruth)

Eliot, George Deneau, Feltes, (imagery) Hardy, Steinhoff, Thale

Eliot, T. S. Feltenstein, Foster, Hyman, Jeffrey, H. McLuhan, John Steadman, Wasserman, Whalley

Eliseo, Thomas Vetter

Elizabethans (conceits) Alden, (m) Carpenter, (wit and rhetoric) W. Crane, (m, imagination) Halio, E. Holmes, T. Marsh, (poetry) Richards, Sharp, Tuve

Ellison, Ralph Bloch

Elster, Ernst R. Meyer, Nyman

emblem S. Brown, Gracian, E. Hill, Martyn, Mazzeo, Praz, Selig, Wasserman

Emerson, Ralph R. Adams, N. Baym, Keller

Empson, William (m) Dorfles, Olsen

Ennius, Quintus (m) Lefkowitz

epithet (cf. m, as substitution) (compound) Groom, (transfer of) Headlam, Hense, Quayle, Roberts, Robertson, Rohrich, Spicer

Ernst, Max Ellmann

Esnault, Gaston Migliorini

Estella, Diego de McCann

Estiennes, Henri E. Weber

euphuism (Lyly's) Carpenter, Konrad, Lyly

Euripides Hodler, Magdeburg, Pauer, Pecz, Rappold, M. St. John, E. Schwartz

Evans, Maurice Brewer

evolutionism (m of) Landau

extra-metaphorization Lauretano

Fabius A. Weiss

fame (as m) Mahoney

fancy (see imagination)

Faraday, Michael Vaihinger

Farre, George (seeing-as) Burlingame

Faulkner, William Flanagan, Gold, Guetti, J. Simon

Feidelson, Charles Jr. (see R. Ellmann) Mackey

Fenollosa, Ernest Dorfles, Kennedy, Liu

fiction (see m, as fiction)

Fillmore Lambert

Fitzgerald, Francis S. Burleson, Weimer

Flacco, A. Persio Parisi

Flaubert, Gustave   Demorest

Fleming, Noel   (seeing-as) Stadler

Fletcher, I.   (see W. Martin and Woolmer)

Flint, F. S.   Ellmann

Fodor, Jerry   (grammar) Barone, (m) Bickerton

Fonseca, Pedro da   Slattery

Forberg, Friedrich   Vaihinger

force   Nietzsche, (as m) Urbach

Force, Maryanne   (see Roland Force)

Ford, Ford Madox   Baernstein

form   (symbolic) Cassirer, (dramatic, lyrical, epic) Dallas, (symbolic) Langer, Pepper, (gestalt) Reichling, (symbolic) Urban

Forrest, David   Vetter

Forster, Edward   Raina

Foss, Martin   L. Knights, (R) Wheelwright, (R) Wimsatt

frame   (context frame) Black

Francastel, P.   Schiavina

France, Anatole   Rew

Frederick, Harold   See

Freud (cf. m, Freudian theories of)   (m) C. C. Anderson, (influence on Thomas) Chaneles, Lacan, H. Nash, Pederson-Krag, Pongs, Sarbin, Heinz Werner

Fronto, Marcus   McCall

Frost, Robert   (on m) Cole, Ogilvie, H. Ward

Funk, Robert   (R) Perrin

Garbutt, John (see R. Knapp)

Garcia Lorca, Federico Allemann, Friedrich, E. Huber, Llie, Turcato, Zardoya

Garcilaso de la Vega Alonso

Garnier, R. Raeder

Gautier, Theophile Rivers, E. Ullmann

George, Stefan Konrad

Gerber, Gustav Bauer, R. Meyer, Tupper

gesamtvorstellung (whole representation) Pluss

gestalt Reichling

gesture, as metaphor (see m, behavioral)

Gide, Andre Ellmann

Giono, Jean S. Ullmann

Giraud, Pierre Pasini

Giraudoux, Jean Charpentier, (m) LeSage

Gobineau, Count Joseph de Riffaterre

Godwin, William Rothstein, Storch

Goethe, Johann von Bauer, (m) Biese, Burckhardt, Diez, Henkel, Hocke, Mauthner, Pongs, Ryder, Schiff, Sohngen, Urbach, Vianu

Gogol, Nikolai Proffer

Gold, J. (R) Flanagan

Goll, Yvan Hesehaus

Gomez, Ramon Jackson

Gongora, Luis de Alonso, Atkinson, Gates, Gracian, (m) Guillen, Hocke, E. Kane, Mazzeo, Montes, B. Muller, Palley, L. Thomas, Uhrhan

Gorgias Isocrates

Gottfried of Strassburg Leistner

Gottschall, Rudolf von (on m) Beyer

Gottsched, Johann C. Adelung, Breitinger, D. Knight, Mansfeld, Nyman, Phelps

Gournay, Mlle de Rousset

Gracian, Baltasar (pen name: Lorenzo Gracian) Beinhauer, Bethell, Coster, Croce, Gonzalez, Hafter, Hatzfeld, Hocke, Lazaro, May, Mazzeo, C. Pellegrini, Sarmiento, Selig, Terry, Woods, Yndurain

grammar (generative) Lambert, (Fillmore Case) Lambert, (generative) Pavy, Ryle, (generative) Strang, (generative) O. Thomas

grammatical terms (as m) Curtius, Greenfield

Grant, C. K. Olscamp

Greek literature and poetry (figures) Barczat, (imagery) Becker, (m) Blumner, Bonnet, Buchner, (imagination) Bundy, (attic) Coenen, (analogy) Damon, de vocabulis . . . , (lyric) Dietel, (poetry) Disep, (rhetoric) Fraunce, (personification) A. Gerber, Hangard, Hans-Werner, Hardie, Hense, Hesehaus, Hoppe, (tragedy) Hormann, Keith, (m) Marzullo, (skeptics) Pappenheim, Roschatt, (philosophy) Shibles, R. Thomas, Tryphon, T. Webster

Green, Henry M. Turner

Greene, Robert (m) Carpenter

Gregory the Great Kathleen

Grimm, Jakob Bauer

Groby, Miss G. James, Thurber

Groos, Karl Nyman

ground (of a m) Ushenko

Gryphius, Andreas (imagery) Fricke, (m) Joos

Guevara y de Norona, Antonio Brinkmann

Guieysse, G. (see M. Schwob)

Guillen, Jorge Palley

gunas De

Gynt, Peer Roppen

haiku   Miner, Thompson, Yasuda

Hamann, Johann   (imagery) Blackall, Phelps

Hanson, Norwood   (seeing-as) Burlingame, (seeing-as) Soltis

Harding, D. W.   Knights

Hardy, Thomas   (m) Hornbeck, Littmann, A. Smart, A. Tate

Harris, George Washington   Rickels

Hawthorne, Nathaniel   A. Griffith, Shroeder

heart   Hermann, Shroeder

Hebbel, Friedrich   Feldkeller, Selina Meyer

Hegel, Georg W. F.   (dialectic) Chaneles, Specht

Heidegger, Martin   Nielsen

Heine, Heinrich   Silz

heiti (cf. kenning)   Einarsson

Hempel, H.   Pasini

Henle, Paul   C. Myers

Henning, Hans   Pongs

Henryson, Robert   Hyde

Hense, C.   Bauer

Heraclitus   Wheelwright

Herbart, Johann   Vaihinger

Herbert, George   Van Buren

Herder, Johann G. von   (m) Barnard, D. Knight, Phelps

hermeneutic   S. Brown, Funk, Klaus Lange

Herodotus   (m) Blumner

Herrick, Robert   Wentersdorf

Hesiod   Hirzel

Hesse, Mary   (R) Bennet

Hester, Marcus   Wajid, Wittgenstein

Heyms, Georg   Schneider

Hibbard, A.   (see Thrall)

Hidalgo, Jose Luis   Lorenz

Hildum, D.   (see Roger Brown)

Hispalensis   Vendome

Hjelmslev, L.   Pavel

Hobbes, Thomas   (conceit) Gang, George Watson

Hoffman, Robert   (see Wragg)

Hoffmann, E. T. A.   Rippley, Stock

Hofmannsthal, Hugo von   Mauser

Holderlin, Friedrich   Hof, Schottmann, Watt

Holman, C.   (see Thrall)

Homer, imagery and similes of   W. Anderson, Barclay, Basset, Bauer, (and Vergil) Baur, (oxmoron) Buchner, Coffey, Creore, Dahl, Damon, Duntzer, Egen, (synaesthesia) Engstrom, Frankel, Gerlach, Gertel, Greverus, Hirzel, (m) Keith, Ker, Kittlitz, (m) Konig, Krupp, LaRoche, D. Lee, Moog, Newton, Notopoulos, Parry, Pecz, Platt, Rambo, Rank, Semler, Shorey, Sickel, Silver, (synaesthesia) Stanford, (m) Viravsky, Wann, R. Wellek, Wier, Wilkins, Wittich

homology   Trier

Hopkins, Gerald Manley   (m) R. Boyle, (influence on D. Thomas) Chaneles, (compound words of) Chaneles, (R) Hess, Hines

Horace   (on metaphor of origins) Albert, Andrewes, (m) Baker, (ut pictura poesis) Haight, Lindstrom, Page, Robson, Schneider, Wilkinson

Housman, A. E.   W. Greene

Hugo, Victor   Baudelaire, (m) Brunetiere, (m) Degenhardt, (m) Duval, (m) Huguet, Konrad, Lucchetti, Matt, Nyman, Patterson, Robertson, Rousset

hui-i   Wu

Huizinga, Johan   Margolis

human body (as m for state) Hale, A. Taylor

Hume, David Mackey, Manser

humor (as expression of intellectual maturity) O. Asch, (in Spanish m) Beinhauer, Bergson, (in attic comedy) Blumner, (jokes) Boulton, (and category-mistake) Cross, (Mallarme) G. Davies, (of literary m) Demidoff, Freud, (as m play) Fry, Groesbeck, Jenkins, Kern, Koestler, Kohfeldt, Kuusi, Leisi, LeSage, Lucas, May, "Amusing Metaphors," "On the Mixing of Metaphor," Monro, Pasini, Peacock, C. Pellegrini, M. Pellegrini, Raimondi, Shibles, Shipley, Thurber, Wells

Husserl, Edmund Heinz Hulsmann, Nielsen, John Steadman

Huxley, T. H. Blinderman

Ibsen, Henrik Johnston, Reinert

icon (cf. substitution) (verbal) Bacon, (a standing-for) Brower, (representation) Bullinger, Henle, (symbolizing) Lemmon, C. Myers, H. Read, Sohngen, C. Williams, Wimsatt, Wu

iconography (Spenser) Aptekar, Widmer, F. Wilson

id (see m, Freudian theories of)

ideas (inseparable from reality) Bally, "Idea and Image," (of conceptism) Kane, (inseparable from word and object) Leondar, ("m of an idea") Leroux, ("idea" from "shape") Lucas, (m as) Manser, (as images) Olivero, Stutterheim

ideogram, Chinese Babcock, Fenollosa, Frye, Kenner, Liu, Wu

idiom F. Vonessen

image Agarwala, (meaningful) Aldrich, (management) Aldrich, (as comparison of real and unreal) Alonso, Antoine, (of creatures to God) Aquinas, Baernstein, (surrealist) Balakian, (concrete, dead, affective) Bally, Bauer, N. Baym, Becker, (violent) Bigsby, (pictorial) Bland, Bloch, Bodkin, Boillot, (and m) Boulton, (dynamic, non-visual) Brandenburg, (as recalled sensory experience) K. Brooks, Bruneau, (anti-) E. Burke, Clemens, Colvin, Comstock, Daiches, (in schizophrenia) Delmond, (in acting) Dodge, (as not accompanying m) Downer, Downey, (in Pope) T. Edwards, (in French romanticism) Eigeldinger, Eisenstein, (in H. James) P. Evans, (origin of) R. Frazer, Friedman, (definition of) Furbank, (reflexive) Gide, (definition of)

Gluskina, Gourmont, (heart) A. Griffith, (figurative) Groos, Hegel, Hoernle, G. Hughes, Hulme, Hynes, "Idea and Image," (surreal) F. Jones, Juilliere, (autism) Kanner, Kenner, (not necessary) Khatchadourian, Leiter, C. Lyons, (definition of) Manser, (human) Meadows, Miller, (dominant) Musurillo, (complex) Musurillo, Newman, O'Dea, Olivero, J. O'Neill, Pacernick, Peres, Pongs, Ponomariff, Pound, H. Read, Reverdy, Skelton, Smythies, Sohngen, Sperry, (definition of) Spurgeon, E. Stern, Sterzinger, W. Stevens, (voluntary, involuntary) W. Stevens, Storz, Taillardat, Thompson, Turnbull, Tuve, S. Ullmann, Urbach, Vaihinger, Van Ghent, A. Weiss, R. Wellek, Heinz Werner, Whalley, (imageless) Woodworth, Yeats

imagery (partial list) (of Rimbaud) Ahearn, (Horatian) Andrewes, (thematic, in The Faerie Queen) Apteker, (of Keats) Arestad, (as expression of intellectual maturity) Asch, (of Milton) Banks, Barfield, (of Spenser) Baroway, (oriental) Baroway, (scientific) Beaver, (of animals in Spanish) Beinhauer, (of Pindar) Bernard, (distribution of) Betts, (in Hamann) Blackall, (of Poe) Blanch, (of E. Taylor) Blau, (of Coleridge) Bliesener, (of Bismarck) Blumner, (in literature) K. Brooks, (Biblical) S. Brown, (of Jean Paul) Buchmann, E. Burke, (of killing) K. Burke, (color) Burleson, Church, Coombes, Dallas, (of H. Crane) R. Day, (in Greek poetry) Disep, (and recall) Eaton, (in drama) Ellis-Fermor, (in philosophy) Eucken, (in education) Fennema, Filzeck, (of N. West) Flavin, F. S. Flint, (archetypal) G. Foster, (eidetic) S. Foster, (defined) Friedman, (classification of) Friedman, (definition of) Furbank, Galton, (in brain-damage) Goldstein, (Egyptian) Grapow, (erotic) R. Harrison, Hemingway, E. Hesse, (in love-poetry) Hindermann, Hornstein, Hortnagl, (eidetic) Jaensch, (metaphysical poets) Kermode, (eidetic) Kluver, (psychological) Lay, (of Ruskin) G. Levin, (Chinese, defined) Liu, (alchemical) Mazzeo, McCabe, Miles, Mincoff, T. Moore, Muir, Nyman, (Frost) Ogilvie, Pear, Prior, (dictionary of) Provenzal, Reinert, Rickert, (verbal) Robbins, A. Rosenberg, (kinaesthetic) Sunesen, Tuve, Wells, Heinz Werner, Wordsworth

imagination Addison, Aikin, Alden, Aldrich, (Coleridge's theory of) J. Baker, (as grasping concrete images) Bally, (in W. Stevens) Betar, (child's) Biese, (metaphorical) Biese, Bodkin, (and fancy) Bodmer, (and fancy) Breitinger, (and fancy) Bullitt, (and invention) Bundy, E. Burke, (and reality in Stevens) Carruth, (primary and secondary; and fancy) Coleridge, (and fancy) Dallas, Durand, Esnault, (true and false) Fordyce, (as sense images) Gourmont, (ingenio) Gracian, (and fancy) H. Greene, (Elizabethan) Halio, D. James, Jordan, Lentricchia, H. Lewis, Lowes, Manser, Marignac, Montes, H. Myers, Nyman, (and fancy) Peacock, Ribot, (and fancy) Richards, (as m) Richards, Riddel, Romagnoli, (and fancy) Ruskin, (and fancy)

Scoggins, Shakespeare, Speranski, (and fancy) W. Stevens, (source of m) Stutterheim, Trowbridge, Turnbull, Vaihinger, F. Vonessen, (fancy) Wells, (types) Wheelwright, Woodhouse, (and fancy) Wordsworth, (and fancy) Zall

imagism Aldington, Coffman, Davie, Fang, F. S. Flint, S. Foster, Angus Graham, G. Hughes, Hulme, A. Jones, W. Martin, Miles, Miner, Pagnini, Pound, Pratt, W. Ramsey, Woolmer

impressionism (m of) Lazaro

incipits (and m) Kathleen

infinity (as m) Vaihinger

ingenio Coster, Gracian, (ingegno) Marzot, (ingegno) Mazzeo, (ingegno) Minozzi, (ingegno) M. Pellegrini, (ingegno) Raimondi, Sarmiento, (ingegnio) Terry, (ingegno) Tesauro

irony (as dialectic) K. Burke, Konrad, (antithesis) MacGill, Quinlan, Reinert, (as m) Speranski, Tschizewskij, Wells, Heinz Werner

Isaeus Baden, Lincke

Isaiah B. Robinson, C. Robinson

Isidore (see Hispalensis)

Jacobs, Vivian (see Wilhelmina Jacobs)

Jaensch, Erich (on images) S. Foster

Jakobson, Roman Erlich, Lacan, Pasini, Riffaterre, Stankiewicz, Wald

James, D. G. Knights

James, Henry P. Evans, R. Gale, P. Gibson, W. Gibson, (m) Hemstead, (m) Holder, Holder-Barell, V. Leonard, Short, Terrie, Todasco, Weimer

James, William (m) C. C. Anderson

Jauregui y Aguilar, Juan M. de Lazaro

Jean Paul (see Johann Richter)

Jevons, William Vaihinger

John of the Croſs McCann

Johnson, Samuel (personification) Bronson, Carnochan, (on criticism and m) Hagstrum, Page, Perkins, Ricks

Jonson, Ben (m) Carpenter, South

Jordan, E. Whittier

journey Fergusson, (as m) Roppen

Joyce, James (influence on D. Thomas) Chaneles, (extended similes of) B. Collins, Isaacs, Kronegger, Manso, Thornton

Jung, Carl G. (on archetypes) Bodkin, (R) Wheelwright

Juvenal (m's of) Genther, (hyperbole) E. Harrison

Kafka, Franz (as antimetaphorical) Allemann, Hillmann

Kainz, Friedrich Pongs

Kaiser, Wolfgang Hocke

Kames, Lord Henry Home (m) Blair

Kaminsky, F. Olscamp

Kanner, L. R. Saussure

Kant, Immanuel (on symbol as absolute metaphor) Blumenberg, Croce, Emerson, Esnault, Eucken, Mackey, Manser, Margolis, Mauthner, Nyman, Ortega, Sohngen, Specht, Takeda, Tarbet, Vaihinger, Veca

Kaplan, B. (see Heinz Werner)

Kaplan, Werner (picture sentence of) Church

Katz, Jerrold (see also J. Fodor) (grammar of) Barone, (m) Bickerton

Keats, John Arestad, (m) D'Avanso, (synaes.) Downey, Fogle, Haworth, Kaufmann, Kauvar, Mahoney, S. Ullmann, Van Ghent

Keller, Gottfried (similes of) Fleissner

Keniston, K. (see A. Couch)

kenning (kenningar cf. heiti, reknar) Bode, Borges, (varying, and concealing) Browne, D. Collins, Einarsson, Hollander, (anti-) E. Kane, Marquart, R. Meissner, Merwe, Mizener, M. Muller, Quayle, Rankin, Reichardt, Spitzer, Vigfusson, Waern, H. Ward

Kerenyi (R) Wheelwright

Killy, Walter Pongs

King, Bishop (on analogy) A. Collins

King, Martin Luther Andrew King

Kleist, Heinrich von Kanter, Ritzler, Senger

Knights, L. and B. Cottle (R) Rau

Komornicka, Anna Pasini

Konrad, Hewig (R) Bruneau, (R) Marcel Cohen, (R) Louis, (R) Marouzeau

Koran, metaphors of al-Baquillani, (m) Ibn al-Sharif, Quṭb, Sabbagh, Sister

Kreutzfeld Nyman

Kuhn, Thomas Nicolson

Kyd, Thomas (m) Carpenter, Wells

La Creppede, Jean de Solard

Lange, Konrad Margolis, Nyman, Vaihinger

Langer, Susanne (on m) Dorfles, Logan

language (picture) Aldrich, (constitutes objects) Allemann, (origin of) Barfield, (constitutes thought) Beardsley, (Spanish) Beinhauer, (symbolic and mythical) Cassirer, (logos and m) Coleman, (as constituting reality) Coleridge, (as intuition and thought) Croce, (figurative) Grindon, (analogous with life) Kalmus, (as game) Mandelbaum, (picture theory of) Schwyzer, Shibles, Strang, Urban language, as all or nearly completely metaphorical   Adler, Allemann, (almost) S. Baker, Barfield, (political as m) Barnard, (not) Bilsky, Child, T. D., Demetrius, Edie, Fenollosa, F. C. Flint, Foss, (everyday speech) Foultz, (as entirely images) Gourmont, Hamann, (has Metapherngeist) Herder, (as image) Hulme, Kaufmann, Lucas, M. McLuhan, Nietzsche, Richards, Schlanger, Stutterheim, Wald, Walsh, A. Ward, (vocabulary as m) Warfel, P. Weiss, Wheelwright

language-game   Mandelbaum, Petrie, Wittgenstein

Lanier, Sidney   (scientific image in poetry) Beaver

Larsson, Hans   Nyman

Lauretano, Bruno   (R) Francioni

Lawrence, D. H.   (imagery of) Beutmann, (m) Hinz, Isaacs, Jeffries, (simile) Nicholes

Lazamon   (similes of) H. Davies

Leconte de Lisle, Charles   E. Ullmann

Lee, I.   (R) Wheelwright

Leiter, R.   (see Roger Brown)

Leon, Luis de   McCann

Leroux, Pierre   D. Evans

Lessing, Gotthold   Phelps

Levin, Samuel   Ellis

Lewis, C. S.   Norwood, Stewig

Lewis, Hywel   Knights

light   (m use of) Bausani, Blumenberg, (as m) Knauber, Olken, Osborn, Pardee, Rowley, Sharkey, Tarrant, Tschizewskij

linguistics   (as metaphorism) Valesio

Lipps, Hans   Pongs

Lira, T.   (pseudonym of Harry Feltenstein)

l'isti'arah ("metaphor" in Arabic)   Sabbagh

Liszt, Franz   Silz

literal (cf. steno-language)   Adler, (in religion) Aldrich, (descriptions) Allers, (as basis of m) Aschenbrenner, (as only conventionally distinguishable from metaphorical) Ballard, (achieved and born) Barfield, (as deriving from metaphorical) Barfield, (as dictionary meaning) Carney, (in science, philosophy prose, oratory) Croce, (no non-metaphorical definition of) Ferre S. George, H. Greene (least figurative), Harrell, (humanizing) Kohfeldt, (achieved and born) Leondar, (no) C. S. Lewis, Nemetz, (based on frequency) A. Paul, (as bold) M. St. John, Shibles, Sohngen, (as belonging to a universe of discourse) Urban, Zipf

literalization   (as rhetorical device) Quinlan

Locke, John   Addison, Bauer

Longfellow, Henry W.   S. Ullmann

Longinus, Dionysius   R. Lee, Page, A. Tate

love allegory of   C. S. Lewis

Lowell, Amy   Miles

Lucian   O. Schmidt

Lucretius (Carus), Titus   (simile) Hohler, Raumer, Spangenberg

Lukacs, Georg   Hagopian

Lusitano, Candido   (see F. Freire)

Lydgate, John   J. N. Smith

Lyly, John   (m) Carpenter

Machado, Antonio   Alonso, Llie

Machiavelli, Niccolo   Lauretano

machine   (see metaphor, machine)

MacLaren, Alexander   Martyn

Madiros, A.   Olscamp

matter (as m) Urbach, Vaihinger

Maupin (see Cain)

Maximus, Bishop (imagery of) Conroy

Maxwell, James Clerk J. Turner

Mays, W. Olscamp

McCann, E. Simmonds

McCloskey, Mary Kames

meaning (cf. m, as meaning) (pictorial) Aldrich, (meaning of) Aleksandrowicz, D. Allen, Asche, Aschenbrenner, W. Austin, Barfiel Berggren, Bradford, Breal, Brodbeck, J. Brown, Du Marsais, (of m) Eicke, Embler, Esnault, (connotative) Frentz, Frye, (image as) Friedman, Greenfield, (change of) Hecht, (and m) Henel, Henle, Hester, Hoernle, (change of) Kroesch, Lambert, Lazlo, Leckey, Leondar, Lieb, Logan, ("whole meaning") Mackey, (as imagery) MacNeice, Manser, Needham, Nemetz, Novakova, Ogden, Osgood, Philbrick, Shibles, (as a m translation) Sohngen, G. Stern, ("whole meaning") Tilden, S. Ullmann, Urban, Walpole, Weinrich, Welby

Mechthild of Magdeburg Luers

medicine, metaphor in Begelman, Calvi, Minkowski

Medina, Jose Ramon Lorenz

Meier, Hugo (R) Lieb, (R) Soll

Meireles, Cecilia Mendes

Melville, Herman Guetti, Key, Rowland

memory Esnault, (m as relation between sensation and memory) Fiser (basis of m) Fruit, (of images) Galton, Hardy, Hecht, (m as trans formation and forgetting of original meaning) Hytier, (image) Jaensch, (as basis of m) Peacham, Stutterheim

mental illness (as myth) Sarbin, Szasz

Mercier, Louis-Sebastian Patterson

Meredith, George Littmann

Merleau-Ponty, M. Edie

metafora; Revista Literaria (see same)

metagogia (pathetic fallacy) Torre

metamorphosis (see m, as metamorphosis)

metapherein (metaphor) (Webster's Dictionary) Metaphor

Metaphern-freundlich Eicke

Metapherngeist Herder

metaphora Isocrates, (E.B., 11) Metaphor

metaphorally (O.E.D.) Metaphor

metaphorical (as different from metaphor) Biese, (as embodying spirit) Biese

metaphorical license Urbach

metaphorical twist Beardsley

metaphorician Vaihinger

metaphorics Curtius, (Schrift- und Buch-) Curtius

Metaphoriker Vaihinger

Metaphorisch Mayrocker

metaphorist (O.E.D.) Metaphor

metaphorize (O.E.D.) Metaphor

metaphorologie Blumenberg

metaphorous (O.E.D.) Metaphor

Metaphysical Poets (conceits) Alden, Kermode, Mazzeo, McCann, W. Moses, Mourgues, Perkins, (based on m) Ransom, Sharp, Shepherd, Tuve, George Watson

metaphysics (cf. m, Thomistic theories of; and m, as metaphysics) (m) Ballard, (as basis of analogy) Ballard, N. Baym, Borges, (mad) Chesterton, (and m) Chesterton, (and seeing-as) Copleston, Costello, Emmet, (of symbol and m) Flesch, (and m) Heidegger, Henderson, (analogy) MacIntyre, Masiello, McInerny, Nemetz, Pepper, Reichenbach, Rousset, Sohngen, Stutterheim, Sweet, Terry, Tindall, Turbayne, Urban, C. Wagner, Whittier, Wisdom, Zoll

metaplasm (alteration for meter or ornament) Sacerdos

metecsemie Carnoy

metonymy (as a real relation) Alonso, (as a substitution) Alonso, S. Brown, (as reduction) K. Burke, (as cause-effect relation) Church, Dannehl, H. Greene, Heylen, Holz, R. Meyer, Sayce, See, Sherry, Warfel

Meyer, Theodor Nyman

Meyers, C. M. Olscamp

Michaux, Henry Zaubitzer

middle ages Arbesmann, (rhetoric of) Arbustow, (imagination) Bundy, Curtius, (analogy in) Damon, Debaisieux, (m in) De Bruyne, (arbor picta) Dieter, Diomedis, (symbol in) Dunbar, Ker, (imagery of) Kohler, C. S. Lewis, Luers, A. Wellek, Whitbread

Migliorini, Bruno Sala

Mill, John Stuart Sanderson

Milo, Titus Itzinger

Milton, John (imagery of) Banks, (m in) J. Cope, (simile) Grose, Lerner, Mackin, Ricks, Shawcross, Sherwin, Tuve, Whaler, Widmer

mind-body (as m) Vaihinger

Minozzi, Pierfrancesco Mazzeo

mirror (cf. speculum) St. Augustine, (as m) Hugede, (of God) Slattery, Sohngen, Wasserman, O. Weise

mistro (mystery) Gracian

Mittner, L. (R) Browne

models (cf. m, as model) (scientific) Achinstein, (of Freud, Plotinus) Allers, (psychological) C. C. Anderson, (scientific) Apostel, (political science) Barnard, (biological) Beament, (psyc) Begelman, (constitutive of object) Berggren, (explanatory) Berggren, (scale, analogue, theoretical, submerged, archetypal) Black, (scientific) Brodbeck, (biological) Canguilhem, (scientific) Denbigh, (engineering) Finzi-Contini, Freudenthal, (of reality) Hagopian, Shibles, Stogdill, Strang, (game-model) Szasz, Toulmin

modification (principle of) Uhrhan

Moliere (pseudonym) (m's of) Degenhardt, D. Meier, Meyer

Monroe, Harriet (see Hart Crane)

montage, as metaphor (in film) Balazs, Eisenstein, (i.e. Struktur)

Schlotthaus, L. Wagner

taigne, Michel de   Coupland, Mayer, Rousset, Schnabel

re, Marianne   Olsen

ike, Eduard   Kappenberg

ris, Charles   Dorfles

ler, Max   (on poetic m) Barfield, (on radical m) Barfield, Bauer, (on m) Beyer, H. Frost, Jesperson, Mauthner, Stanford, (anti) A. Ward

ro, D.   Olscamp

set, Alfred de   (m) Brand

h (cf. m, as myth)   Alden, Alvarez, Biese, (as m) Brooks, (as reciprocally determining language) Cassirer, Christiansen, (m-to-myth transformation) Chun, (Irish) D. Clark, (m-to-myth transformation) Morris Cohen, (and m) Daiches, (and m) Dorfles, J. Frazer, (as m) Frye, Gertel, Hsia, Keith, Konrad, Lauretano, Law, M. Lewis, Littlefield, Madge, Mauron, F. Muller, Nemerov, (as m) Rank, (based on m) Ransom, Riddel, (m-to-myth transformation) Sarbin, Snell, Stutterheim, Trickett, Trzynadlowskiego, R. Wellek

hopoetic   Marshall Cohen, Wheelwright

el, Ernest   (see Morris Cohen)

e, as metaphor   Gracian, Lever, Lord, Mendelsohn, Nemerov, Vaihinger

he, Thomas   Liedstrand, Wells

ura cursus   Galinsky

ure   (as trope) Emerson, (as universal m) Turbayne

ro   (as m) L. Johnson, (oratory) Andrew King, (literature) Klotman

logisms   Vetter

val, Gerard de (pseudonym)   Schicker

rology   Sperry

ell, A.   (see H. Simon)

iger, Hans   (R) Moraux

Newman, John P. Scott

Nicole, Pierre Rousset

Nietzsche, Friedrich Groos, Hesehaus, Lawler, Urbach, Vaihinger

novel, as metaphor Embler, Hagopian

objective correlative Eliot, Feltenstein, Fogle, Jeffrey, H. McLuhan, John Steadman, Wasserman, (pointing m) Whalley

objects (used metaphorically) Brinkmann

Ockham, William Menges

Okey, L. (see K. Brooks)

Olbrechts-Tyteca, L. (see Perelman)

Ortega y Gasset, Jose (m's of) Arroyo, Jaurrieta, (E.L.) Metafora, Pongs, Vela, Heinz Werner

Osgood, Charles (connotative measurement scale) Frentz

Ovid (similes of) Brunner, Owen, Richardson, Washietl

Owens, Joseph (Thomism) J. Anderson

oxymoron (cf. m as antithesis) Abel, Breitinger, (in Greek poetry) Buchner, (masochism) Gracian, (anti) Kane, McCann, A. Phillips, Simmonds, Weinrich, R. Wellek, Wheelwright

Pallavicino (see Sforza-Pallavicino)

parables (of Rabbis) Feldman, (as m) Funk, Ibn al-Sharif, Moogan, (as m) Rhys-Davids

Paracelsus, Philippus Singleton

Parkhurst, H. Shipley

Parmenides Vaihinger

parody Rohrich

Pasternak, Boris Jakobson

pathetic fallacy Abrams, Breitinger, K. Burke, Dick, Miles, Noel, Pasini, Ruskin, Schlauch, Torre

Paul, Hermann   Pongs

Paul, Saint   (m's of) Albani, S. Brown, Frye, (analogies of) H. Gale, (m's of) Gryglewicz, Heylen, (m) Howson, Hugede, Ramsay, B. Robinson

Paulhan, Fr.   Nyman

Pavel, Toma   Pasini

Peacham, Henry   Susenbrotus

Pederson-Krag, Geraldine   C. C. Anderson

Peele, George   (m) Carpenter

Pellegrini, Camillo   (Peregrini) Sarmiento

Pellegrini, Matteo   Croce, (Peregrini) Hocke, Mazzeo, Woods

pendulum-theory   (Lange) Nyman

perception (cf. m, perceptual)   (physiognomic) Gombrich, (as knowing) Gombrich, Soltis

Peregrini, Camillo   (see Pellegrini, C.)

Peregrini, Matteo   (see M. Pellegrini)

Persius   Pierson

person (persona)   (as m) Breal

personification   (of abstractions) Aikin, Alden, Biese, (allegory) M. Bloomfield, Bronson, S. Brown, (of fate) Browne, (as conveying moral worth) Chapin, (in 18th century) Chapin, (lyrical form) Dallas, (dramatic form seems to be a reverse personification) Dallas, (of Romans) Engelhard, (m as) C. Ferguson, <u>Figures of Speech</u>, (in history texts) Flaum, Freud, (nature-) A. Gerber, H. Greene, Harrington, Hense, (anti) Hobbes, (as misleading) Huxley, Jackson, Keith, Komornicka, Lauretano, Lever, (allegory) C. S. Lewis, Mackel, (extended) G. Martin, Morel, ("fundamental metaphor") F. Muller, H. Nash, Petersen, Pongs, Quayle, Reinhardt, Robbe-Grillet, (criaturalismo) Rodriguez-Alcala, Schlauch, Shelley, Slattery, Spacks, W. Stevens, Stutterheim, Trickett, (reversal of) Tschizewskij, Urbach, Vaihinger, Wasserman, T. Webster, Weisgerber, Yasuda

Peters, R. S.   Louch

Petronius   (m) Downer

phoros Perelman

phraseoplerosis (Bentham) Ogden

Picasso, Pablo (on plastic m) Aldrich

picture (cf. m, as pictorial) (meaningful) Aldrich, (T or F) Aldrich, (juxtaposition of) Benamou, (theory of meaning) Daitz, (as m) McLuhan, (theory) Schwyzer, (philosophical) Shibles, G. Myers, Urbach, Vaihinger, Wittgenstein

picturesque Hillenbrand, C. Hussey, (anti) Kevin, H. McLuhan

Pindar Bernard, Hardie, Hense, Hines

Plato (analogies of) J. Anderson, (m) Berg, Bertram, Burrell, Courcelle, (and hieroglyph) Dieckmann, Grenet, F. Harrison, J. Huber, G. Hussey, Lauretano, Lingenberg, Louis, Mackey, Marignac, Sambursky, Sihler, Tarrant, Tigner, Urbach, Vaihinger, Wiegandt

Plautus, Titus (m's of) Forehand, Graupner, Inowraclawer, Langen, Mendelsohn

Pleiad (of Parnassus) Le Hir

Plotinus (on use of conscious models and metaphors) Allers, (image of) Brehier, C. Wagner

plurisignation (cf. m, and multiple-meanings) Wheelwright

Plüss, Theodor Nyman

Plutarch (m) Dronkers, McCall

Poe, Edgar Allen (images of) Blanch, (synaesthesia) Downey, Kronegger

poem, as painting (cf. m, as pictorial; m, as drawn) Babbitt, Benamou, Bodmer, Breitinger, Dankmeyer, C. Davies, Dryden, Hagstrum, Haight, Horace, Howard, Lamotte, Landow, (imitation of) R. Lee, Lessing, Park, Schlegel, Wimsatt

poetic license Dryden, (metaphorical license) Urbach

poetic metaphor (as conscious m) Barfield, Lever

poetry (20th century) Alleman, (as algebra of m's) Arroyo, Barquen (as m's) Biese, (metaphysical) Brandenburg, (as m's) Brooks, (revolution in) Brooks, (metaphysical) Brooks, (and mathematics) Buchanan, (as m's) K. Burke, (as m's) Burkland, (as m's) G.

Carter, (as m; Yeats) D. Clark, Coenen, (Romantic) Conzelmann, (as universal analogy) Croce, E. E. Cummings, (Sanskrit) De, (Canadian) Djwa, (rose in) Friend-Pereira, (Nahuatl) R. Gonzalez, (not m's, Housman) W. Greene, (as m's) W. Greene, (grammar, meaning) Greenfield, (as m's) Gummere, (imagery) Hardt, (as not m's) Hess, (Czechoslovakian) Horak, Horrell, Housman, (as m's) D. James, (not m's) Jennings, Johann, (as m's) Lanier, Lodge, (as m's) Nair, (as m's) Olivero, (as m's) Ortega, (as m's) Parkhurst, (as m's) Pasini, (as imitation) Peacock, Perry, Petsch, (as m's) Ransom, Rew, (as m's) Rousset, (as all m) Shelley, (as m) Shklovskii, Sidney, Skelton, (French) Spicer, Spire, Sterzinger, (as m's) W. Stevens, Storz, Strich, (as m's) Sucre, (as m) D. Thomas, Tyler, Valentine, Wahl, (about poetry) R. Wallace, (as m's) Wasserman, Wheelwright, R. Willis, (as naked) Yasuda, Zimmermann

Polybius   Wunderer

Pongs, Hermann   Deutschbein, (R) Fink, Laan, (R) Seidler

Pope, Alexander   (suppressed m in) Bluestone, (image cluster of) T. Edwards, (m's of) Fogle, (image) Kallich, Mack, Mengel, Page, Pettit, Warburton, A. Williams, Wimsatt

portmanteau words   (of L. Carroll) Ferdiere

Porzig, Walter   Pongs

Postal, P.   (on m) Bickerton

Pound, Ezra (see also F. S. Flint)   Ellmann, Fenollosa, G. Hughes, Kennedy, Kenner, Liu, Miner, Wajid

Praz, Mario   Mazzeo

precieux   (of Giraudoux) LeSage, (poetry) Mourgues, (Preziositat) Riniker

pretending   J. Austin, S. Baker, (games) Berne, (psychiatric) Caruth, Haworth

Price, H.   Manser

Prodicus from Ceos   Lauretano

Propertius, Sextus   (m) Marcellino

Proust, Marcel   Fiser, V. Graham, (m) Guichard, Kolb, Linn, Matore, Pardee, S. Ullmann, Virtanen, Waber

Prudentius, Aurelius   Kudlien

puns   Alden, (of Petronius) Downer, Empson, Gracian, (anti)

Kane, (méssage, messáge) M. McLuhan, Mendelsohn, Monro, Sherry, Wilhington

Quevedo y Villegas, Francisco G. de   Brinkmann

Quintilian   (m of) Assfahl, Bauer, Capella, (didactic m's of) J. Carter, McCall, M. Pellegrini, Vendome, Wackernagel

Rabelais, Francois   Coupland, La Juilliere

Racan, Honore de   Solard

Racine, Jean   Cretin, N. Gross, Sayce, Schurmeyer, Vercel

radical metaphor   (see m, radical)

Ramsey, Ian   (R) Gill, Tesauro

Ramus, Petrus   Tuve, Zoll

Ransom, John Crowe   K. Knight

rasa   De, Nair

ratio communis (cf. m, Thomistic theory of)   McInerny

reality, as analogical   J. Anderson, (as conceited) Gracian, (as literal) W. Stevens, (a book) Sucre

regulative ideas   Vaihinger

Reichard, G.   Wheelwright

Reichling, A.   Stutterheim

reknar (cf. kenning)   Einarsson

renaissance   (m) D. Allen, (rhetoric) Brennan, (imagination in) Bundy, (wit and rhetoric of) W. Crane, (English) Hablutzel, (political analogy in) Hale, Laguardia, Mazzeo, Wasserman, A. Wellek, Zoll

repetition   (as the unexpected in art) Battcock

resultant   (of m) Ushenko

Reyes, Alfonso (m) Himelblau, Robb

Reynolds H. Gerber

Rhetorica ad Herennium McCall, Vendome

rhetorical terms (as m) Curtius

Richards, I. A. (m) Bilsky, Bland, Dorfles, Fogarty, Frentz, Hotopf, Hyman, Kames, A. Kaplan, Lauretano, Ransom, Jerome Schiller, Ushenko

Richter, Johann Paul (Jean Paul, pseudonym) (as richest of German m's) Biese, (imagery of) Buchmann, Koffka, Mauthner, Musken, Pongs, Rasch

riddles (see metaphor as puzzle)

Riffaterre, Michael Ellis

Rig-Veda (m) Hirzel, (m's of) Weller

Rilke, Rainer Kobayashi, Krummacher

Rimbaud, Arthur (images of) Ahearn, Kloepfer, Schicker

Robbe-Grillet, Alain (m's) Hagopian

Robinson, Richard (on Thomistic analogy) J. Anderson

<u>Roland</u> Bulatkin

romanticism (theory of) Abrams, (style of) Barat, (American) T. Boyle, (Volkslied) Conzelmann, (1900-1950) Craddock, (German) Dieckmann, Krummacher, Lewy, Newman, Petrich, H. Read, Rousset, S. Ullmann, M. Vonessen

Ronsard, Pierre de Riniker, Silver

rosa mystica (in middle-English poetry) Friend-Pereira

Rousseau, Henri R. Lee, Schlanger

rupaka (m) Nair

Ruskin, John Landow, Miles

Ruston, P. (see Norton)

Ryle, Gilbert A. Baker, (on category-mistakes) Cross, Erwin, Hillman, (on category-mistake) Khatchadourian, Manser, Orpinela, J. Smart, Smythies

Sacerdos (on figures of speech) Cassiodorus

Sachsphare Deutschbein

Sahagun, P. (Aztec m) Holtker

Saint-Armant, Marc de Solard

Saint-Gelais, Mellin de Riniker

Samson, Richard (see Albert Upton)

Sapir, Edward Leondar

Sappho (similes of) Damon

Sartre, Jean Paul Manser, S. Ullmann

satire (of Horace) Baker, Gracian, Horace, Rodriguez-Alcala

Saussure, Ferdinand de Lacan, Mandelbaum

Scalds (see kenning)

Schaar, Claes (see J. N. Smith)

Scheer, Richard (see James Carney)

Schelling, Friedrich von F. Vonessen

Schiller, Johann Margolis, Nyman, Johann Schiller

schizophrenia (art in) Basaglia, Caruth, (figures of speech of) Chapman, (image in) Delmond, Ekstein, Ferdiere, R. Johnson, Navratil, Pavy, Piro, J. Read, (as myth) Sarbin, Heinz Werner, White

schlemiel (as m) Pinsker

Schopenhauer, Arthur Mauthner, Nyman

Scott, Sir Walter Fiske

Scriblerus, Martinus (see A. Pope)

sea (storm) Kahlmeyer, Keith (as mythical), E. Schwartz

seeing-as Aldrich, Bevis, Bouwsma, Burlingame, Copleston, Daiches, Downey, Farre, (m as) C. Ferguson, Ferre, Fleming, (as knowing) Gombrich, Hanson, (reading as) Hester, (aspect-seeing) Hester, Hick, ("experiencing-as") Hick, Hungerland, (Valery) Hytier, Jaensch, Kuhn, Langer, (as participation) Lauretano, May, Mehrabian, Nicolson, Norwood, Ortega, Petrie, Richards, Soltis, Sperry, Stadler, Sterzinger, W. Stevens, Tilghman, Toulmin, Van Steenburgh,

Vesey, (aspect) Wajid, Wasserman, Wheelwright, Wittgenstein

Sein und Scheitern (as m's) Blume

semasiology (and m) Gardner

semejanza (m or simile) Gracian

Seneca, Lucius H. Lyons, McCall, Ryba, C. S. Smith, Stewig

sensus litteralis Nemetz

sentence, metaphoric J. Brown

separation (principle of) Uhrhan

seventeenth century Cabeen, (logic and rhetoric) Howell, Marzot, Mazzeo, Nicolson, Praz, Pride, Ragsdale, Rousset, Solard, A. Wellek, Windfuhr, Woods, Zoll

Sevigne, Marquise de (list of images) Kogel

Sforza-Pallavicino, Cardinal (conceit) Mazzeo, Praz

Shakespeare, William Armstrong, Brooks, Carnochan, Charney, Clemen, Coleridge, M. Crane, Daiches, Elliot, Ellis-Fermor, Foakes, Galinsky, M. Golden, Greenberg, Hankins, Harrier, Heilman, Hense, Hobday, Hubner, Helene Hulsmann, Jenkins, Joseph, Kanzer, G. Knight, Knights, F. Kolbe, Lambrechts, Lawlor, Leskov, Marheineke, T. Marsh, H. Matthews, Mauthner, Mizener, Morozov, Mrozkowski, Muir, O'Dea, Pettet, Praz, Prior, Rubinstein, Sanford, Schnemann, E. Smith, B. Spencer, Spevack, Spivack, C. F. Spurgeon, Stauffer, Vianu, H. Voigt, Wietfield, Yoder

Shapiro, Karl L. Wagner

Sharpe, Ella F. (m) Caruth

Shelley, Percy B. Butter, (synaesthesia) Downey, Fogle, Freydorf, Mortenson, O'Malley, Schulz

Sherry, Richard Peacham

Shibles, Warren (R) G. Myers, Urban, Wittgenstein

ship (as m) Allen, Goldammer, (wreck) Kahlmeyer, (drunken) Kloepfer, (of state) Wolf

sickness (as m) Spamer

Sidney, Sir Philip T. Marsh, Wells

sign Lauretano, Pelc

Sihler, E. (on Plato) Berg

simile (cf. m, as simile) E. Adams, Alden, (dictionary of) Aguilar, (Homer) W. Anderson, (Dante) Applewhite, (as m) Aristotle, (Quintilian) Assfahl, Bandyopadhyay, Basset, (Vergil, Homer) Baur, S. Brown, (Ovid) Brunner, Cameron, (in Elizabethan drama) Carpenter, (collection of) Cawdry, (as God's master plan) Cheyne, Christiansen, (Wordsworth) Ciesielski, Coffey, "Comparisons Beyond Compare," (Vergil) Cooley, (Brantome) Coupland, (unanalyzable) Croce, (Aeschylus) Dahlgren, Dankmeyer, (Lazamon) H. Davies, Degen, (French) De Lozier, (types) Deutschbein, (Greek lyric) Dietel, (collection of) Dony, (Plutarch) Dronkers, Duntzer, (Homer) Egen, (as play) Eichholz, (in Kant) Eucken, (in prose) Eusebio, (of Rabbis) Feldman, (in historical texts) Flaum, (of Keller) Fleissner, (in science) Gimeno, (in Sanskrit) Gonda, (confused) Goodsell, (in H. Beecher) A. J. Graham, (of Conrad) Graver, (Spencer) Green, (stated) H. Greene, (Miltonic) Grose, (conscious) Gummere, (French) Hachtmann, Hegel, (Vergilian) Hornsby, (in Catullus) Howe, (strange) Hutchinson, (Arabic) Ibn Abi 'Aun, Keith, (Dante) Ker, Kleiser, (Bengali) Lahiri, D. Lee, (closed) Leondar, (Miltonic) Lerner, Lucas, Margolis, McCall, Meszaros, Moseley, (upama) Nair, O. Nash, (French) Nazaryan, Nicholes, Nyman, Odell, Owen, Paradkar, Pluss, Proffer, (recurring) Rees, Rew, Rhys-Davids, Rieser, Ronnet, Sarv, Schultes, Seidler, (detached) Sherwin, Showerman, "New Similes Each Year," E. Smith, (dictionary of) J. Spencer, Spurgeon, (bee-) J. Steadman, Steele, A. Taylor, Vico, H. Voigt, E. Webster, Whaler, E. Wheeler, Wheelwright, Widmer, Wilkins, (dictionary of) Wilstach, Wohlberg, Yasuda

similitudo templi Flasche

Simonides of Ceos Horace

sixteenth century (m and symbol in) Brewer, (m and symbol in) Evans, (logic and rhetoric in) Howell, Huguet, Lea, R. Lee, Michaelsson, Ragsdale, Solard, A. Wellek

slang (insight in) Andrews, (as m) Andrews, (jargon) Brooks, (jargon) Brunot, (French) Esnault, (student) Kluge, (African) Kok, Lauretano, Liebesny, Mausser, Nosek, B. Porter, Randolph, (French) Schultz, (French) Schwob, Tomkins, Wakeman

Slattery, Michael (m) R. Boyle

Smith, Adam Vaihinger

Smyrnaeus, Quintus Niemeyer

Snider, James (see Osgood)

Snorri Sturluson (on the kenning) Borges, (categories of) Brodeur

Solana Llie

sone Whalley

Sophocles Goheen, Hense, Hirzel, Lindner, Musurillo, Pecz, Rappold, Rieger, M. St. John

sound (as m) A. Stein

space (picture) Aldrich, Vaihinger

Sparshott, F. Olscamp

speculum (mirroring) Nemetz

Spenser, Edmund Aptekar, Baroway, Glazier, Gottfried, Green, (simile) Heise, Sam Meyer, Wells, Yuasa

spirit (=breath) Lucas, F. Muller

Sponde, Jean de Solard

Sprachbild (collective m) Vonessen

Sprat, Bishop A. Rosenberg

Spurgeon, Caroline (anti) Friedman, (anti) Hornstein, G. Knight, F. Kolbe, (pro) M. Smith

Stadler, Ernst Schneider

Stahlin, Wilhelm (on Spanish m) Beinhauer, Laan, Pongs

Stalin, Joseph Pongs

Stanford, William Wimsatt

Stanislawski, Ryszard (see "Zwiazek . . . ")

Statius, Publius Papinius H. Wilson

steno-language (cf. literal) Marshall Cohen, Wheelwright

Stern, Gustaf Dorfles, Shibles

Sterne, Laurence Isaacs, Singleton

Sterzinger, Otto Nyman, Pongs

Stevens, Wallace (on poetry and painting) Benamou, (on imagination) Betar, (m's of) Bevis, Brumleve, (R) Carruth, Egan, Ellis, Ench, Frye, Isaacs, Bruce King, Lentricchia, Liddie, Logan, Morse, Nassar, Ransom, Riddel, Sheehan, M. Turner

Stewig, John   Zale

Stöcklein   Hecht

stoic   (rhetoric) Barwick

Stowe, Harriet Beecher   See

structuralism   Riffaterre

struktur   (see montage)

Sturluson   (see Snorri)

Sturm, H. G.   (see Sara Sturm)

Stutterheim, Cornelis   (R) Laan, (R) Meeussen, (R) Rooth

style   (German) Adelung, (of images) Antoine, S. Baker, Bally, (of romanticism) Barat, Craddock, Demetrius, Gerlach, Gourmont, (paradoxical) Groos, (French) Hachtman, Haugsted, Huttig, Kafka, Kent, K. Knight, Kramer, Lambrechts, Lauretano, Leech, Le Hir, Leroux, Lindstrom, Lucas, (as constituting what is said) Mackey, Manso, Marquart, Mincoff, Mizener, Moseley, Nowottny, R. Parker, Pasini, Petrich, Raleigh, H. Read, Riffaterre, Ronnet, Sayce, Schnabel, (determined by m) Schorer, Seewald, Seidler, Sforza-Pallavicino, H. Spencer, Spitzer, Svennung, S. Ullmann, (as m) Valesio, Vianu, Way, Wheelwright, Yndurain

Suci, G. J.   (see Osgood)

Supervielle, Jules   G. Martin

surrealism   Llie, McCabe, H. Read, (superrealismo) Svanascini

Susenbrotus   Peacham

Swanson, J.   (models) Farre

Swedenborg, Emanuel   Mazzeo

Swift, Jonathan   Lindstrom, Quinlan, Swaim, K. Williams

Swinburne, Algernon   (synaesthesia) Downey

symbol   (as m) Alain, (as m) Berry, (as m) Boulton, (as m) Brewer, (as m) Brooks, (as m) K. Burke, (as m) Caracostea, (as m) Cargill, (symbolic form) Cassirer, (and m) Coleridge, Danielou, (in religion and metaphysics) Debaisieux, (in Flaubert) Demorest, (ambivalent) Dempe, Dillistone, Donelly, Dorfles, Dumas, (in Dante) Dunbar, Emerson, M. Evans, Feidelson, Feldkeller, (as m's) Feltenstein, (dynamic) Fiser, (metaphysics of) Flesch, Foss, Friedman, Frye, Goldammer, Gombrich, (in Nahuatl poetry) R. Gonzalez, Haacke, Hagopian, (in Kafka) Hillmann, (French)

E. Huber, Hynes, (is m) Iberico, Jacobs, D. James, John, E. Jones, Kahlert, B. Kaplan, Khatchadourian, K.Knight, (in art is m) Langer, (presentational or discursive) Langer, Lauretano, (inversion) Leckie, (symbolizing) Lemmon, Leondar, (symbolic style) Leroux, Lever, Lorenz, (bibliography) Lurker, (symbolic stage) Manso, H. Matthews, W. Matthews, McCabe, Mindel, Minkowski, Muir, Nashat, Nietzsche, Ogilvie, J. O'Neill, A. Parker, Percy, Robbe-Grillet, R. Ross, Rousset, Rowland, Royce, (as expanded m) Schlauch, Shibles, Shroeder, Sieffert, Silberer, Strich, Stutterheim, Taupin, Thurber, Tilden, Urban, Vela, Vischer, (= "Throw-together") R. Wellek, Heinz Werner, Wheelwright, Yelton

symbolism Balakian, Kronegger, (French) Lehmann, Liu, Pacernick, W. Ramsey, Sarmiento, F. Vonessen, Yelton

synaesthesia Babbitt, (color imagery) Baudelaire, Burleson, Correia, (in Mallarme) G. Davies, (literary) Downey, Engstrom, (in romanticism) Erhardt-Siebold, (in 19th century) Erhardt-Siebold, (in Verlaine) Fleischer, Fogle, Fonagy, Garcia-Giron, Ginsberg, (origin in) Hagopian, Hornbostel, Hugnet, Huysmans, Jacobs, Kramer, Leakey, (lack of) Liu, Migliorini, Morelle, Ogden, O'Malley, Richards, Roedig, Rowley, Schlauch, Schlegel, Seidler, Siebold, Silz, Skard, Sohngen, Stanford, Stock, Tarrant, E. Ullmann, (bibliography) S. Ullmann, (conceptual) S. Ullmann, (imaginal) S. Ullmann, Vetter, Waern, K. Weise, (Doppelempfinden) A. Wellek, Wells, Heinz Werner, Whalley, Whorf

synecdoche (cf. m, as synecdoche) (as representation; as part whole relation) Church, Dannehl, Eastman, G. Gerber, H. Greene, Holz, Sherry, Vaihinger, Warfel

synectics Gordon

Szasz, Thomas Sarbin

Taaffe, James (see R. Wallace)

Tacitus, Cornelius Kitt, Stitz

Taillardat, Jean Pasini

Tannenbaum, P. H. (see Osgood)

"tarning" (as striking use of single term) Barfield

Taulers, Johann Vogt-Terhorst

Taylor, Edward (imagery of) Blau, (m of) C. Griffith, (imagery) Halbert, Shepherd

Tennyson, Alfred Gunter, H. McLuhan, Nodelman

tenor and vehicle Abrams, Bilsky, Blair, (as "principle idea" and "accessory idea") Blair, (as "visual sense" and "figurative sense") Blair, (in organic m) T. Boyle, (as "independent variable" and "dependent variable") Feltenstein, (as subject and transposed term) Feltenstein, Frentz, S. George, (m as tenor and/or vehicle) Hotopf, [principle object (tenor) and accessory (vehicle)] Kames, A. Kaplan, (tenor embodied in vehicle) A. Kaplan, (tenor) K. Knight, Lauretano, Leakey, Leondar, (subject is literal, predicate is not) Lord, O'Dea, Osborn, Ransom, Richards, (unconscious tenor and conscious vehicle) Rohovit, Ruiz, W. Stevens, Ushenko, Wajid

Terence Forehand, Graupner, Langen

Teresa, Saint McCann

terms (and m) Litvinenk

Tesauro, Emmanuel Bethell, J. I. Cope, Croce, Donato, Hatzfeld, Hocke, Mazzeo, Praz, Raimondi

theatre (as m) Sanford, Schnabel

thinking (picture) Aldrich, (as metaphorical) Ballard, (plastic thought) Schiavina, (thought as m) Vaihinger

Thomas, Dylan (poem analysis of) Barone, Carman, (m's of) Chaneles, (on imagery) Ellmann, (imagery of) Greiff, Hornick, Knauber, Korg, Morton, Moynihan, Schoff

Thoreau, Henry (on wit and m) C. Anderson, (water image of) N. Baym, (circular imagery of) Boies, (m's) Houston

Thorild, Thomas Nyman

Thurber, James G. James

Tieck, Ludwig Bauer, Petrich, Pongs, Rowley, Urbach

time (imagery of) Knapp, Rank, Ryder, Shibles, Vaihinger, Wasserman

Tirso de Molina (pseudonym) Morris

topics, theory of Woods

Vaihinger, Hans   Biese, Nietzsche, Nyman

Valery, Paul   Guiraud, E. Huber, Hytier, Spoerri, Tindall, Urbach

Vaughan, Henry   Simmonds, Wiehe

Vega Carpio, Lope F. de   (concetos) Erdman, Sturm

Vendome, Matthew of   (animate, inanimate transfers of) Bede

Vergil   (Homeric comparisons of) Baur, (imagery of) Bovie, (figures of) Braumuller, (simile) Cooley, (pastoral of) Damon, (simile) Hornsby, Ker, Krondl, Preuss, J. Steadman, Wier

verisimilitude   Jaurrieta

Verlaine, Paul   (synaesthesia; m) Fleischer

Vianu, Tudor   (R) Dumitrescu, (R) Galdi, (R) Lazarescu, (R) Makarov, Wald

Viau, Theophile de   Solard

Vico, Giovanni   (m) Biese, Croce, Dorfles, Edie, Mauthner

Vigny, Comte Alfred V. de   C. Sauvage

Vischer, Friedrich T. von   (m) Bauer, Beyer, R. Meyer, Nyman

visions   (metaphorical) Aldrich, (mythic in American literature) Ballowe, Blake, R. Boyle, (in Yeats) K. Burke, D. Clark, (on Blake) Corrigan, (multiple) Ernst, (m as a form of) F. C. Flint, Friedman, (pro and con) Haworth, Kaufmann, Alec King, Lauretano, LeSage, F. Marsh, O'Malley, (twinned) Ong, Pardee, Pasini, Rousset, Ruin, Shook, E. Stern, Sucre, Heinz Werner, Wimsatt, Woodhouse, Zimmermann

Vogelweide, W. von der   Rehbold

Voltaire, Francois   (m in drama) Friedland

Vossler, Karl   Pongs

Wackernagel, Wilhelm (on m) Beyer

Wagner, Richard (on symbol) Fiser

Wallerstein, Judith (see Ekstein)

Walsh, Dorothy Dorfles

Warnke, F. (see A. Phillips)

Warren, Austin (see R. Wellek)

Warren, R. P. (see C. Brooks) Strandberg

Warton, Joseph Page, Trowbridge

Washington, Booker T. Andrew King

Watson, G. (reply) T. Gang

Webster, John (m) Carpenter

Weeks, D. Olscamp

Weiler, G. (see Mauthner)

Weinrich, Harald (m) Henel, Lambert

Weisgerber, Leo Pongs

Weitz, Morris Dorfles

Wells, Henry Pasini

Werner, Hans Nyman

Werner, Heinz Laan, Pongs

West, Nathanael (animal imagery of) Flavin

Whalley, George Ellis

Wheelwright, Philip (R) R. Boyle, (R) Marshall Cohen, J. Cope, Egan, T. Greene, Knights, Logan, (R) McMullin, (R) Mooij, Olscamp, (R) Rau, (R) Stallknecht

Whitman, Walt (basic m of) Brumleve, (imagery of) Dudding, Fang, Isaacs, Toperoff, Weimer

Whorf, Benjamin L. Leondar

Wieland, Christoph (m of) Calvor

Wilde, Oscar S. Ullmann

Williams, C. A. S. Pelliot

Williams, William Carlos L. Wagner, Weimer

Wilson, Edmund Hyman

Wilson, George P. (see V. Randolph)

Wilstach, Frank (R) Gilman, (R) Littell, (R) Teale

Wimsatt, W. K. (R) Bacon, (R) Davidson, Dorfles, (R) Humphreys, (R) Keast, (R) Nowottny

wit (Thoreau) C. Anderson, (as m) Aristotle, [as initially misleading (cf. logical-absurdity)] Aristotle, (as revealing correspondences) Barton, (metaphysical) Bethell, (in 16th century) W. Crane, (simple and compound) Gracian, (Gracian) Hafter, S. Johnson, Lyly, Mack, T. Marsh, Ong, Peacham, Perkins, Praz, Ricard, Stanford, Tesauro, Wells, Williamson, Woods

Wittgenstein, Ludwig (seeing-as) Aldrich, (seeing-as) Bouwsma, (seeing-as) Burlingame, Dorfles, Hanson, Harriman, F. Harrison, Hester, Mandelbaum, Manser, M. McLuhan, Petrie, Schwyzer, Shibles, Tilghman, Toulmin

Wolfe, Thomas (imagery of) T. Boyle, Maddock, W. Voigt

Wordsworth, William (m) Ciesielski, (imagery) V. Hill, Alec King, F. Marsh, Miles, Peacock, Ransom, Scoggins, C. J. Smith, Sonn, Zall

Wundt, Wilhelm Nyman

Wyatt, Sir Thomas Wentersdorf

Yeats, William B. Agarivala, K. Burke, D. Clark, Ellmann, Frye, Lentricchia, Mazzeo, Raines, Rutledge, Scanlon, Vendler, F. Wilson

INDEX

SECTION III METAPHOR:

A

absolute Allemann, Blumenberg

to describe abstract (abstract to concrete is circular) Bevis, Borges, Boulton, (as abstract) K. Burke, (Stevens) Carruth, (anti) Coleridge, (immaterial by material) Fenollosa, C. Ferguson, (based on abstraction) Fogarty, Fogle, (defined) Gray, Hecht, (generalization) Kanner, Konrad, Langer, Lieb, (as abstraction) F. Muller, Urban, Vaihinger, Wald, A. Ward, Wasserman, (ideal) Watt

to describe abstract by concrete Allers, Barfield, Bevan, Borges, Brooks, S. Brown, T. D., G. Davies, Feltenstein, Fere, Ferre, Fogle, France, T. Gang, Gardiner, Gertel, Gottsched, Gray, (general and particular) T. Greene, Herder, Iberico, Jenyns, Jesperson, (imperceptible by sensuous) K. Knight, Langer, LeSage, Liebesny, (the spiritual) Marignac, McInerny, (E. L.) Metafora, R. Meyer, Pally, Pardee, Rew, Richards, Ruin, Schlauch, (and vice versa) Adam Smith, Sohngen, Speranski, E. Stern, Stutterheim, S. Ullmann, Vianu, Wackernagel, L. Wagner, Wells, (concrete universal) Wheelwright, C. Williams

in actions (see metaphor, behavioral)

as adjective (rich adj.) Eastman, Friedrich, Garcia-Giron, (simile as adj.) Hillyer, Holz, Arvid Smith, (attribution) Tesauro

in advertising Bonsiepe, G. Graham

as belonging to aesthetics Gregory, Haugsted, Herschberger, Jackson, Keller, Kent, K. Knight, Kohfeldt, Laguardia, H. Meier, T. Meyer, J. Muller, Nyman, Ortega, Pasini, Pongs, Randolph, G. Stern, Sterzinger, M. Vonessen, Wajid, Wheelwright

alchemical Mazzeo

as ambiguous Allers, (obscure) Aristotle, Birch, (obscure) Croce, Dempe, (obscure) Eastman, (and chaotic) Edie, Empson, (not) Feltenstein, Fenollosa, Fowler, Friedman, Gracian, Hobbes, (D. Thomas) Hornick, E. Kane, A. Kaplan, (open-texture) Khatchadourian, Lauretano, (oscuridad) Lazaro, Mehrabian, (two terms not distinct) F. Muller, Schiavina, (not obscure) H. Spencer, Stevenson, (equivocation) Tesauro, Tindall, (ambivalent) Tschizewskij, Heinz Werner, Wheelwright

anagogic   Frye

as analogical (cf. m, Thomistic theory of; analogy)   (as analogical transfer) E. Adams, G. Adams, G. Allen, (not) Allers, C. C. Anderson, (four term) Aristotle, (four term mathematical) Barfield, (in later stage) Morris Cohen, Elster, Emerson, Fogle, Fordyce, Freud, (formal m; four term) Frye, G. Graham, T. Greene, Hoffding, Holz, Ioannou, Jenyns, H. Jones, (substitutive analogy) Kanner, Khatchadourian, Laguardia, (anti) Lauretano, Leger, Lemmon, Lloyd, MacDonald, Margolis, McInerny, (O. E. D.) Metaphor, (Webster's) Metaphor, (E. B. 10) Metaphor, (abbreviated analogy) Migliorini, Nowottny, Nyman, (of two spheres of being) J. O'Neill, M. O'Neill, Oppian, Osborn, Owens, Pepper, Perelman, Pongs, Raleigh, Ransom, Robillard, Schlanger, Sharkey, (m based on analogy) Sohngen, Srzednicki, Stutterheim, Tesauro, Tilden, (homology) Trier, Albert Upton, Urban, (as argument) Warburton, Watts, R. Wellek, (four term) Whalley, Wheelwright

animal (cf. bestiary)   Brinkmann, Davoine, Handel, A. Kolbe, Lemos, Marcus, (as witty) Mazzeo, McCann, Morel, Muller-Graupa, H. Nash, Olken, Oroz, Preis, Rees, Saineanu, Schultz, South, W. Stevens, Whaler, Yoder

as animating   Aristotle, Demetrius, (Pongs) Fink, Hecht, T. Hughes, Jackson, Keith, Olken, Pongs, Ruskin, Schlauch, W. Stevens, Tesauro, Torre, Urbach, R. Wellek

as antithesis (cf. oxymoron; m, as illogical)   (instructive) Aristotle, Borges, Brooks, K. Burke, D. Clark, Elster, (contradictory) Empson, (dissonance) Friedrich, Fry, Garcia Lorca, Gertel, (of extremes or contexts) Gracian, Hempel, (clash of terms) Henle, Hungerland, Iberico, (incongruous) Jenkins, Khatchadourian, Koestler, Leisi, MacGill, Mackey, MacLeish, (relation of) May, (contrast) McCall, Nietzsche, (dissolving of) Nowottny, (affirm and deny) Nyman, Ogden, (imagery of conflict) Olken, Parkhurst, (between life and spirit) Pongs, (polarity) Przwara, Raleigh, (m gives counterpoint) Schorer, (contrariety) C. J. Smith, Steinhoff, W. Stevens, Tesauro, D. Thomas, (contradiction) O. Thomas, Tschizewskij, (antonym or apposition) Turcato, Van Ghent, (of proverbs) Wakeman, (concordia discors) Wasserman, (contradiction) Weinrich, (incongruity) Wells, Heinz Werner, Wheelwright, Wisdom, Wohlberg

as apperception   Elster, (relation between sensation and memory) Fiser, Nyman

appositive (cf. m, as juxtaposition; m, as parataxis) Friedrich, Pettit, Turcato as appropriate Peacham, Ransom, Reinert, (not) Schlotthaus, Shibles, Welsh

Arabic al-Jindt, al-Samargandi, al-Tha'alibi, Ibn Abi 'Aun (simile), Mehren, J. Muller, Qutb, Sabbagh, Stutterheim

archetypal (cf. archetype) Frye, Lorenz, Osborn

in architecture (cf. architect) Biese, (dissonance) Friedrich, (edifice m) Griffin, Kohfeldt, Mackey, Schlegel, Weimer

in art Dorfles, Embler, (as basis of all art) D. Ferguson, (and m of value) Gombrich, A. Kaplan, Kaufmann, Keller, Konrad Lange, (as basis of all arts) Madge, M. McLuhan, H. Meier, Nietzsche, (basis of) Pasini, Perelman, Rank, H. Read, Rieser, Rousset, Royce, (not basis of all art) Sarmiento, Schiavina, Speranski, (m as world view; m in every art) Stutterheim, "Zwiazek"

artificial (cf. conceit) Borges, Friedrich, Gracian, Kafka, (not) Mazzeo, F. Muller, Peacham, Rousset, Sarmiento, Schiavina, (artifice or trick) Shklovskii, John Smith, Stanford

as basis of arts and sciences (cf. m as basis of philosophy) Aish, M. Baym, (tensional basis) Berggren, Black, Blinderman, Burkland, Denbigh, (Valery) Hytier, Lauretano, (as basis of all the arts) Madge, Pepper, Perelman, Royce, Schlanger, Slattery, J. Walker

as as-if (see as-if) (in lyric) Krummacher, Meszaros, Mrozkowski, Nyman, Ogden, Shuford, Szasz, Turbayne, Vaihinger, Watts

as association (increased) C. C. Anderson, Armstrong, Baroway, (basis of m) Blair, (free-association) Fonagy, (free association) Gordon, (of sense ideas) Gourmont, (nearness) Jakobson, (bisociation) Koestler, Linn, MacGill, (of images) Martino, Mauthner, P. Moses, F. Muller, Ortega, C. Read, Riffaterre, Ruskin, G. Scott, Speranski, (contiguity) Stankiewicz, W. Stevens, Tarbet, Vaihinger, Wasserman, Wheelwright

as influencing audience (cf. m, rhetorical) Osborn, Pasini, Schiavina, Wheelwright, Wimsatt

as reflecting author's tastes (cf. m as descriptive of persons) (not) Friedman, Rankin, Schiffhorst, Spurgeon, E. Stern, Tarbet

autoerotic Isaacs

avoidance of Benn, Bentham, Birch, (Kafka) Hillmann, Kafka, (purge language of) Kevin, Nyman, Reichenbach, (as determinative) Richards, Robbe-Grillet, Spratt, W. Stevens,

Stutterheim, Urbach, Vonessen, Watts, Yasuda

B

as beautiful (cf. ornament) (not ugly) Cicero, (not ugly) Gottsched, Gracian, Haworth, Jennings, May, Mazzeo, Miles, Nietzsche, Ogden, Peacham, Quintilian, Richards, (not) Rousset, Sarmiento, (noble) John Smith, (not ugly) Taillardat, Wells

behavioral J. Austin, Caruth, (constitute) Embler, (in religious ritual) Feldkeller, Fere, (mysterious) Gracian, (conceited) Gracian, (response change) Hungerland, (gesture) Hytier, Jakobson, (gesture) A. Jones, (in theatre) Kern, Lever, (mimicry) Mauser, A. Parker, Rohrich, Skinner, (gesture and action) Slawinska, Steinhoff, Szasz, Albert Upton, Vela, Wittgenstein

bibliography of (cf. Section I Extensive works on metaphor) (m) M. Baym, (m) Beardsley, (personification) M. Bloomfield, (personification) Chapin, (imagery) Friedman, (imagery of ancients) Gartner, (analogy) Hoffding, (imagism) Hughes, (rhetoric) Kitzhaber, (analogy) Leger, (definition and classification) Lieb, (symbolism) Lurker, (imagists) W. Martin, (on Thomistic analogy) McCanles, (m) Mendes, (m) Mora, (Sanskrit poetics) Nair, (synaesthesia) Pavy, (tropes to 1886) Pecz, (schizophrenic language and m) Piro, (ancient figurative language) Poschl, (emblems) Praz, (m) Shibles, (m and synaesthesia) Siedler, (synaesthesia) Silz, (synaesthesia) Skard, (on Spratt) Spratt, (m) Stutterheim, (conceit) Tesauro, (imagery) Thavenius, (synaesthesia) S. Ullmann, (synaesthesia and language deviation) Vetter, (rhetoric) K. Wallace, (Crashaw) Warren, (synaesthesia) A. Wellek, (imagery) Heinz Werner, (Wordsworth) Zall

body (body politic) Love, (body of Christ as m) Poteat, (body functions as m) Pott, Rohrich, Schlauch, (body of a work) Schoeck, (Christ's body) Sohngen

bold (cf. conceit) (in Spanish language) Beinhauer, Brooks, Freud, (fantastic) Friedrich, (bold) Hecht, Hocke, S. Johnson, Keith, Kloepfer, (E. B., 8) Metaphor, (not) M. St. John, Weinrich, (violent or fustian) Wells

as a borrowing (cf. m, transfer of; m, relation of)

in brain damaged patients Chapman, Goldstein, (aphasic) Jakobson, Heinz Werner

C

in Canadian poetry   Djwa

being captivated by (cf. m, unconscious of) Ballard, Barnard, (m controls man) Coleman, Albert Day, Ferre, (fooled by) R. Frost, S. George, Gombrich, Kuhn, Lauretano, Mackel, MacNeice, (obsessional m) Mauron, (slippery m's) Mehrabian, Mindel, Monson, F. Muller, C. Myers, Nicolson, Nietzsche, Norwood, Ogden, Pederson-Krag, Richards, Royce, Sarbin, Schlanger, Stelzner, W. Stevens, Thurber, Turbayne, Urbach, Vaihinger, Welby, Wells

catachresis   Tryphon, R. Wellek

as category-mistakes   A. Baker, Cross, (type-crossings) Drange, Erwin, Haworth, (deviant utterance) Hillman, Khatchadourian, Lauretano, Leondar, R. Martin, Orpinela, Pap, Percy, (cross sorts) Richards, Ryle, Sarbin, J. Smart, Watts

as catharsis   Ruin

chains of (cf. m's build on m's)   Brinkmann, Denbigh, (as allegory) Gibbons, Hardy, (cluster) Harrier, Hornick, Lauretano, Marias

as <u>chia-chieh</u>   Wu

in Chinese   Baroway, Ch'i, Fang, Fenollosa, Frankel, Angus Graham, Hsia, G. Hughes, Kennedy, Kenner, Liu, J. Muller, Pelliot, Pound, A. Williams, Wu

as clarifying   Alcuin, Boulton, Breitinger, C. Brooks, K. Brooks, Buchanan, Cicero, Coombes, Demetrius, (illuminating) Eastman, Edie, C. Ferguson, (illuminates) Ferre, Fitzosborne, H. Fowler, Grierson, Hecht, Ioannou, Jennings, (vivid) Keith, (not logical) Lauretano, Lockwood, Lucas, (vivid) McCall, (vivid) McCartney, (precision) Murry, Nyman, Peacham, Pederson-Krag, Quintilian, Stutterheim, Warfel

based on new class inclusion   Aschenbrenner, Cassirer, Goodman, (two instances of a general notion) Gregory, Leisi, Schlanger

classification of   (he suggests) Blumenberg, Blumner, Brinkmann, W. Fraser, Friedrich, Frye, Gertel, Gracian, H. Greene, Hempel, M. Hesse, T. Hughes, Hungerland, Ioannou, Knapp, Leakey, J. Lees, Leondar, Lieb, MacGill, Madge, Meadows, Molhova, F. Muller, Musurillo, (Freud's) Nash, Nietzsche, Olken, Palley, Pasini, (conceit) C. Pellegrini, (kenning) Rankin, Rew, (as reclassification) Richards, Rodale, Ruin, Sabbagh, Schlauch, Schnabel, Shipley, Adam Smith, Speranski, W. Stevens, Taillardat, Tesauro, Tomkins,

Torre, (classif. as m) Vaihinger, (anti) Vela, Watts, R. Wellek, Wells, (types of imagination) Wheelwright, Zardoya

as cliche LeSage, (slogan) Warfel

cognition (see m, intellectual)

as collage Khatchadourian

collective Vonessen

common (cf. slang) W. Fraser, (everyday German) Haubrich, (everyday) A Johnson, Liebesny, (everyday) "The Metaphor of Everyday Life," (lang.) (E.B. 8) Metaphor, (colloquial) Nosek, E. Weber

as comparison (cf. simile; m, as simile) (emphatic) G. Allen, (of real and unreal) Alonso, Bally, (of unlike things) Beardsley, (pictoral) Berggren, Beyer, Biese, Carney, (mechanical) Coleridge, (partial) Cooper, (with third thing) Deutschbein, (of meaning) DuMarsais, (of reverie) Eastman, (illuminating) Eastman, (of bodies of knowl.) C. Ferguson, (of one to many ideas) Fitzosborne, (of diff. planes of consciousness) Fogle, Goodman, Gracian, (analogical) T. Greene, Groos, (poetic) Henning, (Kafka) Hillmann, T. Hughes, Huttig, Jamieson, Juilliere, Kok, A. Kolbe, Kramer, Leroux, Liedstrand, Mackel, A. Martin, McCall, D. Meier, Ramsay, Rew, Richards, E. Stern, Stossel

as not a comparison Allemann, Barfield, Berggren, Biese, Black, Celan, Murry, Reverdy, Rieser

as complex Page, Stutterheim

composite S. Ullmann

as concealing (cf. m, indirect)

as concise or brief Alcuin, Aristotle, Berry, Beyer, Cicero, Coombes, Esnault, (simplifying) "Figures of Speech," Friedrich, H. Greene, Haworth, Hornick, (economize) T. Hughes, (simplifying) Kaufmann, Kenner, Koestler, McCall, McCloskey, Nemerov, Nyman, (rapid) Peacock, Perelman, (brief) Rousset, Schlanger, Arvid Smith, (intensive) Stanford, Tesauro, Vico, Wells, Heinz Werner

as concrete Elster, Fogle, Gracian, Gray, Grierson, Haworth, Hornick, Hungerland, Kenner, Kern, K. Knight, Kohfeldt, Konrad, Liddie, Lieb, Migliorini, (universal) Ransom, Richards, Speranski, W. Stevens, Wells, Wheelwright, Wisdom, Wu

as condensation (cf. m, Freudian theories of) Freud, Hungerland, Koestler, Lacan, Mayer, Patterson, Rohovit, Ruiz, Sharp

as representing a culture or age Beinhauer, Birch, Blumenberg, Brinkmann, Ch'i, Eicke, Embler, Erixon, Force, Hecht, Herder, Hocke, (in culture) Holtker, (repres. the social side of man) Holz, Hornstein, (constitutes it) Kaufmann, Mackel, Mizener, H. Myers, Pongs, Samborn, Schlanger, W. Stevens, Sucre, Tschizewskij, Weekley, O. Weise, R. Wellek

in cursing (cf. slang) Lemos

in dance (cf. m, behavioral) Hornbostel, Lawler

dead Barfield, (faded) Bjorkman, Boillot, Clutton-Brock, (indistinguishable from live) H. Fowler, Leondar, (E.B. 8) Metaphor, Migliorini, Nietzsche, Schlauch, Ushenko, Wheelwright

as defense mechanism (cf. m, Freudian theories of) Freud, Rohovit, R. Saussure

as delusion (cf. m, as misleading) Addison, Birch, Borges, Freud, Gummere, Hobbes, Bishop King, Lentricchia, Nietzsche, (superstition, illusion) Nyman, (trickery) C. Pellegrini, (illusion) Speranski, E. Stern, (allusion) Thornton, S. Ullmann, Heinz Werner

as dense Ransom

as description (cf. m, as possible explanation) (of unfamiliar in sci.) Figures of Speech, Fruit, (descriptive m) Frye, (explanation) Gracian, (not) Henderson, (as qualification) T. Hughes, Kaiser, (interpretative) Landau, McCall, (explicative m) C. Myers, Norwood, Rieser, Schlanger (as interpretation) Schorer, H. Simon, (interpretative) Stelzner

as deviation (cf. m, as transfer) Bevis, (from noun-adj. categ.) Borges, Boulton, Brooke-Rose, Brooks, G. Brown, (varying kenning) Browne, Bullough, (to gain insight) K. Burke, Burkland, (of word order) Carnoy, (incongruity) M. Clark, (to gain insight) Coleman, (from usual association of terms) Coombes, (by comparison or synecdoche) Eastman, (impractical) Eastman, (of lang.) Eliot, (strange-making) Erlich, (displacement) Freud, (dissonance) Friedrich, (of syntax) Friedrich, (abnormal) S. George, (lang. in brain damage) Goldstein, (from habit or custom) Goodman, Gottsched, Gracian, (of sound pattern) H. Gross, (grammatical) H. Gross, (from expectation)

H. Gross, (from custom) Henle, ("deviant-utterance") Hillman, (of speech) Holz, (from convention) Hulme, (from normal rules of use) Hungerland, (from normal use) R. Johnson, (syntax, meaning, letters) E. Kane, (irrelevant utterance) Kanner, (distorts) Kaufmann, (from self-evident) Kaufmann, (from custom, context) Lecky, (grammatical) Leech, Leisi, (from usual) R. Meyer, (of order of events, etc.) Monro, (grammatical imperfection) F. Muller, Nietzsche, (from literal) Norton, (from usual categories) Nowottny, Pavy, (of speech and thought) C. Porter, (from proper meaning) Quintilian, Ramsey, (of sound, grammar, meaning) Randolph, (distortion) Rousset, Sacerdos, (word-circuit) Schlanger, (from culture) Schlanger, (to gain insight) Shibles, (from context) Shklovskii, Slawinska, Speranski, (from normal) E. Stern, W. Stevens, (modification) Uhrhan, (lang.) Vetter, (of context) Weinrich, (emotive and causal) Wheelwright, (from established order) Winter

diagrams of   James Brown, Deutschbein, Nowottny, Richards, Stutterheim, Albert Upton, Vaihinger, Heinz Werner

as dialectic   K. Burke, (in Plato) Burrell, (in Hegel and D. Thomas) Chaneles, Bruce King, Lanier, Marignac, Nietzsche, Pongs, Schiavina, D. Thomas, Vaihinger

as diaphora   F. Muller, (diaphor) Wheelwright

dictionary of   (similes) Rodale, J. Spencer, (French) Varinot, (similes) Wilstach

didactic   (in Quintilian) J. Carter, Croce, Lewontin, Mackel, R. Meissner, Ogilvie

direct   Wells

as disclosure   Ramsey

as displacement   Muncie, Rohovit, Schon, (contextual) Shklovskii

as dissolving distinctions (cf. m, as deviation; m, as transfer)

as dissonance   Friedrich, Gracian

as distance   (symbolic) Buchanan, (psychical) Bullough, (in therapy) Caruth, (between actual and metaphoric image) Elster, Horace, (anti) Lauretano, Osborn, Reverdy, Riffaterre, E. Stern, (psychical) Wajid, Heinz Werner, Wheelwright

distrust of (cf. m, as misleading; m, avoidance of)   Benn, Bentham, Raleigh

in drama (cf. dramatists by name; m, behavioral)   Freud, (comedy) Kern, Lemmon, LeSage, Linn, D. Meier, Nietzsche, Preston,

Radtke, Rieser, Romilly, A. Rosenberg, Sanford, Johann Schiller, Schurmeyer, Slattery, Spurgeon, (plays as m's) Stutterheim, Vianu, Hans Werner

as dramatic Carpenter, Dallas, P. Gibson, Jaurrieta, Morris, A. Rosenberg, Wimsatt

as drawn or sketched (cf. m, as pictorial) Addison, Blair, Church, Hulme, W. Kaplan, Heinz Werner

and drugs Heinz Werner

as dualism (metaphoric stage) Manso, Vaihinger

E

in education (cf. m, didactic; m, in reading; m, test for) Cooper, Dempe, Fennema, C. Ferguson, "Figures of Speech," Flaum, Fordyce, R. Frost, Frye, Fucke, Gordon, Groesbeck, Groff, P. Gross, Hillenbrand, E. A. Holmes, T. Hughes, Kevin, Liebesny, Looby, Lord, Mackel, McCabe, R. Meissner, Monson, Nietzsche, C. Porter, Richards, E. St. John, Samson, Semler, N. Smith, Stewig, Stogdill, Stone, Tomkins, Albert Upton, Anne Upton, Watts, E. Webster, Winchester, Zale

Egyptian Grapow, J. Muller

as ellipsis Buchanan, Lord, (for all its qualities) Mackel, Ogden, Olscamp, (kenning as) Rankin, Sharp

as emblem (cf. emblem) S. Brown, Gracian, Leroux, Ogden, O'Malley

as constituting emotions Hotopf, Ioannou, Pasini, (m controls feeling) Richards, Stevenson, A. Ward, Whalley

as descriptive of emotions (cf. objective correlative, pathetic fallacy) Beinhauer, Bett, Borges, Breitinger, Brooks, Deutschbein, Dickey, Eliot, Feltenstein, Fogle, Freud, Hagopian, Hotopf, (makes us more aware of them) Lea, H. McLuhan, Osborn, Rousset, Voltaire

as expressing emotions Arrom, E.B., Beardsley, Bodkin, (intense) Borges, Boulton, Breitinger, Brooks, (and ideas) Burkland, Carnoy, Clutton-Brock, Deutschbein, (objective correlative) Eliot, (unity of) Elster, Esnault, Feigl, (as physiological) Fere, D. Ferguson, Freud, Grierson, Hecht, (D. Thomas) Hornick, Hotopf, T. Hughes, Hulme, Kaufmann, Lea, R. Lee, Longinus, Morier, Murry, Peacock, Rousset, Ruskin, (deep emotion) Sarmiento, Sucre, Vela, Wasserman, Wells, Whalley, Wimsatt

as stimulating emotions (cf. m, as pleasing) Boulton, Coombes, Cosmo, Eastman, Feltenstein, (to action) Ferre, Figures of Speech, Gardiner, (conceit) Gracian, T. Greene, Groos, Hecht, Ioannou, (vitalize) Jaurrieta, Kaiser, Khatchadourian, Bishop King, Olivero, Peacham, Quintilian, Sherry, Stevenson

as emotive E. Adams, (emotive-intellectual) Adank, C. C. Anderson, (emotive-descriptive) Aschenbrenner, Bally, Berggren, Black, Burkland, Carpenter, Morris Cohen, H. Crane, Croce, (generalized emotive susceptibility) De, (rasa) De, Dickey, Eisenstein, Feigl, Ferre, Fink, Freud, Gertel, Goldsmith, Grierson, Hempel, (induced similarity) Henle, G. Hughes, (psych. attitude) Hytier, Iberico, (not) D. James, Jamieson, (excessively) Jamieson, Jaurrieta, A. Kaplan, (not) Keith, Khatchadourian, Koestler, Kohfeldt, (as love) Lanier, Leakey, MacLeish, Madge, Molhova, (rasa) Nair, Nyman, J. O'Neill, (sentiment) Ortega, Osborn, Pongs, Rhys-Davids, Richards, Rieser, Ruiz, (based on violent feelings) Ruskin, (transfer) Sarmiento, Arvid Smith, (not) Speranski, Srzednicki, Stanford, G. Stern, W. Stevens, Stevenson, Stutterheim, D. Thomas, Tilden, S. Ullmann, A. Ward, Welsh, Heinz Werner, Wheelwright

emotive theory (cf. m, as emotive) Beardsley, MacNeice, Richards, Rieser, Tilden

as empathetic Dorfles, Fogle, Ortega, Pongs, (other minds) Thomson

as energy Foss, Lauretano, Mindel, Vaihinger, Whalley

as epic or historical form Dallas

as epiphor Olscamp, Wheelwright

as escape (cf. m, based on taboo) (impractical) Bullough, (in Hegel's dialectic) Chaneles, (from laws and causes in nature) Chaneles, (in D. Thomas' poetry) Chaneles, De, Dickey, (from single universe of discourse) Ferre, Freud, (freedom) Friedrich, (from tension) Gracian, (from taboo) Hempel, (from oppression) Hocke, Leisi, Lentricchia, LeSage, Madge, (release) Mawardi, (E.L.) Metafora, Monro, Muncie, (Daedalus of discourse) Nemetz, Ortega, Pongs, Ruin, R. Saussure, W. Stevens

essential Whalley

as ethical term (as disclaimer) Stanford, (of abuse) Stutterheim

in ethics (cf. m, value; m, as parable) Edel, (captivating) Ferre, Gracian, G. Graham, (as value-charged) Hagopian, Henderson, (as appraisive) Henderson, Kaufmann, Mazzeo, Nietzsche,

Ogden, Oppian, Osborn, Rhys-Davids, Rousset, Stauffer, Turnbull, Urban, Vaihinger, Wasserman, A. Weiss, Wheelwright

as basis of etymology Abrams, Bett, Birch, Boillot, Breal, G. Brown, Ch'i, Diderot, Edie, France, Fruit, (dict.) Klein, Lauretano, Locke, Lucas, Mauthner, Migliorini, F. Muller, Sala, (latent basis) Schlauch, Sharpe, Trier, Tschizewskij, F. Vonessen

as euphemism (cf. euphemism; m, based on taboo; m, Freudian theories of) Cicero, Hempel, Pasini

examples (to be learned) Beinhauer, Bodmer, (compiled) Croce, Dickey, Dony, Embler, (to be learned) Gracian, (should be compiled) Hecht, (to be learned) Jenkins, Kames, (get repertoire of m's) Kaufmann, McCabe, H. Nash, Nietzsche, Ogden, Osborn, Parkhurst, Samson, Schlanger, Speranski, Stallknecht, Albert Upton, Anne Upton, Virtanen, Wilss, Wilstach

excess of Demetrius, Goldsmith, (not) Irving, Jamieson, Kane, (not) Kevin, Longinus, (not) R. Meyer, (not) O. Nash, Pope, (pro.) Sarmiento

exercises in (cf. m, test for; m, examples of) "Figures of Speech," Lord, Mackel, McCabe, Albert Upton, Anne Upton

expansion of K. Brooks, Buchanan, K. Burke, Cicero, Dondua, M. Evans, (as allegory) Gracian, (novel) Hagopian, (in Aeschylus) Headlam, (anti) Kevin, (implications) Landau, (limited) R. Lees, Monson, (generalization) F. Muller, C. Myers, Pepper, (excessive) Pope, (as allegory) Quintilian, (anti) Ramsay, Ransom, Regnaud, Richards, (limited) Rousset, Scanlon, Schlauch, Shibles, Snell, Srzednicki, W. Stevens, Stutterheim, Tupper, Wackernagel, Warburton, (expansive) Wells

as experience (cf. m, behavioral) Buchanan, (social) K. Burke, (Stevens) Carruth, (transformed into lang.) Cassirer, Daiches, (rasa) De, (and adventure) Dickey, Dorfles, (of heightened consciousness) Eastman, (existential and phenomenological) Edie, (a participation) Funk, (possible exper.) Gertel, Gombrich, (conceit) Gracian, ("experiencing-as") Hick, (identity of) Hornbostel, (of emotions) Hotopf, Hytier, (lived-through) B. Kaplan, (enjoyed) B. Kaplan, (imitative of) Kenner, Klubertanz, Langer, (participatory) Lauretano, (as single experience) Madge, M. McLuhan, (rasa) Nair, Riddel, (man-in-world) Robbe-Grillet, Schivina, Stanford, Stutterheim, (as lived) Vela, (organizing of) Warfel, Goodwin Watson, Whalley, Whorf, Wittgenstein

as expressing the inexpressible Boulton, Osborn

expression theory of Berggren, Croce, Edie, Schiavina

as expressive (cf. m, as expressing emotions; m, as intellectual) Iberico, Leakey, Pasini, Porzig, G. Stern, Stutterheim, S. Ullmann, Urban, Vela, Wald, Wheelwright

F

as fable Diez, Eastman, Fordyce, Frye, La Fontaine, Lindstrom, (compressed) Nemerov, (condensed) Rhys-Davids, Vico, Warfel

faded (cf. m, dead) Bjorkman, Gerhard

in fairy tales Diez, Rohrich, Rowland

false (cf. m, as misleading) (as allegory) Barfield, (as conscious hypostatization) Barfield, (literally false) Beardsley, Berggren, Carney, (false analogy) Chase, (if taken literally) Morris Cohen, (attribution) Angel Day, (type-crossings are false) Drange, (a priori) Drange, (literally) Ferre, H. Greene, Nyman, (mistake) Percy, Rousset, Ruskin, Stanford, E. Stern, W. Stevens, Sucre, Urbach, P. Weiss, (pseudo) Heinz Werner

familiar Allers, Ogden, (habitual) Pasini, A. Paul, Wheelwright, Zipf

fantastic Friedrich, (D. Thomas) Hornick

as fantasy Fonagy, Rousset

far-fetched (pro) Bett, (anti) Cicero, (as from our experience) Coombes, (anti) Demetrius, Elster, (anti) Gibbons, (anti) Gottsched, (pro) Gracian, Guillen, (D. Thomas) Hornick, (anti) Irving, Jamieson, S. Johnson, Kafka, Kane, (anti) Longinus, Mariani, Mazzeo, F. Muller, (pro) Ong, (anti) Peacham, (incredible) C. Pellegrini, (anti) Quintilian, (anti) John Smith, (anti obscure) H. Spencer, (anti) Speranski, E. Stern, (anti) Voltaire, (exuberant) Wells

as fiction Barfield, (legal) Bentham, Bevis, Mackel, Nietzsche, (lie) Nyman, Ogden, Riddel, Schorer, Speranski, E. Stern, W. Stevens, (lie) Stutterheim, (lie) Urbach, Vaihinger

in film (cf. montage)

as filter Berggren, Black, Bullough, Farre, Ferre, Swanson

Finnish Kuusi

fixed (of Homer) Parry, Rank, Rees, (not) Ushenko, (or ritual) R. Wellek

in folklore (cf. m as representing a culture or age) (folksongs) Kahlert, Lemos, E. Parsons, Randolph, Rohrich, Rosaldo, Rowland, Schultz

forced (anti) Irving, (anti) Jamieson

formal Pasini

as formula Jaurrieta, (codifies) Kaufmann, (anti) Kohfeldt, (law) Mindel, (schema) Nyman, Schlanger, Tesauro, Tindall, Vaihinger

Freudian theory of Abraham, Aleksandrowicz, (as model not reality) Allers, Begelman, Downey, Ferdiere, Fonagy, Freud, Gordon, Jeffries, E. Jones, Knapp, Lacan, Lewin, Mawardi, Muncie, H. Nash, Rohovit, R. Saussure, Sharpe, Heinz Werner

function of Pasini, (functional) Turcato

fundamental Blumenberg, (personification) F. Muller, (or symbolic m) Urban

as fusion (cf. m, as synthesis; m, as interaction) E. Adams, Aldrich, Biese, Black, Brooke-Rose, Burkland, (synthesis) Cosmo, Downey, (resolution) Empson, (blending) Gardiner, T. Greene, Hempel, (synthesis) Hulme, Leondar, Nyman, Perelman, Pongs, Prescott, Richards, (of image and concept) Sohngen, E. Stern, G. Stern, Sterzinger, Vela, (nuclear-fission) Whalley, Wheelwright

G

in games (cf. m, as play; language-game) Berne, Louch, (chess) Mandelbaum, Nietzsche, (as game) Tschizewskij, Urbach, Wittgenstein

of gender Nietzsche, Vonessen

genitive-link (cf. m, as all parts of speech) Aristotle, Brinkmann, Brooke-Rose, Friedrich

as a work of genius Adelung, Aristotle, Boillot, (of imagination) Coleridge, Emerson, (to gain fame) Gracian, (conceit) Gracian, Hagopian, (m reinforces greatness and vice versa) Longinus,

Lucas, Marzot, (as work of insane) Mazzeo, Pepper, W. Stevens, (as work of insane) Tesauro, Urbach, Voltaire

as genus of all tropes Bede

based on genus-species transference Aristotle, Aschenbrenner, Donatus, Feltenstein, (identity of) Frye, Goldthwait, (as inadequate) Ioannou, Maurer, (not) Ogden, (not) Stanford, Albert Upton

good (reevaluation of) Allers, G. James, Kohfeldt, (by insane) Mazzeo, Mehrabian, "The Metaphor of Everyday Life" M. St. John, (Liebesmetaphern) Schuchardt, Stutterheim, Tesauro, S. Ullmann, Weinrich, Wheelwright

grammatical (e.g., metonymy) F. Muller, ("formal m") Pasini, (pure m) Turcato

Greek (naval terms, art, science, carpentry) Fischer, McCall, Morel, Morello, Pongs, M. St. John, Shibles, Stanford, Tarrant, Verdenius

H

as harmony Gracian, Kohfeldt, May, Richards, (harmonium) Riddel

in Hebrew and Accadian Dhorme

hidden (cf. m, as taboo; m, indirect)

of hieroglyphics (cf. emblem; imagism) Dieckmann

in Hindi Pandey

in history (cf. memory) Flaum, Girardot, M. Lewis, Mindel, Sanderson, Sidney, (as deviation) Speranski, Sucre

as honest (sincere) Brooks, Page

as humanizing (cf. personification) Dorfles, Koch, Kohfeldt, Lauretano, Lentricchia, McInerny, Meadows, Pongs, Rieser, Royce, Schlotthaus, W. Stevens, Todasco, Weisgerber

as humor (cf. humor) Aristotle, S. Baker, Bally, Blumner, (jokes) Boulton, Brooks, M. Clark, (category-mistake) Cross, (literary m) Demidoff, Freud, Fry, Groesbeck, Jenkins, Kern, Koestler, Kohfeldt, Kuusi, Leisi, LeSage, Lucas, May, "Amusing Metaphors,"

"On the Mixing of Metaphors," Monro, Nyman, Pasini, Peacock, C. Pellegrini, M. Pellegrini, Preston, Raimondi, Randolph, Rohrich, Rousset, Shibles, Shipley, Thurber, Wells

as hyperbole   Cicero, "Figures of Speech," Gracian, Harrison, Konrad, Law, Tesauro

as hypothesis (cf. m, in science; m, as possible explanation; m, as new)   K. Burke, Denbigh, (hypostatize entities) Feltenstein, Ferre, (hypoth. identity) Frye, Gordon, Gregory, (prescriptive) Henderson, M. Hesse, Hillmann, (analogy) Hoffding, (interpretation) Hutten, Huxley, (a groping) Hytier, (as law of universe) Jaurrieta, Kaufmann, Landau, Lea, (does not explain) Madge, Mawardi, (m guides observ.) Mehrabian, Meszaros, Mindel, (explicative m) C. Myers, H. Nash, (hypothetical) Nyman, (exploratory) Osborn, Pepper, Raleigh, Ribot, Rieser, Schlanger, Schon, Shibles, H. Simon, Stelzner, Albert Upton, Vaihinger, Wisdom

I

ideal   Jaurrieta, Pongs, (ideal as a m) Vaihinger, Watt

as expressing ideas (cf. m, in thought; m, intellectual)   Blumenberg, Borges, (as based on ideas) Brinkmann, (ideas necess. for m) Morris Cohen, D. Collins, Croce, (m as idea) Friedman, Lauretano

as identity (cf. m, origin of; m, as immediate experience; m, as unity in difference)   Barnard, (indifference) Berggren, Brinkmann, Buck, Church, (original identity) Morris Cohen, (as kenning) D. Collins, (impractical) Eastman, (of qualities) Elster, (of several things) Esnault, (emotive) Freud, Friedrich, (species-genus) Frye, (hypothetical) Frye, Gertel, (of real and unreal) Hagstrum, Hillyer, (originally) Hornbostel, (of exper.) Hornbostel, (unverified) Jaurrieta, (in schizophr.) R. Johnson, Kames, Mazzeo, (not) H. Nash, (not) Nyman, (ideal) Ortega, Robbe-Grillet, (of subj. and obj.) Ruin, Schiavina, Shipley, (original unity) Stanford, (simultaneity) Sterzinger, Stutterheim, (tautology) F. Vonessen, A. Ward, (naive) Watts, (descriptive or as-if) Watts, (of perception; of sense and imagination) Heinz Werner, Whalley, Wheelwright

as illogical   Allemann, (incongrous) Baroway, Beardsley, (not) Esnault, Feldkeller, Murry, Ransom, Richards, Stanford, Whalley, Wheelwright, Winter

as illustrating   E. Adams, Aristotle, (not just) Blumenberg,

of Indian peoples E. Parsons

indirect (cf. m, Freudian theory of) (not) Eastman, (implied) H. Greene, (Gongora) Guillen, Leisi, (indirect communication) J. Lewis, (hidden) M. Muller, Richards, (latent) Schlauch, (hidden) Selig, (concealing) Sharpe, (implicit) Tindall, Urbach, Vianu, (implied) Wells, (concealed) Heinz Werner, Wheelwright, (submerged) A. Williams

an inexhaustible concept Baym, Breal, Isenberg, (inexplicable) Jaurrieta, (E.L.) Metafora, Murry, Richards, Van Steenburgh, Whalley

inflection (in music) D. Ferguson

representation of inner by outer (cf. m, to describe mind; m, as descriptive of emotions) S. Asch, (synthesis of inner/outer) Biese, S. Brown, Edie, Embler, Emerson, Empson, Feltenstein, France, Freud, Hempel, Holz, Jeffrey, Jenyns, H. McLuhan, Richards, Robbe-Grillet, Ryba, Ryle, Sarbin, Schlauch, Arvid Smith, E. Stern, Vaihinger, Vela, Vico, Wakeman, (physiognomic perc.) Heinz Werner

as giving insight (cf. m, as source of knowledge) Aristotle, Arrom, Bally, Boulton, Brooks, Bullough, K. Burke, (in Hegel's dialectic) Chaneles, Coleman, Emerson, Gordon, Gracian, T. Greene, Hecht, Hick, (into emotions) Hotopf, Irving, Jaurrieta, R. Johnson, Knights, Mazzeo, McInerny, Meszaros, C. Meyers, Monson, (revelation) Murry, (rasa) Nair, H. Nash, (any supreme insight is a m) Parkhurst, Percy, (revelation) Pongs, Prado, (disclosure) Ramsey, Randolph, Richards, Shibles, Shklovskii, (revelation) W. Stevens, (revelation) Stutterheim, Temkin, Tschizewskij, S. Ullmann, Warfel, Whalley, Wheelwright

caused by inspiration Borges, R. Johnson, Ruskin, Sarmiento, Schlanger, Stutterheim

as intellectual Adank, Alden, Bally, G. Carter, (as based on knowledge) Coleman, (and empathy) Dorfles, Eisenstein, (not) Feigl, Gracian, Gray, (reaction) Groos, (cognitive) M. Hesse, G. Hughes, R. Johnson, (not) Kames, Bruce King, Knights, (anti) Lauretano, Logan, (cerebral) MacNeice, Madge, May, (serious) C. Pellegrini, (not) Ruskin, (too) Sarmiento, (erudite or learned) Selig, Adam Smith, Terry, Tilden, (cognitive) Van Steenburgh, Vico, A. Ward, Yndurain

intentional Boulton, G. Brown, Cain, (phenomenological) Edie, W. Fraser, Gibbons, (Kafka) Hillmann, (intentionality) B. Kaplan, Leakey, McInerny, Molkova, Prado, Richards, G. Stern, (voluntary) W. Stevens, Watts

as interaction Black, Buhler, K. Burke, Downer, (of meanings) Eliot, Feidelson, Feltenstein, (of meaning) S. George,

M. Hesse, Hotopf, Khatchadourian, Needham, (of thought) Osborn, (of usual and contextual meaning) Osborn, Richards, Ruiz (of two objects) Adam Smith, (between two intellectual objects) Adam Smith, Stanford, (oscillation between) Sterzinger, L. Wagner, (resonant) Whalley

as introjection   Freud

as intuited   Aldrich, Aristotle, (lang. is intuition) Croce, (culturally) Dorfles, Elster, (intuited memory) Esnault, Feltenstein, Gardner, Girardot, Hulme, Iberico, Jordan, Langer, Larsson, MacNeice, May, Nyman, Ogilvie, J. O'Neill, Parkhurst, Rieser, Royce, Ruskin, Schlanger, Shibles, Stanford, Urban

inverse   (stress on major term) Wells

in Ireland   Kevin

as irrational (cf. m, as illogical)   Korg, Lentricchia, Madge, Pasini, Ransom, Speranski, W. Stevens

as an isomorphic relation   Bochenski, Leondar

J

in Japan   J. Muller

in jazz   E. Kane

in journalism   Balston, Ch'i, Eicke, H. Fowler, Rowntree, Wilss

as juxtaposition (cf. m, as parataxis; m, as appositive)   (wild) Bally, Battcock, Benamou, Biese, (mere and extreme) Brooks, Coombes, (not mere) Dickey, (mere) Downey, (montage) Eisenstein, Eliot, (parallel images) Elster, (visual) Fenollosa, S. Foster, (literal m) Frye, G. Graham, T. Greene, Hegel, G. Hughes, T. Hughes, Jenkins, (of images) Kenner, Bruce King, (contextual) Koestler, Lauretano, Liu, (of incongr. images) MacLeish, (without copula) H. McLuhan, M. McLuhan, (of dissimilar) Parkhurst, (without is) Pound, (of dissimilar obj's.) Rousset, Schlauch, Silz, Tilden, L. Wagner, Whalley, Wisdom, Wu

as kenning (see kenning)

as source of knowledge (cf. m, as insight; m, as new; m, to express unknown by known) G. Adams, St. Augustine, Bevan, Black, Boulton, Brooks, Buchanan, Bullough, Cassirer, Day-Lewis, Deutsch, Dickey, (and discovery) Feidelson, (to know is to use m) H. Frost, R. Frost, Funk, Gordon, Gracian, Harriman, (explanatory) M. Hesse, (objective emotive) Hotopf, (discovery) Huxley, Irving, R. Johnson, (relig.) Kessler, Kohfeldt, R. Lee, Logan Mackel, MacLeish, R. Meissner, Morier, (revelation) Murry, H. Nash, Nyman, Ortega, Pasini, (knowl. by mistake) Percy, Pongs, Quintilian, Royce, Ruin, Schlanger, Shelley, W. Stevens, Stutterheim, Tarrant, (not) Tilden, Heinz Werner, Whalley

to express unknown by known (cf. m, as a source of knowledge) Brooks, S. Brown, Morris Cohen, Edie, Esnault, Ferre, Fonagy, Foss, Hocke, Bishop King, (spiritual) K. Knight, Kohfeldt, (spiritual) Marignac, Ortega, Pepper, Pongs, Schlanger, Sewell, (not) Tilden, Urbach, (precinding m) Van Steenburgh

of the Kwakiutl Indians Boas

L

as based on a theory of language M. Baym, Painter, Stutterheim, Urban

latent (see m, indirect)

in law Barfield, (analogy) Kalinowski, (civil rights) Andrew King, Nietzsche, Ogden, Samborn, Tarbet, Toulmin, Vaihinger

as lens Berggren, Farre

as likeness (cf. m, as simile) J. Anderson, Aquinas, Aristotle, E.B., Barnard, Bede, Berry, Bodmer, Breal, G. Brown, Carney, Cicero, (physical) G. Davies, Deutsch, Esnault, Feltenstein, Fenner, (descriptive m) Frye, Gardner, Gibbons, (between figure and thing) Gottsched, Gracian, (analogy) G. Graham, (of thought) Hecht, Hempel, (antecedent similarity) Henle, (induced or emotive similarity) Henle, (of unlike) Herschberger, Hobbes, (analogy) Hoffding, (contingent m) Holz, (of two diff. fields) Hungerland, Iberico, (true) Ioannou, (of relations) Ioannou, (of qualities) Ioannou, Jakobson, Juarrieta, Jenyns, Khatchadourian, Konrad, Lacan, R. Lees, Lord, MacGill, MacIver, Mawardi, (E.L.) Metafora, (Webster's) Metaphor, (E.B., I) Metaphor, Migliorini, Molhova, (implicit)

Nemerov, Olscamp, Ong, Parkhurst, Peacham, Phelan, Prescott, (old and new) Richards, (of feelings) Richards, Riffaterre, Rousset, Sherry, Arvid Smith, John Smith, Speranski, Srzednicki, Standiewicz, W. Stevens, Stutterheim, (in unlikeness) Tindall, Tupper, S. Ullmann, Albert Upton, A. Ward, (in diff.) Wells, Welsh, (induced) Wheelwright, Wimsatt

as not based on likeness (of a single quality) Allers, (kenning) D. Collins, Isenberg, Jenyns, Khatchadourian

linguistic theory of Adank, Bally, Barone, Bickerton, L. Bloomfield, M. Bloomfield, J. Bowers, Breal, Brinkmann, Brooke-Rose, Buhler, Carnoy, Chomsky, Coseriu, Ellis, Fodor, Fonagy, Gardiner, G. Gerber, Greimas, T. Hughes, Jakobson, Jesperson, Katz, Koen, Lacan, Lambert, Leech, S. Levin, Liebesny, Mandelbaum, Mauthner, H. Meier, P. Moses, Nosek, Osborn, Painter, Pasini, Pavel, Pelc, Randolph, Reichling. Riffaterre, F. Saussure, H. Schmidt, Schultz, Stanford, Stankiewicz, G. Stern, Strang, Stutterheim, O. Thomas, Todorov, Uhrhan, S. Ullmann, Valesio, Vianu, Vossler, Warfel, B. Wheeler, Whorf

as indistinguishable from literal Beardsley, Robert Brown, Morris Cohen, Friedman, (response) Kaiser, (same wd. as lit. and fig.) Lecky, Leondar, C. S. Lewis, Sohngen

as irreducible to literal Allers, Beardsley, Berggren, Blumenberg, (not paraphrasable) Brooks, Carney, Carpenter, (but is paraphrasable) Cavell, Morris Cohen, (irrational) Cosmo, Croce, Dickey, Ebersole, Feidelson, Feltenstein, Fenollosa, F. C. Flint, S. Foster, France, Friedman, Funk, Gombrich, Hungerland, Iberico, Ioannou, D. James, Jaurrieta, R. Johnson, A. Kaplan, Kendall, Khatchadourian, Bruce King, Knights, Lauretano, (no literal) C. S. Lewis, Love, Mackey, Martino, May, McCloskey, Meszaros, (E.L.) Metafora, C. Myers, H. Myers, O. Nash, Nyman, Osborn, Pasini, Pepper, Perelman, Prado, (m contrasted with) Quinlan, Raleigh, (not logical) Ransom, Richards, Robbe-Grillet, (i.e., plastic thought) Schiavina, Shibles, Slattery, Speranski, Stanford, W. Stevens, Stevenson, Stutterheim, (non-literal) Tilden, Tschizewskij, Ushenko, Van Steenburgh, Vianu, F. Vonessen, Walsh, A. Ward, P. Weiss, Whalley, Wheelwright

as reducible to literal statement Aristotle, Aschenbrenner, Bentham, (except imagery) Carney, (can be paraphrased) Cavell, Herschberger, Hobbes, A. Martin, Meszaros, (E.B., 3) Metaphor, H. Myers, (operationally) H. Nash, Needham, A. Paul, Spratt, Stevenson, Van Steenburgh, Whalley

literalist theory of Beardsley, Black, A. Martin, Spratt

taken literally (cf. m, as myth; m, logical absurdity theory of) (by primitive) Beinhauer, (as preceding the literal) Biese, (as source of literal) Buck, (two terms of) Bullinger, (is false) Carney, (in schizophrenia) Chapman, (is myth) Morris Cohen, (a new type of literal) Daiches, (is false) Ferre, (simple juxtaposition) Frye, (becomes the literal) Kaufmann, (is error) R. Lees, (derived from) Lemmon, (is false) Mackel, McCabe, Mindel, (anti) C. Myers, O. Nash, (anti) Ogden, Sarbin, Sohngen, (is false) P. Weiss, (is myth) Wheelwright

live Pressler, Stanford, Ushenko, Wakeman

in logic (of logic) Britton, S. Brown, Morris Cohen, (in syllogism) Cole, Feigl, M. Hesse, Howell, (poetic) Larsson, (anti) Lauretano, MacIver, (Ramistic) Mazzeo, McInerny, Menne, (logic is inferior to rhetoric) H. Myers, Nietzsche, Nyman, Olscamp, Pacernick, Painter, Picard, J. Ross, Shuford, Y. Simon, Snell, Tesauro, Tuve, (logic based on m) Vonessen, (anti logic) Walsh, Wheelwright

logical absurdity (cf. m, controversion theory of) Beardsley, Carney, Celan, (m as the impossible) Coon, Cosmo, Empson, Feidelson, Ferre, Frye, H. Greene, Henel, Hulme, Khatchadourian, Leondar, McCloskey, Nemetz, Ortega, (puzzlement-recoil) Osborn, Percy, Schlotthaus, Srzednicki

lyrical Pasini, Tumlirz, (rhyme) Turcany, Ziemendorff, Zoll

M

machine Ballard, (mechanical) Carter, (models) Deutsch, Embler, Harre, (mechanism) H. Jones, Korg, (mechanism) Landau, (mechanical) Lauretano, (mechanical) Meadows, (atomistic) Meadows, Norwood, Pepper, (mechanical) Stelzner, Turbayne

mad Chesterton, Fry, (madness needed for m) Mazzeo, W. Stevens

and make-believe Friquegnon, Jakobson

material Scudamore

as maxims Gracian

as meaning Aschenbrenner, (apprehend one meaning through another) Barfield, Erwin, (double meaning) W. Stevens, (double meaning) Stutterheim, Tilden, (as meaningful; whole meaning) Vonessen, (meaningful) Wheelwright

mediational processes of (thermal cues) C. C. Anderson, Gordon as metamorphosis (cf. m, transfer of) (Breton) Balakian, (of seen through subjective sensitivity) Biese, Jaurrieta, Lauretano, Madge, Michaelsson, J, Simon, W. Stevens, Ushenko

of metaphor Bachelard, (m as metaphorical) T.D., Doblin, (m about m) Ferre, Murry, (m as itself m) Nemerov, (m is itself m) Pongs, Ransom, Richards, (no such thing as) W. Stevens, Stutterheim, D. Thomas, R. Wallace

built on metaphors (cf. m, chains of) Brower, Edie, Hornick, Lauretano, (m itself a m) Lucas, Marias, (contrast of) Quinlan, (multiple m) Rousset, Schlanger, (theories of) Slawinska, E. Stern, (anti) W. Stevens, D. Thomas, Vianu, (collective m) Vonessen, Woodhouse

as metaphysics (cf. metaphysics) Chesterton, Costello, Ebersole, Emmet, Henderson, (metaphysical) MacNeice, C. Myers, Pepper, Rousset, Sohngen, Stutterheim, (m as metaphysical necessity) Sucre, Tindall, Turbayne, Urban, C. Wagner, Whittier, Wisdom, Zoll

as metonymy Brinkmann, Dannehl, G. Gerber, (cause-effect) Gracian, Jakobson, Lacan, (cause-effect) MacGill, (grammatical imperfection) F. Muller, Nietzsche, Stankiewicz, Urbach, Wheelwright

to describe mind (cf. m, as repres. of inner by outer) Abrams, G. Adams, Allers, C. C. Anderson, S. Asch, Barfield, Bally, Benamou, Bland, (dynamic image) Brandenburg, (in sensuous terms) S. Brown, Buchanan, Carvalho, Dickey, (in terms of body) Edie, (by nature) Emerson, (by body) Empson, Freud, Hecht, Ioannou, Jesperson, H. Jones, Lawlor, Lewin, F. Muller, Ogden, Olken, Richards, Ryle, Sarbin, Stutterheim, (other minds) Thomson, Vaihinger, Vonessen, Wakeman, (by physical obj.) Welby

as misleading (initially) Aristotle, (if unrestricted) Arrom, (initially) Beardsley, Birch, (misrepresents) Gottsched, Gummere, Hobbes, E. A. Holmes, (not) Horsburgh, Huxley, Bishop King, Locke, MacIver, F. Muller, (circular) C. Myers, N. Nash, Nietzsche, Nyman, Ogden, Pederson-Krag, (trickery) C. Pellegrini, Reichenbach, Rousset, Ryle, Sarbin, Shibles, Stelzner, Sternheim, (degeneration) W. Stevens, Strang, Temkin, (deception) Tesauro, Turbayne, Urbach, Warfel

misuse of (in psychology) Allers, Berggren, Birch, Borges, (in prose) Breitinger, (in logic) Britton, (mixed m, conceit) Buck, (in context--mixing) Carney, Chesterton, Clutton-Brock, Morris Cohen, (about deity) A. Collins, (in science, philos., prose, oratory) Croce, (dangerous analogy) Farber, H. Fowler, S. George, Gottsched, (not) Hagopian, (not) Horsburgh, H. Jones, E. Kane, Kevin, Lauretano, R. Lees, MacIver, A. Meyer,

(moment of) Schlanger, (enigma) Selig, Stutterheim, (mysterious) Tesauro, (magic) R. Wallace, (mystery) Walsh, (mystery) Wheelwright, (mystical) Wimsatt, (magical) Winter

as myth (cf. myth) Alden, Barfield, Berggren, Blumenberg, K. Burke, Cassirer, Christiansen, Chun, (if taken literally) Morris Cohen, Dorfles, Fink, (if terms identified) Frye, Keith, Lauretano, M. Lewis, Littlefield, Madge, Mauron, Mauthner, F. Muller, (condensed) Nemerov, Nietzsche, Norwood, Pongs, Rank, Ransom, (myth to m) Sarbin, (myth to m) Speranski, Stutterheim, Trzynadlowskiego, Turbayne, Urbach, Wheelwright

N

as a naming (improper) Aristotle, Beach, Begelman, Edie, Esnault, Fonagy, Goldthwait, (in Hawthorne) A. Griffith, (confused) Gummere, Hecht, Hempel, McInerny, Murry, (done by story-telling) Nemerov, (pseudo) Ogden, Ortega, Pasini, Pongs, (of already found truth) E. St. John, Schlanger, Shakespeare, Tilden, (names) Vaihinger

as narrowing Richards, Schlauch, Turbayne

as natural Adelung, Augustine, Coleridge, Croce, Emerson, Fenollosa, Gardiner, Girardot, Goldsmith, (originally) Grierson, Haworth, Hytier, Irving, Kenner, Kohfeldt, (conceits) Lea, LeSage, Longinus, R. Meyer, F. Muller, Osborn, Pasini, (to ordinary man) Peacock, Reinert, Rhys-Davids, Ruskin, Speranski, W. Stevens, (imitate actual speech) Sucre, S. Ullmann, Urban, Wasserman, Wheelwright, C. Williams

as agreeing with nature (cf. analogy, universal) St. Augustine, S. Baker, (by imagination) Breitinger, Brooks, B. Brown, (not) Coleridge, Eisenstein, Emerson, Fenollosa, Gottsched, (as more than) Gracian, Haworth, Hesehaus, Hillyer, Keller, (experience) Kenner, (nature-m's) Lanier, (conceit) Lea, LeSage, Mazzeo, Murry, Pongs, Rhys-Davids, Semler, W. Stevens, Terry, Tesauro, Turbayne, Wasserman, (setting as a m) R. Wellek

as necessary principle of language development Ballard, Barfield, Bede, Beinhauer, Biese, Borges, Boulton, Breal, Brooks, Burmester, (and symbolic forms) Cassirer, Coleman, Croce, Donatus, Edie, Egan, Fenollosa, C. Ferguson, Fonagy, H. Fowler, France, W. Fraser, H. Frost, Gardiner, Gardner, S. George, Gertel, (in style) Gourmont, Gummere, (all men use m) Hecht, Hempel, Holz, Hytier, Jesperson, Kafka, Klein, Langer, Mackel,

Migliorini, F. Muller, Nietzsche, Ogden, Pasini, Peacham, Regnaud, Richards, E. St. John, Schlauch, Stutterheim, Urban, Wakeman, Wasserman, B. Wheeler, (radical m) Wheelwright

need for (to cultivate use) C. Ferguson, Kafka, (drive to create them) Nietzsche, Ogden

negative (cf. m, of silence; m, of omitting) Aristotle, Wajid

as a net Black, Mauron, Swanson

as a "neutralization" Pasini, Pavel

as new Beinhauer, Berggren, Berry, Blumenberg, Boillot, (absurdity of) Borges, (to create connections) Boulton, Breal, (discovery) Brooks, K. Burke, (new) Burkland, (creates) Burkland, (discovery) Canguilhem, Ch'i, Clutton-Brock, (the new is always metaphorical) Morris Cohen, Dickey, Edie, Eisenstein, Eliot, Elster, (a new seeing) Ferre, (unique) S. Foster, Funk, Gardiner, S. George, (anti) Gertel, Gordon, Holz, Hulme, Kaufmann, Kohfeldt, Kuhn, Langer, Lea, (to improve language) Mackel, (in old) MacLeish, Monro, Parkhurst, Pasini, (in old) Pavel, Pepper, Ramsey, (in old) Reichling, Reverdy, (in old) Rice, (as hard to create) M. St. John, Schlanger, (as emergent concept) Schon, (in old) Stutterheim, (no new m) Sucre, Taillardat, S. Ullmann, Ushenko, (m old) Vela, (neologisms) Vetter, Wheelwright, Winter, Wu

of Newfoundland B. Porter

as nonsense Gill, Hobbes, Kevin, Manso, Monro, (represents nothing) Stutterheim, George Watson, White

object-comparison view of Beardsley, Schipper

of omitting (cf. m, of silence; m, negative) Richards, Schlotthaus, Vaihinger, (m is seeing an object in terms of its negation) Wajid

in oratory (cf. m, in rhetoric) (only) Hegel, (rhetorical m) Hempel, Hoffmann, Inviolata, Kaufmann, Andrew King, Osborn, Roschatt, Stelzner, Wimsatt

organic R. Adams, T. Boyle, Brumleve, (organicist) G. Carter, Denbigh, Fogle, (organon) Jordan, M. Lewis, (organismic) Meadows, (organism) Mehrabian, (organicism) Pepper, (biological)

Stelzner, Vaihinger

oriental (cf. m, in Chinese) Wiener

origin of (cf. m, as immediate experience; m, as necessary principle of language development) [p = primitive immediate experience] (p) Barfield, (p) Boulton, (p) Buck, Carvalho, (p) Morris Cohen, (p; in myth) Dorfles, (preverbal) Edie, Gerhard, (in myth) Gertel, Grierson, Grindon, (p) Gummere, (synaesthesia) Hagopian, Hempel, (of poetic comparison) Henning, (in poetic m) Hester, Hornbostel, Isocrates, (as unknown) Jaurrieta, Jesperson, (history of) Kohfeldt, (in love) Lanier, Lauretano, Lawler, Liu, (sensible to non-sensible) Locke, Manso, Migliorini, F. Muller, (pre-analytic) C. Myers, Pasini, Ransom, (image prior to language) H. Read, Regnaud, Richards, (in sense) E. St. John, Sala, A. Scott, Speranski, Stanford, Turcato, Vela, Vico, Heinz Werner, Wheelwright, Whorf, Wundt, Zipf

as ornamenting Addison, Bede, (anti) Beinhauer, Berggren, (anti) Biese, Birch, Blair, (anti) Boulton, Breitinger, Cicero, Clutton-Brock, Croce, Demetrius, Donatus, C. Ferguson, Fitzosborne, S. George, Gottsched, Gracian, Hegel, (anti) Lauretano, Leakey, Macbeth, McCall, (anti) Murry, (anti) H. Myers, (alamkaras) Nair, Nietzsche, Olivero, Ortega, Quintilian, (as mask) Rousset, Sacerdos, (ameliorative) Schlauch, Stutterheim, (lively) Voltaire, (decorative) Wells

as ostrannie (estranging) Shklovskii

P

in painting Biese, Burkland, Dryden, (painting as silent poetry) Horace, Irving, Speranski, Turnbull

as a parable (condensed) Arminius, Bozon, S. Brown, Eastman, Fink, Fordyce, R. Frost, Funk, Gracian, Perrin, (Buddhist) Rhys-Davids, Turnbull, Wackernagel, Warfel

as paradigm Kuhn, Leiter, Ramsey, Vaihinger

as paradox (cf. m, as mystical) Abel, Alden, Brooks, J. Cope, Fry, Gracian, Groos, E. Kane, LeSage, Macquarrie, B. Spencer, Vela, Wajid, R. Wellek, Whalley, Wheelwright, Wisdom

parallelism Bonsiepe, Elster, Gertel, McCall, Albert Upton

as parataxis Pound, Whalley, Wu

perceptual (cf. m, visual; m, as drawn) Carnoy, F. C. Flint, Force, S. Foster, (anti) Hotopf, Hungerland, Kuhn, Langer, Manser, May, Nietzsche, Nyman, Ortega, Osborn, Petrie, H. Read, Richards, M. St. John, Soltis, Stanford, E. Stern, (wholes) A. Ward, (physiognomic) Heinz Werner, Wheelwright, Wittgenstein

in Persian poetry Nashat

as descriptive of persons S. Asch, Friedman, Hornstein, Jeffries, G. Knight, Kuypers, Mehrabian, R. Muller, Nietzsche, (reveals author) Rankin, Sarmiento, Spurgeon, Steinhoff, Tarbet, Weekley, Wells, (not) White, Wisdom, Yoder

as perspective (by incongruity) K. Burke, Friquegnon, Girardot, Hulme, (many models needed) Hutten, Jackson, Kohfeldt, Lauretano, Leisi, (no single m) Marias, (no single m) Mehrabian, Muncie, (no single m) Musurillo, C. Myers, (perspectivism) Nietzsche, Nyman, (no single m) Pepper, (no single m) Ramsey, Sarbin, (no single m) Schlanger, Sheehan, (no single m) Shibles, (no single m) Strang, (world view) Stutterheim, (perspective m) Van Steenburgh, (conceptual variation) Wheelwright, Wittgenstein

as persuasive (cf. m, as stimulating emotions; m, as true) Henderson, Peacham, B. Robinson, Sherry, S. Ullmann

as language of phenomenology (cf. m, intentional) Binswanger, Edie

philosophical Costello, Van Steenburgh, Veca, Vischer

as basis of a philosophy (not) Allers, Blumenberg, K. Burke, G. Carter, (not) Croce, Embler, Feltenstein, (banish from philosophy) Fitzosborne, Girardot, Henderson, Horsburgh, Hulme, (Valery) Hytier, Kaufmann, Kuhn, Lauretano, Luca, Mackey, Marias, Meszaros, Mizener, C. Myers, H. Myers, Norwood, Pasini, Pepper, Perelman, Prado, Ransom, (not) Reichenbach, (m reveals philosophy) Rhys-Davids, Richards, Schwyzer, Shibles, Sidney, Sohngen, (not) W. Stevens, Stutterheim, Sucre, Tarbet, Tschizewskij, Turbayne, Turnbull, Urbach, Urban, Van Steenburgh, Vianu, Wald, J. Walker, Warburton, Whalley

in philosophy (cf. m, Thomistic theory of) Aldrich, J. Anderson, Aschenbrenner, Aristotle, J. Austin, A. Baker, Ballard, Barfield, Beardsley, Bennet, Bentham, Berg, Berggren, Bertram, Biese, Black, Blumenberg, Britton, Robert Brown, E. Burke, K. Burke, Burlingame, Carney, Cassirer, Cavell, M. Clark, Morris Cohen, Copleston, Costello, Croce, Cross, Daitz, Delaney, Derbolav, Deutsch, Ebersole, Edelman, Edie, Eisler, Emmet, Erwin, Eucken, Farre, Feigl, Feltenstein, Fleming, Foss, Friquegnon, S. George, Gill, Grenet, Groos, (analogy)

Hagner, Hampshire, Hanson, Harre, Harriman, F. Harrison, Hayner, Heidegger, Henderson, Henle, M. Hesse, Hester, (analogy) Hoffding, Horsburgh, (on Plato) J. Huber, Hulme, Hussey, Isenberg, Jordan, Kaminsky, A. Kaplan, Khatchadourian, Kohfeldt, Kranz, Lalande, Langer, Lauretano, Leondar, C. I. Lewis, Lloyd, Locke, Logan, Luca, MacDonald, MacIntyre, MacIver, Mackey, Manser, Margolis, Marias, A. Martin, R. Martin, Marty, McCloskey, McPherson, Meszaros, C. Myers, G. Myers, Nietzsche, Nyman, Ogden, Painter, A. Paul, Pepper, Perelman, Petrie, Prado, Reichenbach, (existentialistic) Robbe-Grillet, Ryle, Santayana, Schipper, Shibles, Smythies, Sohngen, Sojcher, Soltis, Specht, Srzednicki, Stallknecht, Stevenson, Stutterheim, Swanson, Sweet, Takeda, Tarbet, Tigner, Tilden, Tilghmann, Tomkins, Toulmin, Turbayne, J. Turner, Urban, Ushenko, Vaihinger, Van Steenburgh, Vesey, F. Vonessen, C. Wagner, Wahl, Wajid, Walsh, George Watson, P. Weiss, Welsh, Whittier, Wisdom, Wittgenstein, Zimmer

based on physiological states (cf. m, Freudian theory of) C. C. Anderson, Fere, Fonagy, Kaiser, Madge, Sharpe, Spire, (not) Szasz

as pictorial (cf. m, as drawn; picture; poem, as painting; imagism) Addison, Aristotle, Babbitt, S. Baker, Bally, (comparison) Berggren, Bett, Bevis, Biese, Blair, Bland, Bodmer, Breitinger, (of unfamiliar) S. Brown, Carpenter, Church, Cicero, (to imagination) Coleridge, Daitz, C. Davies, Deutsch, Deutschbein, Dickey, Dieter, Dryden, Elster, Feigl, Fenollosa, C. Ferguson, Frankel, R. Frazer, Freud, Fruit, Gardiner, (not) Goldsmith, Goodman, Gottfried, (not) Gray, (not always) Groos, (picturesque) Gummere, (pictorial) Gummere, Hagstrum, Haight, (not) M. Hesse, (not) Hester, Hillyer, Hocke, Holz, Horace, (not) Hornick, G. Hughes, Hulme, Irving, Jaensch, Jamieson, Jennings, W. Kaplan, Kaufmann, Kenner, Kern, Khatchadourian, Kohfeldt, LeSage, Lewontin, Liebesny, Lockwood, Mackel, Madge, Manser, Martyn, (not) Mazzeo, M. McLuhan, R. Meyer, G. Myers, Nietzsche, Norwood, (not) Nyman, O'Dea, Ogden, Quintilian, Ramsey, H. Read, (painting) Rieser, Rohrich, Rousset, (not) Sharp, Sherry, Shibles, Shook, A. Smart, Sohngen, Tupper, Turnbull, Urbach, Van Steenburgh, Walsh, Wasserman, (false) Welby, Wells, Heinz Werner, Whalley, C. Williams, Wu

plastic Aldrich, Goodman, Parkhurst, Rieser, (plastic thought) Schiavina

in plastic art Burkland, Khatchadourian, Madge, Rieser, Schiavina, Speranski, (setting) R. Wellek, "Zwiazek"

as play J. Austin, (games) Berne, (simile) Deutschbein, (comparison) Eichholz, Fonagy, Fry, Groesbeck, Margolis, Mendelsohn, Nietzsche, Nyman, Peacock, Szasz

proportionality (see m, as analogical; analogy)

in prose Gracian, H. Gross, Hagopian, Havighurst, (as dead m) Hulme, Lane,Lecke, Lucas, Parkhurst, (as m) Pasini, Pongs, Rees, Rew, Richards, A. Rosenberg, Scheer-Schazler, Schon, Shklovskii, G. Stein, S. Ullmann

as proverb Alain, Church, Lang, Maass, J. Read, A. Taylor, (proverb as argument) Wakeman, (contradictory proverbs) Wakeman, Wasserman, (contradictory proverbs) Watts

psychological or psychiatric theory of (cf. m, Freudian theory of; schizophrenia; m, as therapy) Abraham, Adank, Aleksandrowicz, Allers, C. C. Anderson, Armstrong, S. Asch, Basaglia, Begelman, Biese, Bodkin, Boulton, R. Brown, Bruchmann, Buck, K. Burke, Cain, Caruth, Chun, Church, (on image) Colvin, (on image) Comstock, Couch, Downey, Frentz, Freud, Galton, Gordon, Gourmont, Isaacs, Jung, Kainz, Kaiser, Kanner, B. Kaplan, Knapp, Koch, Koen, Lacan, Lemmon, Lewin, Louch, Mauthner, Mehrabian, Mellon, Minkowski, Muncie, H. Nash, Navratil, Nyman, Ogden, Oppenheimer, Osborn, Osgood, Pacernick, Pear, Pederson-Krag, Pongs, C. Read, Richards, Robbins, Rohovit, Royce, Ruin, Sarbin, R. Saussure, Schon, Sharpe, Silberer, H. Simon, Skinner, Speranski, Sperry, Stahlin, G. Stern, Stevenson, Stogdill, Szasz, Valentine, Vetter, Wasserman, Watts, A. Wellek, Heinz Werner, Wundt

as pun (see pun)

pure (pure figure) H. Greene, (not) D. James, (as giving awareness of m's) Madge, (as grammatical m) Turcato

as puzzle (-resolution) C. C. Anderson, Aristotle, Borges, Ebersole, Praz, (enigma) Rousset, Wittgenstein

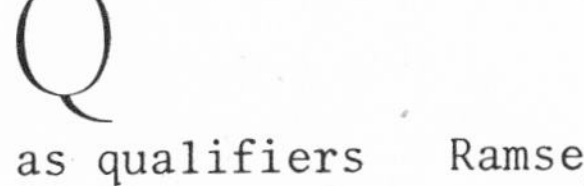

Q

as qualifiers Ramsey

having a common quality Aschenbrenner, Buck, (aspect) Elster, Esnault, (quality) Hayner, (quality, relation) Ioannou, Knapp, Molhova, (not) C. Myers

R

radical (as natural and unconscious) Barfield, G. Gerber, Jesperson, B. Kaplan, Kaufmann, F. Muller, Schon, Urban, Wells, (A-B, A is B) Whalley, Wheelwright

in reading Cooper, Fennema, C. Ferguson, Friedman, Groesbeck, Groos, Hester, Kaiser, Khatchadourian, Kohfeldt, Lauretano, Looby, Richards, Shawcross, N. Smith, Thompson, Albert Upton, Ushenko, Vaihinger

as constituting reality (cf. m, as constituting thought; m, as constituting emotions) Barnard, Berggren, Black, Blumenberg, K. Burke, (Stevens) Carruth, (symbolically) Cassirer, (reveals) J. Cope, (to think is to express) Croce, (intuition is expression) Croce, Denbigh, Dickey, Dorfles, Egan, Embler, (as essential) Farber, (models do not) Farre, (hypostatize entities) Feltenstein, Ferre, Force, Frye, M. Hesse, Holz, (emotive) Hotopf, (verisimilitude) Jaurrieta, Jordan, Kuhn, Leondar, Mackey, Marias, Martino, M. McLuhan, Meadows, Mehrabian, Minkowski, Murry, H. Myers, H. Nash, Nietzsche, Norwood, Robbe-Grillet, Royce, Sarbin, Schiavina, Schlanger, Shibles, Sohngen, Sterzinger, W. Stevens, Tesauro, Tindall, Urban, Vela, Vico, Wald, Wasserman, (as creating reality) Welsh, Wheelwright, Whorf, Wimsatt, Wu

to describe reality Allers, C. C. Anderson, St. Augustine, (conceit) Gracian, (Gongora) Guillen, Hamann, Herschberger, Hocke, Holz, (emotive) Hotopf, Hulme, R. Johnson, A. Kaplan, Kendall, Kohfeldt, (not) Laguardia, Lentricchia, Manser, (as conceited) Mazzeo, (not) McInerny, Meadows, (not) A. Meyer, Nietzsche, Norwood, Nyman, Ortega, Pongs, Ramsey, Ransom, Reinert, (not) Robbe-Grillet, Rousset, Royce, Sarbin, Sheehan, Shibles, Slattery, W. Stevens, Stutterheim, (reveal) Sucre, (not) Temkin, (reveal) Tesauro, Urban, Vela, (reveal) Vonessen, Whalley, Wheelwright, Winter

reciprocal Aristotle, (transfer) Biese, Black, (reflexive) Ellmann, Friedrich, S. George, (reflexive image) Gide, (symmetrical) Guillen, (in analogy) Hoffding, (mutual) Jaurrieta, Leakey, Leondar, Madge, Migliorini, Richards, Sala, (reversal) Tschizewskij

reification of Sarbin

rejuvenated Beinhauer, Brooks, Clutton-Brock, (recreate) Girardot, Migliorini, Morris, Pasini, Schlauch, Taillardat, Vaananen, Wheelwright

as relation (cf. m, transfer of, esp. for names beginning with a-g) (of theory and experiment) Hutten, (of diverse images) Iberico, (of emotions and objects) Irving, (spiritual and physical) Jaurrieta, (of old and new experience) B. Kaplan, (as all sentences with "is") Kaufmann, (without "is" also) Kaufmann, (God to world) Kendall, (God to man) Kendall, (of things known) Bishop King, (dialectic between intellect and sensation) Bruce King, (of incompatible contexts) Koestler, (of sound to imagery) Kohfeldt, (of two objects) Konrad, (not by third thing) Lauretano, (of contradictory classes) Leisi, (of unlike contexts) Lemmon, (of general and specific) Lieb, (of literal subject and figurative predicate) Lord, (superimposition of ideas) Lucas, (real-theoretical, exist-become) Mackel, (old and new) MacLeish, (extreme elements) Mariani, (body-soul, religion-eroticism) McCann, (of environments) "The McLuhan Metaphor," (synthesis) Meszaros, (two levels of truth or causality) Nemetz, (image-object) Nyman, (moral-sensory, various senses, spiritual-sensuous) O'Malley, (ideal) Ortega, (subject-object, mind-body) Ortega, (abstract-concrete) Pasini, (coalescence) Pavel, (extensive and intensive) Pavel, (male-female poles) Pongs, (two different fields) Porzig, (mysterious) Ramsey, (distant realities) Reverdy, (new-old, modern-traditional) Rice, (subject-object, inner-outer) Richards, (as inexhaustible) Richards, (borrowing, intercourse of thought) Richards, (context transaction) Richards, (combine, contiguous) Riffaterre, (sympathetic) Robbe-Grillet, (subject-object) Ruin, (different fields) M. St. John, (of different perceptions) M. St. John, (different fields) Samborn, (animate-inanimate) Schlauch, (human to non-human) Schlauch, (different spheres) Schlotthaus, (man-cosmos) Sewell, (two contexts) Shibles, (misused) Slattery, (thing stated and restatement) W. Stevens, (words to reality) Stutterheim, (different fields) Temkin, (sense-sense, static-dynamic, animate-inanimate) Torre, (world and moral truth) Turnbull, (meanings) Valesio, (qualities) Van Steenburgh, (old and new) Wells, (primitive) Whalley, (image and object) Nyman

religious (cf. m, Thomistic theory of; analogy, universal) Aldrich, Aquinas, Augustine, Bede, Beinhauer, Berggren, Bourke, Brewer, S. Brown, Bullinger, (analogy) Burrell, (analogy) J. Butler, (in D. Thomas) Chaneles, Cheyne, D. Clark, Coleman, Conroy, J. Cope, Copleston, Courcelle, Cranfield, Debaisieux, Dhorme, Dieckmann, Dieter, Dillistone, Downing, Eichholz, Emerson, Ericson, Feldkeller, Feldman, (models in) Ferre, D. Fraser, Friquegnon, Funk, Gill, Goldammer, Gracian, (of St. Paul) Gryglewicz, Habbel, Hermann, Heylen, Hick, Hoffmann, Howson, Hugede, Inviolata, Ioannou, (anti) D. James, Jenyns, W. Jones, Jung, Keach, Keller, Kendall, Kessler, Bishop King, F. Kolbe, Klaus Lange, R. Lees, J. Lewis, Loeb, Macmillan, Macquarrie, Martyn, Mondin, Moogan, C. Myers, Nelson, Nietzsche, Ong, Penido, Perrin, Pongs, Poteat, Przwara, Ramsay, Ramsey, Rankin, Ransom, (Buddhist) Rhys-Davids, Robillard, B. Robinson, C. Robinson, J. Ross, Royce, Ryan, E. St. John, G. Sauvage, Sawhill, Schlegel, Sheen, Slattery, Sohngen, N. Stevens, Stutterheim,

Tesauro, Ungewitter, Vaihinger, Vogt-Terhorst, Goodwin Watson, Wimsatt, Wunsche

as repetition Battcock, (of ratios) Berggren, (of sound) Erlich, (avoid) "Figures of Speech," H. Gross, Hardy, (of imagery) Matlaw, Schlauch

as repression Freud

as resemblance (see likeness)

as response Osborn

in rhetoric (partial list) Aristotle, Bacon, Baden, Bain, Baker, Barfield, Blair, Bonsiepe, Boulton, J. Bowers, S. Brown, K. Burke, Campbell, Cicero, E. Cope, Cox, Craddock, W. Crane, Demetrius, DeMille, Empson, Fenner, Fogarty, Fonagy, Fraunce, Gerlach, Gibbons, Gracian, Greenough, Grierson, Hermogenes, Hobbes, Holland, Hook, Howell, Inviolata, Jamieson, Jewel, M. Joseph, Kames, Kitzhaber, (terms) Lanham, (anti) Lauretano, (dictionary) Lausberg, Leech, Le Hir, Lord, Macbeth, MacGill, McCall, Mehren, Osborn, W. Parsons, Peacham, Perelman, Puttenham, Quintilian, Ragsdale, Richards, C. Robinson, Sherry, Adam Smith, John Smith, Stirling, Stutterheim, Susenbrotus, W. Taylor, Tesauro, Tryphon, Vaihinger, Vinsauf, Volkmann, Wald, K. Wallace, Whately, Williamson, T. Wilson, Wimsatt

rhetorical Osborn, Pasini, Reynolds

rhythmical Erlich

as a riddle Gracian, Hocke, E. Parsons, Praz

ringing Whalley

ritual (see m, fixed)

as governed by rules (not) H. Crane, (not) De, (rules unknown) Dickey, S. George, Goodman, Gracian, (not) Herder, (not) Hester, (not) Hungerland, Hutten, (not) Isenberg, Jamieson, Kohfeldt, (not) Lecky, S. Leonard, (not) McCloskey, (E.B., 3) Metaphor, J. Muller, (linguistic rules) Nowottny, (not) Pepper, Phelps, Rousset, (not) Sharp, Taillardat, Uhrhan, (not) A. Ward

Russian Erlich, (literature) Peretts, Shamota, Shklovskii, Volkov, Zirmunskij

S

in Sanskrit De, P. Kane, Nair

as not a simile Beardsley, Margolis, H. Spencer

sinking (relating terms of high and low value) (debasing) Alcuin, (anti) Cicero, (not) Demetrius, (anti) Jamieson, Junker, (pro) Bishop King, Murry, Pope, (pejorative) Schlauch, Swift, (sunken) Wells

as slang (see slang)

slippery (cf. m, being captivated by) Mehrabian

as slogan (see m, as cliche)

in social relations K. Burke, Holz, (constitutes) Kaufmann, Konrad, (social theory) Meadows, Mindel, H. Nash, Nietzsche, Osborn, Pongs, Schiavina, Taillardat, Vaihinger, Westendorpf

sound Fonagy, G. Gerber, Gottfried, H. Gross, Hess, Hungerland, B. Kaplan, Kohfeldt, Lecke, P. Moses, Nietzsche, Stanford, A. Stein, (phonetic) Tupper, Turcany, (synaesthesia) S. Ullmann

Spanish Beinhauer, Lang, Lemos, Lorenz, McCann, (Chile) Oroz, (Chile) Ortiz, Preis, Roberts, Sarmiento, Uhrhan

spatial Freud, (reveal non-spatial) Holz, (not) Lauretano, Prado, Rank, Ryle, Heinz Werner

influence on speaker (cf. m, in oratory) Osborn, Wimsatt

as any part of speech Black, Brinkmann, Brooke-Rose, Brower, G. Brown, Cummings, Friedrich, (any term) Goldsmith, (conceit) Gracian, Joyce, Lord, Molhova, Nosek, Wackernagel, Whalley

as representing spiritual by sensual (see m, to express unknown by known)

as spontaneous (cf. m, as immediate experience) Gertel, Girardot, Gummere, (lightning-thought) Hecht, (not) Hillmann, G. Hughes, Jenkins, Lauretano, LeSage, Nemetz, (simultaneous) Nyman, (simultaneous) Ortega, Pasini, Peacock, Pongs, Ransom, H. Read, Schiavina, Sharp, Speranski, E. Stern, Stutterheim, S. Ullmann

sports Gryglewicz, Haubrich, Pressler, Sawhill, Spurgeon, Weekley

stages of Manso, (levels of) Nemetz, Osborn, Urban, Heinz Werner

static-dynamic Gertel, Torre

statistics of Fonagy, E. Huber, (no. of image) Hulme, Kaiser, P. Moses, Rew, Spurgeon, Stahlin, Whaler as stereoscope of ideas E. Adams, Berggren, (spectroscope) Raleigh, Stanford, Turnbull, A. Ward

as stimulus Osborn, Skinner

as story (cf. m, as fable; m, as parable) (compressed) Nemerov

as striking (cf. m, as surprising) (shocking) "Force of Metaphor," Gracian, McCloskey, Reverdy, Silz

structural Berggren, Turcato

subject (content) of Pasini, Rew, Schnabel, (m can have content) John Smith, Snell, W. Stevens, Taillardat, Torre, Wajid

subjective (private or personal) (anti) Coleridge, J. Cope, (and objective) Deutschbein, Dickey, Esnault, Feldkeller, Holz, Iberico, Jaurrieta, Kohfeldt, Konrad, Madge, (immature solipsism) Manso, H. Nash, Ortega, Osborn, Pongs, (personal) R. Saussure, E. Stern, Urban, Vaihinger, Vela

as sublimation Freud

as the sublime E. Burke, Gracian, R. Lee, Longinus, Mansart, Praz, Quintilian, Wasserman, Whalley

as a substitution Alonso, Aristotle, (of one reality for another) Arrom, (of m by m) Ballard, (of non-verbal) Berggren, Beyer, Black, (representation) Bullinger, Elster, (synecdoche) Kanner, Lacan, Leroux, Lewontin, Liu, (psychological) Martino, (take one thing for another) Mazzeo, (Webster's) Metaphor, (of strange word for proper word) (E.B., I) Metaphor, Nemetz, Ruiz, Shibles, Shipley, E. Stern, Sterzinger, Tindall, Uhrhan, Vaihinger, Vianu, (in different contexts) Warfel, Whalley

subtle (in Crane) Fuller, (conceit) Gracian, Voltaire

as suggestive (cf. m, as hypothesis) Arrom, Fenollosa, (simile) Hillyer, Hungerland, (of emotions) Ioannou, Page, Reinert, M. St. John, Stevenson, Urbach, Walsh, Goodwin Watson, (alluding) Heinz Werner, Wheelwright, Yelton

supervenience theory of Beardsley, Foss

as suppositio McInerny, Vaihinger

suppressed (in Pope) Bluestone

as surprise (cf. m, as unexpected) Aristotle, Brooks, Bullough, (strange-making) Erlich, Goodman, H. Gross, Henle, Kohfeldt, (striking) McCloskey, "Force of Metaphor," Peacock symbolic (one term is implied) Barfield, Blumenberg, Buhler, (not) Madge, (polysemous) L. Wagner

symbolism theory of Berggren

synaesthetic (see synaesthesia) Carnoy, Correia, Gertel, Gracian, P. Moses, Olken, Stanford

as a syncretism Pasini, Pavel, Heinz Werner

as synecdoche S. Brown, K. Burke, Kanner, (as congruity) MacGill, F. Muller, Quintilian

as synolon Lauretano

as synthesis (cf. m, as fusion; m, as unifying) Biese, (of acts of spirit) Cosmo, Croce, Hulme, Nyman, Stanford, E. Stern (of images) Stutterheim, (of intellect and emotions) Winter

T

as based on taboo (cf. kenning, concealing) Browne, (to conceal ugly) Browne, (not just) Dorfles, Hempel, Monro, Ortega, Pasini, Pongs, Heinz Werner

technical W. Fraser, Lauretano, (professional) Samborn, Schlanger

as tension (tensive) (type-tension) Berggren, (in W. Stevens) Bevis, Brooks, Buch, Morris Cohen, Daiches, (heightened consciousness) Eastman, Foss, Gracian, T. Greene, Guillen, Herschberger, Khatchadourian, Lauretano, Leisi, Leondar, McCloskey, (between essence and existence) Nielsen, Nyman, Osborn, Pongs, Porzig, Richards, W. Stevens, Stutterheim, A. Tate, Wheelwright, (between values, speaker, audience) Wimsatt

as a single term (cf. m, as substitution; tarning) Barfield, S. Johnson, (latent m) Madge, (not) Stanford, Tindall, Tupper, Van Steenburgh, (never) Vonessen

test for (seven scale preference) Knapp, A. Martin, Miller Analogies Test, H. Myers, Osgood, Pavy, Prior, J. Read, Robbins, Rohovit, Samson, Sarbin, Taillardat, Albert Upton, Anne Upton, Watts

in theory (constitutes) M. Hesse, (constitutes) Hutten, (no one theory of m) Khatchadourian, (constitutes) Kuhn, (of language; origin of theory) Lauretano, (anti theory of m) Louch, (theory of) Marques, Mehrabian, H. Meier, N. Nash, (basis of) Pasini,

rieta, (transcendental) Keller, (transcendental) (E.L.) Metafora, Nielsen, (not) Nowottny, (not) O'Dea, Pardee, Peacock, Pongs, (revelation) Slattery, W. Stevens, Stutterheim, (not) Tilden, Vogt-Terhorst, Wheelwright, Wimsatt

as transfer (of contexts) G. Adams, (name, attribute) G. Allen, (improper) Aristotle, (name) Arminius, (of both words and things) Bede, (animate-inanimate) Bede, (over type-boundaries) Berggren, (by picture, analogy, emotion) Berggren, (space-time) Borges, (sensuous-unsensed) Brinkmann, Brooke-Rose, (of meaning) Brooks, (of one field to another) Buhler, (of contexts) K. Burke, (of contexts) Burkland, (of contexts) Carney, (of word or thought) Cassiodorus, (symbolic form) Cassirer, (of one thought content by the name of another) Cassirer, (m to myth) Chun, (of name) Cicero, (of proper to another meaning) Angel Day, (from one plane of speech to another) Deutschbein, (context interchange) Dickey, (animate-inanimate) Donatus, (from proper meaning to another) DuMarsais, (concrete-abstract) Edie, (not) Edie, (from sphere to sphere) Elster, (intuitive) Esnault, (between categories) Feidelson, (of speech) Feltenstein, (of meaning or use) Fere, (of feeling) Ferre, (of attribute) Fogarty, (realm exchange) Friedrich, (non-material to material) H. Frost, (name) R. Frost, (real-unreal) Fry, (finite-infinite) Fry, (process-void) Fry, (of contexts) Frye, (of judgment) Funk, (of context) Funk, (of different worlds) Garcia Lorca, (of object and language) Gardiner, (of name) S. George, (of improper, of meaning) Gibbons, (reclassification of two realms) Goodman, (cause-effect) Gracian, (cause-effect) G. Graham, (of name) T. Greene, (conversion from one context to another) Harrell, (sort-crossing) Haworth, (change of meaning) Hecht, (fuse two different spheres) Hempel, (iconic) Henle, (of feelings) Henle, (not) Hester, (of names) Hobbes, (of things) Hocke, (non-sensuous to sensuous) Holz, (of spheres of knowledge) Holz, (not) Hornbostel, (relating animate and inanimate) T. Hughes, (of meaning) Hytier, (of name) Ioannou, (of emotions) Ioannou, Jaurrieta, (of meaning) Kanner, (of name, idea or picture on part of reader) Khatchadourian, (of tenor) K. Knight, (from one sociological sphere to another) Konrad, (transposition or sliding of meaning) Lacan, (anti) Lauretano, (literally "carry across") Lucas, (of name) MacIver, (of name) Madge, (of attributes) G. Martin, (of meaning) Martino, (of meaning) Mawardi, (O.E.D.) Metaphor, (Webster's) Metaphor, (of meaning, attribute or name) (E.B., 2) Metaphor, (literally improper) (E.B., 2) Metaphor, (of name) R. Meyer, (from proper idea to another) Migliorini, (emotive and intentional) Molhova, (classification of) Molhova, (of situations) Monro, (imagined) Morier, (name) F. Muller, (cause-effect) F. Muller, (sign-signified) F. Muller, (meaning) F. Muller, (psychical from latent to manifest content) Muncie, Nemerov, (perception to image; image to language) Nietzsche, (from perception to cognition) Olivero, (transpositions) Olken, (of names) Ortega, (of two thoughts producing a third) Palley, (physical to spiritual) Pongs, (animate-inanimate, part-whole, rational-irrational) Quintilian, (import the irrelevant) Ransom, (of word) Richards, Ruiz, (m to myth) Sarbin, (emotional) Sarmiento, (of qualities) Schipper, (of different fields) Schlanger, (of activity) Schlauch, (synaesthesia) Schlauch, (name) Schlauch, (physical to psychical) Sharpe, (word) Sherry, (body-mind, reasonable-unreasonable, living-inanimate) Sherry, (of universe of discourse) Shibles, (intellect-physical) Adam Smith, (name or meaning) Stanford, (inner-outer, narrow-wide, dark-light, death-life) Steinhoff, (of meaning) G. Stern, (meaning to sound, of meaning and sound from speaker to listener) Stutterheim, (name) Tupper, (name) Tryphon, Uhrhan, E. Ullmann, (sense) S. Ullmann, (of meaning or emotion) S. Ullmann, (of universe of discourse) Albert Upton, (of actual and less actual) Urbach, (internal-external, physical-spiritual) Urbach, (space-time, cause-effect, material and object) Urbach, (of all things) Urbach, (universes of discourse) Urban, (unjustified) Vaihinger, (abstract and concrete) Wald, (of two contexts) P. Weiss

as transformation   (diaphora) F. Muller, (m to myth) Sarbin, (physical to spiritual) Urbach, (of objective to internal) Vela, (semantic) Wheelwright

as translation (translatio)   Dannehl, (from proper meaning) Peacham, Sherry, (from proper meaning) John Smith, (of species) John Smith, (of object into words) Sohngen, (of realms, concepts to images, of languages) Sohngen

as transmutation   Cassirer, Schon, Slote

as transubstantiation   S. Ullmann

as true   (poetic truth) Abrams, Adler, Aquinas, Aristotle, Aschenbrenner, Barfield, (as containing both true and false statements) Beardsley, (as true say-ing) Beardsley, Berggren, (pragmatic) Blumenberg, (as true) Brooks, (and truth) Morris Cohen, Croce, (as belief and disbelief) Daiches, (as true) Daiches, (creating truth) Dickey, Edie, (to life) Elster, Embler, (for imagination) Esnault, (as true or false) Goodman, (conceit) Gracian, (not true or false) Gracian, (true or false) G. Graham, (self-evident) Gray, Hecht, (not true or false) Hutten, (to schizophrenic) R. Johnson, Kendall, Kohfeldt, (etymon) Lauretano, C. S. Lewis, May, Mazzeo, (not true or false) McCloskey, Meszaros, Murry, (not true or false) C. Myers, (not) H. Myers, (true or false) Nietzsche, Olscamp, (m has own logic) Pepper, Phelps, Pound, Ramsay, Ransom, Richards, Royce, Ruskin, Sarbin, Shibles, Stanford, W. Stevens, Sucre, Terry, (not true or false) Tilden, Urbach, Vaihinger, (to describe truth) Voltaire, Walsh, (not true or false) A. Ward, Welby, Wheelwright, Winter

Turkish   Agakay

as type-crossing (see m, as category-mistakes)

U

unconscious of (cf. m, captivated by) Lauretano, Nietzsche, Norwood, J. O'Neill,Pepper, Ramsey, Richards, Sarbin, Schoeck, (involuntary) W. Stevens, Urban, Wakeman, Welby, Zale

derived from unconscious (cf. m, Freudian theory of) Biese, Buck, (preconscious) Dorfles, Elster, Feldkeller, Fonagy, Freud, Gardiner, Gummere, Hempel, (collective) Jung, Lacan, (of extra-metaphorization) Lauretano, (pre-logical) Lauretano, Lawler, (subconscious) Lorenz, MacNeice, Mauthner, Mawardi, F. Muller, Pongs, (preconscious) Vico

understanding of (cf. m, in education) (in history texts) Flaum, E. A. Holmes, T. Hughes, G. James, Kaiser, Kohfeldt, (one thing through another) Langer, Looby, Mackel, Madge, Morier, Richards, (valuational) Rieser, Shibles, Thompson, Albert Upton, Urban, Wajid, Wells

as unexpected (cf. m, as surprise) Monro, Ong, C. Pellegrini, Shklovskii, Urbach, R. Wallace

unfamiliar Allers, (strange-making) Erlich, Shklovskii, Urbach

as representing unfamiliar by familiar E. Adams, (picture) S. Brown, Edie, Hutten, Irving, R. Meyer, H. Nash, Sarbin, Speranski, E. Stern, Stutterheim, Weisgerber

as unifying (cf. m, as synthesis; m, as unifying) K. Brooks, Coleman, Croce, Day-Lewis, Feidelson, (both thought and images) Ferre, Fogle, Foss, (of meaning) S. George, Girardot, (conceit) Gracian, (spiritual) Hecht, (image and meaning) Holz, Iberico, (real and ideal) Kohfeldt, (man with nature) Lanier, (soul and body) Lanier, (spirit and nature) Lanier, Lauretano, Lewontin, Manso, May, Meszaros, Nemetz, Ong, (resolution) Osborn, Parkhurst, Pongs, (synthesis) H. Read, (of form and meaning) Reichling, Richards, (experience) Richards, (of value) Rieser, Schon, Shipley, (of history and philosophy) Sidney, (poetry and philosophy) Slattery, Sohngen, Stanford, Vela, (of experience) Warfel, Watt, Heinz Werner, Wheelwright, Yelton

as unique (partial list) Prado, Taillardat, Tschizewskij, Walsh

as unity in difference (or diversity) Aristotle, E.B., Berggren, Blinderman, Borges, Brooks, Croce, Daiches, Esnault, Feltenstein, Fogle, Freud, Garcia Lorca, Gordon, (conceit) Gracian,

V

as rendering the invisible by visible (cf. m, to describe abstract by concrete) Dieckmann, R. Wellek

visual (cf. vision; m, as pictorial) Aldrich, Battcock, Benamou, (substitution) Berggren, (visual-verbal parallel) Bonsiepe, (not) Brandenburg, (not) E. Burke, Morris Cohen, Downey, Fenollosa, Ferre, (in renaissance tragedy) Fishman, F. C. Flint, Friedman, (visual juxtaposition) Frye, Gombrich, Gottfried, Gourmont, (not) (D. Thomas) Hornick, G. Hughes, Kaufmann, Kenner, Lockwood, MacNeice, Matt, Nietzsche, Pardee, W. Ramsey, H. Read, Shibles, Sohngen, E. Stern, Stock, Vonessen, Warfel, Wasserman, (double) R. Wellek, Heinz Werner, Whalley

war Albert Day, Hocke, Mackel, Mauron, McCann, Tarbet

as wit (cf. wit) Aristotle, (clever) Croce, (simple and compound) Gracian, S. Johnson, Mauthner, May, Mazzeo, Praz, Tesauro, Wakeman, Wells, Williamson